EUROPEAN REGIONAL COMMUNITIES

EUROPEAN REGIONAL COMMUNITIES

A New Era on the Old Continent

MELVIN G. SHIMM, *Editor*
HANS W. BAADE, *Associate Editor*

ROBINSON O. EVERETT
Special Editor for this Symposium

OCEANA PUBLICATIONS, INC.
DOBBS FERRY, NEW YORK
1962

© Copyright 1962 by Duke University

Library of Congress Catalog Card Number 62-20226

Originally Published in Summer 1961

by

LAW AND CONTEMPORARY PROBLEMS

DUKE UNIVERSITY SCHOOL OF LAW

PRINTED IN THE UNITED STATES OF AMERICA

TABLE OF CONTENTS

	PAGE
FOREWORD .... *Robinson O. Everett*	1
THE ECONOMIC AND POLITICAL PROBLEMS OF INTEGRATION .... *Albert Coppé*	3
THE EXTERNAL POLICY OF THE EUROPEAN ECONOMIC COMMUNITY .... *J. F. Deniau*	18
JURIDICAL AND INSTITUTIONAL ASPECTS OF THE EUROPEAN REGIONAL COMMUNITIES .... *Paul Reuter*	35
THE ROLE OF THE COURT OF JUSTICE OF THE EUROPEAN COMMUNITIES AS SEEN THROUGH ITS CASE LAW .... *Maurice Lagrange*	54
THE IMPACT OF THE EUROPEAN ECONOMIC COMMUNITY ON THE MOVEMENT OF THE UNIFICATION OF LAW .... *A. Grisoli*	72
PARLIAMENTARY CONTROL AND POLITICAL GROUPS IN THE THREE EUROPEAN REGIONAL COMMUNITIES ...... *Franz C. Heidelberg*	84
PROBLEMS CONNECTED WITH THE CREATION OF EURATOM .... *Pierre Mathijsen*	92
THE CONCEPT OF ENTERPRISE UNDER THE EUROPEAN COMMUNITIES: LEGAL EFFECTS OF PARTIAL INTEGRATION .... *Gerhard Bebr*	108
RULES GOVERNING COMPETITION WITHIN THE EUROPEAN REGIONAL COMMUNITIES .... *Jochen Thiesing*	118
THE RULES OF COMPETITION WITHIN THE EUROPEAN COMMON MARKET ...... *Fernand Spaak and Jean N. Jaeger*	139
CAPITAL MOVEMENTS AND INVESTMENT IN THE EUROPEAN COMMUNITIES .... *Hermann J. Abs*	162
THE STRUCTURE AND FINANCIAL ACTIVITIES OF THE EUROPEAN REGIONAL COMMUNITIES .... *Giandomenico Sertoli*	169
TARIFFS AND TRADE IN THE COMMON MARKET .... *Hans W. Gerhard*	193
THE EUROPEAN COMMON MARKET AND THE GENERAL AGREEMENT ON TARIFFS AND TRADE: A STUDY IN COMPATIBILITY .... *James Jay Allen*	213
LABOR AND THE EUROPEAN COMMUNITIES .... *Meyer Bernstein*	226

FOREWORD

For decades Americans have been asking, "Why isn't there a United States of Europe?" Generally, in posing this question, the questioner has ingenuously disregarded the existence of time-honored barriers to unification, such as the rise in nationalism and differences in language, governmental institutions, economic system and development, culture, religion, and historical tradition. Since the days of Rome, it has been apparent to many Europeans that substantial advantages might inhere in union; but the lure of these possible gains has not sufficed to induce Europe to surmount the ancient obstacles to unification. Indeed, when Napoleon and later Hitler attempted forcibly to impose a form of unity, the attempt was fiercely resisted. By reason of the intensified national hatreds left in the backwash of the two World Wars, the prospects for a United States of Europe seemed especially dim a few years ago. Although the Soviet threat created an urgent need for Western Europe to investigate whatever strength there might be in union, it seemed that this same threat might induce a despondency which could paralyze the initiative of European leaders. Also, it was clear that the Communists and several other groups would seek to sow such discord in the West that a united Europe would be impossible.

The gloomy postwar prognosis has proved misleading; today there is a realization that since the inception of the Marshall Plan—and to a considerable extent as a product of that Plan—Europe has made giant strides towards political, economic, and juridical union.[1] The American awareness of this recent progress has been demonstrated in many ways: by a flow of investment into Europe; by governmental action to cooperate with newly created European institutions; by recent books and articles about doing business in the Common Market and the problems that this customs union may create for American exports; and by the picture on the cover of a widely circulated American magazine of Jean Monnet, an outstanding proponent of European unity.[2]

If a United States of Europe ultimately does result, the creation of the three European Regional Communities—the Coal and Steel Community (E.C.S.C.), the Atomic Energy Community (Euratom), and the Economic Community, or Common Market (E.E.C.)—will constitute a major milestone on the road to union. These Communities embody a spectacularly successful political, economic, and legal experiment. Among the evidences of their success are: the prosperity and economic growth experienced in recent years by the six Member States; the establishment of the perhaps short-lived European Free Trade Area (E.F.T.A.)—which may be considered, in some respects, one of those imitations constituting the sincerest form of flattery and which was intended to provide seven Western European countries outside the Communities with some of the economic and commercial benefits enjoyed by the Six; the efforts to create customs unions like the E.E.C. in other parts of the world—notably Latin America; and the discussions undertaken between

---

[1] Although the reference here is to Western Europe, the Soviet Union has also enforced some integration of its satellites.
[2] Time, Oct. 6, 1961.

the Common Market, on the one hand, and Greece, Turkey, and Great Britain, on the other, with a view to some form of membership or association for those countries. Indeed, the willingness of the English to consider abandoning their traditional insularity—and possibly even their Commonwealth ties—is a striking testimonial to the benefits of Community living. Another testimonial is afforded by the remarkable rapprochement between the French and the Germans, who were adversaries in three wars during the last hundred years.

The significance today of the three Communities and of the movement towards European unity which they represent made them a suitable subject for a symposium in *Law and Contemporary Problems*. Indeed, a study of these Communities and their institutions suggests any number of interesting questions. For example, how feasible are the new concepts of federalism and supranationalism utilized in the treaties establishing the three Regional Communities? Has a satisfactory system been created for parliamentary control of action by the E.C.S.C. High Authority and the Commissions of Euratom and the E.E.C.?[3] To what extent should a responsibility be imposed on official bodies to compensate persons whose interests are injured by their action?[4] What institutional framework, if any, should be provided for participation by labor groups in governmental activities and in the management of business enterprises?[5] To what extent should there be a duty for governments to facilitate and finance the "readaptation" of workers who are the victims of sociological or technological change; and, if there is such a duty, how can its performance be assured and be financed? What is the proper sphere for judicial activity?[6] Can the exercise of national veto rights feasibly be subjected to judicial review?[7]

In preparing a symposium which would treat some of the contemporary problems pertinent to the Communities, the editors have been confronted by a formidable task. Obviously, the contributors of articles should be persons—in most instances Europeans—who were familiar with the operations of the Communities; moreover, it was desired to obtain a balanced presentation of viewpoints. To select the most suitable writers, correspond with them, and ultimately to persuade them to provide articles proved difficult. Frequently delays occurred—especially in obtaining satisfactory translations of articles submitted in languages other than English and in obtaining approval of editorial changes. Documentation of citations was also sometimes a problem. These burdens had been foreseen from the outset; and in some ways, the very difficulty involved in publishing this symposium convinced us that its value would be great. *Ad astra per aspera.*

ROBINSON O. EVERETT.

---

[3] *Cf.* E.C.S.C. Treaty art. 24; Euratom Treaty art. 114; E.E.C. Treaty art. 144. See also Heidelberg, *Parliamentary Control and Political Groups in the Three European Regional Communities, infra,* p. 431.
[4] *Cf.* E.C.S.C. Treaty arts. 34, 40; Euratom Treaty arts. 151, 188; E.E.C. Treaty arts. 178, 215.
[5] See Bernstein, *Labor and the European Communities, infra,* p. 572.
[6] The Court of Justice, under certain circumstances, has a consensual jurisdiction. E.C.S.C. Treaty art. 42; Euratom Treaty art. 153; E.E.C. Treaty art. 181. It may arbitrate certain disputes between Member States. E.C.S.C. Treaty art. 89. And on certain occasions it may rule on fundamental modifications proposed jointly by the High Authority and the Council for Assembly approval. E.C.S.C. Treaty art. 95. Certain issues must be certified to it by national tribunals for decision. E.C.S.C. Treaty art. 41; Euratom Treaty art. 150; E.E.C. Treaty art. 177. The Court's scope of review is not easy to define *Cf.* E.C.S.C. Treaty arts. 31, 33, 37, 38, 66(5); Euratom Treaty art. 146; E.E.C. Treaty art. 173.
[7] *Cf.* E.C.S.C. Treaty art. 10.

THE ECONOMIC AND POLITICAL PROBLEMS OF INTEGRATION

Albert Coppé*

I

The Task Involved

The task of integrating the economies of the six member countries of the Community, as set out in the Treaties establishing the European Communities, involves action over the whole field of economic activity. Since the aim is not merely to provide a free-trading area, but, in fact, to weld six national markets into a single Community market and a single Community production area, this integration involves a fundamental recasting of the economic structure over a period of time.

The system of integration chosen by the Six, with its three Communities, is not an ideal system. The European Coal and Steel Community (E.C.S.C.) was the pilot plant of European unity, and the defects of partial integration—integration of a sector of the economy only—were accepted for this reason. The European Atomic Energy Community (Euratom) arose, to some extent, because of the great need for a spectacular achievement on the road to unity at a moment when atomic power seemed to be one of the most important phenomena in the world. Then came a shift in emphasis—and how right it has proved—towards the European Economic Community (E.E.C.)—the Common Market. The development of the integration of the Six was thus a pragmatic evolution, with all the imperfections and inconsistencies, as well as some very great advantages of flexibility, that the system provides.

A pattern does emerge, however, from the different structures of the three Communities. It is possible to see this pattern both in the tasks that the Communities must accomplish and in the instruments— the institutional features—created to achieve them.

The tasks themselves can be summarized as follows:

1. *The abolition of trade barriers within the Community area*

This has involved removal of customs duties and all similar levies making the sale of goods from the rest of the Community more difficult than the sale of goods produced within a national market. It has also involved removal of quotas—*i.e.,* all quantitative restrictions on imports and exports. This problem has become very

* Licenciate in Political and Social Sciences 1933, Doctor of Economic Sciences 1940, University of Louvain (Belgium). Vice President, High Authority of the European Coal and Steel Community; Chairman, Board of Management of the Statistics Office of the European Communities; Member, High Council of Statistics; Extraordinary Professor, School of Economic and Social Sciences, University of Louvain (Belgium); Minister for Public Works, 1950; Minister for Economic Affairs and Middle Classes, 1950-51; Minister for Reconstruction, 1952.

much less acute following the restoration of the French economy to health and the much more rapid progress of the industrialized western countries towards the removal of the quantitative restrictions. Finally, it has involved removal of currency restrictions—*i.e.,* all barriers presented by difficulties in acquiring the currency of one or another of the member countries. This question has now been largely solved by the rapid move towards convertibility.

2. *Free circulation of factors of production*

The free circulation of goods has its counterpart in the free circulation of the factors of production—labor and capital—and in the free movement of services. It would be inconceivable to allow the free movement of goods to those areas of the Community that are underdeveloped and overpopulated if its counterpart did not exist in the form of the free movement of labor, and if these areas were not given the opportunity to import the capital that would enable them to close the gap. It looked at one time as if the free circulation of labor would present difficulties, but since the provisions of the E.E.C. Treaty allow workers to move from one country to another only to take up a specific job, the bulk of trade-union fears were assuaged.

The free movement of capital enables the spreading of the Community's investment resources. The free movement of services extends the principle of competition and the exploitation of a large market to all the auxiliary activities involved in the trade in goods—banking, insurance, the wholesale and retail trades, and so on.

3. *A common external tariff*

The E.E.C. Treaty stipulates the establishment of a common external tariff by the end of a transition period of ten to twelve years—a process that is now being speeded up, as is the abolition of trade barriers. The common external tariff is the factor that makes the Community of the Six a customs union and not a free trade area. By treating the Community as a single tariff area with a common tariff, the Treaty obviates all the innumerable problems—and, above all, bureaucratic complications—that would be presented by control of the origin of goods. The aim of the Community is to do away with customs formalities within its frontiers, not to redouble them.

The E.C.S.C. Treaty did not involve a common external tariff. The harmonization of the existing national tariffs was, however, effected at the low rate of the Benelux tariff plus two points, with an additional allowance for geographical protection.

4. *Common rules of competition*

A common market would not last long if the conditions of competition, in so far as they are determined by governmental and private measures, showed wide differences in the component parts of the area. The national and regional authorities would vie with each other in creating unfair advantages for their own industries, and the resultant distortions in competitive power would mean that the industries that has clear sovereign powers. Even in the E.C.S.C., where sovereign powers over a limited field have been transferred to the High Authority by the Governments, the panoply of sovereignty over the broad lines of economic policy as a whole remains in the hands of the Governments. In the E.E.C., the power of decision is retained by the Governments through the Council of Ministers. The Community might, therefore, appear at first sight to be very largely a form of confederate system, in which the ultimate powers are wielded by a body composed of representatives of the member Governments.

In fact, however, the institutional structure of the Communities, even in the form adopted for the E.E.C., has certain features going well beyond a confederate system and distinguishing it sharply from the organizations based on simple intergovernmental cooperation. These distinguishing features include the existence of strong independent executives, making their decisions by majority vote, and with clearly defined and fundamentally important powers.

1. *The European Coal and Steel Community*

The High Authority of the E.C.S.C. is able to make major decisions in the field of prices, investments, and the rules of competition without consulting the Council of Ministers. Even in the fields of transport and social policy, the High Authority has been able to make substantial progress, simply because it is a Community body with a kind of vested interest in ensuring that a Community solution is achieved to Community-wide problems.

2. *The European Economic Community*[1]

In the Common Market, the Commission proposes and the Council of Ministers disposes. But, after the initial four-year stage of the transition period, decisions in the Council of Ministers will be made mainly by a weighted majority vote. There is thus no question of a veto being exercised by one of the member countries.

In addition, the power of proposal by the E.E.C. Commission is an extremely efficient and potent instrument. It enables the Commission to gauge the climate of Community opinion and to push forward with measures that might never come to fruition if they had to have been formulated, proposed, and pushed through by national Governments or their representatives. The speeding-up of the Common Market timetable is a perfect example of the functioning of this process. It was the Commission that all along acted as the driving force. Not only did it produce the actual proposals that were discussed by the Council of Ministers, but it also worked hard on the proposals during the difficult discussions in the Council and was instrumental in producing the final compromises that were incorporated in the final draft.

Thus, the Communities' executives act as a motor or dynamo, in a way that has been conspicuously absent in the ministerial bodies of some organizations for simple

[1] The powers of the Euratom Commission are not dealt with here, since they occupy a position somewhere about halfway between those of the High Authority of the E.C.S.C. and those of the E.E.C. Commission.

would do best would not necessarily be the most efficient. Many efficient, and normal conditions, viable, industries would be driven to bankruptcy, and many efficient industries would be preserved.

Integration must, therefore, inevitably include common rules of competition. In the Community, these cover, in general, the following fields:

a. Nondiscrimination—the application of comparable terms—among others, price and transport rates—to all consumers in the Community who are in comparable conditions.

b. A ban on subsidies and other state aids that favor industries in one part of the Common Market against those in others.

c. A ban on agreements in restraint of trade—*i.e.*, agreements to restrict production, regulate prices, allocate markets or production, or restrict technical progress. In the E.C.S.C., this ban is backed by the requirement that all proposed agreements between firms must receive the prior authorization of the High Authority to become valid; authorization may be refused if the High Authority considers that the agreement is not in conformity with the Treaty's stipulations. The task of the Common Market is much broader, covering the whole field of economic activity.

d. There must be no abuse of a dominant power in the market by any firm or group of firms. Here, again, the High Authority has greater facilities, since mergers between firms require prior authorization by the High Authority. In the general Common Market, moreover, the executive must seek out abuses before interdiction. While the bans on restrictive practices apply only when trade between Community countries is involved, the antitrust laws of the E.C.S.C. Treaty are not subject to this limitation.

5. *Common policies*

The fundamental principle of all three Community Treaties is their insistence on action going far beyond the setting up of a customs union. In fact, it is quite clear that it would be impossible to remove trade barriers if the six Governments were to pursue their economic, financial, agricultural, transport, and foreign-trade policies on national lines, while industry and commerce were busy exploiting a vast new market. Deflation in one country while another inflated would mean that the former's goods would flood the latter's market. Differing forms of protection for agriculture would mean the maintenance of disparate price levels and would create such havoc in the markets that the establishment of a single market would become impossible. Divergent action by national Governments in their foreign trade agreements would make nonsense of the common external tariff. Many more examples could be given.

II

The Instruments of Integration

To achieve the task set out above, the European Communities provide an entirely new type of structure. They do not provide a federal system in which an executive intergovernmental cooperation, and effectively fulfill their role of dealing with problems in the European Community interest, which is rarely the sum of the (conflicting) national interests. It is this realization of the common interest, and the spectacular benefits that its application is already bringing, that makes the proposals of the executives acceptable to the national Governments.

3. *The European Parliament*

The European Parliament is not a legislature, nor does it have any say in the appointment of the Governments of the European Community; but the 142-member Parliament can remove any of the three Communities' executives on a motion of censure voted by a two-thirds majority. Moreover, the European Parliament must be consulted before certain specific decisions are made, and it has a right to scrutinize the Communities' budgets. Through its thirteen standing committees, the Parliament also keeps a close watch on the work of the three executives and calls on their members to testify before these committees. Plans for direct election of members by universal suffrage have been drawn up by the Parliament itself, and this may well be a steppingstone to the further extension of the Parliament's powers.

4. *The Court of Justice*

Another common institution is a supreme court of seven judges having the sole power to decide whether the acts of the Communities' executives and the Council of Ministers should be upheld or quashed. The innovation as far as the Court is concerned is in the fact that its judgments have the force of law throughout the European Community and are directly binding on individuals, firms, national governments, and the Communities' executives.

Thus, the structure of the Communities presents something half-way between a true federal structure and the kind of intergovernmental cooperation we have seen in the past. It distinguishes itself from the latter systems by its dynamism and its effectiveness. It can and should logically result one day in a full federation; but in the meanwhile, it has shown itself fully capable of standing on its own two feet.

III

The Problems of Integration

A. The General Difficulties—Real and Imagined

It was always clear that a gigantic task such as the integration of the economies of six countries would present a complex series of problems. In the first place, since the structure of the Communities was something entirely new, the task of fitting it into the existing national and industrial framework was bound to give rise to differing viewpoints among business men and politicians on the political approach in general and the methods of action. Those whose wishes were not met naturally felt aggrieved.

Secondly, a vast undertaking such as the economic union of the six countries was also bound to run up against vested interests over a wide area. There are always persuasive reasons for retaining the status quo in almost any field, particularly if it involves a good deal of protection. In business, it allows a relative degree of peace and quiet; and even if the economy lacks dynamism, industrialists and businessmen may find the additional security a more than adequate compensation. Some of the trade unions, too, felt at the start of the integration process that it might be the workers who would suffer from the expansion of competition in a six-country market of 160 million consumers.

Many of these anxieties were, in fact, dispelled when the Common Market actually came into being. This was true with the common market for coal and steel in 1953, as it was true for the general Common Market in 1958. Once industrialists and workers are caught up in the new spirit of dynamism and rapid advance of the Common Market and come to recognize the very great improvements it brings in sales, production, and living standards, they experience a sudden change of opinion and, it seems, a sudden change in outlook. Today, the results of the Common Market are being anticipated by the Community's industries, which are all basing their future production and sales plans on the existence of a market of continental size. The trade unions, on their side, are the most fervent supporters of European integration and of continued moves towards full unity.

Some industries, however, were clearly bound to experience genuine difficulties. The classic example is the Belgian coal industry. On the one hand, the common market for coal and steel has prevented the protraction of this industry's agonies by placing bounds on the national protection it can be granted; on the other, it has enabled reorganization to go forward with far less disagreeable social consequences than would have been possible if the E.C.S.C. were not providing the aid for reemployment, retraining, and resettlement of miners, known as "readaptation." In the general Common Market, moreover, there will undoubtedly be other cases where industries that were previously highly protected will have considerable difficulties in adapting themselves to new conditions.

Here, however, a conscious policy of economic expansion can greatly ease the change. It is in times of recession that firms go to the wall. During expansionary periods, adaptation to the new conditions of increased competition in the Common Market occurs through more rapid expansion of the more efficient firms, rather than through an increase in the number of firms compelled to close down. At the same time, experience in the E.C.S.C. has shown that booms can mask a good deal of uneconomic activity. Thus, when the rate of economic expansion slackened at the end of 1958, the structural difficulties of parts of the Community's coal industry were suddenly revealed with full clarity.

The E.E.C. Commission regards a rapid rate of expansion as the fundamental pillar of the Community's economic policy, and has urged that an expansion rate of between four and five per cent per annum in the gross national product be achieved over the coming years.

B. Problems of Partial Integration in the European Coal and Steel Community

Before dealing with the major practical problems, it is worth looking back on the problems of partial integration faced by the E.C.S.C. before the Common Market and Euratom came into being. The first and most obvious of these was the absence of the formulation of general economic policy and trade cycle policies from the field of power of the High Authority. Since this remained the responsibility of the six national Governments, cases could—and, in fact, did—arise in which the Community's price policy could be regarded as contrary to the general economic policy being followed at that time by individual member Governments. Freedom of coal and steel prices enables firms to charge prices during a boom that will not only finance a rapid rate of investment, but also permit these firms to mass reserves sufficient to finance price cuts during a recession. The Governments' interest during a boom, however, is to avoid inflationary pressures, and some of the Community Governments exerted considerable pressure on the prices of E.C.S.C. products—pressure that was incompatible with the E.C.S.C. Treaty. When this particular problem arises, as it must from time to time, it should be remedied by recourse to article twenty-six of the Treaty, which provides for coordination of the High Authority policy with the general economic policies of the six Governments.

Secondly, the failure of the Treaty to grant the High Authority any powers over external trade meant that, before and during the coal crisis, the Governments were able to follow contradictory import policies. Some Governments feared the dislocation of their coal markets by the arrival of excessive quantities of coal from other Community countries, and the free circulation of coal in the Common Market was thus endangered. In the E.E.C. Treaty, this defect regarding external trade is remedied, and the Commission has important powers over the coordination of external trade policies.

Other problems of partial integration were apparent in the field of labor policy and transport. The labor policy of the High Authority, by granting especially favorable conditions to coal and steel workers, particularly in cases of unemployment and in housing questions, created difficulties, since the other sectors of industry were less favored. There were also problems of harmonizing transport rates and conditions, but these problems may well be repeated on the broader plane of the general Common Market.

The E.C.S.C. has also faced some extremely difficult problems in the field of competition. Articles sixty-five and sixty-six of the E.C.S.C. Treaty are quite unequivocal; banning agreements in restraint of trade and mergers that result in an excessive restriction of competition. These articles make agreements between firms and mergers of firms subject to authorization by the High Authority. They have been instrumental in enabling the High Authority to ensure that the trade barriers eliminated in the transition period were not replaced by private restrictions.

The strict nature of these two articles has applied much more exacting standards to the coal and steel industries than those applicable to other industries. Evidently the coal industry found this disparity even more burdensome when the coal crisis started. The sales organization for Ruhr coal provides a classic example. Believing that unbridled competition between the coal firms of the Ruhr was impracticable, the High Authority in 1956 ordered the dissolution of the monolithic sales cartel known as GEORG and authorized a system comprising three sales agencies that were to compete with each other. In fact, however, actual competition did not result. This system, which would have expired in March 1959, was extended for a year, while a new solution compatible with the Treaty was sought. The High Authority then refused a request of the Ruhr coal agencies for authorization of a single sales agency. The High Authority believes that should the Governments consider that competition is not capable of ensuring the efficient operation of the coal market in present conditions, the E.C.S.C. Treaty should be modified. This can only be done in accordance with the rules laid down for Treaty modifications, and, until that happens, the High Authority must apply the Treaty's rules of competition. In any event, there should be no doubt that, if living standards are to be raised, the maintenance of competition on the market is of fundamental importance, whatever the private interests involved, and the rules adopted to ensure this must be adequate and effective.

Although the E.C.S.C. has presented particular problems, its experience has been invaluable not only as a pilot operation which proved that integration could work successfully, but also as a model for the supranational pattern of organization that precludes domination by any of the Member States and guarantees the rights of the smaller countries.

C. Agriculture

It is impossible here to do any more than indicate the nature of the extensive problems faced by integration in such key fields of policy as agriculture. Agriculture presents a special problem in all highly developed industrial societies. In all of them, these problems have led to more or less extensive government intervention. This ranges from complete central organization of the internal market for particular products to relatively free systems. In all cases, however, agriculture is protected from foreign competition by a great variety of methods designed to raise the incomes of farmers, which tend to be lower than those of other groups.

In a common market, there can be no question of excluding agriculture. This would not only distort the whole integration system, but it would also discriminate against those countries in whose economies agricultural exports play a vital part. On the other hand, it would be unthinkable that the present basis of the Common Market's agriculture, which is the family holding, should disappear. The problem is, therefore, not whether there should be agricultural protection, but what degree of agricultural protection there should be and what methods should be used to achieve it. At the same time, ways must be found to ensure structural improvements and greater productivity, and protection should not be so great as to suppress any incentive in this direction.

D. Transport

The E.C.S.C. Treaty abolished transport discriminations for coal, steel, iron ore, and scrap. It also directed the High Authority to try to find, in cooperation with the national governments, ways of harmonizing transport conditions for E.C.S.C. products. The E.E.C. Treaty requires the formation of a common transport policy, the basic principles of which the E.E.C. Commission expects to finish working out in the course of this year.

The major problem in this field, which has already come to the fore, is similar to that which has proved such a hard nut to crack in the E.C.S.C.—that of ensuring nondiscrimination in transport rates and conditions. While some of the Governments are strongly in favor of price publicity as the only really effective means of preventing discrimination, others are equally strongly opposed. Perhaps in the not too distant future, publicity for transport rates will be as widely accepted in the Community as it already is in the United States. There, the regulatory role of the Interstate Commerce Commission is accepted in the interests of fair competition, and no one would dream of calling it *dirigiste*.

E. Competition

The problems of competition will play an essential part in determining the form that the Common Market will eventually take. Such measures as the ban on state subsidies and other aids likely to distort competition by favoring certain firms will be difficult but should present no fundamental problems of principle. The real problems will rather arise when the E.E.C. Commission has defined its antitrust legislation and begins to enforce it.

So far, the E.E.C. Commission has been working to make it legally possible to apply in uniform fashion the rules of competition laid down in the E.E.C. Treaty. Belgium, Italy, and Luxembourg had no antitrust legislation at all and have had to adopt new measures that will enable a common policy on competition to be put into practice. The E.E.C. Commission has already presented to the Council of Ministers draft regulations on the control of cartels, which would greatly strengthen its hand in achieving effective control. At all events, the Commission is determined that abusive control of the market in the main industrial sectors shall not pass into the hands of cartels or a small number of enterprises, since this would be contrary to the aims of the Treaty.

F. The Underdeveloped Regions of the Community

One of the problems that has always beset customs unions has been the danger that investment from the whole area would tend to become increasingly concentrated in the well-developed areas, thus making the richer areas richer and the poor areas poorer—or relatively poorer, at any rate. The classic examples of development of this kind are the southern United States and southern Italy after the union of the peninsula. This tendency is attributable to the attraction that a high degree of economic development exerts on new industrial investment. Clearly, firms and individuals with capital to invest are likely to move towards regions that will have an adequate economic intrastructure, roads and railways on which to bring in their raw material and get out their finished products, schools and technical colleges to train a skilled and productive labor force, hospitals to treat their workers when they are ill, power stations to provide energy, and so on.

This problem has been faced in the E.E.C. by the establishment of the European Investment Bank, with a capital of $1,000,000,000, of which $250,000,000 has been paid up. This feature of the E.E.C. Treaty was particularly insisted upon by Italy, as the country of the Community with the largest underdeveloped region. It is a fact that investment in the rapidly developing industrial regions of northern Italy is still far outstripping investment in the underdeveloped South, despite the efforts of the Cassa del Mezzogiorno[2] and the initial operations of the European Investment Bank. Ways may well have to be found to step up the operations of the Investment Bank in this field.

G. The Associated Countries

One of the most adventurous and spectacular features of the Community has been the association in a free and equal partnership with the Community of the countries and territories that had or have particular links with one of the Community's member countries. This forged a direct link between the Community and African territories with a population of about 53,000,000. It was particularly favorable to the associated countries in that it gives them free entry for their products into the Common Market, while they themselves were allowed to retain customs duties required to protect their young industries. In addition, an Overseas Development Fund of $581,250,000 was set up for an initial period of five years, to encourage social and economic development in the associated countries. The problem so far has been to find a rapid enough procedure to ensure speedy approval of all worthwhile projects. This problem is now on the way to being solved, however, and it is expected that projects will be approved more rapidly in the coming months. By the end of 1960, the Commission had already approved the financing of 126 projects involving a total contribution of $121,000,000. Among social projects, schools and hospitals were most prominent, while economic projects consisted mainly of roads, harbors, railways, and other infrastructure development.

The Commission not only has speeded up its procedure for examining and approving investments by the Overseas Development Fund, but it is also ready to help where associated countries find it difficult to finance or undertake global studies on which to base their development needs. One country that the Commission has already helped to overcome this difficulty is Ruanda Urandi, where it is financing a project for a general study of development possibilities.

The most urgent problem connected with overseas countries, however, concerns

[2] The Italian Government Fund set up to aid development in southern Italy.

the future of association itself. As these countries become independent, one after the other, they find it unsuitable to be linked to the Community in a form of association in which they themselves have no say, and which, to the new and sensitive nationalism of Africa, may savor of the old colonial days. At the same time, association with the Common Market offers very great advantages, and enlightened African statesmen realize that the Six have much to offer as sources of aid and as markets. It is essential, therefore, to devise as quickly as possible new legal forms through the use of which the overseas countries can be made to feel free and equal partners in an association from which all taint of subordination, however superficial, or even imaginary, has been removed.

H. Labor Policy

Labor policy has always occupied a somewhat anomalous position in the development of the European Communities. All three Community Treaties leave the bulk of direct responsibility for labor policy firmly in the hands of the national Governments. At the same time, the E.C.S.C. Treaty grants the High Authority very important powers in the field of employment policy, and similar although perhaps less far-reaching powers are vested in the E.E.C. Commission under the E.E.C. Treaty. The problem in the E.C.S.C.—and it is one that is likely to be even more acute in the E.E.C.—has been that of exploiting the Treaty provisions sufficiently to make a powerful enough impact on reemployment, retraining, and resettlement of workers. In the E.C.S.C., the High Authority cannot itself initiate readaptation projects: the proposals have to come from the national Governments. In the E.E.C., readaptation aid is given post facto by the Common Market's Social Fund for projects already undertaken by the existing public authorities. The real testing time for the Social Fund's operations will thus be in the future, and a great deal will probably depend on pressure from the trade unions and on the willingness of the national Governments to make use of the Fund.

In the initial stages of readaptation in the E.C.S.C., the Treaty provisions seemed to be of relatively minor importance. The coal crisis has, however, proved them to be what the French negotiators of the Treaty had envisaged—the major innovation of the Treaty in the social field.

In other fields of labor policy, the function of the Communities has been, and will almost certainly continue to be in the future, to take action and exert their influence in fields where the Treaties grant them only indirect or negligible powers. The E.E.C. has already stated that it intends to make full use of its wide freedom of choice for indirect action, particularly in aiding occupational mobility through training programs. In the E.C.S.C., the High Authority's housing programs, covering roughly 60,000 dwellings, are a typical example of action in a field on which the E.C.S.C. Treaty is silent. Moreover, the wide range of studies undertaken by the Communities—particularly of labor costs and real incomes in the six countries, and also on such subjects as social security, occupational training, industrial health, and safety—provide accurate data on which the executives, national Governments, and employers and trade unions can base their policy so as to take account of the whole of the Community's economic area.

I. The Harmonization of Turnover Taxes

One of the underlying assumptions of integration through the Communities has been that one cannot remove one or several kinds of trade barriers and leave the others in existence. If one does, the remaining trade barriers can be magnified to supply the protection that has been lost through the abolition of the others. Similarly, the E.C.S.C. has shown that it would have been extremely difficult, in the long run, to integrate parts of the Community's economies and leave other parts unaffected.

This does not mean, as Paul-Henri Spaak pointed out in a memorable debate in the Common Assembly of the E.C.S.C., that one must harmonize everything before one can have a common market. Obviously, the value of a common market is in the real differences between resources and conditions in some parts of the common market and those in other parts—differences in suitability of location, in raw material resources, in geographical features, in aptitudes of the labor force for different operations, and so on. If there were no differences, if some areas did not have advantages over others in particular fields of activity, the advantages of a common market would be far fewer. At the same time, however, it is clear that one cannot leave major distorting factors in the economy.

The E.E.C. Commission has stated unequivocally that the field of fiscal impositions provides one of these major distorting factors. Above all, turnover and sales taxes, imposed at different levels in the member countries, cause artificial differences in production and cost schedules that lead many exporters to feel that despite the removal of trade barriers, they are up against greater difficulties than domestic producers on certain of the Community's national markets. The Commission has recognized the need for a common turnover tax, possibly combined with a sales tax. This is clearly the only ultimate solution, although we may have to be content with partial solutions before the ideal can be achieved. A working party of Commission and Government experts is now examining ways of solving the problem.

J. The Community and the Outside World

The E.C.S.C. and Euratom, with their limited fields of operation, have had few major problems in the field of external policy. It is true that the levels of export prices for coal and steel were attacked from time to time in the General Agreement on Tariffs and Trade (G.A.T.T.), but the High Authority was able to show fairly conclusively that taking recessions and boom periods together, outside consumers had paid no more than Community consumers. Euratom was able to conclude cooperation agreements with the United States, Britain, and Canada, and although the technical operation of the United States-Euratom agreement has presented difficulties, no one could say that either the High Authority or the Euratom Commission has felt itself directly threatened by problems of external policy.

In the case of the Common Market, however, the problems of its relations with the rest of the world, and particularly with its European neighbors, have dominated a large part of its existence. It seems clear that in the long run, the influence of the Common Market must be to produce a general expansion in world trade. Rapid growth within the Common Market will, in turn, bring greater requirements of imports and should be a potent force for rapid economic expansion in the free world. This has been called the creative effect of an economic union on world trade. At the same time, as tariff barriers are removed within the economic union, it is possible—and for some highly sensitive products, probable—that users within the area will switch their purchases from outside suppliers to producers within the area. In this way, they will obtain cheaper products, since, when all internal tariff barriers have been removed, goods produced within the Common Market will not be subject to customs duty.

Another fear of third countries has been that a long-term trend towards self-sufficiency in certain products could appear in the Common Market. The United States has had particular fears on the score of exports of its farm products to the E.E.C. This whole problem depends on whether the undoubtedly expansionary effects of the Common Market are greater, and reveal themselves more rapidly, than the diversionary effects, and also on whether political pressures for self-sufficiency, such as the farmers' lobby, can be kept within reasonable bounds.

All the signs in the Common Market so far point to a generally beneficial effect. In the first place, not only has the Community itself been adopting increasingly liberal policies in the field of its common external tariff and the speedy removal of quota restrictions, but the creation and existence of the Common Market have also generated increasingly liberal and free-trading tendencies in the rest of the world. Rarely have G.A.T.T. negotiations for mutual world-wide tariff reductions been approached in such a liberal spirit as the major free-world countries approached the 1960-61 round of negotiations. In addition, the predictions of rapid expansion of production and trade have been fulfilled up to the hilt. Industrial production in the Community in 1959 was about seven per cent greater than in 1958; and in 1960 it was thirteen per cent higher than in 1959. Trade within the Community in 1959 rose by seventeen per cent over 1958, and in 1960 by twenty-eight per cent over 1959. The Community's trade with other countries in 1959 was eight per cent higher than in 1958, and in 1960 it was sixteen per cent higher than in 1959.

One of the most important problems raised by the Community's external affairs has been its relations with Great Britain. This has been not merely a question of the threat that Britain seems to have seen for its foreign trade, but also a political question. At the time of writing, a general, if as yet ill-defined, British desire to draw closer to Europe may set us on the road to a solution of this fundamental problem, which has, indeed, dogged the course of European integration ever since it began in 1950.

Finally, the Community is becoming increasingly aware, as recent pronouncements of the members of the E.E.C. Commission have shown, of the need to help underdeveloped countries. The Community, like other highly developed industrial countries, must aid developing countries by:
    a. ensuring that severe price fluctuations for the primary products on which they are largely dependent do not dislocate their development plans;
    b. buying their industrial products as their new industries develop, even if their wages are lower; and
    c. making a greater effort to provide aid in the form of grants, investment loans, and technical assistance.

These duties are all part of the price that the advanced countries must pay to the rest of the world for being wealthy.

IV

SOME MAJOR LINES OF DISAGREEMENT

A. The Supranational Idea: the Letter and the Spirit

The Community system, whether more supranational, as in the case of the E.C.S.C., or less supranational, as in the case of the general Common Market, has features that could not be provided either by traditional national alliances or by intergovernmental cooperation. Through its voting systems—simple majorities in the three executives, and weighted majorities in the Council of Ministers—it prevents the domination of the Community by any of the larger Member States. This is an inestimable advantage for the three small Benelux countries, which are vitally interested in European unity, but not in the resuscitation of the old power blocs.

Moreover, the system has shown its efficacy. It does admittedly demand great understanding on the part of the national Governments, and there have been times when the Governments have wished to brake rather than encourage further development of the Community system. This is hardly to be wondered at when one considers the period of ten years, which is, after all, but a short thread in the loom of history. There are bound to be times when some Governments want to go faster, and times when they want to go slower.

Perhaps the most outstanding and at times unexpected feature of the system's development has been the resilience of the European concept. Time after time, when the drive towards unity seemed to have faltered, it has sought strength in new ideas and new directions and has pushed forward with redoubled momentum.

B. Dirigisme and Laissez-Faire

The words *dirigisme* and *laissez-faire,* representing the two extremes of economic thought, are much in vogue among those who dislike the Community. This is because the Community, like national Governments, has had to steer a sane course between intervention in the economy and total freedom. The decisions made in choosing this course were bound to be the object of major attacks. A great deal of misunderstanding has been created on occasion by the unthinking or unscrupulous use of these terms, and it is well to see where the Communities stand in this respect.

In the first place, positive action is clearly needed to get rid of trade barriers and the private forms of restriction and protection. Otherwise, there can be no single market and competition is doomed. It is easy, but quite unjust, to attack such action as *dirigisme,* when its aim is to produce a truly competitive economy.

Secondly, it has long been clear that industry cannot be allowed complete and unfettered freedom to act as it thinks fit. *Laissez-faire,* in fact, died long ago, and most liberal economists recognize this. Indeed, what matters is fair competition, and it is the task of governments to safeguard it and to restore it when it has been destroyed. The economy should, therefore, allow a maximum of freedom to initiative and expansion; it cannot, however, allow industrialists the freedom to act in a restrictive way by rationing production or markets, by fixing prices, or by suppressing technical progress.

Thirdly, even if the Community institutions wanted to, they would be unable to follow a *dirigiste* policy. The Treaties are in themselves liberal documents, and the measures they lay down are almost invariably based on persuasion rather than direct control. The competitive economy has amply proved itself in western Europe in the last ten years, and the Soviet Union itself is now busy introducing competition between firms to increase productivity, having already, in the form of *stakhanovitism,* introduced cut-throat competition among workers, which is anathema—and rightly so—to our own trade unions.

There is nothing doctrinaire about the Treaties, however. The provisions covering the European Investment Bank, the Social Fund and the Overseas Development Fund, and the conception of agricultural policy show that the Community is prepared to use direct central action and the organization of the market where it considers this necessary.

C. The Future Development of Integration

The future development of European economic integration is closely linked with political trends. Will there be a federal system of the type to which the three Community Treaties aspire, or will Europe move towards a confederated system, in which the supreme body will consist of Government representatives? At the time of writing, much hangs in the balance.

For the moment, we must try to advance through concrete measures, as Robert Schuman said in his historic declaration of May 9, 1950, for "Europe will not be made in a day." The next stages on which we have set our sights are the merging of the executives of the three Communities and the institution of a system of direct elections, rather than nomination, to the European Parliament.

Whatever the current controversies, one comes back to the experience of the United States, where a confederate system lasted for only a few years. It is hard to avoid the conclusion that confederation can only be a stage on the road to real unity.

THE EXTERNAL POLICY OF THE EUROPEAN ECONOMIC COMMUNITY

J. F. Deniau*

In a world where things, and in particular things economic, are becoming more and more interlocked, it is not always easy to make a neat distinction between the domestic policy of a country or group of countries and its policy for dealing with external affairs. This is what the six countries of the Common Market have been finding since the inauguration of the European Economic Community (E.E.C.).

They have been finding it, first of all, in a very practical way in the implementation of the internal machinery of the Treaty of Rome—that is to say, with the elimination of customs duties and quantitative restrictions between the Member States. This has led much more quickly than expected to technical problems that involve coordination of their relations with nonmember countries, especially with those practicing state trading or those where abnormal conditions of competition obtain. It may, indeed, be difficult to establish the free circulation of certain goods within the Common Market so long as the aims of each Member State's bilateral agreements with nonmember countries—that is to say, their import policies—remain widely different. This being so, unification of the policies adopted by Member States towards nonmember countries must advance strictly in step with unification of the internal market.

When the six countries were negotiating the Common Market, they no doubt felt that the most difficult problems, or at least the most immediate ones, would be those relating to trade among the six countries themselves. This may explain the fact that the Treaty of Rome does not contain a special chapter on the Community's external relations. Apart from the provisions on the establishment of the common external tariff itself[1]—that is to say, the application of one of the constituent elements of the customs union of the Six—the expressions used are in most cases of a fairly general nature:

1. declarations of intention, stating the liberal intentions of the Community;[2] and
2. procedures under which to participate in future negotiations, to elaborate, step by step, a common commercial policy,[3] to pursue this common policy after the end

* Licence en droit et Diplôme de doctorat d'Etudes Supérieures de Droit 1949, (Economie Politique), Diplôme de l'Institut d'Etudes Politiques 1949, Licence es Lettres, Ethnologie et Sociologie 1947, University of Paris. Ecole Nationale d'Administration. Inspecteur des Finances; Directeur, The Association with the Third Countries, Commission of European Economic Community, Brussels, Belgium. Author, Le Marché Commun (1958; rev. ed. 1961).

[1] E.E.C. Treaty arts. 18-29.
[2] *E.g., id.* art. 110.
[3] *Id.* art. 111.

of the transition period;[4] and finally, to enable nonmember countries either to join the Community[5] or to associate themselves with it.[6]

Experience has shown that the internal machinery of the Common Market has so far functioned well and has even made possible a considerable speed-up in the implementation of the Treaty, but it has also shown that what may be very pressing and very difficult questions have arisen in the Community's relations with nonmember countries. These questions have a direct bearing on the life and character of the Common Market as a whole; and ever since the entry into force of the Treaty of Rome—that is to say, since January 1958—much of what has been done by the Community, and especially by the officials of the E.E.C., has revolved around the issues they pose.

The first need was to coordinate the activities of the six Governments and to find a common position on a certain number of problems that had existed before the establishment of the Common Market, but that could be reviewed in the light of the new situation. The second was to have the E.E.C. recognized for what it was and to define in broad outline the relations it could have with its partners. There are, therefore, always two parts to the definition of the Common Market's attitude: first, the consultation and coordination procedure between the various organs of the Community—especially the Commission and the Council of Ministers; and second, liaison work and the elaboration of a common position with regard to nonmember countries. The emergence of the Common Market on the international plane has been observed in many ways. The Community has taken part as such in the work of many international organizations, such as General Agreement on Tariffs and Trade (G.A.T.T.) and Organization for European Economic Cooperation (O.E.E.C.). With some of them—O.E.E.C., the International Labor Office (I.L.O.), the Council of Europe, and certain specialized agencies of the United Nations—it has concluded agreements for practical cooperation covering such items as the attendance of observers at meetings and the exchange of information. Moreover, a number of nonmember countries (seventeen at present) have accredited diplomatic missions to the Community in Brussels; they include the United States, most European countries, and other countries as different in character as Japan, Australia, and Brazil. In this way, recognition of the international role that the Community could and should play has found a first practical expression.

I

To begin with, the Community faces a series of major problems that would have confronted the Governments of the Member States even if they had not set up a Common Market among themselves. These are mainly such problems as the coordination of cyclical policies, the development of certain countries in order to ensure a better equilibrium in their trade with the industrialized countries, the stabilization

[4] *Id.* art. 114.
[5] *Id.* art. 237.
[6] *Id.* art. 238.

of the basic commodity markets, the situation of agriculture in the industrialized countries, and the problems of commercial relations with low-wage countries or countries practicing state trading. All these problems face the western countries as a whole and call for a greater measure of international cooperation. Far from making them more difficult, the establishment of the E.E.C. is intended to facilitate their solution. It is easier to reach international understanding if six of the parties concerned have already agreed among themselves, and it is also very much easier to make an effort on the required scale if the resources of some of the partners have already been pooled and their positions coordinated. Moreover, the existence of an independent body, such as the E.E.C. provides, able to objectively appraise the questions for discussion and settlement, must serve to facilitate agreement on any solution proposed. The Common Market, therefore, introduces a twofold new element: *politically,* the revival of international cooperation inherent in the Common Market's own unification; and, from a more strictly *economic* point of view, its own weight and the responsibilities that this entails.

The second set of problems derives from the establishment of the Common Market itself and from the reactions of the nonmember countries faced with this considerable change in international economic conditions. If these reactions and the weight of the Common Market and its responsibilities are to be fully understood, it may be useful to recall certain figures concerning the part played by the E.E.C. in world trade.

A large part of the trade done by the countries of the Common Market is with other members of the Community: it varies from twenty-five to more than forty per cent, for both imports and exports. The average amounts to about one-third. Trade with European nonmember countries accounts for about another third. The final third is covered by relations with the non-European countries, especially the United States. Taken as a whole, the E.E.C.'s share in world trade, as is shown in table one, often places it above the United States and on an approximately equal footing with as vast an association as the Commonwealth.

TABLE I
World Trade
(1959 figures in £1,000 million)

	Imports	Exports
World trade	104.4	99.9
United States	15.0	17.4
E.E.C.	24.1	25.2
Sterling Area (including United Kingdom)	24.8	21.5[a]
United Kingdom	11.2	9.3

[a] 1958.

As importer of foodstuffs and raw materials, the Community accounts for about thirty-one per cent of world trade, the United States for sixteen per cent, and the United Kingdom for eighteen per cent. In other words, the Community offers an outlet for these products that is almost double that of the United States and greater by two-thirds than that of the United Kingdom.

As an exporter of industrial goods, it covers some thirty-three per cent of world trade, whereas the United States accounts for twenty-six per cent and the United Kingdom for sixteen per cent. In other words, its sales are double those of the United Kingdom and almost thirty per cent higher than those of even the United States.

If, finally, we exclude trade between the Community countries, the United States, and the United Kingdom, in order to find out the significance of these three great trading partners for the rest of the world, we see that industrial exports from the United States to the rest of the world are still ahead of those of the Community, which, in turn, exceed British sales by forty per cent; however, as a purchaser of primary products from these regions, the Community already outstrips by one-third both the United States and the United Kingdom.

From these figures, one can draw certain conclusions that will illustrate the attitude of the Community towards nonmember countries:

1. The Community is the world's greatest importer of raw materials. This is of direct interest to the countries in course of development and, therefore, to a sphere in which the Community has a particular responsibility and where it can exercise a positive influence, if only by the volume of its trade.
2. The Community can in no way be regarded as a closed, inward-looking entity. It is, in fact, in large measure open to the world and for the greatest part of its activities depends on its relations with the rest of the world.
3. Its relations with the rest of the world are spread almost equally over the various geographical areas. It is, therefore, very difficult to grant privileges to one sector rather than to another. In particular, the problem of the relations of the Common Market with its European neighbors should not be considered in isolation, but must on the contrary be seen in the wider setting of the over-all western or even world policy of the Common Market.

II

At the same time, it is this very importance of the Community that has given rise to anxiety in certain countries. Quite apart from any political consideration and looked at merely from the point of view of trade, the establishment in Europe of a customs union, with all the advantages this entails for the participating countries and with the change it could bring about in the habits of the nonmember countries, was bound to arouse certain reactions. The customs union of the Common Market is, it is true, in conformity with the rules of G.A.T.T. and the level of its external tariff, calculated on the principle of the arithmetical mean of the tariffs of the Member States, is also in conformity with G.A.T.T. Its level is comparable with, or even lower than, that of other major industrial countries. Moreover, though the customs duties of certain of the Member States must be raised to the level of the common external tariff, others must be very considerably lowered, and it might even be considered that the reductions will be much more important than the increases, since they will more especially affect two of the countries of the Community with the largest populations—namely Italy and France (the German tariff is already very close to the future common external tariff). For the products contained in List G—that is to say, those that had been excluded from the general rules of calculation and for which the tariff was fixed in special negotiations after the entry into force of the Treaty of Rome—the average of all the rates agreed is also below the average of the previous tariffs, and is, therefore, in conformity wth the G.A.T.T. rules. But in this matter, it is not the legal aspect that constitutes the main problem.

Anxiety was first expressed within G.A.T.T. itself, and in particular by non-European countries in the process of development.. It should be remembered that the Treaty of Rome includes the association with the Common Market of a number of countries, mainly in Africa, and provides that there shall be both commercial arrangements and financial aid to help these countries. This association, and in fact, the Treaty itself, seemed to other countries to constitute a danger to their own exports or their own development. Replying to these fears, the Community has restated its confidence in the beneficial effects of the Common Market on all nonmember countries as a result of the internal expansion that is expected to result from the machinery of the Treaty of Rome. It is the basic philosophy of the Common Market that leads the Community to adopt this position. Previous experience, such as that gained with Benelux, has, moreover, shown that the development of trade among countries forming a customs union has had no ill effect on trade with outside countries. On the contrary, the growth of investments and consumption within the customs union, in fact, brings with it an expansion of imports from nonmember countries. One can point, for instance, to the fact that, on the basis of the provisional figures for 1960, the Common Market's internal trade has increased by twenty-five per cent over the previous year and its external trade by more than eighteen per cent, imports gaining considerably more than exports. In this light, it may be considered that the internal *expansion* of the Six is one of the best guarantees of the beneficial effects that the Treaty will have for the countries outside the Common Market. Table II shows this increase of trade with nonmember countries, both on a European and a world scale. The Community has, moreover, repeated its readiness to discuss with its partners any practical difficulty that might arise and to seek ways of dealing with it. But discussion is difficult, since it turns on hypothetical cases and largely concerns a gamble on the future consequences of the Treaty, since so far no concrete difficulty has arisen.

This, however, does not, of course, relieve the Community of the duty to make special effort in its relations with the countries in the process of development. As has been stressed before, the Community has a definite responsibility in this respect. Without prejudice to the machinery laid down in the Treaty for the benefit of the directly associated countries, this regional assistance must be supplemented by par-

External Policy

TABLE II
Development of the Imports of the E.E.C.
(Intra-community trade excluded)

Imports to the community and their source	1958 millions	1959 millions	1960 millions	Per cent increase from 1958 to 1960
World	$14,610	$15,411	$17,753	+21.5
Near-East	1,904	1,893	1,980	+ 3.9
Far-East	912	899	1,139	+24.8
Latin America	1,561	1,630	1,812	+16.0
North America	3,238	2,981	4,276	+24.2
European countries non-member of the E. E. C.	4,263	4,623	5,368	+25.9

ticipation in other forms of aid that will be open to all countries in the course of development. Under this heading, the Community as such is already sharing in the work of the Development Assistance Group, the first meeting of which took place in Washington in 1960. This is, moreover, one of the fields in which coordination of the positions adopted by the Community and the leading industrial countries, especially the United Kingdom and the United States, is particularly desirable.

There are also some European countries, whose attitude towards the unification of the Six and the changes that this can bring about, has been very reserved. The report of the Spaak Committee, which was to serve as the basis for the Treaty of Rome, was adopted by the six countries at the Conference of Venice in May 1956. In July 1956, the Council of Ministers of the O.E.E.C., acting on the initiative of Great Britain, undertook to study a draft for a free trade area, which reflected the desire to set up as soon as possible a means of extending the commercial advantages of the Common Market to all its neighbors and of eliminating from the very outset any possibility of differential treatment. These negotiations were suspended at the end of 1958 without a satisfactory conclusion having been reached. It may be appropriate at this point to recall the reasons for this state of affairs, which are to be found both in the main lines of the agreement proposed and in a deep-rooted misunderstanding of the true nature of the Common Market.

First, the *technical* difficulties. It is clearly more difficult to reach agreement among seventeen countries than among only six, especially if the agreement in question would have very considerable importance and would provide for the eventual complete elimination of all customs duties and quota restrictions among the member states. Moreover, while the six countries of the Common Market are very similar in their structure and are already closely linked by trade, if only because they have common borders, the proposed free trade area embraced countries differing widely from one another in their economic development and in their trade patterns. Some of them do a very important part of their trade with the Common Market, whereas others at present have very much bigger outlets outside Europe than in the Common Market, so that the specifically European commitments that they can undertake are correspondingly limited. On the political plane also, their situation is different: for while the six countries of the Common Market belong to the same alliances, some of the countries that took part in the negotiations for the free trade area maintain a position of strict neutrality.

Furthermore the very system proposed—that is to say, a free trade area in which each member would be free to maintain its own customs tariffs vis-à-vis nonmember states at the level, high or low, that suited its convenience, and to preserve its own autonomy in commercial policy—gave rise to a number of practical difficulties. It is true that this system took into account the very great diversity of economic goals and political wishes of the countries promoting the free trade area. But against this advantage, it had the drawback of creating a number of technical and administrative problems (*e.g.,* the diversion of trade, the determination of origin, the calculation of added value, and, possibly, the imposition of compensatory charges) that added to the other difficulties of the negotiations and made them even more complex.

While in the Common Market the six countries considered that the attainment of the commercial aims, and in particular the total elimination of customs duties, must be backed by a series of undertakings and by a certain common discipline in other fields, which, in fact, affect the development of trade, the basic attitude of the other European countries was rather the reverse of this. To them, for either the political or the economic reasons already mentioned, the free-trade-area agreement would have had to be strictly limited to certain commercial benefits, with undertakings in other fields kept to a minimum. Quite apart from any ideological conflict, this undeniably involved technical dangers for the Common Market and its development. There was, in fact, the risk that difficulties might arise among the Six in the implementation of the Treaty, from motives that would have had nothing to do with the Community itself, but that would have been due to imperfections or to the lack of adequate undertakings on the part of the other members of the free trade area. It has been pointed out that the first years of the implementation of the Treaty have shown how unification vis-à-vis the outside world was essential to ensure internal unification. In these circumstances, to extend to a large number of widely different nonmember countries much of the internal machinery of the Treaty, but in the context of very different undertakings, and in particular without any commitment on commercial policy and on relations with the outside world in general, could have been tantamount to preventing the Common Market from reaching its goal. The force of this argument can be seen from the institutional point of view, when it is remembered that the Common Market has, as it were, to be the motive force for political unification in Europe; but it can also be appreciated from the strictly economic point of view.

The main benefits to be hoped for from the Common Market, in fact, do not lie in the first reductions of duties or increases of quotas. Their effect, though certainly favorable, is limited. The main benefits—the growth of investment, the increase of consumption, and structural reorganization—are to be expected from the *conclusion* of the measures agreed on—that is to say, from the complete establishment of a single market and the fusion of existing national economies. If this is borne in mind, it is clear that one must avoid anything that might seriously prejudice the chances of completely implementing the Treaty or that might change it into an agreement creating a mere preferential area, in conformity neither with its vital economic and political aims nor even with the rules of G.A.T.T.

This, in fact, is where it may be said that the negotiations for the free trade area involved not only technical difficulties, *but a deep-rooted misunderstanding of the true nature of the Common Market*. Some countries, in fact, wished to look upon the latter as no more than a mere commercial arrangement that could easily, with a little goodwill, be replaced by another and wider commercial arrangement of a different character. For the Six, however, the purely commercial aspects of the Treaty of Rome are indissolubly linked, as has been said before, with a series of broader economic commitments that would lead to the degree of unity they are seeking to attain. They believe that over and above the free movement of goods, they must ensure freedom of movement for persons, capital, and services; that a number of fundamental conditions of competition must be established or brought into line, especially in the social field and also by the elaboration of a common agricultural policy; and, finally, that in external relations, the establishment of a common customs tariff is one of the elements indispensable to the completely free movement of goods within the Community.

Furthermore, the magnitude of these economic commitments in itself gives a clearly political character to the whole operation. In the first place, it is necessary, if these economic commitments are to be fulfilled, to take extremely important decisions in the whole field covered by the Treaty and to arrive at very difficult compromises on issues vital to the Member States. This is not possible unless there is a constant political will. Secondly, the economic unity thus reached must make possible further progress in political integration.

This is, moreover, in accordance with the spirit of G.A.T.T., which permits deviations from the most-favored-nation clause, but subject to an assurance that what is being done will really lead to unification, to the establishment of a new economic unit among the countries concerned. In such cases, differential treatment becomes no more than a transitory tariff measure, justified by the end in view. To the extent, however, that such an operation would be likely to bring about no more than partial trade advantages and thus to set up a new preferential area, it would amount to a totally unjustified disruption of international trade. This criterion provides the touchstone for any wider solution in Europe. To the extent that such an association represents a serious step towards unification, that it offers a chance of ultimate success, that it constitutes a major srengthening of both economic and political cohesion in Europe, a differential treatment covering all the European countries could be justified. On this latter point, however, and especially with regard to the United States, the recent trend in economic relations between Europe and North America calls for additional caution.

III

Economic relations between Europe and the United States are very different from what they were twelve years ago when the O.E.E.C. was set up. At that time, the economic and monetary situation of Europe was extremely serious owing to the ravages caused by the war. It is to the honor of the United States that it recognized the dangers of this situation and sought to remedy them. To serve this purpose, the O.E.E.C. was given a twofold task: to ensure the allocation of Marshall aid credits; and to promote in Europe a liberalization of trade and a greater degree of cooperation, by which European recovery could be speeded. In view of the situation in Europe and especially the marked imbalance in its trade with the United States, which was reflected in a disastrous shortage of dollars, it was accepted that this liberalization of trade might be operated for the benefit of the European countries alone and, therefore, with a certain degree of discrimination against the United States.

Today the situation, although not reversed, is very different. Europe is selling more and more to the United States, and there is increasing stability in trade balances. Most of the European currencies have regained some degree of strength, and since the beginning of 1959, almost all of them have again become largely convertible. One of the first consequences of this has been the transformation of the European Payments Union into something more flexible. Another consequence is that Europe as a whole can no longer be regarded as a partner requiring the assistance of the United States and entitled to privileged treatment in relation to the United States. On the contrary, in view of the American situation, it is necessary to avoid all discrimination—that is to say, all differential treatment. It is important to promote a liberal policy in European-American relations, based on equality, which will be to the advantage of both sides and will avoid any action which might provoke a return to protectionism.

The E.E.C. has been fully conscious of this fact. It seemed that neither economically (the American balance-of-payments situation), nor legally (because the return to European convertibility makes quota discrimination against the dollar no longer acceptable), nor politically, was there any justification for Europe as a whole to envisage a system based on differential treatment of the United States. Such a system could only be considered if, through its various mechanisms, economic as well as institutional, it offered a guarantee of a positive and really constructive contribution on both the European and world level.

This anxiety not to establish in Europe a commercial system that would amount to unjustified discrimination against others, especially the United States, is certainly well-founded as regards present relations between the United States and Europe;

but the same applies equally to other nonmember countries. The developing countries in particular would be hard pressed to understand why the richest countries should establish amongst themselves a preferential area for the sole benefit of their own commercial interests and should do this at a moment when it was essential that the efforts of the leading countries should be coordinated in order to improve international trade.

IV

Nevertheless, this does not mean to say that the Common Market has done nothing with regard to its European partners. On the contrary, it has worked out a policy and has already adopted a number of important measures to implement it. After the suspension of the negotiations on the free trade area in the "Maudling Committee" at the end of 1958, the Commission of the Common Market drew up a memorandum in which the following principles and lines of action were set out:

1. The Community remains open. Any European country can associate itself with it or even join it, and in this way participate in all the commercial advantages of the Common Market. But it must be realized that such participation in the advantages implies the acceptance of a certain form of discipline or commitments *that will ensure both the smooth functioning of economic integration in Europe and the conformity of the operation with the general principles referred to earlier.*
2. Over and above this serious and constructive possibility of association, which remains desirable, the Common Market can at once adopt a liberal policy vis-à-vis its European partners that will mitigate any anxieties or difficulties they may experience and that will take account of their specific problems.
3. Such a liberal policy vis-à-vis its European neighbors must not be divorced from the Common Market's attitude to other countries or groups of countries. On the contrary, the Community should make a positive contribution as part of a world-wide liberal policy without any discrimination.

Such a liberal policy has already shown fruit in a certain number of concrete measures adopted. In the case of quantitative restrictions, the Community decided, when the first quota enlargements were made within the Community on the way to the full Common Market, to allow the other European countries to share in the benefits derived from the major part of these enlargements. The same was done at the time of the second enlargement, made in accordance with the provisions of the Treaty of Rome. In order, however, to take account of the changes in the situation between Europe and the rest of the world and in particular the United States, discrimination for the benefit of one geographical area and against another was no longer considered justifiable. Under these conditions, the enlargements were made in a way that would benefit all the contracting parties of G.A.T.T. to whom the most-favored-nation clause applies. More recently, in May 1960, it was decided, in connection with the speedier implementation of the Treaty, that all industrial quotas amongst the Member States should be completely abolished at an early date. Here, again, the benefit of the operation would be extended to nonmember countries. It can, therefore, already be said that the problem of differential treatment in the field of industrial quotas virtually no longer exists, although at the end of 1958, it was considered by the European partners of the Common Market to be the most difficult of the problems and gave rise at that time to fairly serious objections of principle, especially when at the time of the first quota enlargement already mentioned, the Community decided not to extend to other European countries the three per cent enlargement of oil quotas.

There remains, therefore, only the tariff problem; but this is a question not of principle, but of degree. It is true that a very high tariff can be prohibitive or can bring with it diversions of trade, especially in the traditional pattern of trade. On the other hand, a sufficiently low tariff is perfectly compatible with the normal development of international trade. The E.E.C. has acted along those lines.

When the first internal tariff reduction of ten per cent was carried out within the Community, on the way to the full Common Market, a certain extension for the benefit of nonmember countries was granted; once again, it covered all the contracting parties of G.A.T.T. to whom the most-favored-nation clause applies. The same procedure was envisaged at the time of the second tariff reduction amongst the Six, subject to the Community's trading partners and especially its European neighbors being prepared to grant a certain degree of reciprocity. More important, however, was the decision, taken in connection with the speedier implementation of the Treaty, that the first approximation towards the common external tariff, to be carried out on January 1, 1961, should be carried through on the basis of that tariff *reduced by twenty per cent*. This reduction was practical proof of the Community's will to follow the most liberal tariff policy vis-à-vis the outside world. The twenty per cent reduction may be made permanent, provided that nonmember countries, especially the European countries, agree to grant a certain measure of reciprocity. In thus making concessions on its tariff—which are to be taken into account in later negotiations but to be applied forthwith—the Community wished not only to mitigate any difficulties that nonmember countries might experience, but also to commit the world's leading industrial countries to new tariff negotiations that could bring about a considerable improvement of trading conditions throughout the world.

In the same spirit, the E.E.C. was the first to take up the proposals made by the American Government (Dillon proposals) for a series of tariff negotiations in G.A.T.T. Indeed, it was largely with these negotiations in mind that the Community made the advance gesture of the twenty per cent reduction on the common tariff. The Community has not excluded the possibility of other similar reductions being made later.

V

The establishment of the "Seven" of the European Free Trade Association (E.F.T.A.) in November 1959 introduced a new element into the situation, but without fundamentally altering the facts. The Association is made up of seven countries (Great Britain, Sweden, Switzerland, Denmark, Norway, Austria, and Portugal) that do not belong to the Common Market. It does not include five European members of the old O.E.E.C.—namely, Ireland, Iceland, Greece, Turkey, and Spain.

In as much as this association of the Seven is based on principles and machinery that are very close to the original British plan for a free trade area, and, therefore, very different from those of the Common Market, it does not facilitate the search for a comprehensive solution. This is, however, true from the technical point of view, and has nothing to do with any purely tactical considerations. It might also be said to lend further emphasis to the need for a liberal policy in Europe, reflected in reciprocal tariff concessions. Only if and when actual difficulties were created for trade by unduly high customs tariffs would it be possible to speak of an "economic division of Europe," which might even lead to some political tension. This situation has not arisen and is not likely to arise. In fact, the problem of differential quota treatment has already ceased to exist—as has been pointed out. If the two groups agree to some reduction of their tariffs either in G.A.T.T. or other negotiations, the risk of any damage to the established pattern of trade will become extremely slight. The action taken so far by the Community reflects this aim.

After the decision of January 1960, a committee was set up for discussions and negotiations between the Common Market and its European partners, especially those belonging to the E.F.T.A. This committee, which is known as the "Committee of Twenty-one" (since apart from the other European countries, the United States and Canada are full members), has done a great deal of work in the course of this year. On a number of occasions, the Community has made the following proposals:

1. A reduction of the common tariff, in the light of certain reciprocal concessions from the members of the E.F.T.A.; and
2. further studies to cover any particular difficulties that might arise in the discussions concerning specific solutions in conformity with the rules of G.A.T.T.

This is, as it were, a double approach: first, a liberal policy that *a priori* reduces the scope of any possible difficulties by reducing the level of tariff barriers; and then additional action, case by case, wherever it is required because of continuing specific difficulties.

Some remarks must be made about these proposals. While their effect is European, they also have world-wide repercussions because of the play of the most-favored-nation clause. Further measures of this kind have a long-term incidence that is not to be neglected, although they have sometimes been described as purely short-term or partial solutions. They commit the Community to a liberal approach, and this can have a considerable influence on its internal structure as well as on its future development; they also commit, or endeavor to commit, the leading industrial countries in the same way. As for the specific difficulties, it must be pointed out once again that so far none of them has arisen, and that on the contrary the Common Market is an area that is importing more and more; and the more firmly the liberal policy can be applied, the smaller will be the risk of specific difficulties arising in the future. Table III gives details, for the members of the E.F.T.A., of the development of trade with the E.E.C., and shows their increased trade with the Community as a result of the latter's economic expansion.

TABLE III
DEVELOPMENT OF THE IMPORTS OF THE E.E.C.
(Intra-community trade excluded)

Imports to the community and their source	1958 millions	1959 millions	1960 millions	Per cent increase from 1958 to 1960
Total E. F. T. A.	$3,571	$3,906	$4,600	+24.8
Austria	440	452	535	+21.5
Denmark	391	422	419	+ 7.1
Norway	207	211	237	+14.4
Portugal	76	72	83	+ 9.2
England (or Great Britain)	1,160	1,363	1,534	+32.2
Sweden	692	730	381	+27.3
Switzerland	605	656	771	+27.4

It is, of course, true that the way trade will develop cannot be judged simply from the statistics of the day; and it is perfectly understandable that some countries, especially those who do a large part of their trade in the Common Market, should feel some concern about more long-term economic developments and should wish for an immediate share in the internal advantages of the Treaty. The trade aspect is not the only one; the question of investments may also be of importance. To such countries, anxious to obtain definite or over-all commitments and guarantees, the possibility of association with or membership of the Community remains open.

The distinction between these two possibilities, based on two separate articles of the Treaty, must be clearly understood. Membership[7] would normally mean the acceptance of all the principles and the entire machinery of the Treaty of Rome. It would mean that the Community would increase its members, the new Member States subscribing fully to its objectives, both economically and politically. Association[8] is a more flexible formula. It creates no new member of the Common Market, but establishes between a given country and the unit formed by the Six a series of undertakings and mutual bonds, while each partner retains a certain measure of autonomy. The flexibility of association as a solution of the problem can show itself in two ways. On the one hand, particular account can be taken in practice of the specific problems of the countries seeking association. On the other hand,

[7] E.E.C. Treaty art. 237.
[8] *Id.* art. 238.

on questions of principle, the contents of the agreement to associate can also be widely varied. It may range from institutional consultative machinery based on common objectives and, as in the case of the association agreement between the E.C.S.C. and the United Kingdom, containing nothing that, from the economic angle, conflicts with the most-favored-nation clause, to an agreement of very great economic substance such, for example, as a customs union.

Negotiations between the Community and Greece and between the Community and Turkey were begun under article 238 of the Treaty. These negotiations have been conducted by the Common Market Commission. The two countries named were not invited to take part in the talks that led to the establishment of the E.F.T.A., since these were of a strictly commercial and industrial character that had little connection with the problems facing these two countries; both are in process of development, and any agreement necessarily implies an element of assistance to them. The E.E.C. felt that it was a political necessity to respond to their request.

At the time of writing, the negotiations with Turkey are still proceeding; but those with Greece culminated on March 30, 1961, in the signature of a draft agreement of association which is shortly to be concluded. The draft agreement is based on a customs union to be established between Greece and the Community over a transition period and intended to enable Greece to become, at a later date, when its economic progress allows, a full member of the Community. It also includes a number of protocols to take account of special aspects of the Greek economy, which had to be in a position to continue and even to accelerate its drive for modernization and industrialization. For this reason, it was necessary to include special measures such as the establishment of a longer transition period for certain products, or the protection by Greece of her new industries; the Community, for its part, will provide financial aid and will also take exceptional steps to improve Greek outlets in the Member Countries.

The draft agreement is not limited, moreover, to a mere customs union. Following the example of the Rome Treaty, and at the same time taking account of Greek needs and possibilities, it includes sections on the free movement of persons, services, and capital, transport, competition rules, and economic policy.

Most of these proposed measures refer expressly to the rules or principles of the Rome Treaty, but leave the details and conditions of their application to decision by the institutions set up under the Association Agreements.

It should also be pointed out that the association of the overseas territories as it was laid down in outline by the Treaty of Rome may be subject to certain amendments, if only because most of these countries have now become independent. This is one of the many points on which the particular responsibilities of the Community must be judged in the light of its wider role.

At the beginning of 1961, therefore, the E.E.C. found itself engaged in a series of negotiations stemming in part from its various responsibilities and in part from the clarification of its relationships with its main trading partners.

The normal forum for these discussions is G.A.T.T. Talks are proceeding for the recognition of the common tariff, which, of course, is one of the essential elements of the customs union of the Six. It is certainly in conformity with the G.A.T.T. rules; nevertheless, its establishment implies a number of changes, and in particular the unbinding of duties, which must be studied by the nonmember countries under article XXIV (6) of the G.A.T.T. Convention. A difficulty, which is mainly one of timing, arises for agriculture: much of the common agricultural policy of the Six still remains to be worked out, whereas certain nonmember countries would like to obtain immediate and very precise guarantees on the effects of this policy on their trade.

As soon as the negotiations on the recognition of the Common Market's external tariff have ended, it will be possible to go on to the stage of tariff negotiations in the real sense of the word—that is, to reciprocal tariff concessions. In this field, the Community has proposed across-the-board reductions for the entire common tariff; these have already been mentioned in connection with the decision for the speedier implementation of the Treaty. In the Committee of Twenty-one, the Community has also proposed that, in view of the European problems, efforts should be coordinated in order to ensure that these negotiations produce the maximum effect.

Moreover, the Community shares in the other work of G.A.T.T.—that is to say, it is represented on the committees that deal more particularly with agricultural problems and with the relationship between countries in process of development and the industrialized countries. This does not exclude the search for solutions to any specific difficulties that may arise. Consultations have, for example, begun with certain Latin American countries.

Finally, on December 14, 1960, the O.E.E.C. was recast and a new body set up under the name of the Organization for Economic Cooperation and Development. This reorganization is largely in line with the principles that have guided the Community itself. The new Convention puts the United States, Canada, and all the European countries on an equal footing. Also, the traditional functions of the O.E.E.C. must now be considered in the light of the new situation in Europe and from the angle of the ever-growing importance of the relations not only between Europe and the rest of the world, but, more accurately, between the industrialized countries (be they European or American) and the countries in course of development.

It is against this background that the action of the industrialized countries should be coordinated, because it involves the most important of the responsible industrial countries, especially the United States, the Community, and the United Kingdom. The commercial problems of relations between the Six and the Seven could also be studied in this setting. Lastly, the more general coordination of western economic policies, and in particular of cyclical policies, should be examined in this framework.

Without encroaching upon the rights of G.A.T.T., which remains the organization with the widest membership, the importance of this intermediate group between G.A.T.T. and the Europe of the Six is obvious, since it comprises both North America and the European countries. Permanent consultation and the preparation of decisions to be taken in the other organizations, either of a wider geographical compass such as G.A.T.T. or of a more specialized technical competence (monetary organizations, for example), could occur at this level.

VI

One finds, therefore, that by virtue of its novelty the establishment of the Common Market has given rise to apprehension in certain countries. But one must also remember that it has so far produced no real difficulties. Paradoxically enough, however, it is very much easier to tackle concrete difficulties and to find means of removing them than it is to allay fears. This leads one, I think, to the following concluding observations:

1. The Common Market must not be judged from the commercial point of view alone, or without taking into account its contribution to European unification. But even from the economic point of view, the expansion that the Common Market is expected to bring should produce a favorable development of world trade from which all nonmember countries will benefit. In addition, the unification of the Six constitutes a new fact that will make it possible for these countries to play a greater positive part in attaining world equilibrium. Undeniably, the emergence of the Common Market has provoked a certain amount of rethinking in this field and has already brought forth proposals for reciprocal tariff reductions that are having a healthy influence on the trend of the world's economy.

2. This role of the Common Market as a driving force in both the economic and the political field is one of its essential features. The stronger the Community becomes and the more rapidly it is united, the more easily will it be able to play the positive role that can be rightly expected of it. This is the real significance of the fact that it was possible to couple the decision to accelerate the application of the Treaty with a decision at the same time to reduce the level of the common external tariff.

3. The Community remains open to any country wishing to join it or to associate itself with it. Clearly, this is the most complete sort of coordination the Common Market can offer; but it is not the only kind. A liberal policy practiced by the Common Market should also have excellent general results and should meet the problems of most nonmember countries.

The question of confidence in the future effects of the Common Market has been repeatedly brought up in the course of this paper. It is admittedly difficult to expect nonmember countries to accept more confidence in the internal expansion of the Six as an answer to their anxieties, just as it is difficult to ask the Community to doubt its own success, which would be contrary to its aims and contrary to the production and trade statistics already at its disposal. But it is here that one sees the full value of the liberal policy that the Community has proposed and begun to apply. This policy will further strengthen nonmember countries in their relations with the Common Market; and in the kind of gamble on the future represented by the unification of the Six, it will further reduce the measure of possible risk and increase the likelihood of a favorable outcome. Finally, moreover, this developing policy is a sign of the six countries' good will, a pledge that they are pursuing their unification not in the spirit of setting up a closed shop, but in that of making a new and fundamental contribution to the development of the free world.

JURIDICAL AND INSTITUTIONAL ASPECTS OF THE EUROPEAN REGIONAL COMMUNITIES
PAUL REUTER*

I

GENERAL CHARACTERISTICS OF THE THREE COMMUNITIES

A. Economic and Political Characteristics

Three Communities form the subject of this study—namely, (a) the European Coal and Steel Community (E.C.S.C.), (b) the European Economic Community (E.E.C.), and (c) the European Atomic Energy Community (Euratom). All three are regional international organizations, economic in character. Their object is to unify the economies of the member countries by creating among them a common market—in one case for coal and steel (E.C.S.C.); in another case for the products and substances relating to nuclear energy (Euratom); and finally, for the generality of the bases and products of economic life (E.E.C.). At the heart of these enterprises, there is a common economic philosophy that can be defined by the concept of regulated competition or institutional markets. By this it must be understood that the economic regime of these unified areas entails two combined elements—on the one hand, competition and, on the other, an organization charged with the duty of elaborating and applying rules, supervising their application, and fixing penalties for their violation. Naturally, this characteristic of organization varies with the products and the circumstances involved. Thus, it is very marked for the fissionable materials and minerals subject to the control of the Agency created by the Euratom treaty.[1] The characteristic is almost equally visible with respect to coal and steel in the event of a grave economic crisis and, even in a normal period, includes strict rules about publicity and nondiscrimination with respect to coal and steel.[2] As for the E.E.C., although the organization of the market can be rigorous with respect to agricultural products,[3] it is fairly light for the bulk of other products subject to the Treaty and tends toward antitrust legislation of the American type.

Against this backdrop one is better prepared for a technical analysis of the powers which have given the European Regional Communities their juridical importance. These powers were not intended merely for the supervision of a completely private and liberal economic movement, but instead for the performance of a more active governmental role. The powers delegated to the Communities, such as legislation,

* Professor in the Faculty of Law and Economic Sciences of Paris; jurisconsult-adjoint to the French Ministry of Foreign Affairs.
[1] Euratom Treaty arts. 52-76.
[2] E.C.S.C. Treaty arts. 71-75.
[3] E.E.C. Treaty arts. 38-47.

jurisdiction over individuals, and imposition of penalties on enterprises, are not those generally delegated by countries to international organizations. From this delegation the Communities derive great political importance.

It must be added that the States concerned in the three Communities have considered that their creation would open the way towards the political unification of Europe. This intention was clearly expressed in the Schuman declaration of May 9, 1950 and in the preamble to the E.C.S.C. Treaty; and it is also demonstrated by the attempt to create a European Defense Community in the Treaty of May 27, 1952. But, when the Defense Community, as well as its projected extension into a political community, never saw the light of day, the authors of the Rome treaties of 1957 constructed the E.E.C. and Euratom in such a way as to mask their political importance and to foster the illusion that, in the modern world, economic unification could operate while leaving national sovereignty intact. Even if there is a possibility of doing this while the object is limited to partial economic unification along the lines of the E.C.S.C. and Euratom, it becomes less likely in the framework of the general common market.

Nonetheless, the ambiguity of the Rome Treaties (Euratom and E.E.C.) is real. Not only is there visible an opposition between the exterior presentation and the real strength of certain institutions, but—what is even more serious—these agreements include a large number of matters left undetermined, especially in the case of E.E.C. In fact, with respect to E.C.S.C. and, to a lesser extent, Euratom, the Member States could set forth in the very text of the signed agreements the essentials of the rules to be applied. Such was not true as to the E.E.C. because of the wide range of the subject matter. The agreement creating E.E.C. contains certain relatively precise rules on some points (such as the timing for disappearance of customs and quantitative restrictions); but, as for the rest, it contains only principles and promises. What appears is the framework for a treaty! On the other hand, the real form of E.E.C. is still not determined; and to make concrete the principles put forward in the treaty depends upon the constancy of the political determinations made by the Member States.

These remarks tend to caution the jurist to prudence in drawing general conclusions. The political scientist makes the inventory of the forces working for the unification of Europe and of the obstacles encountered by those forces. The jurist can only point out what is certain, what is doubtful, and by what paths evolution is possible.

B. Institutional Framework of the Communities

In a general way, the three Communities show the same over-all framework for their institutions—namely, a two-headed Executive, a parliamentary assembly, and a Court of Justice. In each Community the executive power reposes in two groups—on the one hand, a body of independent persons nominated in common accord by the Member States but acting outside the scope of national influences, and, on the other hand, a council of national ministers, who take part, subject to varying conditions, in deliberations which, more or less and according to the particular case, bind governments and private enterprises. These two groups collaborate in governing each of the Communities. The Council of National Ministers corresponds to the central organ of all international organizations; by contrast, the body composed of independent persons is a relative innovation. No doubt, in all international organizations—and in the political life of all countries[4]—there are groups of independent individuals which, within the organizational framework, have the authority to offer proposals for action by the organization or to exercise quasi-judicial functions. However, an especially significant feature of the independent executive organs created for the three Communities—E.C.S.C.'s High Authority and the Commissions of E.E.C. and of Euratom—is that they foreshadow a European parliamentary regime, since the members of these organs, though originally government nominees, are politically responsible to a European assembly. In fact, however, the membership of those bodies has been made up not only of politicians but also of experts.

The European Parliamentary Assembly, which has authority to act within the framework of each Community, has so far been constituted only of delegates selected by the respective national assemblies from their own membership. However, the treaties anticipate that Assembly members may be elected by direct universal suffrage; and a project recently approved by the Assembly concerns making this prospect a reality.

The Court of Justice, which is open not only to Member States but also to private enterprises and, in a certain measure, to the organs of the three Communities, has a complex role to play, the most important part of which is the control of the acts of the executive organs of the Communities. This control is exercised through the procedure for annulment of a decision made by the Executive.

C. Relations Between the Communities

In light of the similarities in the general institutional frameworks of the European Communities, the question suggests itself: Is the time not ripe to merge the three Communities? In connection with this important question, one notes that juridically, each Community has a distinct and precise basis; the international agreements relating to them are formally distinct for each Community. The explanation for this is obvious in the case of the E.C.S.C., which stood alone at the outset in 1952. Then, in 1957, the negotiators at Rome took enormous care to ensure that each of the two new Communities should rest upon its own juridical instruments. Even so, the three Communities have numerous and delicate relationships—a great number of which are poorly defined.

For one thing, the Rome agreements sought to avoid a disorderly multiplication of organs; and, in a special Convention it was agreed that certain organs would be common to all three Communities (Assembly and Court of Justice), or to two of

[4] *E.g.*, regulatory commissions, such as the Federal Trade Commission in the United States.

them (Economic and Social Committee). This solution has been extended without formal agreement to other new organs (Secretariat of the Council of Ministers and the Information Services). It constitutes a new and original adaptation of an institution—union of personnel—well known to public law. This device can render great service; but at the same time it creates considerable juridical difficulties, many of which have not yet been resolved. Carried too far, these measures for union of personnel might result in the complete suppression of the organic independence of each Community. In this same vein, suggestions are made daily for unifying in one body the E.C.S.C.'s High Authority and the Commissions of E.E.C. and Euratom; but realization of such proposals is far from simple.

In connection with efforts to harmonize and unify the three Communities, juridical hurdles must often be surmounted. To cite only one example, the national governments are still competent under the E.C.S.C. Treaty to negotiate commercial agreements relating to coal and steel; but when the provisions of articles 110-116 of the E.E.C. Treaty are applied, they will not be authorized to negotiate such agreements as to other products. Moreover, the E.E.C. Treaty contains a monetary clause safeguarding the free circulation of all the products which it governs, but the E.C.S.C. Treaty lacks such a clause. Should it then be concluded that the provisions of the E.E.C. Treaty (*lex generalis*) apply where the E.C.S.C. Treaty (*lex specialis*) is silent? Such an effect can be doubted, since this question is too complex to permit its solution by so summary a formula.

What can be said without danger of error is that the working out of the Treaty establishing the E.E.C. will be necessarily accompanied by a unification of the three Communities; but that result will be neither immediate nor complete, and the methods employed may be diverse.

D. Conclusion

In concluding this section of the paper, the dynamic character of the Communities must be stressed. They are built to an economic plan, and with an implicit political objective. They are equipped with four main organs (Council of Ministers, body of independent executives, Court of Justice, and Parliamentary Assembly), and that may well lead to the pre-eminence of one or the other of those organs. Further, though separate in their juridical foundations and in their respective personalities, the three Communities nevertheless tend to become unified.

These wide possibilities of evolution raise a fundamental question which encompasses all the others. To what extent do the European Communities establish a European federalism? Or, to use an adjective which has already given rise in Europe to passionate controversy, to what extent are the European Communities supranational? The question must be posed in these terms because public opinion so poses it; but it must be stressed that, from the scientific point of view, such questions use a vocabulary which may engender considerable confusion. Although it will be seen in the course of this study that the European Communities display certain very pronounced federal aspects, it would be wrong to adopt any rigid notion of federalism with respect to them. There is no absolute distinction between federal and international structures, and there are numerous varieties of federalism. The federalism of the United States today is not the same as it was in the time of Chief Justice Marshall; that of India does not resemble that of Canada; and it may well be questioned whether, in a more general way, the technical evolution of the modern world, the mode of evolution of military problems, economic relationships, and transport will not lead to extensive regrouping of States in the second half of the twentieth century on the basis of formulae very different from those of the nineteenth century and the early part of the twentieth.

Two important characteristics enable one to fix the degree and the nature of the federation of all political structures: the equilibrium of political forces and the relationships affecting the juridical organisms. Indeed, in its most general form, the spirit of federalism is simple. It relies upon equilibrium between the federal and the local powers; and in the sphere of juridical technique it leads to a harmonious system of relationships between the federal and local laws—a system which transposes political equilibrium to the juridical sphere. It is from these points of view that the Communities should be studied in order to determine what evolution may take place from the initial steps traced by the Treaties.

II

THE EQUILIBRIUM OF POLITICAL FORCES

The situation at the outset is simple to describe. There were no European political forces but only national states, national political parties, and national enterprises. The founders of the E.C.S.C. wished to create European forces by an interplay of institutions. Although the organs of the E.C.S.C. do not all exhibit to the same degree the aptitude to represent and evolve a European political force, it is possible— starting with the E.C.S.C. Treaty and examining at the same time the structure, relationships and powers of its organs—to discern an initial plan. It will then be shown how this plan has evolved and what transformations have been achieved by the Treaties of Rome and subsequent events.

In the E.C.S.C. Treaty the central governmental organ is the High Authority, which is placed under the ultimate control of the Court of Justice. The advantage accruing to the European forces from this arrangement is considerable, since the High Authority and the Court are absolutely independent of the national governments. Although their members are nominated by the governments, it is for a relatively long period of six years, and, at least in the case of the High Authority, a principle of co-option by the members first designated by the States arises in combination with that of governmental designation in such a way as to reinforce still further the independence of the members. The character of the Assembly was not fixed at the outset; since it is made up of delegates chosen by the component national parliaments, its role will move in different directions according to the influence of the European or nationalistic tendencies which will appear in the Assembly.

Contrariwise, the Council of Ministers would appear essentially to represent the national governments. However, its role is secondary because it is to intervene only in limited cases—either by giving conforming advice when confronted with certain important decisions of the High Authority (*i.e.*, advice which must be favorable if effect is to be given to the decisions), or by itself making certain decisions relating to the administration of the Community. Thus, at least in principle, the Council can function as a federal organism without being impeded by the unanimity rule which so often paralyzes international organizations.

A first general impression would support the view that the Paris Treaty of 1951 has accorded a very important place to organs by means of which European political forces can gain expression. Nevertheless, other considerations point in a different direction. In the first place, the Treaty itself has set out a very important part of the rules which are to be applied in the Community. To this extent, the functions of the High Authority are limited to the application of these rules and the control of their operation without the assumption of real political responsibilities. The conclusions which can be drawn from the structure of the E.C.S.C. must, therefore, not be exaggerated. This observation is all the weightier since the sphere of the powers of the E.C.S.C. is limited with precision. Reference can undoubtedly be made to powers transferred exclusively to the E.C.S.C.—for example, in regard to the prices of coal and steel payable to the producers. However, besides these powers of the Community, there exist certain powers exercisable by the Member States in competition with the Community; and there are many such powers affecting coal and steel. Some of these powers are governed by the Treaty, while others are subject to an obligation, rather badly defined, to ensure harmony. It would be quite erroneous to believe that coal and steel come within the powers of the Community; such a formula is almost void of meaning. What should be said is that as regards coal and steel the Community exercises precise and limited powers.

Finally, it must be noted that, even for the independent organs, a weighting effect arising from national political influences has intervened with respect to the designation of members. Thus, the figure of nine members fixed for the High Authority is the result of a series of minute considerations relating to national influences,[5] and the designations of members for the Court of Justice have likewise been forced to bear those considerations in mind. Furthermore, the impossibility of reaching agreement as to the permanent headquarters of the institutions—an impossibility which to this day has not yet been overcome—shows at the outset the force of national resistances to unification.

[5] It was, of course, necessary that each State have at least one national among the members of the High Authority. It was, moreover, necessary that the total number be uneven. A seven-member authority would have led to the presence of two German or two French members—a prospect to which neither country would have agreed. A nine-member authority composed of two German, two French, four Benelux (Belgium, the Netherlands, and Luxembourg) and one Italian member was found amenable, and therefore adopted.

Such being the initial situation, how far has experience allowed these diverse forces confronting one another to find their equilibrium? Any general evaluation in this regard must be very shadowy. It should take account of factors external to the Communities and notably of the general political and economic situation. The first years (1952-53) were marked by the expectation of a reinforcement of the E.C.S.C. by new treaties. Then the rejection of the European Defense Community, together with the opposition of Mr. Mendès-France (1954-55), considerably slowed down the affirmative recognition of European political forces. These revived, however, after the conference of Messina (June 1955) and the conclusion of the Rome agreements (March 25, 1957). The general economic situation was very favorable to the E.C.S.C. until 1958; but since that date the coal crisis has imposed a heavy burden on that Community, and at the same time the E.C.S.C. has had to face the most difficult problems which it had not been able or willing to resolve earlier—such as the elimination of discriminations in transport and reform of the selling and buying organizations relating to coal. Meanwhile, from 1958 to 1960, the new Communities, particularly the E.E.C., were making brilliant opening advances, which placed the E.C.S.C. somewhat in the shade.

The powers of the High Authority have proved to be less than was foreseen in the provisions of the Treaty. The members of the High Authority, being at the same time both European functionaries and men of politics, when faced by the national forces which they had to encounter, have not been able to affirm their responsibility and to demonstrate their political energy. These members seem to have been profoundly divided among themselves and more anxious to use the provisions of the Treaty to avoid assuming responsibility, than to reach fixed objectives. These causes of internal weakness are inevitable when it is realized that the members of this body are not recruited in accord with any political affinity which could and should bind a team called to undertake so heavy a task, but in accord with the play of national politics in the six countries concerned. To these causes of weakness has been added a deliberate determination on the part of the national governments to cease making new concessions to the E.C.S.C.

In practice, the special Council of National Ministers has shown the reality of its power. Actually, the national Ministers themselves are not the sole depositaries of this power. Their episodic meetings and the changes of membership resulting from events of national political life prevent them from bearing exclusively the weight of the functions granted them by the Treaty. However, the permanent national functionaries, who from the national standpoint oversee the relationships between the Community and the national States, have experienced a growth of their importance over the whole of this period. They are the people who prepare for the regular meetings of the Council; and they are to institute on the European plane a coordinating committee, whose meetings are to form the effective base for concerted activity.

From the outset the Assembly has established itself as a parliamentary organ and has sought to extend its powers;[6] it has claimed the honor of being the most active instrument in the progress of European unification. With a view to constituting homogeneous European political forces, the national delegates at this Assembly have established groups based on ideological affinities without regard to nationality. This initiative has been hailed—and rightly so—as a step in the development of European federation; but even here it is necessary to preserve a fairly balanced view of the development of European institutions. The Assembly as a protagonist of European unification has seen its role made easier by the fact that the political forces hostile to that unification have not been represented among its members[7] and that, up to the present, absolutely vital interests have not been at issue in the E.C.S.C.[8] Otherwise, the Assembly has scarcely any influence upon the national governments who are responsible for the delay in unification, nor even upon the Council of Ministers. Its debates up to the present time have had no direct important repercussions on the national parliaments.

As for the Court of Justice, its functioning in the framework of the E.C.S.C. has confirmed the lessons of federalism. In its jurisprudence it has defended the supranational character of the High Authority—sometimes, but rarely, annulling the decisions of that Authority when it appeared that the Authority had made too wide concessions under pressure from national politics.

Contrary to what has often been said on this subject, the Rome arrangements have confirmed, rather than modified, the experience of the E.C.S.C. Since 1958, the number of members of the Assembly is double what it was under the E.C.S.C.; but its role and its attitude have not changed. The Court of Justice has still not had to pronounce any important judgment relating to the application of the new Treaties, but there is no reason to consider that tendencies it has already displayed will change.

The most profound modification, it is well known, concerns the respective roles and the relationships of the independent executive and the Council of Ministers, the executive having in the Rome agreements changed its name from "High Authority" to the less colorful one of "Commission." Appearances appear to confirm an effacement of the organ most typically European—namely, the Commission. Besides the very significant change of name, it is noteworthy that the members of the E.E.C. and Euratom Commissions are nominated for four years only, and that co-option has

---

[6] The confident spirit of the Assembly best appears in M. P. Wigny, The Parliamentary Assembly in the Europe of the Six (1958). For a more detached view, see Stein, *The European Parliamentary Assembly—Techniques of Emerging Political Control*, 13 International Organization 232 (1959). The same movement has tried to manifest itself, but unsuccessfully, in relation to the Assembly of the Union of Western Europe. See Haas & Merkl, *Parliamentarians Against Ministers—The Case of Western European Union*, 14 *id.* 37 (1960).

[7] The Communist Party is not represented in the Assembly, a fact which appreciably affects the composition of the French and Italian delegations.

[8] It was perhaps different when the coal crisis was discussed in 1959 at the European Parliamentary Assembly; but, when the Assembly wanted to throw the responsibility for a difficult situation back to the Council of Ministers, its resolution received only 44 votes out of 142. Resolution of April 16, 1959, [1959] Journal Officiel de la Communauté Européenne du Charbon et de L'Acier 560 [hereinafter cited as Journal Officiel].

disappeared. Further, the most important powers are vested in the Council and not in the Commission. The Commission's role, apart from secondary methods of execution, appears on the surface to have been reduced to a simple right to make proposals to the Council of Ministers; the Council makes the decisions. Such are the appearances, but they are largely deceiving.

Actually, the proposals of the Commission have an important juridical effect. In the majority of cases the Council has the right to adopt the proposals of the Commission by a qualified majority or to reject them, whereas a decision contrary to those proposals requires a unanimous vote. In this way the Rome agreements have led the way to a veritable political impasse. Unless the Council can achieve unanimity within its own body, all it can do is to accept the views of the Commission, or leave the problem unsolved. In practice, the Commission prepares its proposal for action along lines indicated by the course of debates within the Council, with whose members the Commission has had indirect contact in advance. Moreover, there are common meetings between the Commission and the Council. If the first proposal of the Commission is rejected, the Commission sometimes presents another in the course of the same meeting in order to achieve a result—with the possibility of reverting to the first proposal if the second one also meets with rejection. In reality, the Commission is an organ of mediation in the national conflicts which break out within the Council; and in this way it can play an extremely important role.

Doubtless, it will be said that this system is very imperfect since the result may be that no decision at all is taken. This is quite true, as unfortunate examples have already revealed. However, it must be pointed out that in the E.E.C. the problem is quite different from that confronted in the E.C.S.C. In the E.E.C. it is a question of arriving at decisions, each of which is the equivalent of what the E.C.S.C. Treaty has stipulated in its economic provisions. It cannot be too often repeated that the E.E.C. Treaty is a framework, a carte blanche, which for the generality of matters considered is confined to announcing general principles, while remanding to Community decisions the task of applying those principles. Instead of concluding twenty or more treaties of the E.C.S.C. type, the Member States have evolved this new mechanism—which certainly has imperfections, but is manifestly more progressive than repeated international conferences of the traditional type, each leading to the conclusion of a treaty submitted for ratification pursuant to national constitutional procedures. Each of these decisions can, and undoubtedly will, take into account the competency of the Commission to execute them in the same conditions as those which apply when the High Authority effectuates its own decisions, at least in certain well-determined cases. A part of the objection still remains, since the execution of the E.E.C. Treaty depends finally on the good will—the European will—of the Member States. But does this circumstance astonish anyone? Starting from zero, a federal political force cannot be created in a day.

It may be suggested that, up to the present, Member States have not given proof of a desire for political unification and have not fulfilled the subscribed commitments.

Attempts could also be made to show that the established rules have not been respected as to coal[9] and transportation.[10] Thus, it could be established that the persistence of national positions founded on economic and geographical realities is sufficiently permanent to raise doubt that these positions will be easily abandoned. Economic unification and the realization of a common market, since they cannot be accomplished solely by recourse to such simple measures as the abolition of customs and other quantitative restrictions, presuppose common action in varied and extensive fields; and the States do not show any wild enthusiasm to venture upon the route towards such common action. The whole regime governing coal and the atom needs to be recast to embody an energetic policy; and the decisive test of the vitality of the E.E.C. has not yet been undergone. This test will occur in the adoption of the more specific measures and institutions required for a common agricultural policy.

However, exaggeration in whatever form must be avoided, and a pessimistic conclusion concerning European political forces would not be realistic. The policies and decisions resolved upon by national governments are not arbitrary; they reflect social realities impinging upon those governments.[11] While social realities and social institutions may not be in complete harmony, there cannot be a complete discord between them. Have, then, the institutions of the Communities permitted, in the broad sense, the development of European political forces? If the reply is in the affirmative, it must be anticipated that these forces, as they gain strength and develop, will, in turn, induce the further development of the institutions. To the present writer, it seems clear that the treaties establishing the three European Communities have given rise, with short delays, to relatively important European political forces. European parties are seen in outline; labor unions in various countries must coordinate their action; business enterprises become Europeanized—all this without taking into account the development of a vast European bureaucracy composed of experts, officials, economists, and jurists.[12]

[9] At the present time, not all the States permit the free circulation of coal coming from third party countries; former organizations of sale and purchase continue to function; and the Belgian market has been isolated from the rest of the common market on the initiative of the High Authority itself. It has been argued that these measures were contrary to the Treaty; and this is so under one interpretation of the Treaty. If this interpretation were to be accepted as valid, it would be necessary to conclude that the draftsmen of the Treaty committed a fundamental economic error. In our view, the European market for coal cannot function unless it is strictly organized.

[10] The harmonization of the conditions of transport laid down in the E.C.S.C. Treaty (Convention Containing the Transitional Provisions § 10) has never been realized. The provisions are quite insufficient and the anodyne provided by article 79 of the E.E.C. Treaty concerning the elimination of discriminations has not yet been applied (because of the absence of a majority vote by the Council of Ministers).

[11] It is not possible to accelerate without limit the process of unification; neither can that process be stopped on grounds of pure ideology, since it is already a fait accompli. The French Government, after the elections of 1958, was not in favor of the European Communities; the present Prime Minister has often opposed their development. In spite of this, the movement has continued. The French Government has not only insisted on executing the Treaties, but in fact it has desired to go beyond that and has often submitted itself to the Commission and to action by the Commission. This extremely curious political phenomenon arises quite simply from the pronounced need of every government destined to last to accept a certain number of realities. European solidarity is not the fruit of a free decision by governments.

[12] This typically European political force marks its strength by having compiled a statute guaranteeing

Yet, if these phenomena (which in the final analysis involve only a fairly limited number of persons) are alone considered, the insight into the development of European political forces and the birth of federalism would be quite incomplete. It is wrong to imagine that Europe is a super-structure attracting to itself ever more numerous elements which will, at a given moment, counterbalance national structure in a really federal equilibrium. Actually, if Europe is to become a meaningful entity, there must be established conditions for a veritable intellectual, social, and juridical harmony which can overcome the obstacles to the development of a common conscience. It serves no purpose to superimpose the action of 5,000 officials and 300 European politicians upon the millions of national officials and national politicians if the latter preserve a strictly national mentality. The functioning of the three Communities has already permitted to a perceptible degree the transformation of the habitual psychological perspectives of the national officials and politicians. Although it is difficult to assess the extent of that evolution, its existence has been made evident by the breadth of the contacts and exchanges between the Communities and the national governments. This situation is the outcome of a state of affairs which cannot be disputed—namely, that solely by reason of their central location at the crossroads of six national influences, the Community organs are better informed and technically better equipped to resolve many problems posed in a purely national framework. If power has a centralizing influence, the converse is no less true, since the fact of being at the center gives more power. In this respect Community institutions play their role. By the fact of their existence and the still rudimentary powers which they exercise, they have impelled the national forces to take part in a contest which slowly transforms the purely national bases of social life.

These observations are not intended to minimize the important problem of the structure of the Communities in relation to that of the Member States; but it suggests a more serene consideration of that problem. In practice, the question is to determine to what extent the administration of the Communities is to be direct or indirect. A recent example can be cited with respect to the rules of non-discrimination in transport.[13] Should only the national governments and the national tribunals be charged with the application of these rules (in which case one is confronted with a regime of indirect administration), or should certain powers be given directly to European institutions (controlling agencies, Commissions and Court of Justice)? In discussing this problem at the Council of Ministers, the Member States have shown hesitancy in this matter; but the sheer logic of the system requires acceptance up to a certain point of direct intervention by European authorities. Indeed, each State which has accepted European rules will fear that these rules may be twisted or poorly applied if national authorities alone are entrusted with their administration; and so,

---

European officials against all national influences. Each government ends by consenting thereto, although with regret, under fear of the influence of the neighboring State.

[13] E.E.C. Treaty art. 79.

to avoid a greater evil, the State will itself submit to control. The real problem will be to fix the degree and the limits of this partially direct administration.[14]

In light of the previous discussion, certain conclusions can now be stated. At present it would be an extreme exaggeration to speak of an equilibrium between European and national forces, since the latter have by far the upper hand in all spheres;[15] and it would be an abuse of language to speak of federalism in any strict sense with respect to Europe and the Communities. However, by their structure and by the approach to problems which they compel, the Community institutions tend to develop the social reality of Europe; and, thanks to them, it is possible to perceive the development of European forces which someday perhaps will be able to work in equilibrium with national forces.

III

COMMUNITY LAW AND NATIONAL LAW

In the general political sphere, the Communities display the beginnings, fragile as yet, of federalism; in the juridical sphere an analogous statement may be made—but with a difference. Although still very imperfect, the juridical construction of European federalism shows advances over the political. This is not surprising, for in the general evolution of federalism the establishment of juridical rules always precedes the creation of specific organs charged with application of those rules. The situation of the present international community as a political system is the most striking demonstration of this fact. Most of the rules of international law already show a certain consistency; and yet the international community does not really possess the differentiating organs which would give it an autonomous structure nor does it rest upon powerful political forces.

The European Communities, which suffer by reliance on political forces less strong than national forces, do not themselves possess any power of restraint.[16] Nevertheless, a Community juridical system—relatively diverse, coherent, and fortified by a well-developed judiciary—grows in strength from day to day. Both the legislative and judicial functions are exercised in the European Communities in a much more perfect form than in the international community; and European Com-

---

[14] If a common agricultural policy ever sees the light of day, what are the elements of this policy which, in relation to decision or management, will be delegated to European organisms?

[15] One of the most important factors of this transformation of national administrations, which has been alluded to earlier in this study, is the temporary employment of national officials in the higher posts of the European administration. National administrations, however, do not yet employ European officials.

[16] The European Communities do not have at their disposal any physical constraining force. In regard to the States, the powers of the Community are no stronger than in international relations. In regard to individuals, the Communities can exercise acts of constraint only through the intermediary of the national governments. (Decisions which impose financial obligations on enterprises or private persons are executory, and are to be enforced in each of the Member States through their legal procedure with no formality other than certification of the authenticity of such decisions. E.C.S.C. Treaty arts. 44, 92; E.E.C. Treaty art. 192.) The control and inspection functions which the Community authorities can exercise with regard to individuals (E.C.S.C. Treaty arts. 47, 86) and sometimes even with regard to States (Euratom Treaty art. 81) do not have provision for the use of physical constraint.

munity law thus emerges as a real juridical system[17] having complex relationships with national law.[18]

A. Community Law as a Juridical System

Every international organization develops, more or less extensively, its own law concerning its relations with its agents or officials, with those subject to its control (when it has direct powers of control), sometimes with its suppliers, and also sometimes with its Member States (this last category of relationships being more delicate and subject to controversy).[19] This remark applies in an eminent degree to the European Communities, because they exercise direct powers of administration and control with respect to numerous and important enterprises and because the States have agreed to place themselves in a subordinate position to the Communities concerning numerous spheres of activity and concerning the most important State functions—the legislative and judicial functions.

Not surprisingly, controversies have arisen at the outset as to the characteristics of this Community Law. To some persons it would appear as pure administrative law developed from a Treaty which forms its base—the unique foundation of Community law. According to this view, such law would develop from the Treaty by virtue of whatever general legal principles are common to the national jurisprudences of the six Member States. In this perspective, international law, contemplated with the greatest reticence, is practically excluded from Community relationships; and the fear apparently is entertained that international law, because of the principles of coordination which are at its base, would not be conducive to the evolution of the Communities.[20]

For other persons, the relationships between States within the Communities, as well as those between the States and the organs of the Community, spring from international law. It goes without saying that in this case the thought is for protecting the independence of small or medium States, which feel themselves menaced more than the other members by the federal regime. The political objects associated with these different positions are evident. Indeed, this is only a more technical aspect of the quarrel about supranational institutions which has developed since 1953 on the political scene of several countries—notably in France.

From the scientific point of view, the study of organizations such as the European Communities would show that, in reality, international law and internal law are not at all separated in so absolute a manner as certain German and Italian doctrines have tended to assert. As the Treaties which created the Communities have pro-

---

[17] See subsection A, *infra*.
[18] See subsection B, *infra*.
[19] See P. REUTER, INTERNATIONAL INSTITUTIONS 227 (1958).
[20] Although the Community Court of Justice avoids, as it should, taking any position in regard to this question, lawyers in general evidence a preoccupation with it in studies as well as in conclusions submitted to the Court. See, *e.g.*, Lagrange, *Juridical Order of E.C.S.C.*, REVUE DE DROIT PUBLIC 841 (1958); Conclusions of Roemer, in Case Nos. 24/58 and 34/58, Oct. 30, 1958, [1958] JOURNAL OFFICIEL 484.

vided in relation to the role of the Court of Justice, the international agreements which created the Communities are undoubtedly the principal source of Community law;[21] but the Court can be called upon to apply the provisions of other Treaties and particularly the general rules of international law, in so far as there is no derogation from the basic agreements.[22] Naturally the Court is called upon to apply the general principles of internal law—particularly on the basis of the national law of the six member countries.[23] Thus, the existence of a Community juridical order of great richness is apparent. It comprises numerous juridical sources—*e.g.*, treaties, custom, general principles of international law and of internal laws, numerous legislative or regulatory decisions emanating from the European Communities, as well as international agreements concluded by the latter with third-party States or other international organizations. It is impossible to deal here with the mass of problems presented by this variety of juridical sources; but two examples can be given that will show to what extent Community law brings into issue problems of federal technique. The first example will relate to the constitution of the Communities; the second, to their legislation.

In what sense and up to what point can it be said that the European Communities have a constitution? This problem is not specifically a Community one; it would arise in connection with other international organizations, notably those whose constitutive charters bear the title of "constitution," as in the case of the International Labor Organization. But the title or denomination of a juridical act is neither conclusive nor essential. It is quite clear that, from a formal point of view, the different agreements which have founded the European Communities are international treaties. At first sight, if one speaks of "constitution" in relation to those Communities, that term can only refer to the material character of those treaties. They would be constitutions in so far as they establish institutions and fix the fundamental and general rules that are to govern the relationships with which they are concerned.

In this sense, what would be the consequence of the constitutional characteristic of these treaties? It is not necessary to invoke this characteristic in order to force the Community organs or the Member States to respect the Treaties; this consequence results from their being treaties between States. However, recourse might be had to this characteristic to explain either certain problems of interpretation of the Treaties or certain peculiarities of their revision. It has already been pointed out that the interpretation of treaties creating international organizations is subject to special rules, notably as regards the implied authority of the organization.[24] The revision of these treaties is in the same way subject to particular rules of practice paralleling

---

[21] E.C.S.C. Treaty art. 31; E.E.C. Treaty art. 164; Euratom Treaty art. 136.

[22] In the decree No. 8/55 of Nov. 29, 1956, 2 RECUEIL OFFICIEL DE JURISPRUDENCE DE LA COUR 305 (1956) [hereinafter cited as REC.], the Court applied "a general rule of interpretation admitted alike in international and national law."

[23] See Dec. Nos 7/56 and 8/57, 3 REC. 223 (1957). As to the general principles of law, see P. REUTER, INTERNATIONAL PUBLIC LAW 87 (1958).

[24] C. de Visscher, *Judicial Interpretation of Treaties of International Organizations*, RIVISTA DI DIRITTO INTERNATIONALE 167 (1958).

the rules applicable to the reservations which Member States can introduce when signifying their adherence.[25] In this connection, if certain Community agreements were analyzed, notably those which have instituted the E.C.S.C. and Euratom, it would be evident that these agreements contain provisions of quite different juridical dignity and that the procedure for the revision of these agreements takes note of that fact. In fact, the E.C.S.C. Treaty has prescribed simplified procedures for revision, in which certain provisions of the Treaty are placed on a higher hierarchical level than that which relates to the ordinary articles.[26] These privileged provisions are those which define the principles of the common market and the equilibrium of the institutions. Taking a contrary course, the Euratom Treaty has reduced to a lower class certain of its provisions—particularly those which contain technical rules—in order to permit an easier revision than for the other provisions of the Treaty.[27]

These observations, of whatever interest they may be, are still secondary. The Court of Justice has annulled a decision emanating from the executive organs of the Communities on the ground that it was contrary to the constitutional equilibrium of powers.[28] However, in any case, the annulment of such a decision would have been decreed as a violation of the Treaty. A further step may be taken pursuant to the constitutional theory by contending that the agreements creating the European Communities have definitely become constitutions with regard to the Member States, so that these States have lost the power to modify the agreements by means of international treaties. If the revision clauses contained in these agreements are examined, it is seen that, in fact, all the revision procedures authorized there contain the obligation to bring the Community organs into action, at least for purposes of consultation. It is then arguable that the States can no longer modify these agreements by international treaties concluded in an entirely free manner, outside of the revision procedures laid down in the original agreements. In other words, the States would no longer be free to undo what they had done by using the same method or even by their unanimous agreement. Thus, they would have delegated a part, small but certain, of their treaty-making power. Such is the thesis finally accepted by the Netherland Parliament (although initially the Dutch government had taken the contrary position) under political pressure from an eminent protagonist of European unity, Mr. van der Goes van Naters.[29] Here one is at the threshold of federalism in the strict sense; but the point of view just outlined is probably not that of all the governments. Against it the adversaries of European unification would argue once again—as they did concerning the Defense Community in 1954—that the Treaties setting up the European Communities are unconstitutional according to internal law.

[25] *Cf.* E. C. HOYT, THE UNANIMITY RULE IN THE REVISION OF TREATIES—A RE-EXAMINATION (1959).
[26] E.C.S.C. Treaty art. 95.
[27] Euratom Treaty arts. 92, 197, 215, 76, 85, 90.
[28] Meroni v. Haute Autorité, Dec. Nos. 9-10/56, June 13, 1958, 4 REC. 36 (1958).
[29] See Reuter, *The Revision of Supranational Treaties*, NEDERLANDS TIJDSCHRIFT VOOR INTERNATIONAAL RECHT 120 (1959). The E.C.S.C. Treaty has, in fact, been modified outside of the procedures laid down on Oct. 27, 1956, as to a point of detail connected with the settlement of the Saar question.

The practice on points of detail often stresses the constitutional nature of the agreements creating the Communities. Thus, to cite a recent example, the Treaty setting up the E.C.S.C. was recently modified under the special procedure provided in the last paragraph of article ninety-five. According to classical treaty technique, notice of this modification should have been given to the French government, the depositary of the Treaty, which would have informed the Member States. Instead, following a technique more federal than international, the text of the modification was published in the *Journal Officiel* of the European Communities[30]—the Council of Ministers confining its action to notifying the Member States, so that they could take all measures eventually required according to their internal law.

The second example to be briefly cited relates to Community legislation. The Communities can establish, under different titles, general rules which are binding not only on governments but directly on individuals. In the case of the E.C.S.C., this power is limited to certain rather technical measures, and has been regarded by certain writers as a secondary legislative or rule-making power. In the E.E.C., the power has been considerably extended, and so its legislative character is even more striking. In fact, as has been pointed out several times, the E.E.C. Treaty contains only general principles, general directives; real Community laws are necessary to make the execution of the Treaty possible. As the texts of these Community laws can relate to matters which in the member countries are regulated by national laws, the importance of the powers of this Community can easily be assessed.

Numerous problems arise in connection with this legislative power, the most frequent form of which in the E.E.C. is that of regulations adopted by the Council of Ministers. In certain instances these regulations are based on a proposal by the Commission—sometimes with the advice of the Assembly. In other cases, they are decided upon by the Council alone; and the Council in some cases must come to a unanimous decision.

The decisions of the Council passed on a unanimous vote cannot fail to give rise to numerous reflections. In fact, the difference between an internal convention signed by the representatives of the six countries and a unanimous decision of the Council of Ministers is, at the same time, very superficial and very wide. It is superficial because in both cases the national States indicate their consent; and it is wide because the decision of the Council is valid in its own right and will receive its full application by publication in the *Journal Officiel* of the European Communities, but a convention will be subject to all the other procedures laid down by the national constitutions, including national parliamentary sanction. In this sense, it can be said that the creation of the Communities, and particularly that of the E.E.C. (founded on a Treaty which is a mere framework), results in a lessening of the powers of the national parliaments, rather than of the national governments.

---

[30] This is the case of a veritable promulgation (not laid down by the Treaty) effected jointly by the President of the Council of Ministers and the President of the High Authority on May 16, 1960, [1960] JOURNAL OFFICIEL 781.

These two juridical categories—the Convention of the Six and the decision of the Council—are so similar to each other that, in practice, they are sometimes confused. Many of the articles of the Treaties founding the Communities are not precise, and the question arises: Do they refer to one or the other of these procedures? One single example will be cited—that of article 235, which, in the case of gaps in the Treaty, authorizes the Council, acting by unanimous vote, to take the appropriate measures. The Treaty texts are often ambiguous; and by virtue of this mechanism, the six governments have been able to avoid recourse to the conventional international procedure.[31] They may be tempted to do so again in less certain circumstances.[32] Indeed, it is the evolution of the European political forces which will determine what use can be made of so sweeping a power conferred upon six governmental delegates.

B. Relations between Community Law and National Laws

Just as in an authentic federal system, the relations between Community law and national laws are very complex—even apart from the phenomenon noted above that the common general principles of the several systems of national law are themselves a source of Community law. To illustrate the complexity of the relations between Community law and the extensive domain which, to varying degrees, is allotted to national laws, it will be well to observe the framework of the E.C.S.C. A certain number of matters—restrictively defined by the Treaty—have been transferred to the Community, sometimes with a reservation of concurrent jurisdiction for national laws. Other matters have rested within the primary jurisdiction of the Member States and their national laws. In some cases the States have obligated themselves to exercise their jurisdiction in accord with rules laid down by the Treaty; in other cases, to harmonize their exercise of jurisdiction with the aims of the Treaty; and in the majority of cases, the States have undertaken no obligations as to the exercise of their jurisdiction. A greater uncertainty prevails in the case of the E.E.C. because—it must be repeated once again—the Treaty establishing this Community is a skeletal agreement which provides no choice between direct and indirect administration. Without fear of being disproved by future event, the forecast can be made that, for the greater part, the powers of the Member States will not be transferred to the Communities. Instead, the Communities will fashion rules and limit their functions to the supervision of the applications of these rules, with the assistance of the Court of Justice—while, by methods varying from multilateral convention to parallel legislation, the Member States will seek to harmonize their national laws dealing with a wide variety of activities.

Even with reduced intervention by the Communities, the relations between Community law and national laws call for adjustments. How are the national States

[31] E.E.C. Regulation No. 3, [1958] JOURNAL OFFICIEL 561, has authorized the bringing into force, without ratification, of the contents of an earlier International Convention of Dec. 9, 1957, signed at Rome.

[32] Compare the hesitations which appear in INTERIM COMMITTEE FOR THE EUROPEAN UNIVERSITY, REPORT (April 27, 1960).

going to make room in their juridical order for Community regulations and decisions? This is a very difficult question which should be examined separately with respect to each country. Cases can well be imagined where it will be a delicate matter to make Community regulations supersede the national laws, to which, however, they are superior in the hierarchy of legal authority.

The relations between the Community Court of Justice and the national tribunals cannot by their interaction alone resolve all these difficulties; nevertheless they have a great importance for the establishment of harmonious relations between the Community juridical system and the national ones. In this regard, it must be pointed out that generally the tribunals of the Member States do not depend on the Court of Justice of the European Communities for their authority or look to it for their control; and they even may be said to avoid any control by this Court. Furthermore, the power of the Court of Justice is limited quite precisely and is far from extending to all matters where a violation of Community law is alleged. For example, if a State or an individual violates Community law, another individual who is aggrieved must normally resort to the national tribunals.[33] The Treaties contain certain indispensable rules for adjusting jurisdictional relations. The Court of Justice of the European Communities has considered itself competent to apply the national law of one of the States each time that the Treaty stipulates a renvoi to that law—as, for example, in matters concerning personal capacity and status[34]—although it does not consider itself competent to decide a suit whose principal object pertains to national law.[35] Conversely, the national tribunals may find themselves called upon to interpret or assess the regularity of Community rules or decisions. The E.C.S.C. Treaty has forbidden national tribunals to assess the validity of the acts of the High Authority and the Council, and obliges these tribunals to certify this question as a preliminary one to the Court of Justice.[36] Similarly, the High Authority has exclusive authority, subject to appeal to the Court of Justice, to rule upon the validity of agreements contrary to the rules of the Treaty relating to cartels.[37] These adjustments are still insufficient and have not operated satisfactorily.[38] The problem has been considered in a more systematic way by the E.E.C. Treaty[39] and the Euratom Treaty,[40] which read as follows:

[33] The individual can first submit a claim to the Community executive and if that body refuses to take the measures necessary to put an end to the trouble, he can start an action protesting this refusal before the Court (this procedure is known as "in carence"). E.C.S.C. Treaty art. 35; E.E.C. Treaty art. 175.

[34] See Nold v. Haute Autorité, Dec. No. 18/57, March 20, 1959, 5 REC. 89 (1958-59), and also—although more clearly expressed in the conclusion of the Avocat Général than in the decree—Mannesman A.G. *et al.*, Dec. of April 4, 1960, Joint Affairs 13/59.

[35] Case No. 1/58, Friedrich Storck & Cie.

[36] E.C.S.C. Treaty art. 41.

[37] *Id.* art. 65.

[38] *Cf.* case No. 1/58 cited above, as well as the cases of OKU before the Stuttgart Tribunal (judgment of Aug. 10, 1953), or the interminable case of Saarbergwerke (decree of the Bundesgerichts of April 14, 1959, 14 BETRIEBS-BERATER 576-78 (1959)).

[39] E.E.C. Treaty art. 177.

[40] Euratom Treaty art. 150.

The Court of Justice shall be competent to make a preliminary decision concerning:
(a) the interpretation of this Treaty;
(b) the validity and interpretation of acts of institutions of the Community; and
(c) the interpretation of the statutes of any bodies set up by an act of the Council, where such statutes so provide.

Where any such question is raised before a court or tribunal of one of the Member States, such court or tribunal may, if it considers that its judgment depends on a preliminary decision of this question, request the Court of Justice to give a ruling thereon.

Where any such question is raised in a case pending before a domestic court or tribunal from whose decision no appeal lies under municipal law, such court or tribunal shall refer the matter to the Court of Justice.

This provision is more logical and more complete than the scattered provisions of the E.C.S.C. Treaty. In order to produce its effects, it presupposes a certain submission on the part of the national tribunals. In fact, these tribunals can always consider that the text of the provision in issue is clear and has a definite meaning, in which case they are not obliged to refuse jurisdiction. This seems to have been the attitude of several national tribunals in certain matters that they already have confronted.

These brief comments show clearly that the relations between the Community law and the national law are not yet completely harmonized, as they would be in a perfected federal system; but they also indicate better than a long commentary that these juridical relations have already reached a degree of complexity and of intimacy which vividly distinguishes them from traditional international relations. The Communities are not at all a federation; but they are progressing in that direction—more so by reason of their institutions than by the play of political forces, and likewise more so by their internal dynamic strength than by virtue of external factors.

THE ROLE OF THE COURT OF JUSTICE OF THE EUROPEAN COMMUNITIES AS SEEN THROUGH ITS CASE LAW*

MAURICE LAGRANGE†

It is common knowledge that a "Convention relating to certain common institutions," signed and ratified at the same time as the Treaties of Rome, has entrusted to a single Court of Justice the jurisdiction of the Court of Justice that each of the three treaties—European Coal and Steel Community (E.C.S.C.), European Economic Community (E.E.C), and European Atomic Energy Community (Euratom)—has established. The same solution has been adopted in respect of the Assembly, which is a common organ of the three Communities. It has, however, been clearly provided that the single Court exercise its jurisdiction in accord with the procedure laid down by each of the three treaties—and depending on whether a claim is introduced within the framework of one or the other of the three instruments. The Treaties of Rome have not modified the E.C.S.C. Treaty in this respect; on the contrary, article 232 of the Treaty establishing the E.E.C. explicitly states that:

The provisions of this Treaty shall not affect those of the Treaty establishing the European Coal and Steel Community, in particular in regard to the rights and obligations of Member States, the powers of the institutions of the said Community and the rules laid down by the said Treaty for the functioning of the common market for coal and steel.

The importance of the part played under these circumstances by the Court in its capacity of sole judge and the difficulties resulting therefrom become at once apparent. The origin of these difficulties does not lie so much in the few differences that the treaties have introduced in respect to the submission of claims and to procedure (the same situation is rather frequent in municipal law, where the same judge may have to exercise different types of authority and apply different rules of procedure); they stem rather from some basic divergences in the very conception of the Common Market and in the economic rules on competition, discrimination, and so forth. The question arises whether the Court should undertake the interpretation of each Treaty in its original context, or whether it should, as far as the texts authorize it, take an approach to the problem that would permit an identical solution of similar conflicts. While such a result might appear desirable, it would be disappointing if it were accompanied by a slowing down of the normally more advanced integration of

* Translated from the French language by Mr. Jean-Aimé Stoll, Officer of the Court's Translation Service, Cour de Justice des Communautées Européennes.

† Advocate General, Court of Justice of the European Communities, since 1958. Formerly Advocate General, European Coal and Steel Community, 1952-58. Contributor of articles to public law and political science publications.

the common market for coal and steel, and by a decrease of the powers of the High Authority of the E.C.S.C.[1]

However, at the time of writing,[2] the Court has not had to pronounce itself on a claim arising under the Treaties of Rome.[3] Its role may, therefore, be studied only within the framework of the Treaty concluded in Paris on April 18, 1951, instituting the E.C.S.C. In this respect, there exists no discontinuity between the Court of Justice of the E.C.S.C. and the single Court of Justice that has been substituted effective October 7, 1958. With the exception of a few details, the rules of procedure have remained unchanged, and the proceedings that had already been instituted under the old Court have been processed without interruption under transitional rules. Continuity has been the more easily ensured as four of the seven judges, as well as the two advocates general and the registrar, have been transferred from the old Court to the new.[4]

In fact, the number of cases has increased at a regular rate;[5] and their number, as well as the importance and variety of contested matters, have not only enabled the Court to create its own case law, but also, through this case law, to exercise considerable influence on the development of the Community.

I

THE COURT'S ROLE ACCORDING TO THE PROVISIONS OF THE TREATY

Article thirty-one of the E.C.S.C. Treaty establishes that

The function of the Court is to ensure the rule of law in the interpretation and application of the present Treaty and of its implementing regulations.

In order to understand the true role of the Court of Justice, its place in the network of institutions established by the Treaty must be ascertained. The Treaty

---

[1] A first interesting example of a confrontation of the two Treaties has arisen in an important case dealing with transport rates (elimination of special rates applicable to the transport of coal for the steel industry and of iron ore in the E.C.S.C.) In its two judgments of May 10, 1960 (Government of the Federal Republic of Germany, Barbara Erzbergbau et al. v. High Authority, Dec. No. 19/58, 6/1 RECUEIL OFFICIEL DE JURISPRUDENCE DE LA COUR 469 (1960) [hereinafter cited as REC.]; Dec. Nos. 3/58 to 18/58, 25 & 26/58, 6/1 REC. 362 (1960)), the Court exclusively applied the E.C.S.C. rules on non-discrimination and the rules governing the establishment of the Common Market based on the "most rational distribution of production," which is obtained by the interplay of competition. It implicitly refused to take account of considerations of "regional policies," whereas article 80 of the E.E.C. Treaty provides that such factors must be considered for the authorization of special rates. In his final observations, the advocate general had advanced a rather more subtle argument, although he reached the same conclusion as the Court. See notes 42-45 infra.

[2] July, 1960.

[3] With the exception of some conflicts in matters of staff relations.

[4] For this reason, the present study quotes judgments rendered by the Court of Justice of the E.C.S.C. before Oct. 7, 1958, and those rendered after this date by the new Court of Justice of the European Communities without distinction. Judgments are cited with the record number of the Court's Record office, the date, and the reference to the Recueil Officiel de jurisprudence de la Cour, published in Luxembourg.

[5] By July 15, 1960, 154 appeals had been lodged, of which 28 had been withdrawn before judgment. One hundred and six judgments had been rendered, 20 cases were pending on that date. Taking into account the cases which represent interrelationships of a variable degree, one may estimate the number of strictly distinct cases judged by the Court at about 50.

establishes a Community composed of the various Member States, whose clearly defined task is, first of all, the establishment of a common market for coal and steel. To this effect, the Community[6] must progressively establish conditions which will in themselves assure the most rational distribution of production at the highest possible level of productivity, while safeguarding the continuity of employment and avoiding the creation of fundamental and persistent disturbances in the economies of the Member States.

In order to meet these ends the Treaty defines its objects[7] and establishes prohibitive rules,[8] as well as ways and means of action.[9] Emphasis ought to be be laid on the fact that these rules concern the Community as a whole—that is to say, each of its institutions, and not only the High Authority.[10]

Thus, the Court appears as an internal judicial organ, the activity of which, within the field of its competence, aims at the smooth functioning of the Community legal order, and which partakes of the life of the Community. In examining the different aspects of the role of the Court in exercising the various powers conferred by the Treaty, this idea must constantly be kept in mind:

1. The main authority of the Court resides in its power to decide on claims for annulment, which Member States—and under certain conditions, coal and steel-producing enterprises (as well as interested third parties in certain cases)—may lodge against decisions of the High Authority. The High Authority is, in fact, the executive of the Community, and it is responsible for the application of the Treaty, in that it must ensure the normal play of competition according to the rules laid down by the Treaty, both by taking action adequate to attain Treaty objectives and by resisting the violation of prohibitive rules by states as well as by enterprises. To this end, the High Authority has been invested with certain powers, the exercise of which, from a formal as well as a material standpoint, has been carefully delimited in each case; the High Authority acts by taking decisions, individual[11] or general,[12] or by creating administrative rules within the framework of powers delegated to it by the Treaty.[13] In respect of these decisions, the Court, whenever they form the subject of an appeal, exercises a control over their legality—a control similar to that

[6] E.C.S.C. Treaty art. 2.
[7] *Id.* art. 3.
[8] *Id.* art. 4.
[9] *Id.* arts. 5 and 6. The most important of these latter is the following: "The Community shall assure the establishment, the maintenance and the observance of normal conditions of competition, and take direct action with respect to production and the operation of the market only when circumstances make it absolutely necessary." This constitutes no less than the outline of the Community's economic policy.
[10] ". . . within the framework of their respective powers and responsibilities and in the common interest, the institutions of the Community shall . . . ." E.C.S.C. Treaty art. 3.
[11] Authorization in matters of agreements and concentrations, see Nold v. Haute Autorité, Dec. No. 18/57, March 20, 1959, 5 REC. 89 (1958-59).
[12] Creation of a compensatory system, see Wirtschaftsvereinigung Eisen & Stahlindustrie *et al.* v. Haute Autorité, Dec. No. 13/57, June 21, 1958, 4 REC. 286 (1958).
[13] *E.g.,* regulation exempting certain concentrations from prior authorization, art. 66(3).

of the municipal legal systems of Member States, of which the most commonly known is the *recours pour excès de pouvoir* [appeal against abuse of power] instituted before the *Conseil d'Etat* of France. As a matter of fact, claims for annulment may be instituted not only against positive decisions, but also against explicit or implicit refusal of the High Authority, after suitable request, to make a decision in cases where it is alleged that the High Authority, by virtue of the Treaty, was under an obligation to act; this is known as *recours en carence*.

2. Apart from the jurisdiction to decide on claims for annulment, the Court exercises in certain cases a "full jurisdiction"—*i.e.*, an unlimited authority to consider all the aspects of the case. The most important of these cases involves the sanctions against enterprises and against Member States. The High Authority may impose fines and daily penalty payments on enterprises alleged to have violated their obligations; and these enterprises may appeal to the Court, which has full powers to consider the case both in fact and in law; this includes the right to consider the *amount* of the fine. A special procedure is provided where a Member State has violated one of the obligations relating to the Treaty.[14] This sanction applies equally to positive acts, such as the grant of illicit subsidies or other means of assistance,[15] and to omissions, such as the nonexecution by a Government of a decision of the High Authority during the course of an appeal.[16] Here, again, the appeal *en carence* may be resorted to: A Member State or an enterprise may request the High Authority to declare that a Member State has violated one of its obligations, and go to the Court if the High Authority refuses to act.[17] As to questions both of fact and of law, proceedings instituted against a Member State under article eighty-eight for a failure in fulfilling its Treaty obligations are of great importance. These proceedings enable the Court to pass on questions that, in themselves, as well as in respect of the principles to which they relate and the interpretation of the Treaty which they render necessary, are of utmost significance. This is especially true since the application and implementation of the Treaty often depends on action to be taken by the Member States, rather than on the exercise of the High Authority's powers.

3. The Court is invested with additional powers—*e.g.*:
   a. to decide on damages where the responsibility of the Community institutions or their staff is involved;[18]
   b. to decide on conflicts between the staff and the administration of the Com-

[14] E.C.S.C. Treaty art. 88.
[15] *E.g.*, creation by the Federal Government of a special allowance for underground miners subsidized by the State, Association des Charbonnages Réunis du Limbourg, Dec. No. 17/57, Feb. 4, 1959, 5 REC. 11 (1959).
[16] Decisions of the High Authority are not suspended in effect prior to judgment when contested by appeal, unless the Court orders their suspension; see E.C.S.C. Treaty art. 39; Government of the Federal Republic of Germany v. High Authority, Dec. No. 3/59, March 8, 1960, 6/1 REC. 17 (1960).
[17] Groupement des Industries Sidérurgiques Luxembourgeoises v. Haute Autorité, Dec. Nos. 7 and 9/54, April 23, 1956, 2 REC. 53 (1956).
[18] E.C.S.C. Treaty art. 40. Several claims for damages have been made on this basis by various steel producers against the High Authority, for alleged faults in the control of the compensatory arrangement for imported scrap iron, which has given rise to considerable fraud. One judgment has been rendered F.E.R.A.M. v. Haute Autorité, Dec. No. 23/59, Dec. 17, 1959, 5 REC. 501 (1958-59).

munities' institutions; the role of the Court in this respect is that of an administrative tribunal similar to those instituted by the United Nations and the International Labor Organization;[19]

c. to annul the acts of the Assembly or the Council of Ministers at the request of a Member State or the High Authority; this power is limited, however, to claims founded on lack of legal competence or substantial procedural violations and has not been exercised to date; and

d. to render an advisory opinion on the constitutionality of amendments to the Treaty that the Assembly may propose under certain determined conditions, at the request of the High Authority and with the concurrence of the Council of Ministers expressed by a majority of five members.[20]

This short summary of the Court's principal functions shows the *twofold aspect* of its role:

1. On one hand, the Court is responsible for ensuring the legality—that is to say, the conformance with the Treaty—of the action of the Community's organs, especially the executive and the Member States. To these latter, the Court represents a guarantee against any arbitrary acts and abuse of power by the High Authority. Conversely, it enables the High Authority to guard itself against interference by the States or against their refusal to honor their pledge of cooperation in the application of the Treaty. The functions of the Court in this regard can, therefore, be summarized as follows:

a. to ensure that the Community does not exceed the limits of the delegation of sovereignty consented to by the Member States; and

b. to enable the Community to exercise the powers so delegated whenever the States resist such exercise; if necessary, the Court may obligate the Community to exercise its powers (the Court appears, therefore, to have been invested with the functions of a constitutional court and, to the extent that the Treaty may be assimilated to a federal system, it can be stated that the role of the Court resembles closely that of a court exercising a federal jurisdiction).

2. On the other hand, the Court is entrusted with the protection of individual rights against the arbitrary and the illegal action of the Administration, and its role in this respect is identical with the functions that the different Member States of

[19] Fourteen judgments have already been rendered in this type of case, of which several are in favor of the claimants. See *e.g.*, Kergall v. Common Assembly, Dec. No. 1/55, July 19, 1955, 2 REC. 11 (1956), where the Court has elaborated a bold theory relating to the "prestatutory character" of a situation founded on a "public law contract," which entitles employees to stability of employment; Miranda Mirossewich v. High Authority, Dec. No. 10/55, Dec. 12, 1956, 2 REC. 365 (1956), in which the Court has annulled a decision refusing a permanent contract to a trainee, on account of the manner in which the traineeship had been accomplished (following the judgment, the traineeship was renewed; and this time the claimant was granted permanent appointment).

[20] E.C.S.C. Treaty art. 95. This procedure has already once been applied, and has resulted in the amendment of a very important Treaty clause, *i.e.*, article 56, concerning grants-in-aid for the readaptation of manpower rendered unnecessary by the structural changes of the coal market. Opinion of March 4, 1960, 6/1 REC. 93 (1960).

the Community have conferred on either administrative or regular tribunals. In fact, the creation of the Treaty and the delegation to supranational organs (particularly to the High Authority) of powers exercised hitherto by national authorities has partly deprived certain citizens of the legal protection otherwise enjoyed in their own countries: national judges are no longer competent to protect them. By ensuring that the supranational authorities exercise their powers in conformance with the Treaty, the Court of Justice substitutes itself for the national judge in affording the legal protection to which these citizens of the Member States continue to be entitled, although certain jurisdiction has been transferred to the Community. This is particularly true whenever the High Authority makes use of its right to impose fines or to levy contributions by way of self-executing decisions that are not subject to consideration by national judges. In this sense, it may be said that the legal order of the Community, which represents the common weal of the Member States, incorporates itself into each municipal legal order; and the Court of Justice itself must be considered, in each Member State, as the complement of the municipal judiciary.

II

How the Court has Interpreted Its Functions

In the following discussion, it is intended to demonstrate how the Court has exercised the functions conferred upon it by the Treaty. First, investigation will be made of the conditions under which the Court has granted access to its forum to claimants other than the States. Then inquiry must be made into the Court's contribution to the solution of some of the most important problems with which it has had to deal.

A. The Direct Access to the Court by Private Individuals

From the beginning, it has become apparent that enterprises, associations of enterprises, and individuals freely instituted proceedings before the Court against—sometimes important—decisions of the High Authority. Proceedings instituted by Member States, however, remained rather the exception. What are the causes underlying this situation?

The main cause of this phenomenon lies in the rather fortunate fact that conflicts arising between the interests of one or more other Member States are rather infrequent, whereas the interests of different economic or social groups are more likely to clash. A decision may be taken with the unanimous consent of Governments and still seriously damage the interests of a whole trade or profession, such as the coal producers.[21] Another reason is the increasing role assumed in fact by the Council

---

[21] E.g., the appeal made by the Federation Charbonnière de Belgique and a certain number of Belgian coal industries against a decision of the High Authority concerning the distribution of funds made available under the compensatory arrangement (mécanisme de péréquation) in order to enable the Belgian coal industry to face the common market after the expiration of the transitional period. Fédération Charbonnière de Belgique v. Haute Autorité, Dec. No. 8/55, July 16, 1956, 2 Rec. 133 (1955-56); Société des Charbonnages de Beeringen et al. v. Haute Autorité, Dec. No. 9/55, July 16, 1956, 2 Rec. 323 (1955-56). In his final observations, the undersigned Advocate General stated: "Associations of

of Ministers in the preparation of decisions by the High Authority. Even in the normal case, where the concurring opinion of the Council is not required, these decisions are generally preceded by extensive common research, or at least by consultations in close liaison with the Council or its Coordinating Committee—which is composed of national civil servants responsible for preparing the sessions of the Council, and which, although not provided for by the Treaty, plays, in fact, a very important role. This procedure results frequently in an effective agreement among the members of the Council, and between these latter as a body and the High Authority. It goes without saying that a minister who has expressed his agreement with a decision that, at least on the essential points, takes into account the concerns of his own government, will, in most cases, hesitate, on behalf of this very same government, to attack this decision on the very day of its publication. Under these circumstances, the interested parties are left alone to defend themselves against these "negotiated decisions," which, notwithstanding their thorough preparation, may well turn out to be illegal. Thus, we have the paradox that the maintenance of state influence within the Community in a larger proportion than was intended by the Treaty calls for a more extensive direct protection of private individuals than had been thought necessary.

The enterprises' right of appeal is rather strictly delimited by article thirty-three of the E.C.S.C. Treaty. Thus, enterprises may only attack

individual decisions and recommendations affecting them, or . . . general decisions and recommendations which they deem to involve an abuse of power affecting them.

The state is considered responsible for the normal safeguarding of its nationals' interests. This is a principle of international law that has been maintained in the Treaty.

Experience has shown, however, that if the Treaty has revealed itself in respect of the functioning of the executive to be somewhat less supranational than one might have expected, it certainly is very supranational in regard to its direct intervention in the functioning of the Community's enterprises, the Community's "subjects." In fact, whatever may be the circumstances in which the High Authority takes its decisions, these are published in the *Official Gazette* and thereby become self-executing. Hence the normal reaction of the victim is to go to Court; and hence also the emphasis on the Court's role as the municipal judge—a role which has already been underlined.

---

enterprises referred to by article 48 are called upon to play an important role under the Treaty, and this role is defined by article 48 itself. We deem it absolutely necessary that they be allowed to play this part also when it comes to defend in the law the collective interests which they represent, and this all the more since—as experience proves—certain decisions of the High Authority may violate these lawful interests, while no Member State deems it necessary to appeal. It may even be said, with regard to coal, that such is almost the normal situation, because usually, and particularly in matters of prices, the interests of the coal producers simultaneously conflict with those of the High Authority whose duty it is to 'seek the establishment of the lowest possible prices' (art. 3(c)), with those of all the consumers, particularly those of the steel producers, and with those of the Governments, whose general policy also tends, in most cases, to reduce the prices of this raw material."

This gives rise to inquiry about the Court's attitude with regard to this development. The question is whether the Court's attitude has been a rigid, negative one, or whether, to the contrary, the Court, inspired exclusively by considerations of equity, ignores the Treaty system and the legal principles which it contains. If the Court had chosen the first solution, it would have been oblivious to the fact that the chief task of a judge is to do justice, and that the Court is one of the organs of the Community, which, by virtue of article three of the Treaty, are under the obligation to realize the objectives laid down therein. In the second case, the Court would have ignored its task, as defined by article thirty-one, to safeguard the respect of law in the interpretation and the application of the Treaty.

Confronted with this dilemma, the Court has tried as far as possible to foster an economic and political development which has become manifest, without, however, prejudicing the Treaty system, and without modifying the legal principles which it contains. It is on this basis that the Court has tried to open its forum as much as possible to private persons. It has been little inclined to attach undue importance to rules of procedure, *e.g.,* as regards the grounds of appeal.[22] Likewise, it has not been very demanding with regard to the grounds of decisions of the High Authority,[23] except in cases where it considered that clearly defined grounds were necessary in order to allow the Court to exercise the jurisdiction conferred on it by the Treaty.[24] Sometimes the Court has had recourse to literal interpretation: in considering the tenor of article thirty-three (enterprises or their associations "shall have a right of appeal against general decisions which they deem to involve an abuse of power affecting them"), the Court declared that "according to this text, which is perfectly clear, admissibility of the claim is sufficiently established if the claimant *formally alleges* an abuse of power affecting him."[25]

The attitude of the Court is illustrated by another example concerning the application of article thirty-three, which provides that enterprises and associations may appeal "against individual decisions and recommendations concerning them." The Court has decided that it is sufficient for the decision "to present the character of an individual decision, although the decision may not be an individual one in respect of the claimant," provided the latter is affected.[26] The Court referred in this case

---

[22] Compagnie des hauts fourneaux de Chasse, Dec. No. 2/57, June 12, 1958, 4 REC. 146 (1958).
[23] Government of the Kingdom of the Netherlands v. High Authority, Dec. No. 6/54, Mar. 21, 1955, 1 REC. 201 (1954-55); Geitling v. Haute Autorité, Dec. No. 2/56, Mar. 20, 1957, 3 REC. 36 (1957).
[24] This goes for the application of art. 65(2), which lays down quite restrictively what are the conditions under which agreements may be authorized. Nold v. Haute Autorité, Dec. No. 18/58, Mar. 20, 1959, 5 REC. 116 (1958-59); Comptoirs de la Ruhr et Nold v. Haute Autorité, Dec. Nos. 36-38/59 & 40/59, July 15, 1960, 6/2 REC. 852 (1960).
[25] Assider v. Haute Autorité, Dec. No. 3/54, Feb. 11, 1955, 1 REC. 138 (1954-55).
[26] Groupement des Industries Sidérurgiques Luxembourgeoises v. Haute Autorité, Dec. Nos. 7/54 and 9/54, 2 REC. 87 (1956). This was an appeal against an (implicit) decision of the High Authority in refusing to take steps against the Government of Luxembourg for having authorized a public official to increase the price of coal intended for other than household purposes—actually the coal exclusively used by the steel industry, since the industrial uses of coal in Luxembourg are almost entirely limited to the steel industry.

to the principle of "interest" which, although not explicitly mentioned in the Treaty, is the underlying principle of the claim for annulment, as the Advocates General have noted on several occasions.[27] Usually the Court has tried, whenever possible, to hold itself to the text of the Treaty. However, in cases where the latter does not furnish adequate grounds for standing to appeal, it does not hesitate to invoke the principle of "interest."[28] Thus, the Court interprets a rigid and careful text *on the basis of general principles of municipal law of the Member States.*

Consider another example of the Court's attitude. With regard to the formal character of a decision, the Court has decided, in its judgments[29] relating to compensatory arrangements in Belgium, that a simple letter of the High Authority published in the "Information" section of the *Official Gazette,* must be considered *parte in qua* as a decision liable to appeal. Still a further example: concerning the objection of illegality, the Court has adjudged[30] that, in view of the lacunae in the texts directly applicable—and after rejecting the argument to the contrary which might have been drawn from another Treaty rule (*i.e.,* article thirty-six relating to pecuniary sanctions, which provides *expressis verbis* the objection of illegality)— the enterprises might, in the course of an appeal against an individual decision, raise an objection of illegality as to those general decisions on which the attacked decision had been based. Moreover, in this situation, they were authorized to invoke against such general decisions *all the grounds* enumerated in article thirty-three and not merely the "abuse of power affecting them," which is the only ground they would be allowed to invoke in case of a direct appeal. This decision is of great importance, since, in effect and by way of exception, it confers the same rights on the enterprises to contest the legality of the executive's decision as are possessed by the Member States.

B. Study of Some Specific Cases

Having thus established that the Court has widely granted access to its forum, and that the claimants have made an equally extensive use of this facility, it will be interesting to demonstrate, by a few examples, how the case law of the Court has been formed and the part such case law has played both in the creation of Treaty law and in the development of the Community's activities.

1. The so-called "Price-List" case was the first case submitted to the Court.[31] Article sixty of the E.C.S.C. Treaty, dealing with prices, prohibits:

... discriminatory practices involving within the common market the application by a

[27] See Final Observations by Advocate General K. Roemer in Groupment des Industries Sidèrurgiques Luxembourgeois v. Haute Autorité, Dec. Nos. 7 & 9/54, April 23, 1956, 2 REC. 123-26 (1955-56). Final Observations by Advocate General Lagrange in Fèderation Charbonniére de Belgique v. Haute Autorité, Dec. No. 8/55, July 16, 1956, 2 REC. 267 (1955-56).
[28] See the judgments already cited, *supra* note 26.
[29] See note 21 *supra.*
[30] Compagnie des Hauts Fournaux de Chasse, Dec. No. 15/57, June 12, 1958, 4 REC. 186 (1958); Meroni, Case No. 9/56, June 13, 1958, 4 REC. 25 (1958).
[31] Government of the French Republic *et al.,* cases 1 to 4/54, Dec. 21, 1954, 1 REC. 10 (1954-55).

seller of unequal conditions to comparable transactions, especially according to the nationality of the buyer.

and, in order to ensure this prohibition, establishes that

... the price-lists and conditions of sale applied by enterprises within the common market shall be published to the extent and in the form prescribed by the High Authority.

Originally the High Authority had, by way of administrative regulation, ordered the publication of price lists and conditions of sale, and had prohibited the application of prices differing from those published; increases and decreases of prices had to be preceded by appropriate and published amendments of the original or preceding price-list. However, the High Authority soon realized that steel producers practiced, in fact, a discount policy which involved sometimes very important discrepancies between the actual price and the price-lists; this practice was motivated by the economic recession which was prevailing in 1953. The High Authority could, of course, have pronounced sanctions; but these would have had to be invoked against practically all enterprises of the common market. In turn, this would undoubtedly have jeopardized the application and life of a Treaty which had hardly begun to become a reality. On the other hand, if the violation by the enterprises of the rules relating to publicity was subject to criticism, it actually reflected in a better way the play of competition than would the artificial application of prices higher than market prices. Thus, the High Authority searched for the means of reconciling the application of the publicity rules, which it considered an essential weapon to eliminate discrimination, with the maintenance of effective competition; and, to this end, it allowed a 2½ per cent tolerance in the application of the price-lists. This became known later as the "rabais Monnet" (Monnet's Discount). The Court annulled this decision as being contrary to the Treaty; in doing so, it disagreed with the present writer who, as Advocate General, expressed the opinion that the High Authority's interpretation of the Treaty might have some merit.

The importance of this first judgment of the Court is striking. From the outset the Court has had to deal with one of the most delicate problems of market economy, *i.e.,* the relation between competition and nondiscrimination. From this, certain commentators have drawn the conclusion that according to the Court's interpretation of the Treaty, there exists a *contradiction* between the two principles and that, in opposition to the E.E.C. Treaty, the Coal and Steel Treaty establishes the *priority* of nondiscrimination over free competition.[32] This theory certainly does not correspond to the intention of the authors of the E.C.S.C. Treaty, who have not considered publicity of prices as an obstacle to the establishment of rules for normal competition, but on the contrary, as a means towards achieving this end. In truth, the problem relates rather to *agreements,* because, while it is relatively easy to control the application of publicity rules,[33] it is much more difficult to detect and to

---

[32] This theory has been advocated, particularly at the important International Conference on Anti-Trust Law, held in Frankfurt from June 7 to 11, 1960.

[33] The High Authority exercises a careful control on this subject and does not hesitate to apply

eliminate agreements between producers if, for instance, all producers of one country issue simultaneously price-lists which are similar. Moreover, the term "common market" must not be considered as being synonymous with "single market"; there can be no doubt that, even in the steel industry,[34] there remains a certain isolation of national markets, despite the elimination of customs tariffs, quantitative restrictions, subsidies and other obstacles which have been abolished by the Treaty. In fact, the potentialities of competition created by the Treaty, however active and beneficial they are, concern the several industries within the national territories, rather than all enterprises of the six countries, each taken by itself.

The Court's judgment is no less instructive if it is considered from a purely legal aspect. The Court had been confronted with one of the classic problems of treaty interpretation—with a conflict between law and opportunity, rather than between the letter and the spirit of the Treaty. It is interesting that the Court was not satisfied by a construction founded on a *literal* interpretation, but that it did use a whole series of arguments in order to establish that the result at which it arrived was the (probably regrettable) effect of a coherent system established by the Treaty and logically inserted in its body of rules.

On a different and, with respect to a general analysis of the Treaty, probably still more important issue, the Court stated that, in taking measures for the application of specific Treaty rules (*i.e.,* article sixty on prices) the High Authority is not only entitled, but under obligation, to pursue the aims defined in the preliminary articles two, three, and four (establishment of lowest prices, fight against illegal agreements, etc.) and that article sixty on prices may be resorted to in order to sustain action taken against agreements. Thus, from its very first judgment onwards, the Court has been careful not merely to limit itself to a literal textual interpretation, but instead to consider the Treaty as a whole and to recognize the interrelation of the Treaty rules. This attitude has been of the utmost importance for the application of an economic treaty, since it is self-evident that in this field a specific problem may present itself in numerous aspects, each of which may be subject to different legal norms.

2. This position was expressly reiterated in the next decision,[35] in which the Court considered that the existence of a situation which possibly justified the application of article 66(7) (predominant market position obtained by public or private enterprises with the result of eliminating effective competition) did not itself bar the High Authority from exercising the powers which article 61(a) (establishment of minimum prices) confers upon it.

---

sanctions to such enterprises as apply prices differing from their price-lists, or whose price-lists contain omissions. See 1/59, Macchiorlatti Dalmas e figli v Haute Autorité, Judgment of Dec. 17, 1959, 5 REC. 415 (1959).

[34] We do not even mention the coal industry, as to which it is common knowledge that the common market is very far from being a reality.

[35] Government of the Kingdom of the Netherlands, Dec. No. 6/54, March 21, 1955, 1 REC. 222 (1954-55).

3. In connection with legal conflicts arising over scrap iron, two interesting cases ought to be mentioned.

(a) The High Authority had created a financial arrangement for the supply of scrap iron to the common market, in order to avoid the rise of prices of scrap iron of internal origin in relation to those of scrap imported from third countries, particularly the United States.[36] The relevant decision had been taken pursuant to article fifty-three of the Treaty, which reads as follows:

... the High Authority may:

(a) after consulting the Consultative Committee and the Council, authorize the institution, under conditions which it shall determine and *under its control*, of any financial mechanisms common to several enterprises which are deemed necessary for the accomplishment of the missions defined in Article 3 ... ;

(b) with the concurrence of the Council acting by unanimous vote, *institute* itself any financial mechanism satisfying the same purposes as referred to above. (Emphasis supplied.)

The High Authority had applied the last rule, which rendered the financial arrangement obligatory. The management of this arrangement had been entrusted to a private body established by the major steel producers of the Community, whose decisions, provided they were taken unanimously, were final. The High Authority retained merely the right to veto. However, some of these decisions, such as the establishment of the compensatory price, clearly exceeded the powers of management and, through the exercise of prerogatives clearly reserved to the High Authority, constituted an authentic market intervention. The mere failure to veto cannot be considered as being equivalent to a decision taken by the High Authority as a collective body in conformance with the procedure prescribed, and under the safeguards established by the Treaty.

Consequently, the Court has rejected the above procedure on the grounds that it entails a delegation of powers by the High Authority to a private body.[37] This decision, which from many viewpoints appears as a rejection of professional *dirigisme*, has in this respect drawn due attention from all concerned within the Community. Lawyers will appreciate this judgment in view of the important contribution to legal science by a decision which, in applying to the Community a theory about the delegation of powers, influences directly the balance of powers established by the Treaty, and, in so doing, touches on the very scope and conditions of delegation of the powers underlying the Coal and Steel Community. The problem is truly one of *federal constitutional law,* and this appears with particular clarity if account is taken of the fact that it is a *private person,* a subject of the Community as well as of a Member State, which receives the safeguard of rules created for the benefit of these

---

[36] As had been expected, the entry into force of the common market created a certain strain on the internal scrap iron market, particularly in Italy, which has no ore mines and has been traditionally a great consumer of scrap iron. Supplies used to be imported freely into Italy from France and Germany, but their resources, formerly in excess of demand, became insufficient. From 1955 onwards, the situation became disquieting because of the considerable increase of the "composite price" of American scrap iron. For some time now, the strain has lessened. The compensatory arrangement has not been extended and is at present being liquidated.

[37] Meroni v. Haute Autorité, Dec. No. 9/56, June 13, 1958, 4 REC. 36 (1958).

"double allegiance" subjects—rules which trace the limits of the power of the "Federal Executive" and lay down the conditions under which it may be exercised.

(b) The second case touches on the substance of the matter. In a first phase, the problem was one of a "simple compensation" between imported scrap iron prices and prices of "internal" scrap iron; compensation was paid on a quantitative pro rata basis. It soon turned out, however, that the moderate prices which were the result of the arrangement expanded, rather than decreased, the demand for this scarce raw material. The very effect of compensation turned out to render the normal functioning of the price mechanism impossible.

Hence came the plan to modify the arrangement, so as to encourage the economizing of scrap iron "without, however, rendering the establishment of new steel-producing centers more difficult." This was obtained by modifying the criterion for distribution of the compensatory funds; these were no longer to be distributed on a tonnage pro rata basis, but in an unequal manner, which tended to penalize use of scrap iron deemed excessive in relation to a determined period of reference. The purpose was to obtain an increase in the consumption of pig iron. This modified arrangement was at the heart of a series of appeals introduced by the Belgian, German, and French steel industries.

These appeals were principally based on the following grounds:

1. Violation of article three, particularly as regards the Community's obligation to:

....

(c) seek the establishment of the lowest possible prices,
(d) ensure that conditions are maintained which will encourage enterprises to expand and improve their ability to produce.

The above rules were invoked in the first place by steelworkers using the Martin and electrical processes, since, to them, scrap iron practically represents the sole raw material which can be used. The High Authority did not fail in their reply to invoke other goals equally established by article three—for example, the goal which obligates the Community "to promote a policy of rational development of natural resources, while avoiding undue exhaustion of such resources." This rule, *mutatis mutandis*, may be so construed as to apply to scrap iron—which, to the steel producer, is as much a raw material as is iron ore.

2. Discrimination.

3. Violation of certain specific rules, particularly article fifty-eight, on shortages. In this respect, the High Authority was criticized for having used a financial arrangement (relevant under article 53(b)) in order to correct a shortage (whereas this situation was deemed covered by article fifty-nine); avoiding thereby the *ad hoc* procedure; and, by so doing, depriving the enterprises of the safeguards provided for by this article (which may be defined as a sort of "procedural abuse").

The Court approved the High Authority's decision and declared:[38]

[38] See Groupement des Hauts Fourneaux et Aciéries Belges *et al.*, Dec. Nos. 8 to 13/57, June 21, 1958, 4 REC. 223 (1958). (Emphasis supplied.)

In pursuing the aims of article three of the Treaty, the High Authority must, in eventual conflicts, ensure permanent conciliation between these aims considered individually and, whenever such conciliation is impossible, grant a temporary preference to such aims as may appear appropriate in the light of facts or economic circumstances in view of which the High Authority, when carrying out the task assigned by article eight of the Treaty, takes its decisions.

After determining the meaning of the term "financial arrangement" in the wording of article fifty-three, the Court continued:

... whereas the High Authority may, by making appropriate use of this powerful means of intervention, ensure *to a very great extent, subject to the needs of the situation,* the necessary conciliation of the aims of article three of the Treaty within the framework of the task assigned to it by the Treaty, and whereas conversely the powers delegated to this end to the High Authority are limited by specific rules contained in Title III of the Treaty; whereas, in particular, such powers must be *considered to have been used for illegal ends* if it appears that the High Authority has used them exclusively, or at least *chiefly* for the purpose of avoiding a *procedure specifically laid down by the Treaty* in order to meet the situation with which it has to deal....

Thus, the Court rendered an exhaustive interpretation of one of the Treaty's basic articles (article three) and to this end used the concept of reconciling legal goals whose concurrent application creates conflicts. Thus was employed one of the most efficient tools of administrative tribunals;[39] and only thereafter has the Court searched for the legal source of the power conferred on the High Authority for such purposes. Finally, the Court undertook to set the limits of this power by using a conception of legal technique well known to the specialist—*i.e.*, the "détournement de procédure."

This case illustrates the role of the Court, not in its capacity of "economic judge," but as an administrative tribunal deciding in economic matters. The Court does not choose between laissez-faire liberalism and *dirigisme*; it does not create a doctrine. By interpreting the Treaty in a coherent manner, and by construing it so as to enable the Executive to attain the aims of the Community, the Court limits its role to that of ensuring that the different Community institutions exercise their powers in accord with the Treaty.

4. One last example will be gleaned from some very recent cases on transport matters. The difficulty in this field stems from the fact that the Coal and Steel Treaty realizes merely partial integration of coal and steel. The transport pool, which had been envisaged at the same time as the Schuman Plan, has not been translated into reality. The Treaty merely provides for a limited intervention by the High Authority, and leaves the task of eliminating discriminations in the transport of coal and steel, as well as that of harmonizing transport rates, to the Governments—which, moreover, in all other matters pertaining to general transport policy, retain

---

[39] One of the classic examples of the application of this theory may be found in the case law of the French Conseil d'Etat, concerning the reconciliation of the powers of police with the protection of individual rights.

their unfettered sovereignty. Thus it is within the framework of the E.E.C. Treaty that the general transport problem will have to be solved. The sole direct power conferred on the E.C.S.C. High Authority concerns special freight rates created for the benefit of coal and steel producers; and these rates must be submitted to the High Authority for approval. In all other matters, the role of the High Authority is limited to that of coordinating and possibly of discerning discriminations; but it does not include the power of imposing a rate system on Member States. Nevertheless, due to the efforts of a Committee composed of experts from the six Member States and inspired by the High Authority, substantial results at first were achieved in the elimination of discriminations within national systems and in the establishment of direct international rates of a digressive character and exempt from the usual procedure of "breaking" the rates on crossing national boundaries.

However, with regard to special domestic rates for transport of ore and coal by rail to the steel industry, the High Authority was less fortunate. After extended exchanges of opinion with the interested Governments and after investigations on the spot, a series of decisions were made on February 9, 1958, ordering the suppression of all rates considered as "supporting rates," while approving at the same time the maintenance of a certain number of other rates, justified by different reasons, such as the existence of competing means of transport. According to the High Authority, the reasonable solution would have consisted in establishing in Germany special rates for whole trains, as had already been done in France and in Belgium; but the High Authority did not have the power of imposing this solution on the German Government and could only "recommend" it— to no avail.[40]

The decision concerning German rates was appealed by the West German Government, seconded by the interested Länder, as well as by a whole series of German steel producers who had benefited from the suppressed special rates. On the other hand, the decision was supported by the steel producers of Lorraine, supported by the French Government. The Lorraine steel producers argued that, in reality, the special rates of the German *Bundesbahn* constituted, *in toto,* a discriminating rate system, since, in fact, the transport of coal from the Ruhr to Lorraine was subjected to the general rates.[41] On the other hand, the Germans protested against the abolition of certain special rates, because they were persuaded that these rates were justified for particular reasons.

This conflict has given rise to several important judgments. First it was ruled[42] that the course of action taken by the German Government in refusing to execute the decisions of the High Authority until judgment in this case had been rendered was

[40] It is known that the Bundesbahn—the German rail system—is not autonomous in matters of transport rates; these must be approved by the federal government. Traditionally, the "freight rates policy" has been an instrument of the government in the service of the latter's general economic policy; it has been used particularly to assist certain industries situated in economically disadvantaged regions, such as Siegerland.

[41] It is common knowledge that the steel industry of Lorraine, situated nearby the iron ore reserves of Lorraine, depends largely on the Ruhr for its supplies of coke.

[42] Government of the Federal Republic of Germany v. High Authority, Dec. No. 3/59, Mar. 8, 1960, 6 REC. 117 (1960).

illegal.[43] The Court stated that the decisions of the High Authority take effect even as to Member States, unless and until the Court has ordered the execution of the decision to be suspended. On the merits, the appeals were rejected. The Court declared that "it would be contrary to the spirit of the Treaty to authorize special rates on the sole ground that adaptation of the interested enterprises to the common market appeared difficult or impossible."[44] This implied the rejection of the so-called "supporting" rates. It also entailed the implicit rejection of "regionalism" within the framework of the Coal and Steel Treaty.[45] Special rates cannot be justified except in special circumstances, for *reasons* inherent in the transport enterprises themselves, such as established competition by other means of transport like water transport (this did apply to certain rates).

Those judgments are interesting not only from the legal standpoint, but also because of their consequences. In fact, the federal government did not await the judgment *in re Sidérurgie lorraine*[46] in order to study a system of rates by whole trains; at the time of writing, these rates are about to be introduced and will grant substantial reductions applicable without any discriminations whatsoever as to any transport of coal to the steel producers, including those situated in Lorraine. This

[43] Government of the Federal Republic of Germany v. High Authority, Dec. No. 19/58, May 10, 1960, 6/1 Rec. 469 (1960); Barbara Erzbergbau *et al.* v. Haute Autorité, Dec. Nos. 3-18/58, 25 & 26/58, May 10, 1960, 6/1 Rec. 367 (1960).

[44] For his part, the present writer stated, in his final observations (6/1 Rec. 441 (1960)): "One of the basic principles which, in the minds of the authors of the Treaty, condition the common market is that of equality under 'natural' conditions, and particularly of maintaining what has been called 'geographic protection.' Here we meet with the fundamental error committed by most of the claimants who base their reasoning on the assumption that transport rates could—or even must—consider the location of enterprises, *as a determining factor,* and adapt themselves accordingly. But, in our opinion, the opposite is true; *the transport is the determining factor* to which enterprises must adapt themselves, and transport must be so organized as not to be discriminating, the suppression of discriminations may eventually entail structural changes and relocation of production units; it being understood that all necessary steps will be taken to minimize the more violent effects of such relocation. This is the condition to which the Treaty subjects the task of progressively establishing 'conditions which will in themselves assure the most rational distribution of production at the highest possible level of productivity' (art. 2), that is to say, an effective common market of raw materials proportionate to Europe."

[45] While admitting that neither the High Authority nor the Court is in a position to judge the *economic soundness* of a Member State's regional policy, the Advocate General expressed the opinion that a "supporting" rate might perhaps be justified, from the carrier's point of view, in cases where, in consideration of other existing measures of regional assistance, this rate represented a temporary measure of assistance which was supposed to disappear on the day the regional policy had obtained results and enterprises would be in a position to accept application of normal rates. Thus, the special rate would have to be considered as a measure justified to preserve customers which might turn out to raise the cost of transport above marginal levels, and could not, in this case, be considered as a subsidy prohibited by the Treaty, or as a discrimination. However, in the case referred to, the above conditions had not been met—either because of failure on the part of the enterprises to prove that they were not in a position to pay normal rates (transport of coal from the Ruhr to the Siegerland industries) or because the need for assistance was of a permanent character (transport of iron ore).

[46] The judgment was read in public sittings on July 15, 1960. As had been expected after the judgment of May 10, on the German claims, the main argument of *Sidérurgie lorraine* has been rejected. The suppression of unauthorized special rates has resulted in the greater part of the internal German traffic being subject to the basic rate which hence becomes in fact, and not merely in law, a general rate without discriminating character. Claimants have nevertheless obtained partial satisfaction since the Court admitted, after hearing the experts, that certain rates aimed at competition with fluvial transport had not been correctly computed. (Chambre syndicale de la noterurgie de l'Est de la France *et al.* v. Haute Autorité, Dec. Nos. 26 & 36/58, 6/2 Rec. 573 (1960).)

solution had at all times been championed by the High Authority, which could, however, not impose it. Thus, a problem has been solved *in a field where the powers of the High Authority are especially limited*—a problem in regard to which responsible governments, due to the divided opinions of their experts, had always been powerless.

Conclusion

The few cases discussed above can give only an incomplete idea of the role played in fact by the Court in the functioning of the Community, as compared to the role assigned to it by the Treaty. Nevertheless, one striking fact stands out quite clearly: The Court's role has undoubtedly been more important than had been foreseen; and, above all, it has been considerably different from that which had been visualized originally.

The authors of the Treaty conceived of the Court of Justice as the *guardian of legality* in the application of the Treaty, according to Western European concepts. According to these concepts, it belongs to the High Authority as the Executive responsible to a Parliamentary Assembly, to take the initiative and select the means by which to attain the aims of the Treaty. To this end, the Executive has been invested with considerable power. As a corollary of this, however, it is for the judge to ensure that this power is exercised within the limits laid down by the Treaty. Among the different tasks of the Court which have been outlined in the introductory part of this paper, the most important, according to the spirit of the Treaty, was most certainly the task of safeguarding Member States and enterprises against possible *abuse of power* on the part of the High Authority.

As a general rule, experience shows, however, that the only criticism that could possibly be leveled against the High Authority would not be that of having abused its power, but rather that of not having, in numerous cases, exercised its power with sufficient determination nor with sufficient promptness. In truth, the High Authority has not always been responsible for this situation; for instance, during 1959, the Council of Ministers did refuse its concurring opinion—required by article fifty-eight—for the introduction of production quotas, which the High Authority deemed to be temporarily required to face the coal crisis. It has, nevertheless, been excessively timid in cases where its powers obviously existed. Thus, in making its decisions relating to the compensatory arrangement introduced to enable Belgian coal mining to face the situation resulting from the common market created after the transitional five year period, the High Authority has not dared to lay down sufficiently selective criteria so as to concentrate efforts on those mines which were the most likely to become competitive ones with the aid of financial assistance. The Court has been led to admit implicitly that such a selective policy would not have been illegal.[47] Evidently, the failure—now generally acknowledged—to integrate the Belgian coal industry into the common market during the transitional period has contributed to

[47] Dec. Nos. 8/55, 9/55, Nov. 29, 1956, 2 Rec. 291-325 (1955-56).

the universal proportions of today's coal crisis, which has become a problem affecting the very structure of the economy. The Belgian coal problem is rendered more difficult to solve because the High Authority is now no longer entitled to use the exceptional measures which were at its disposal during the transitional period.

A further example to illustrate the insufficiently vigorous and speedy application of Treaty rules may be taken from the coal industry in connection with the problem of organizing collective sales groups of coal from the Ruhr and ensuring that such groups conform to the Treaty's anti-trust legislation.[48] Since the Treaty entered into force, no satisfactory solution for this problem has been found; and this has enabled the interested groups to consolidate their position. It goes without saying that today, in the midst of a general coal crisis, solution of the problem has not become any easier.[49]

This state of affairs is in part explained by the influence of the Council of Ministers on decisions of the High Authority which, as has already been set out,[50] is greater than had been provided for by the Treaty. In addition to the influence of states which is thus manifested through the Council, the influence of powerful professional "pressure groups"—whose aims concern practical results, rather than the orthodox application of the Treaty—makes itself felt. However, the consequence of this development has been the increasing importance of the role played by the Court of Justice. The latter is responsible for the correct application of the Treaty and may not ignore the principles and rules which it contains. This fact only increases its responsibility for the functioning of the Community; and there are voices which talk of the prospect of a "Government by Magistrates." Doubtless, this would be far-fetched. For our part, we believe that, whatever may be the Court's desire to take account of economic and political reality and to foster a harmonious development of the Community, the Court cannot neglect its basic duty, which is that of defending the Treaty. As a judge of legality, it has no other choice but to leave the responsibility for its own actions to the High Authority, and to leave it to the governments to decide on such amendments to the Treaty as they may deem necessary.

[48] E.C.S.C. Treaty art. 65.
[49] It ought not to be forgotten that the Court is called in only *a posteriori* and if a case has been submitted to it. Despite its endeavor, as we have seen, to open its forum in the largest possible way, it sometimes happens that essential issues are not submitted to it or that they are submitted in a more or less incidental way, which does not allow for a judgment on the very merits of the case. This is what happened in the case of the organization for the common sale of Ruhr coal. On this matter, several interesting cases were submitted to the Court, but the only one which would have really allowed for a well-timed judgment on the main issue was withdrawn before judgment. This appeal had been lodged by Italian steel producers, but after being granted some satisfaction by the organizations involved, they withdrew their action. Ansaldo Coke *et al.* v. Haute Autorité, case filed under No. 4/56. The appeal had been lodged against the High Authority's decision of Feb. 15, 1956, authorizing the sale in common of Ruhr coal by three sale agencies, under supervision of a common board; that decision still underlies the actual organization. Certainly, the Court alone cannot secure the Treaty's enforcement against an actual agreement of the High Authority, of the Governments, and of the enterprises.
[50] See II(A) *supra*.

THE IMPACT OF THE EUROPEAN ECONOMIC COMMUNITY ON THE MOVEMENT FOR THE UNIFICATION OF LAW

A. Grisoli[*]

I

The Treaty Basis for Approximation of Laws

The general provisions of article three of the Treaty establishing the European Economic Community (E.E.C.) include a directive that Community activities should include the "approximation of . . . municipal law to the extent necessary for the functioning of the Common Market."[1] This general mandate for "approximation of law" is further detailed by the Treaty in two different ways:

1. By express Treaty provisions relating to:
   a. customs and tariff matters;[2]
   b. a number of different situations within the scope of rules envisaging the free movement of persons, services, and capital within the Member States;[3]
   c. mutual regulation of transport matters;[4]
   d. rules governing competition;[5]
   e. certain fiscal matters;[6]
   f. measures to assist the exports from Member States to nonmember countries;[7]
   g. labor legislation and social security;[8]
   h. the situations within the purview of article 220.[9]

---

[*] J. Dr. 1950, University of Pavia (Italy), Ph.D. 1955, Cambridge University (England). Lecturer in Comparative Law, University of Milan (Italy). Associated with the Legal Department, European Economic Community, 1959. Author, La Cambiale in Diritto Inglese, Certain Comparative Aspects of the Carrier's Liability [under the English and French legal systems] (1956). Contributor on subjects of private, commercial, and comparative law to legal periodicals.

[1] "For the purposes set out in the preceding Article, the activities of the Community shall include, under the conditions and with the timing provided for in this Treaty: . . . (h) the approximation of their respective municipal law to the extent necessary for the functioning of the Common Market." E.E.C. Treaty art. 3.

[2] Id. art. 27.

[3] Id. articles 54, 57, 58, and 66 deal with the need to eliminate obstacles to the "right of establishment" and to the free flow of services, so that those engaged in non-wage-earning activities are not restricted to a single country. Article 56 deals with the coordination of special rules which limit the activities of persons or companies from non-Member States and are based on reasons of public order, public safety, and public health.

[4] Article 75.

[5] Articles 85, 86.

[6] These relate to turnover taxes, excise duties, and other forms of indirect taxation, including compensatory measures applying to exchanges between Member States. Article 99.

[7] Article 112.

[8] Articles 117, 118.

[9] This article provides for negotiations between Member States to coordinate rules relating to the

2. A broad authorization, set forth in articles 100-102, for direct intervention by institutions of the E.E.C. to reconcile the legislative and administrative rules and regulations of Member States when:
   a. the existence of a disparity in the legal systems of Member States directly affects the establishment and functioning of the Common Market;[10]
   b. an existing disparity in the legislative or administrative provisions of the Member States distorts conditions of competition within the Common Market;[11] or
   c. it is feared that a Member State's enactment or amendment of a legislative or administrative provision may distort conditions of competition in the Common Market.[12]

Much attention[13] has been devoted to articles 100-102 of the E.E.C. Treaty—three articles which together comprise a chapter, entitled "Approximation of Laws."[14] It is interesting, however, that in the Treaty itself, although article 3(h) refers to the objective of approximating municipal law[15] and article 117 contains a general reference to "the approximation of legislative and administrative provisions," only in article ninety-nine, which deals with taxation, is there a specific cross-reference to the procedures authorized by articles 100-102.[16] The express Treaty provisions relating to approximation of laws in certain specified matters are subject to a more or less rigorous schedule for taking different steps towards the goal.[17] On the other hand, the application of articles 100-102 is unlimited as to subject matter[18] and indeterminate as to time—and clearly the approximation of laws cannot be limited as to time, since it may occur at an advanced stage in the realization of European economic integration.

To what extent was it intended by the Treaty's draftsmen that resort to the procedures of articles 100-102 should be permissible even in instances where the

---

protection of citizens vis-à-vis the state, the elimination of double taxation, mutual recognition of companies, and reciprocal recognition and execution of judicial decisions and arbitral awards.

[10] Article 100.
[11] Article 101.
[12] Article 102.
[13] DEUXIÈME RAPPORT GÉNÉRAL SUR L'ACTIVITÉ DE LA COMMUNAUTE paras. 125-26 (1959); Monaco, *Le rapprochement des legislations nationales dans le cadre du Marché Commun*, 3 ANNUAIRE FRANÇAIS DE DROIT INTERNATIONALE 558 (1957); commentary of Thiesing, in VON DER GROEBEN & VON BROECKH (EDS.), HANDBUCH FÜR EUROPÄISCHE WIRTSCHAFT 3 (1959).
[14] This is chapter 3 of Part three, Title 1.
[15] The chapter on approximation of laws, note 14 *supra*, provides the rules for the realization of the objective stated in article 3(h), just as the objectives stated in other paragraphs of article 3 have corresponding groups of rules elsewhere in the Treaty.
[16] Article 99 specifies that the proposals submitted by the Commission to the Council under its authority shall be "without prejudice to the provisions of Articles 100 and 101."
[17] Unlike the European Coal and Steel Community (E.C.S.C.) Treaty, the E.E.C. Treaty envisages different stages of activity and makes the attainment of the ultimate goal of European integration dependent on several successive phases of development.
[18] Monaco, *supra* note 13, at 560, states with reference to article 100: "The scope of this article is most comprehensive, because it not only covers legislative enactments, but also administrative regulations, both for the execution and the application [of statutes], as well as all administrative acts emanating from each government." [Ed. transl.]

Treaty contained other express provisions relevant to approximation of laws? One should not rule out the possibility that articles 100-102 are not rendered inoperative with respect to matters that the Treaty has subjected to express provisions for approximation of laws, even if those provisions include a timetable for taking the different steps necessary. Of course, under this view articles 100-102 would not be construed in any case to impose a more difficult and complicated procedure for approximation of laws than would be available in the absence of these articles. However, the procedure prescribed in these articles would be applicable in those rare cases, like that of article 220, in which the Treaty, while outlining new fields of activity in the task of approximating laws, does not define the method by which E.E.C. institutions shall achieve this approximation.[19]

II

APPROXIMATION (RAPPROCHEMENT) OF PROVISIONS HAVING DIRECT
INCIDENCE ON THE COMMON MARKET—ARTICLE 100

In so far as the E.E.C. Treaty's chapter on "approximation" of laws is concerned, the provisions in article 100 are by far the most important. According to this article, the Council, acting by unanimous vote on a proposal of the Commission, and after previous consultation with the Assembly and the Economic and Social Committee, shall issue directives for the approximation of such legislative and administrative provisions of Member States as have a direct incidence on the Common Market. In substance, then, there is recognized a prerogative of the Community to ensure within the field of the Member States' domestic legal systems the conditions for realizing the Common Market—either by promoting legislation to give effect to the pledges contained in the E.E.C. Treaty or by causing the removal of obstacles interposed by domestic legislation to such a realization.[20]

The measures made available to the institutions of the E.E.C. to implement this prerogative offer a more effective means to accomplish the objective than any based on a general obligation or pledge of loyalty undertaken when the Treaty was drawn up. Thus, the procedure authorized in article 100 really puts teeth in article five, wherein the Member States pledge generally to take all action appropriate to attain the objectives of the Treaty.

The procedure for intervention by the Community pivots on the directives of the Council—directives which would be preceded by a pronouncement of the Assembly concerning the political opportuneness of the measures the Commission has proposed and by an expression from the Economic and Social Committee as to probable repercussions of such measures on the Common Market.[21] The com-

[19] Article 220 directs that the Member States "shall, in so far as necessary, engage in negotiations with each other" in pursuit of certain objectives.
[20] As is hereafter discussed, the literal meaning of "approximation (rapprochement) of laws" implies the idea of alignment with a pre-established model. In this connection, see Monaco, *supra* note 13, at 568.
[21] Article 100. With reference to the Assembly, see articles 137-44; as to the Economic and Social Committee, see articles 193-98.

plexity of the procedure to be employed is justified by the fact that the intended result impinges upon the sovereignty of the Member States. Directives of the Council, simply by virtue of their existence, have a forcefulness and persuasiveness generally sufficient to ensure compliance with their terms. Nevertheless, under article 189 of the Treaty, a directive lacks direct legislative effect, in that domestic agencies, while bound as to the result to be achieved, retain their competence as to form and means. Thus, the measures utilized by the various Member States to achieve the intended result may vary in form in accordance with the differences in the constitutions of Member States and in their various laws ratifying the E.E.C. Treaty.[22]

The approximation of laws envisaged by article 100 is not designed to operate in specified areas of the juridical systems of the Member States seen in their entirety, but only with respect to those rules that affect the establishment and the functioning of the Common Market. This limitation furnishes a decisive argument against too broad an interpretation of the tasks of the Community in order to promote a uniform law among the Member States.[23] Of course, it remains to be seen which legal and administrative rules will have the effect on the Common Market required to invoke article 100.

III

ELIMINATION OF DISTORTIONS OF COMPETITIVE CONDITIONS—ARTICLE 101

The circumstances under which E.E.C. Treaty article 101 will apply appear more recognizable than those for invoking article 100, since at first glance they refer to a more restricted field. However, in light of the aims of the Treaty, this impression could be misleading. In many ways, the tasks of the Community in maintaining conditions of competition—even though encompassed within a more specific range of competence—are no less vast or binding than those envisaged in article 100.

For article 101 to apply, there must be a difference in the rules of the Member States' domestic laws that is capable of producing a "distortion" in the conditions for competition in the Common Market. In common with other terms borrowed from the language of multilateral economic agreements, the concept of "distortion" has no distinct, strict juridical meaning; nor does the Treaty illustrate its meaning or limits.[24] In its natural sense, the word has implications so wide that it clearly

---

[22] The German law of ratification of July 27, 1957, imposes a duty on the Government to inform the Chamber of every provision of the Community in relation to which active measures of compliance will need to be taken. See Thiesing, *supra* note 13, at 4. In Italy, in the absence of a special ratifying law, the directives may be complied with either by a special law passed to that effect or by delegation by law of the necessary powers to the Government. See Monaco, *supra* note 13, at 562.

[23] See, *e.g.*, Willemetz, *L'harmonisation des législations*, Le Droit Européen, Dec. 5, 1958, p. 176.

[24] An exact idea of its implication may, nevertheless, be obtained from the preliminary documents from which the E.E.C. Treaty was drawn up and from the very aims the Treaty expresses. Indeed, the concept of distortion derives from the conviction that similar competitive conditions should prevail in the Common Market once the economies of the Member States react upon one another. Distortion could arise, with the same consequences as an involuntary discrimination, from factors implicit in the economies of the Member States, such as natural resources, the level of production, fixed responsibilities, etc. On this point, see Tinberger, *Les distortions et leur correction*, in LE MARCHÉ COMMUN ET SES PROBLEMES 256 (1958) [a special issue of the *Revue d'Economie Politique*].

cannot coincide with the concept of distortion in article 101 of the E.E.C. Treaty. In fact, it would be futile to attempt to eliminate some phenomena, which might be labeled "distortions" of competition under an all-inclusive interpretation, resulting from the variations in the political and economic structures of the Member States. Nor should one rule out the possibility that ultimately a general state of equilibrium will be reached whereunder a "distortion," which it is feared will result from one element in a Member State's economy, will be offset through the combined effect of other factors in that same economy.[25]

The aims to which the "harmonizing activity" of the Community are directed by article 101 appear to have regard solely to those disturbances of competitive conditions in the Common Market that, in the language of the Treaty's draftsmen, are described as "specific distortions."[26] Causes of such specific distortions would be, for example:

1. Variations among the Member States with respect to systems of social security, whose effect on industry may vary according to the basis of the system (which may, for instance, be supported by the State out of the general taxes or be based on contributory payments out of wages);
2. Differences among the fiscal systems of the Member States in the extent of utilization of a graduated or progressive tax—of the principle that the greater tax burden should fall on the more profitable sources of production.

Other special factors that might be conducive to distortion include differences among the Member States with respect to use of direct or indirect taxation, systems of financing social welfare, certain price controls, and policies regarding credit and work conditions.[27]

The task of eliminating distortions of competitive conditions requires examination of the most apt means to deal with these special factors conducive to distortions. This task does not necessarily involve juridical measures, and it can be divorced from the process of *rapprochement* of the laws. To a considerable extent the special factors conducive to distortions can be coped with simply by the adoption of mutual economic measures.[28]

---

[25] *E.g.*, differences between the commitments of the various economies deriving from public expenditures, or systems of social security, are usually compensated for by opportune variations of a tax on exchange. National underevaluation, like overevaluation, can act as an incentive to the flow of imports and exports, and, with the tax variations, can contribute to an even balance of payments. Differences in the cost of production attributable to different salary levels may be offset by variations in the index of productivity. On this whole problem, see COMITE INTER-GOUVERNEMENTAL DE MESSINE, RAPPORTS DES CHEFS DE DÉLÉGATION AUX MINISTRES DES AFFAIRS ETRANGÈRES tit. 2, ch. 2 (1956) [hereinafter cited as REPORT OF THE MESSINA COMMITTEE].

[26] *Ibid.*

[27] "Work conditions" would include relationship between male and female salaries, hours of work, overtime, paid holidays, and so on.

[28] The Commission may take suitable economic measures to safeguard industries otherwise placed at a disadvantage. Instead of a system of subsidies, the *Report of the Messina Committee* prefers that the E.E.C. remit customs duties prejudicial to poorly located industries—together with the prompt compliance by all Member States with the rules of the Treaty. On the other hand, direct or indirect subsidies to compensate for heavy burdens created by the Treaty's provisions may be considered inconsistent with the Treaty.

However, differences in the juridical systems of the Member States can themselves promote distortions of competitive conditions; and for these distortions the remedy must be sought in juridical measures—the basis of which would be article 101. Indeed, article 101 of the E.E.C. Treaty—and the whole system of approximation of laws which it envisages—may be regarded as a simple appendix to the chapter prescribing "Rules Governing Competition."

The procedure authorized by the Treaty reflects the difficulty of the subject matter and the arduous tasks that the institutions of the E.E.C. will find in discovering means to resolve such complex problems. As a first step in the process, the Treaty provides for consultation between the Commission and interested Member States—as is also required by article 118, which seeks to "promote close collaboration between Member States in the social field." Should the consultations not achieve their objective, then article 101 authorizes the Council to issue directives. This procedure is considerably simpler than that employed in article 100, no doubt because here the issuance of the directives follows consultations that in themselves are presumably rather complex.

IV
Approximation of Future Provisions—Article 102

Article 102 complements its preceding article by authorizing measures to meet the threat of "distortions" that might reasonably be feared as a result of legislative or administrative provisions enacted after the E.E.C. Treaty came into effect.[29] This article takes on greater importance because, like article 100, it is intended to apply to future stages in the development of the Common Market. Article 101, on the other hand, refers to the juridical conditions prevailing in the different Member States on the effective date of the E.E.C. Treaty. Accordingly, ever-increasing reference to article 102 is to be expected as the Common Market progresses, with a corresponding decline in recourse to the preceding article.

Whenever a Member State proposes to pass a new law or modify an old one so that a "distortion" is to be feared, it is bound to consult the Commission in order to discover probable repercussions on the Common Market. Then, after consulting with other Member States, the Commission will, in turn, recommend the best measures to avoid such a distortion. This procedure differs from that of article 101, both in the duty of Member States to be wary lest their intended new provisions tend to cause a distortion—and, in such event, to inform the Commission of their plans—and in the provisions for the Commission's intervention. The Council is not involved; and no directives are issued—merely nonmandatory recommendations, whose binding power is limited.

[29] "Where there is reason to fear that the enactment or amendment of a legislative or administrative provision will cause a distortion within the meaning of the preceding Article, the Member State desiring to proceed therewith shall consult the Commission. After consulting the Member States, the Commission shall recommend to the States concerned such measures as may be appropriate to avoid the particular distortion." Article 102.

In the not unlikely event that a State ignores the Commission's recommendations, article 102 precludes resort by that State to the terms of article 101 in order to persuade the other States to eliminate the distortion by modifying the provisions of their own laws. However, this would not appear to prevent the use of measures available to the Commission and Council under article 102(2)—*i.e.*, economic measures that do not call for modification of any juridical provisions. Even so, this article seems inadequate in that it permits a Member State to create a "distortion" prejudicial to other states, but removable only by a modification of their own laws. In fact, in these cases the distortion remains, and there is given merely the satisfaction of stating that the blame for it belongs to the State that fails to comply with the Commission's recommendation. One additional sanction provided by article 102 against the non-complying Member States is its elimination of recourse by that Member to the provisions of article 101 should the non-compliance with the Commission's recommendation redound only to the detriment of this Member State.[30]

Article 102 may apply, of course, when the obligation to give notice of proposed legislation is not observed by the Member States; thus, the Commission would be authorized to make recommendations concerning the proposals if it acquired notice from some source other than the State concerned that enactment of the new law might prejudice competitive conditions in the Common Market. In practice, however, it is quite possible that the Commission, if not notified by the Member, may hear of the new statute or administrative regulation only after its adoption—and when the resultant distortion has become apparent. This contingency is not specifically covered by article 102; and so it would probably be necessary to consult article 101, which would seem to apply whenever a State fails to notify the Commission of a legislative or administrative proposal in the erroneous belief that it will have no bearing on competitive conditions in the Common Market, and when the Commission fails to hear of the proposal by some other means.

This conclusion would seem valid, since there is no bar to a broad interpretation of article 101. Article 102(2), which envisages the grave case of a distortion produced in contradiction to a recommendation by the Commission, would lead to recourse, at least in important cases, to the provisions of article 101. Only when the distortion operates solely to the prejudice of the State responsible is the operation of that article entirely excluded. Article 102 seeks to prevent a distortion; but it must yield to article 101 when the existence of a distortion is in fact confirmed.

To adopt, on the other hand, an alternative strict interpretation of article 102, which would lead to recourse to the Court of Justice on the basis that every failure to give notice is itself a violation of the E.E.C. Treaty would, in practice, only

---

[30] "If the State desiring to enact or amend its own provisions does not comply with the recommendations made to it by the Commission, other Member States may not be requested, in application of Article 101, to amend their own provisions in order to eliminate such distortion. If the Member State which has ignored the Commission's recommendation causes a distortion to its own detriment only, the provisions of Article 101 shall not apply." Monaco, *supra* note 13, at 567. [Ed. transl.]

complicate matters, rather than solve them. Indeed, reference to the Court should only be the last resort for the most flagrant violations of the Treaty—violations which may not be resolved in any other way. It can scarcely be justified in this less critical situation of failure to give notice.

Sometimes it may occur that a Member State will not recognize the full consequences of its legislative proposals—will not foresee their possible impingement on competitive conditions in the Common Market. In this event, the State probably will be prepared to make the necessary changes in its new or proposed legislation without being required to do so by either the Council or the Court; indeed, probably then there will be no need to go any further than the consultative procedures envisaged by both articles 101 and 102.

V

Delimiting the Scope of Action by E.E.C. Institutions

In the field of European cooperation, the principle of reconciling and harmonizing the laws and regulations of the Member States has been accepted in preference to the impracticable task of achieving complete uniformity.[31] The difficulties of drafting uniform laws to be ratified simultaneously by several different States are well known. It would be too ambitious to expect States which signed the E.E.C. Treaty, after giving the institutions of the Community the sizable task of promoting European economic integration, to add thereto the task of fostering a uniform European law.

Even a first reading of the Treaty confirms this interpretation. The term "uniformity" is conspicuously absent from the various formulae used to express the tasks of the Community in this field; instead, references are made to "coordination,"[32] "harmonization,"[33] "establishment of common rules,"[34] "abolition of restrictions,"[35] "coordination through negotiation,"[36] and "approximation (rapproachement)."[37] The choice of expressions with respect to the varying methods of intervention by the E.E.C. institutions—and in different degrees—seems, indeed, to be greatly concerned to fix limits well short of the promotion of projects of uniform law, even in the fields of economics and commerce.

In so far as articles 100-102 of the Treaty—which together comprise the chapter entitled "Approximation of Laws"—are concerned, it will be recalled that the initiative of the Commission is limited by the requirement that the legislative and admin-

[31] "It is not possible to attempt to modify in some way by decree the fundamental conditions of an economy, such as those stemming from natural resources, the level of productivity, or the importance of taxation. Part of what is usually called harmonisation can be the result of the functioning of the market itself, of the economic forces that it activates, and of the contacts which it establishes between those affected." Report of the Messina Committee 61. [Ed. transl.]
[32] E.g., articles 54(3)(g), 57(2), 70(1).
[33] E.g., articles 99, 112.
[34] E.g., article 75.
[35] E.g., articles 49, 54.
[36] Article 220.
[37] In addition to articles 100-02, see article 27 and article 117—the latter referring to "harmonization of social systems" and "approximation of legislative and administrative provisions."

istrative provisions as to which it seeks to act must, by reason of their conflicting content, affect the establishment and functioning of the Common Market or cause a "distortion" in the conditions of competition. It might be contended that article 3(h) of the E.E.C. Treaty authorizes a broader scope for approximation of laws. However, in light of the preface to that article,[38] and the use in article 3(h) of a word formula corresponding to that of the chapter composed by articles 100-102,[39] it would seem that these articles are the implementation of article 3(h).[40] Under this interpretation, article 3(h) does not provide any general residual authority for attempting approximation of laws not elsewhere authorized in the E.E.C. Treaty.

Once one abandons the idea that promotion of a comprehensive uniform law for the Community is implicit in all the subjects dealt with in the E.E.C. Treaty,[41] it may be said that in the Treaty's context "approximation (rapprochement) of laws" imports the creation in the various juridical systems of the Member States of groups of similar rules in particular fields. In fact, however much the Member States are bound in terms of solidarity and cooperation, they do not lose their own individuality. The work of reconciliation will simply be a progressive elimination of the most marked juridical discrepancies through the mutual acceptance of common principles. For instance, in corporation or company law, even though article 100 might be invoked concerning a few subjects for which a certain degree of uniformity is required—such as the formalities necessary for incorporation, the principles for determining nationality, the currency law governing the rights of the respective classes of stock

[38] "For the purposes set out in the preceding Article, the activities of the Community shall include under the conditions and with the timing provided for in this Treaty. . . ." Article 3.

[39] Note 14 *supra*.

[40] In this connection it should be noted that articles 100-02 appear to provide a complete system for approximating the different laws to the extent necessary for the functioning of the Common Market. Other Treaty articles dealing with the divergencies in legal and administrative provisions to be reconciled should be deemed special cases in an area generally covered by articles 100-02.

[41] As Monaco, *supra* note 13, points out, this allows one to discount as irrelevant the copious bibliography devoted to the theory and practice of uniform law, even though those contributions dealing with the special field of reconciling legislative systems are now growing in number and importance in view of the increasing attention given to studies devoted to the E.E.C. Treaty. One may, therefore, cite, in addition to the works mentioned by Monaco, *supra,* and Thiesing, *supra* note 13, R. BERTRAND, PRIX, CONCURRENCE ET HARMONISATION DANS LE MARCHÉ COMMUN (1958); N. CATALANO, LA COMUNITÀ ECONOMICA EUROPA E L'EURATOM ch. VII, at 158 *et seq.* (1959); CEASRE COSCIANI, PROBLEMI FISCALI DEL MARCATO COMMUNE 81 (1958); ROGER DUPAGE, DENIS CÉPÈDE & MAURICE LENGELLÉ, LE MARCHÉ COMMUN 26 *et seq.* (1957); H. EICHNER, ANNÄHERUNG DER RECHTSSYSTEME FÜR DEN GEMEINSAMEN MARKT, INSBESONDERE AUF DEM GEBIET DER WIRTSCHAFTS-, FINANZ- UND STEUERPOLITIK IM GEMEINSAMEN MARKT 39 *et seq.* (1957); W. GANSER, HARMONISIERUNG DER STEURSYSTEME IN DER EUROPÄISCHEN WIRTSCHAFTSGEMEINSCHAFT (1957); R. HELLMAN, SOZIALHARMONISIERUNG MIT ZWEI GESICHTERN (1958); FRITZ W. MEYER, HANS WILLGERODT & J. HEINZ MÜLLER, INTERNATIONALE LOHNGEFÄLLE; WIRTSCHAFTSPOLITISCHE FOLGERUNGEN UND STATISTISCHE PROBLEMATIK (1956); UNIDROIT (INSTITUT INTERNATIONAL POUR L'UNIFICATION DU DROIT PRIVÉ), OBSERVATIONS PRÉLIMINAIRES SUR LE RAPPROCHEMENT DES LÉGISLATIONS DANS LE CADRE DU MARCHÉ COMMUN 1-23 (1957); Marchesano, *Armonizzazione dei regimi fiscali nel quardo di un mercato unico*, in Mondo Aperto, Oct. 1957, p. 301; Mattei, *Armonizzazione delle legislazioni*, A.B.J. (Rome) (1958); Mesenberg, *Zu den steuerlichen Fragen des europäischen Gemeinsamen Marktes*, 12 EUROPA ARCHIV 962 (1957); Di Carrobbio, *Armonizzazione delle legislazonia*, in COMMUNITA ECONOMICA EUROPA 27 (1958); Raulin, *L'unification du droit privé et l'unification européenne*, in L'EUROPE NAISSANTE 21 (1955); Willimetz, *L'harmonisation des législations, Nécessite d'unifier les règles de conflict de lois concernant l'existence et la fonctionnement des sociétés commerciales*, in LE DROIT EUROPÉEN 177 (1958).

and bondholders, and the rules governing conflicts of laws—this article could not be brought to bear on the great bulk of corporation law, because any disparity existing in domestic rules of law would have no bearing on the establishment and functioning of the Common Market.

Apart from the approximation (rapprochement) of laws already examined in connection with articles 100-102, the competence of the E.E.C. institutions with respect to the special, more limited cases dealt with in other parts of the Treaty cannot be defined simply by reference to the terms—such as "coordination," "harmonization," and "abolition of restrictions"[42]—used by the Treaty in describing what action the Community institutions are authorized to take. One must also look at the procedures provided for intervention by these institutions. A careful examination of these procedures reduces, and often eliminates, many differences that, at first, might be inferred from the use of different terms—especially when these procedures are considered in relation to one another in the special cases to which they apply, and in contrast to the omnibus procedures under articles 100-102.

When intervention by the institutions of the Community ensues—as it usually does—in the issuance of a directive by the Council, the result is the promotion of the necessary amendments to bring the legislative and administrative provisions of the separate Member States to a point consistent with the terms of the E.E.C. Treaty. Yet, in every case, in accord with the provisions of article 189 concerning directives, the competence of the various institutions of the Member States, in harmony with the provisions of their individual constitutions, is safeguarded so far as the form and means of applying the directives are concerned.[43] Whether the Treaty speaks of "coordination,"[44] of "harmonization,"[45] or in slightly different terms,[46] the directives, when used as the means for implementing the Community policy, will have the same effect on the domestic juridical systems of the Member States under article 189.

Of course, under the Treaty there still remain some cases where differences in laws are not dealt with by means of "approximation (rapprochement) of laws" undertaken through directives of the Council. These cases may vary from the standard model of approximation (rapprochement) in the form and mode of intervention by E.E.C. institutions or with respect to the institution that intervenes. The variations may be better examined by means of the following list of instances in which the Community is empowered to intervene to reduce or eliminate differences in the legislative and administrative provisions of the Member States:

[42] See notes 32-37 *supra*.
[43] With respect to the directives, one must examine their effect on the internal legal system of the Member States. As to this problem, see generally, CATALANO, *op. cit. supra* note 41, ch. 2, at 45 *et seq.*; GIAN STENDARI, I RAPPORTI FRA ORDINAMENTI GIURIDICI ITALIANO E DELLE COMMUNTÀ EUROPEE ch. 4, at 55 *et seq.* (1958); ANGELO SERENI, LE ORGANIZZAZIONI INTERNAZIONALI ch. 9, 2, nos. 8-13 (1958); Theising, *supra* note 13.
[44] See E.E.C. Treaty arts. 54(3)(g), 57, 57(2), 58, 66, and 70(2).
[45] See *id*. art. 112.
[46] Article 87(1) authorizes, in the alternative, the use of directives in applying the principles of

1. to promote approximation of customs laws and harmonization of labor laws by means of recommendations to the Member States under articles 27 and 117;
2. to issue directives for:
   a. approximation (rapprochement) of laws under articles 100-102, as has been discussed heretofore in this paper;
   b. coordination of laws concerning right of establishment and freedom of movement under articles 54(3), 57(2), 58, 66, and 70(2)—a coordination that may come about at the instance of the Member State in the circumstances provided for in article 220; and
   c. harmonization of certain export measures under article 112; and
3. to publish common rules for application in the Member States concerning certain anti-competitive practices under articles 85-87 and transport policy under article 75. (In these cases, the Community institutions may fulfill their tasks by means of general regulations or by decisions addressed to specific addressees.)

The second category—both because it includes the cases covered by articles 100-102, the general authority for coping with significant differences in legal systems, and because it encompasses a far greater number of situations of legal divergence than the two other categories—would seem to provide the "normal form of intervention" by the Community. Or it may be said that the standard competence of the E.EC.. in reconciling different legal systems is by means of directives issued in those cases which come within the second category listed above. Of course, from the standpoint of a movement towards "unification" in the strict sense of the word, the most significant cases are those under the third category—cases in which there is activity similar to some extent to that undertaken by other international organizations.[47]

A further and more detailed study of the E.E.C. Treaty could reveal that, in addition to the substantial differences in the mode of the Community's intervention as

---

competition set out in articles 85 and 86. The Council is empowered to issue directives to eliminate obstacles to the free movement of workers and to the right of free establishment.

[47] A similar progress towards a uniform law is evident in the powers given to important agencies of other international organizations—like the Council of Europe. See, *e.g.*, Statute Instituting the Treaty of London, May 5, 1949, art. 1; Convention, annexed to the Benelux Treaty, of Nov. 5, 1955, art. 3 (creating an Interparliamentary Consultative Council). Yet here, in contrast to the E.E.C. Treaty, the process of creating a uniform law consists of embracing rules affecting whole institutions in a Convention. When the Convention is later approved by each Government (thus giving the rules binding power from the moment of acceptance) earlier inconsistent rules in the domestic systems of each State are replaced. By way of contrast, other international organizations aiming to promote a uniform law in certain matters, lack the binding power of the terms of the Convention on the legislation of the participating states that the decisions and the regulations of the Council of the E.E.C. enjoy. See, *e.g.*, International Labor Organization (which came into force on June 13, 1921); U.N. International Civil Aviation Organization (which came into force on April 3, 1947). The U.N. Economic Commission for Europe, with the goal of reconciling mercantile practices, has pursued many measures in the formation of a conventional law in the commercial field. A more rudimentary task is performed by article X of the General Agreement on Tariffs and Trade, which simply proposes the application and publication of rules relating to international commerce (laws, regulations, judicial and administrative decisions, and so forth) with the ultimate aim of attaining their uniform application.

traced above, there exist other important procedural differences in the methods for confronting divergencies in the legal systems of the Member States.[48] Further pursuit of this inquiry is, however, beyond the scope of the present article.

[48] In some cases, the process of making a decision of the Council is furthered by a proposal of the Assembly or the Commission. Article 99. On other occasions, reference is made to the judgment of the Economic and Social Committee, articles 49, 57(2); sometimes in conjunction with the judgment of the Assembly. See, e.g., articles 54(1), 56(2), and 70(1).

PARLIAMENTARY CONTROL AND POLITICAL GROUPS IN THE THREE EUROPEAN REGIONAL COMMUNITIES*

Franz C. Heidelberg†

The endeavor to give Europe a "new look" after World War II by leading its countries to a workable form of union has found its first practical expression in three international Treaties of a special kind, concluded between the Federal Republic of Germany, the Kingdom of Belgium, the French Republic, the Italian Republic, the Grand Duchy of Luxembourg, and the Kingdom of the Netherlands. The first, signed in Paris on April 18, 1951, and put into force on July 25, 1952, set up the European Coal and Steel Community (E.C.S.C.). The other two, signed in Rome on March 25, 1957, and put into force on January 1, 1958, resulted in the European Economic Community (E.E.C.) and the European Atomic Energy Community (Euratom).

In the traditional manner of multilateral agreements under international law, these Treaties came into being as the outcome of negotiations between the Governments concerned, but their aim is to find new forms whereby a new order can be established in Europe. They endow the three Communities with a federal structure, having central executive organs, representation of the Member States, a common Parliament, and a Supreme Court.

The executive organ of the E.C.S.C. is the High Authority, which corresponds to the Commissions of the other two Communities. The federal element is reflected in a Ministerial Council for each Community, in which each country has one representative. The Court has jurisdiction for all three Communities and renders decisions in first and final instance. Parliamentary and political control is exercised for all three Communities by the European Parliamentary Assembly.

I

It is to the Assembly that we propose to devote our particular attention here. We shall try to show how and why it was founded—for it is by no means self-evident that a predominantly economic union should have a parliamentary organ—to examine the juridical position conferred upon it by the Treaties, and finally to demonstrate how it has developed in practice.

The foundation of the Council of Europe on May 5, 1949, did not lead to the creation of a genuinely parliamentary institution for the fifteen member countries of that organization. All that the founders managed to set up was a Consultative

---

* Translated from the German by Denis M. Moore.
† LL.D. 1932, Heidelberg University. Staff, High Authority of the European Coal and Steel Community, since 1953; Press Department, European Parliamentary Assembly, since 1957. Author, Das Europäische Parlament. Entstehung, Aufbau—Erfahrungen und Erwartungen (1959).

Assembly, which was powerless vis-à-vis the Committee of Ministers. The demand for a Parliament with "limited but real powers" was not met until the Treaty setting up the E.C.S.C. was signed.

The E.C.S.C. Treaty created a parliamentary body known as the Common Assembly and stipulated that it should represent the peoples represented in the Community; that it should have seventy-eight members selected by the national Parliaments from their own ranks; and that, under certain conditions, it could force the resignation of the High Authority. Under the Treaty, then, this Assembly had no very far-reaching prerogatives. Hence, it was claimed that it was "democratic only in appearance" or "at best a stunted growth, lacking real parliamentary powers." Such criticism clearly rests on the traditional concept of a parliament, whose most striking characteristics include the right to legislate and the right to control the budget. In fact, the Common Assembly was invested with neither of these rights. It should be pointed out, however, that the legislative aspect is already covered, at least provisionally, by the Treaties. The important thing is to realize that the absence of legislative powers does not also mean the absence of the right of control.

Although the E.C.S.C. Treaty contained few express provisions concerning the Assembly, it, nevertheless, offered that body the opportunity for dynamic development, since it followed the customary principle of constitutional history on the European continent, which decrees that constitutions shall lay down only the essential organizational and structural provisions governing the parliamentary organ, allowing the latter to decide as a sovereign body upon its internal structure and rules of procedure. In drafting and subsequently applying its procedural rules, the Common Assembly discovered how to ensure for itself an authority, and hence control rights, which at the outset it had certainly not been intended to possess in that degree. Its members at all times staunchly defended the notion of the body's sovereignty. Once sovereignty and independence were recognized, they succeeded in obtaining rights not provided for in the E.C.S.C. Treaty, but at the same time— and this is the crucial factor—not expressly forbidden. In this way, they arrived at the establishment of standing committees and the creation of political groups, and also reinforced their powers of control. The Assembly early decided to hold not only the prescribed regular sessions, but also extraordinary meetings several times a year. Thus, and through committee activities, parliamentary control became a permanent feature and found a logical complement in the deputies' right to put written questions to the Executive. In the field of budgetary control, too, the Assembly was able to gain the right to a limited degree of influence.

The rigid procedure surrounding the vote of no confidence in the High Authority was mitigated in the following manner: the Assembly did not reject or approve the Authority's general report *in toto*, but couched its opinion on the various sections in the form of resolutions reflecting the outcome of the discussions in the competent Committees. Lastly, considerable importance attaches to a proceeding that might be termed the "Government Policy Statement." After it had been informed officially of the resignation of Jean Monnet, first President of the High Authority, the Assembly expressed the wish, immediately after the appointment of his successor, for a statement of the High Authority's political intentions. Monnet's successors in the presidential office acceded to this desire, and their statements were always followed by debates in the Assembly.

The history of the Common Assembly has here been given only in its broad essence, but it shows that the members approached their task as experienced parliamentarians and convinced Europeans. When, on the entry into force of the Rome Treaties on February 28, 1958, the Assembly resolved its formal dissolution and its transformation into the larger Assembly of the three Communities, it was able after six years' activity to present a clean and positive balance-sheet and to bequeath a substantial heritage to its successor.

II

The new Assembly representing the three Communities met for the first time on March 19, 1958. Of its own sovereign volition, it christened itself the European Parliamentary Assembly. Its members are 142 in number. Germany, France, and Italy each sends thirty-six representatives; Belgium and the Netherlands, fourteen; and Luxembourg, six. If the population figures of the six countries are compared, it is at once evident that the smaller States are relatively more strongly represented than the large. The seats had to be distributed in this way, however, as otherwise the different political parties and shades of opinion in the small countries would have been inadequately represented both in the Assembly and in the Committees. Incidentally, though, this question is of scant importance, because the European parliamentarians do not sit as national delegations, but are associated in political groups. They are representatives of the peoples, not of the States.

One of the Assembly's first decisions was to take over the Rules of Procedure of the former Common Assembly *mutatis mutandis*. In view of the much wider field covered, the number of Committees was raised to thirteen:

1. Committee on Political Affairs and Institutional Questions
2. Committee on Commercial Policy and Economic Cooperation with Third Countries
3. Committee on Agriculture
4. Committee on Social Affairs
5. Committee on the Internal Community Market
6. Committee on Long-Term Policy Investment and Financial Questions
7. Committee on the Association of Overseas Countries and Territories
8. Transport Committee
9. Committee on Energy Policy
10. Committee on Scientific and Technical Research
11. Committee on Worker's Safety, Health, and Welfare

Parliament and Political Groups

12. Committee on Administration of the European Parliament and the Budgeting of the Communities
13. Committee on Legal Questions, Rules of Procedure, and Immunities

The first eight of the above Committees are each composed of twenty-nine members of the Assembly; the remainder, of seventeen. Membership of the large Committees should, as far as practicable, consist of seven German, seven French, seven Italian, four Netherlands, four Belgian, and two Luxembourg representatives. On the remaining Committees, there are four German, four French, four Italian, two Belgian, and two Netherlands representatives, and one representative of Luxembourg. Some of the Committees are identical with those of the former Common Assembly.

The special task of the Committees is to guarantee the permanency and effectiveness of parliamentary control. Thus, their activity is not confined to preparing the debates and resolutions of the Assembly—although this is, of course, one of their tasks. Their permanent character is intended to ensure that the Assembly will not simply play a passive role nor be obliged to take cognizance of the acts or decisions of the executive bodies only after the event. The members of the High Authority and European Commissions are under a duty to explain certain problems to the Committees and give them any other information they may need. In addition, the Committees may ask for the attendance at their meeting of any person whom they consider it advisable to hear.

The Assembly has been granted one of the attributes of parliamentary sovereignty in that it is entitled, through the adoption of a vote of no confidence, to secure the resignation of any of the executive organs. The Executive concerned then resigns in a body, but its reconstitution is a matter for the six Governments, which are not prohibited by the Treaties from reappointing the dismissed Executive *en bloc*. Compared with the E.C.S.C. Treaty, however, the Rome Treaties provide a way out of this dilemma: Whereas the High Authority can be called upon to resign only once in the course of a year—on the basis of its general report—votes of no confidence in the E.E.C. and Euratom Commissions are permissible at any time. The result may be that the Assembly gains a say in the appointment of the Commissions, in as much as it can go on moving and adopting votes of no confidence until the Governments finally accede to its wishes.

A further effective means of exercising parliamentary control consists in the members' right to put written or oral questions to the executive organs or to the Councils of Ministers. The institution thus questioned is admittedly not obliged to answer, but it is under a certain moral pressure, because all questions still unanswered after a definite period—a month in the case of the executive organs, two months in that of the Councils—are published in the *Official Gazette* of the European Communities. The fact that to date none of the many questions put has remained unanswered leads to the conclusion that the power of public opinion has been correctly assessed on all sides.

The Rome Treaties have introduced an important innovation by recognizing that the Assembly has the right to be heard by the other organs. The Common Assembly had no such right vis-à-vis either the High Authority or the Council of Ministers. Nevertheless, by laying constant stress on its sovereign powers, it had succeeded in inducing the High Authority, at least, to give considerable weight to parliamentary opinion when making its decisions. An indisputable right was not, however, created by this practice. It is, therefore, all the more significant that the new Treaties give the Assembly an explicit right to be heard: the E.E.C. Treaty names eighteen and the Euratom Treaty eleven cases in which its opinion must be sought. These cases are predominantly connected with the extremely important questions of the harmonization and assimilation of European legislation.

Thus, having a statutory right to be heard, the European Parliamentary Assembly is recognized as possessing, in addition to its power of control, a consultative function, though not the power to make decisions. The Ministerial Councils of the E.E.C. and Euratom are entitled, in formulating their own decisions, to disregard the suggestions and proposals of the Assembly. There is no provision of the Treaties that could prevent them from so doing. But Treaties are not meaningless, and the express introduction of a consultation procedure undoubtedly implies that its outcome must have some binding effect, at least to the extent that the Councils of Ministers would be required to give reasons for not heeding the Assembly's views. The insertion into the new Treaties of the principle of consultation may well be the springboard whereby the Assembly can launch out into legislative functions. Its development along these lines is primarily a matter for the Assembly itself, which, by exercising skill and prudence and taking a leaf from its predecessor's book, can strengthen its position and give added weight to its counsels.

The Common Assembly of the E.C.S.C. had no direct connections with the Council of Ministers under the Treaty; so far as the E.C.S.C. Council is concerned, its relations with the Parliamentary Assembly, too, will remain unchanged. Under the E.C.S.C. Treaty, the High Authority is the "centre and soul" of its Community, a fact that already emerges from its coming first in the list of the Community's organs. It was responsible to the Assembly, whose meetings were only rarely attended by representatives of the Council of Ministers. This lack of contact and of the possibility of discussion with the Governments was regretted and criticized by the Common Assembly. It was not until the occasion of its session in Rome in November 1957, that the E.C.S.C. Council of Ministers offered to meet the Assembly and give concerted replies to its questions by holding a Round Table. This get-together was a useful one, but the Ministers made it clear that they had no wish to create a precedent and that the Round Table meeting was in no sense to be taken as affecting the institutional structure of the E.C.S.C. Treaty. Under that instrument, the Assembly's interlocutor remains the High Authority alone.

The Rome Treaties open up other prospects with regard to mutual relations between the Parliamentary Assembly and the Councils of Ministers. It is true that the concept of consultation does not automatically imply an obligation to discuss; yet, it would quickly become a dead letter if the intention were to give it a limitative or, as it were, a passive interpretation. Consultation by means of correspondence or as a matter of daily routine must not become the rule. The object is not to keep postal administrations, messengers, and office assistants on the run, but to infuse life into the Treaties. Now that the Rome Treaties have brought about a shift in the institutional emphasis by according the Councils of Ministers precedence over the Commissions, it would seem to be in keeping with democratic and parliamentary usage that the Councils should step as often as possible into the limelight of publicity.

III

The formation of Committees is in itself inadequate to maintain a Parliament's capacity for work. One of the factors making for parliamentary activity that is in line with democratic conditions is the possibility for like-minded deputies to associate for purposes of planned cooperation, so that their common political convictions may find expression in a united front. This aim is met by the formation of political groups. Without such groups, a Parliament would resolve itself into a collection of individuals. Like the Committees, the political groups are not an end in themselves, but simply a means of helping the work of Parliament along. From that angle, the idea of forming political groups on a supranational basis was already raised in the Consultative Assembly of the Council of Europe, but was abandoned because of manifold objections. The Common Assembly again took it up and soon put it into practice. The Rules of Procedure were supplemented by a provision to the effect that members might form groups in accordance with their political allegiance; the formation of a group would be deemed to be complete as soon as the President of the Assembly had received an official declaration on the subject, together with the group's title, the signatures of its members, and the names and functions of its officers.

The same Rules apply to the European Parliamentary Assembly, where the minimum membership of a group is fixed at seventeen. To settle the financial problems posed by the existence of the groups, each of the latter is granted from the Assembly's budget a fixed equal basic subsidy, to which is added a further sum in respect of each member. These funds are placed at the disposal of the groups as such and not, for instance, of the individual members. It was in these conditions that in June 1953, the Christian-Democrat Group, the Socialist Group, and the Group of Liberals and Associates were formed. All were duly organized and set up permanent secretariats. In the European Parliamentary Assembly, the members of each group sit together in a body.

The foundation of supranational groups sounds well-nigh revolutionary to

European ears. On closer inspection, however, it will be recognized that the large parties in Europe—especially in the countries of the Six-Power Community—have, for all their national differences conditioned by history or politics, corresponding features that are unaffected by frontiers. Where there is the basis of a common program, it becomes simpler to harmonize divergent opinions—although even so, this is not always easy. Years of regular collaboration in a group lead, however, to a certain community of thought in which opposing views seek to meet each other half-way and a clash is avoided. Nevertheless, agreement on the broad lines should not blind us to the fact that on individual points, considerable differences of opinion may arise at times within the parties, even where their members have had decades of contacts with their counterparts in other countries. It is especially in matters of detail that the influence of the three supranational groups is bound to be most felt, for their task is to be "transformers" in which a multitude of very similar or very dissimilar opinions must first be converted into a foundation for thinking on the European scale.

The Groups are able to master this task the more easily in view of the absence from their domain of any national delegations. Admittedly, the latter designation is customarily used, for "home consumption," as it were, when the people's representatives from one particular country are referred to as a body, but it receives no support either in the Treaties or in the Rules of Procedure. Hence, just as there are no national delegations, so it is impossible to form any sort of national group, not only because this would run counter to the very philosophy of the Assembly, but also because the Rules allow the formation of groups only in accordance with political, and not national, allegiance. It is superfluous to add that the absence of national delegations or groups in no sense means the abandonment of the expression and free play of national characteristics. Europe's wealth and well-being must be based not only on a properly ordered economic life, but also, and essentially, on the manifold springs of its culture, of which the different languages are just as much a part as are variations of temperament, talents and traditions.

IV

The three European Communities represent attempts to arrive at a new order, but they do not in themselves spell its achievement. There are many ways of accomplishing European union, but the task is not simply to discuss ways and means and to seek for a single ideal form, which, to tell the truth, does not exist. The task is rather that of making a start, of overcoming inertia. Even the United States of America began from an initial nucleus of only thirteen States. The establishment of the E.C.S.C. in 1952 introduced a new process that has gone ahead more rapidly than could at first be foreseen. To urge that process further is the supreme task of the Parliamentary Assembly. Experience has shown that despite its limited prerogatives, it is well equipped to do so. The necessary coordination of the three Communities presupposes a degree of political good will that has long since grown up among its members. On all sides, there is an abundance of good will to achieve that coordination; all that is lacking, in some quarters, is the driving force. Parliaments are the dynamic element by which the political flywheel is kept in constant motion.

The rights of the Parliamentary Assembly are still limited, but to the workings of its political and economic imagination and to its keen search for constructive opportunities, no bounds are set. From these premises, it has drawn the proper conclusions, and it has succeeded in off-setting its lack of rights by the indisputable weight of the moral authority that it has from the outset been at pains to acquire. That authority is especially powerful in that it can count upon the European peoples' desire for unity—a desire that must one day be followed by greater European-mindedness on the part of their Governments, whether they will or no! The Assembly is still wanting in many respects: it has no permanent headquarters, its political groups have as yet no prepared programs. But none of this should lead to discouragement. The institution is a new one, its foundation has been revolutionary for Europe. The history of parliamentary government shows that all popular representations have at some time been regarded as a necessary evil and that they have had to fight hard for uncontested recognition of their position. We should be guilty of unfair dramatization if we claimed that for the European Parliamentary Assembly, too, the storm signals have been hoisted. On the contrary, the path has been made smooth for its gradual evolution into a real Parliament. Clearly, the decisive step must be the institution of European elections, and the time when these will take place cannot be predicted. True, in May 1960, the Assembly adopted a draft agreement on European elections, consisting of twenty-three articles, but the last word on this matter lies with the Governments and the Parliaments of the six countries, which have to ratify the agreement.

PROBLEMS CONNECTED WITH THE CREATION OF EURATOM*

Pierre Mathijsen†

In the third annual report of the Commission of Euratom to the European Parliamentary Assembly, it was pointed out that "like the European Coal and Steel Community and the European Economic Community, the European Community for Atomic Energy finds its origin in the will of the Member States to build Europe."[1] This statement is important because it defines the political and organizational framework of Euratom. When examining some of the problems related to the creation of Euratom, one must not forget that although this Community differs from the other two in its tasks, its field of action, and its powers, it must be seen in connection with them and as a means towards the political and economic integration of Europe.

Integration appears particularly urgent in the field of atomic energy. The development of a nuclear industry would be impossible if each country were to act separately and relied exclusively upon its own resources.

As is stated in the preamble to the Euratom Treaty, "nuclear energy constitutes the essential resource for ensuring the expansion and renovation of production and for progressing in peaceful achievements." Belgium, France, Germany, Italy, Luxembourg, and The Netherlands decided, therefore, to "create the conditions required for the development of a powerful nuclear industry which would provide extensive supplies of energy, lead to modernization of technical processes, and contribute in various other ways to the well-being of their peoples." To achieve these objectives, the European Community for Atomic Energy (Euratom) was established by a Treaty signed in Rome on March 25, 1957, by the same six countries that composed the European Coal and Steel Community (E.C.S.C.) and the European Economic Community (E.E.C.).

Euratom can be defined as a union of sovereign states, based upon an international treaty, with institutions of its own, acting independently from the Member States, endowed in the field of nuclear energy with powers not only within the Community, but also competent to act as an international legal person.[2]

There are four institutions: the Commission, the Council of Ministers (assisted

---

* This article only reflects the personal views of the author and may in no way be interpreted as expressing the opinion of an institution of the Community.

† LL.M. 1951, Dr. iur. 1957, University of Leyden (The Netherlands); M.A. 1952, University of Minnesota. Legal Adviser, European Atomic Energy Community, Brussels, Belgium. Author, Le Droit de la Communauté Européenne du Charbon et de l'Acier—une étude des sources (1958).

[1] Euratom, Troisième Rapport Général sur l'activité de la Communauté 7 (1960) [hereinafter cited as Troisième Rapport Général].

[2] The Community is, e.g., competent to conclude treaties with third countries, Euratom Treaty art. 101; and to receive diplomatic envoys. Protocol on the Privileges and Immunities art. 16.

by the Economic and Social Committee and by the Scientific and Technical Committee), the Court of Justice, and the Parliamentary Assembly. The Commission is the central executive body upon which rests the task to implement the provisions of the Treaty. The Council of Ministers is composed of representatives of the governments of the Member States. These two institutions jointly exercise the legislative power of the Community; they are empowered to issue regulations, directives, and decisions that are directly binding not only upon the Member States, but also upon the persons and enterprises that fall within the jurisdiction of the Community.[3] This legislative activity of the Commission and the Council is submitted to the judicial control of the Court of Justice: appeals for annulment may, as a rule, be brought before the Court against all binding legal acts of these institutions. Moreover, an annual report on the activities of the Community is submitted for discussion to the Assembly. This last body can, by adopting a motion of censure, express disagreement with the way in which the Commission carried out its task and thus force the members of this Commission to resign their office.

What Lauterpacht has said about the E.C.S.C. also applies to the legal structure of Euratom: "[I]t exhibits in some respects distinct features of the federal system."[4] A more detailed description of the Community's structure and of its regulatory responsibilities will not be attempted here.[5] The present contribution intends to examine some of the legal, economic, political, and social problems that have arisen for the Community in the various fields in which powers were conferred upon it—namely, nuclear research, dissemination of information, health protection, industrial development, safety control, supply of nuclear materials, and international relations.

I

RESEARCH AND INFORMATION

The task of Euratom in the field of nuclear research is two-fold: (1) coordination of the national research programs of the Member States and, eventually, their completion through direct or indirect financial assistance, through supply of material, or by making available facilities, equipment, and expert assistance; and (2) carrying out of the Community's own research program. The means put at the disposal of Euratom in order to achieve these two aims are numerous.

The most intricate of these tasks is the coordination of the national programs. No direct legal means have been put at the disposal of Euratom to enforce its views

---

[3] According to Euratom Treaty art. 196, these persons and enterprises are natural persons, enterprises, or institutions, whatever their public or private legal status, which are wholly or partly engaged in the territories of the Member States in activities that come within the field defined by the appropriate chapter of the Treaty.

[4] 1 H. LAUTERPACHT, OPPENHEIM'S INTERNATIONAL LAW 187 (1958).

[5] For such a description, see, e.g., Vogelaar, *Euratom: Its Relations to the Other European Communities and Its Regulatory Responsibilities*, in FEDERAL BAR ASS'N, INSTITUTE ON LEGAL ASPECTS OF THE EUROPEAN COMMUNITY 188 (1960); Gaudet, *Euratom, Progress in Nuclear Energy*, in HERBERT S. MARKS (ED.), LAW AND ADMINISTRATION 140 (1959).

in this domain, and much depends on the goodwill of the Member States. However, as the individual members are not always in a position, essentially through lack of funds, to complete their programs, they need assistance from the Community, which consequently reinforces Euratom's position.

As for the execution of its own research program, Euratom may act in various ways. The programs themselves, except for the first five-year program, which is laid down in an Annex to the Euratom Treaty, will be drawn up periodically by the Council of Ministers.

In principle, these programs must be implemented in the Joint Nuclear Research Center of the Community, which the Commission is to establish. For this, the Commission had to choose between either constructing its own center or taking over already-existing national research facilities. Legally, the Commission was free to choose either solution; technically and scientifically, however, it was not justified in building a new research center when, in the Member States, so many installations were standing idle or unfinished. Politically, it was essential for the Community to assert itself as rapidly as possible in this important field. The Commission decided, therefore, to take over the existing facilities of Ispra in northern Italy. The agreement signed in July 1959 between Euratom and the Italian Government, concerning the transfer of this center to Euratom was ratified by the Italian Parliament at the end of July 1960.

This delay in the ratification procedure constituted a serious handicap for the research activity of the Community. It is also a typical example of the kind of problems encountered by Euratom. Although the Commission has been endowed with the necessary legal authority and financial means, the implementation of this particular task was delayed by circumstances beyond its control. This is also true for the installations of the Joint Nuclear Research Center that the Commission has created in Karlsruhe (Germany), and intends to establish in Petten (The Netherlands), and Mol (Belgium).

It is fortunate, however, that the joint research center is not the only means put at the disposal of the Community for the execution of its own research program. Article ten of the Euratom Treaty provides that "the Commission may, by means of contracts, entrust Member States, persons or enterprises, or also third countries or international organizations or nationals of third countries with the implementation of the Community's research program."

During the 2½ years of its existence, Euratom has mainly depended upon such contracts for its research work. This system proved not only satisfactory for the Community, but also useful for European research institutions. Most of these contracts were concluded with persons and enterprises within the Community, but Euratom also participates in two important projects in third countries—namely, the Halden Boiling Water Reactor Project in Norway and the High Temperature Gas-Cooled Reactor Project (Dragon) in Great Britain.

It was within the framework of the Euratom-United States Agreement for

Cooperation[6] that a vigorous impetus was given to this means of research. The interest of private and public organizations in this joint program is clearly demonstrated by the fact that more than 400 proposals were submitted to the Joint Euratom/United States Research and Development Board that was created shortly after the signing of the Agreement in 1958. The various research organizations within the Community were particularly eager to become acquainted with nuclear technology, and for most of them, the financial contribution of Euratom was very welcome.

As for the information resulting from the execution of these research contracts that are financed by the contributions of the Member States, it is obvious that it must be at the disposal of the latter and of the persons and enterprises within the Community. This principle is laid down in articles twelve and thirteen of the Euratom Treaty and applies not only to information acquired through research contracts, but also to information obtained by virtue of international agreements or acquired in the Joint Nuclear Research Center of the Community. While the dissemination of information obtained from the last two sources does not create any major difficulty, because this information is, generally speaking, at the disposal of the Community, the research contracts present the Commission with serious problems.

Although the enterprises and research organizations within the Community are eager to participate in the implementation of Euratom's research program, they are of the opinion that they should obtain certain exclusive rights with regard to information, and especially patentable information. In their opinion, payment of the direct costs does not counterbalance the contribution of the enterprise under a research contract.

The Commission, however, believes that in order to fulfill its obligations with regard to dissemination of information, it must, whenever possible, obtain the fullest rights to communicate information and to grant licenses or sublicenses on the patented results of its research contracts. (Euratom Treaty article twelve). A distinction was, however, made between the nuclear and the nonnuclear applications of such patents and it thus became possible for the Commission, while respecting the provisions of the Treaty, to grant some exclusive rights to Euratom's contractors by conceding to them the patent rights for the nonnuclear applications of their invention. Another solution was to permit the contractor to obtain certain exclusive rights with regards to patent rights outside the Community. But it would be contrary to the Treaty to accept that licenses or sublicenses to exploit patents resulting from Euratom's research contracts may only be granted with the consent of the inventor.

The position of the Commission in this field is strongly reinforced by the extensive powers that have been provided for in chapter two of the Euratom Treaty. Not only are the Member States obliged to communicate to the Commission, at its

[6] Agreement with the European Atomic Energy Community, Aug. 27, 1958, [1958] 9 U.S.T. & O.I.A. 1116, T.I.A.S. No. 4091

request, the contents of applications for patents relating to a specifically nuclear field and patents that appear prima facie to them to deal with a subject that, without being of a specifically nuclear nature, is directly connected with and essential to the development of nuclear energy; but the Community is also empowered to have nonexclusive licenses granted, ex officio, either to the Community or to persons or enterprises. This right to expropriate industrial property is one of the most extensive powers provided for in the Treaty. It also proves that dissemination of information has been considered by the drafters of the Treaty as essential to the public interest, this last aspect being the generally admitted ground for expropriation in municipal law.

It should be noted that the powers of the Commission in this field are in no way arbitrary; the procedure provided for in the Euratom Treaty constitutes a sufficient guarantee for every patent-holder within the Community that his rights, and particularly his right to compensation, will be respected. A special arbitration committee is provided, which can settle all such questions, while appeal to the Court of Justice of the European Communities is always possible. Finally, article eighteen of the Treaty explicitly states that the provisions regarding expropriation "shall not affect the provisions of the Paris Convention for the protection of industrial property."

The problems raised by the Euratom Treaty provisions concerning patents and dissemination of information have an important social aspect as well. The rights of the individual inventor must be protected. According to the municipal law of the Member States,[7] the inventor is basically the owner of his invention, but the law concedes to the employer of the inventor a right to claim the invention, which can only be done against payment of a special compensation, the amount of which depends on the industrial importance of the invention.

The Commission, therefore, states in its third annual report[8] that "certain principles of its policy which are already applied in its research contracts will establish a fair equilibrium between the interests of the Community, of the inventors and of the enterprises."

II .

HEALTH PROTECTION

Article two of the Euratom Treaty provides that the Community shall "establish and enforce the application of uniform safety standards to protect the health of workers and of the general public." Article thirty further specifies this obligation by providing for the establishment within the Community of "basic standards"—*i.e.,* (1) the maximum doses of ionizing radiations compatible with adequate safety, (2) the maximum permissible degree of exposure and contamination, and (3) the

---

[7] See, *e.g.,* German law: Gesetz über Arbeitnehmererfindungen of July 27, 1957, [1957] I Bundesgestzblatt 756; Richtlinien für die Vergütung von Arbeitnehmererfindungen im privaten Dienst of July 20, 1959.

[8] TROISIÈME RAPPORT GÉNÉRAL 39.

fundamental principles governing the medical supervision of workers. However, in matters of health protection, the major responsibility lies with Member States, and according to article thirty-three of the Euratom Treaty "each Member State must enact the legislative and administrative provisions required to ensure compliance with the basic standards." In 1959 the Community issued directives concerning the basic standards;[9] directives, according to article 161 of the Treaty, "bind any Member State to which they are addressed as to the results to be achieved, while leaving to domestic agencies a competence as to the form and means." The directives issued by Euratom constitute the first step towards the establishment of uniform safety standards enforceable in several countries.

Important from a legal point of view is the word "uniform." It is not clear whether it qualifies only the basic standards established by the Community or also the national provisions that are necessary for the application of the basic standards within the Member States. It must be noted in this respect that no direct powers were conferred upon the Community to achieve uniformity. The Commission can only make recommendations[10] in order to ensure the harmonization of the provisions applicable in the Member States.

More important than the powers of the Community are the principles that were laid down and that are now binding upon all Member States. An exhaustive review of this important example of international legislation in the field of health protection will not be made here, but it might be useful to point out a few of the basic principles.

By virtue of the basic standards, all production, treatment, handling, utilization, possession, stocking, transportation, and elimination of natural or artificial radioactive elements must be communicated to the national authorities and eventually submitted for prior authorization. Another essential principle is that a prior authorization must always be required for (1) the use of radioactive elements for medical purposes; (2) the addition of radioactive elements to food, medicaments, cosmetics, and household products; and (3) the use of radioactive elements in the fabrication of toys.

The social importance and implications of these principles are so great that no major obstacles were encountered by the Commission in the drafting of the directives, but it is surprising that as of June 1961, only one country—namely, Germany—has enacted the legislative and administrative provisions required to ensure compliance with the basic standards. And although Belgium, Italy, Luxembourg, and The Netherlands have communicated drafts of provisions to the Commission, the fact remains that, as the Commission stated it explicitly, "one year after the publication of the Basic Standards the situation is not satisfactory."[11] The Community, however, is not a powerless witness, and if a Member State were to refuse to enact the neces-

---

[9] [1959] JOURNAL OFFICIEL DE LA COMMUNAUTÉ EUROPÉENNE DU CHARBON ET DE L'ACIER [hereinafter cited as JOURNAL OFFICIEL].

[10] Euratom Treaty art. 161; recommendations have no binding force.

[11] TROISIÈME RAPPORT GÉNÉRAL 77.

sary provisions, the Commission could consider an appeal to the Court of Justice based on article 141 of the Euratom Treaty.[12]

Although the Community does not, as was pointed out, possess the authority to enact directly binding provisions in the field of health protection, it possesses a sort of indirect legislative power to fulfill an important social task.

III

INDUSTRIAL DEVELOPMENT

The Community is to achieve its aim by "the creation of conditions necessary for the speedy establishment and growth of nuclear industries."[13] Industrial development is, therefore, the first objective of Euratom. In the Treaty establishing the Community, three chapters contain provisions more directly connected with this objective. They endow the Community with certain powers in the field of investment, make possible the creation of joint enterprises, and provide for the establishment of a nuclear common market.

As all the Member States adhere, officially at least, to the principle of free enterprise, very little authority was given to the Community in investment matters. The role of the Commission is purely advisory; it must periodically publish programs indicating in particular the production targets for nuclear energy,[14] and investment projects must be communicated[15] for discussion and advice to the Commission.

This may seem very meager, and, from a purely legal standpoint, it is, indeed; but in reality, the opinion given by the Commission—and which is communicated to the Member State concerned—carries much weight. This was clearly proved by the practice of the E.C.S.C., where the High Authority has similar powers.[16] It appears that the opinion of that Authority is a decisive factor when enterprises seek to obtain bank loans in order to finance their investment. One enterprise even appealed to the Court of Justice for annulment of such an opinion, arguing that it had caused a certain prejudice to the enterprises. The Court declared the appeal inadmissible.[17]

According to article forty-six of the Euratom Treaty, industrial undertakings of special importance to the development of the nuclear industry in the Community may be established as joint enterprises. By joint enterprise is meant an enterprise established by a decision of the Council. The Community itself may participate in the financing, and participation by third countries is also possible. Although these

---

[12] "If the Commission considers that a Member State has failed to fulfill one of its obligations under this Treaty, it shall give a reasoned opinion on the matter after requiring such State to submit its comments. If such State does not comply with the terms of such opinion within the period laid down by the Commission, the latter may refer the matter to the Court of Justice."

[13] Euratom Treaty art. 1.

[14] TROISIÈME RAPPORT GÉNÉRAL 42-55.

[15] Regulation No. 4, [1958] JOURNAL OFFICIEL 417; Regulation No. 5, [1959] JOURNAL OFFICIEL 185.

[16] E.C.S.C. Treaty art. 54.

[17] 3 RECUEIL DE LA JURISPRUDENCE DE LA COUR 205 (1957).

enterprises are subject to the municipal rules applying to industrial or commercial undertakings, the Council may declare applicable to the joint enterprise certain advantages like exemption from all direct taxation or from all custom duties. Up to this time, only one such enterprise has been created by the Council.

Of great economic importance for the development of nuclear industries is the establishment of the nuclear common market. Chapter nine of the Euratom Treaty provides, among other things, for (1) the establishment of a free trade area[18] among the Member States—*i.e.*, abolition of all import and export duties or charges and all quantitative restrictions on imports or exports with respect to a number of products enumerated in an annex to the Treaty; (2) the creation of a customs union[19]—*i.e.*, establishment of a common customs tariff; (3) the abolition of restrictions placed upon access to specialized employment in the nuclear field by nationals of the Member States; (4) the abolition of restrictions based on nationality, which might be applied to natural or legal persons wishing to participate in the construction of nuclear facilities; and, finally, (5) the free movement of capital destined for nuclear industries.

The establishment of the free trade area and the customs union raised a certain number of legal problems. In the first place, the question was asked whether these economic measures were compatible with the provisions of the General Agreement for Tariffs and Trade (G.A.T.T.). The free trade area and the customs union being limited to nuclear products, there might seem to be an incompatibility with said Agreement. It has been argued, however, that the nuclear common market is but a forerunner of the general Common Market established by the E.E.C., which is, indeed, compatible with the G.A.T.T.—the only difference being that the general Common Market is being established progressively, while the nuclear common market came into being on January 1, 1959.

But, if one accepts this last thesis, one may wonder whether the nuclear common market should not coincide geographically with the general Common Market. It should be noted that, according to the E.E.C. Treaty,[20] the Common Market applies to the European territories of the Member States and to Algeria and the French overseas departments, while the provisions of the Euratom Treaty apply "except when otherwise provided . . . to the European territories of the Member States and to non-European territories subject to their jurisdiction,"[21] which covers a much larger area. There is, of course, an answer to this objection: although the Euratom Treaty nowhere states that the nuclear common market is but a part of the general Common Market, this is implied, with the consequence that the E.E.C. territorial provisions also apply to the nuclear common market, thus constituting an exception in the sense of article 198: "except when otherwise provided."

[18] Agreement signed in Brussels by the Member States on Dec. 22, 1958, based on Euratom Treaty art. 93(a).
[19] Agreement signed in Brussels by the Member States on Dec. 22, 1958, based on Euratom Treaty art. 94.
[20] E.E.C. Treaty art. 227.
[21] Euratom Treaty art. 198.

These are but a few of the many questions that arise with the implementation of the nuclear common market; but when one considers the advantages that it entails for the industrial development within the Community, the struggle to solve these problems seems, indeed, worthwhile. A single example may illustrate this: The common customs tariff that was established for nuclear products (*i.e.*, the tariffs applicable to products imported from third countries to the Community) provides for the following duties:[22] fissionable and nuclear materials and radioactive isotopes are completely free from duties; the duty of ten per cent on nuclear reactors is suspended until January 1, 1962; and the duties of five to twelve per cent on the other nuclear products have been partly or completely suspended until January 1, 1964. At the present time, nuclear products circulate practically freely not only within the Community, but also between the Community and third countries.

IV

RESPONSIBILITY AND NUCLEAR INSURANCE

Before discussing the powers and activities of the Community in matters of security control, supply, and external relations, some remarks must be made about a problem that has far-reaching social and legal implications: the responsibility for nuclear accidents and the insurance of the risks involved.

Article ninety-eight of the Euratom Treaty provides that "the Member States shall take all necessary measures to facilitate the conclusion of insurance contracts covering atomic risks." It further enjoins the Council, acting on proposal of the Commission and after consultation of the Assembly and of the Economic and Social Committee, to issue directives as to the particulars of application of said Article.

At the present time, in the absence of the necessary legislation, insurance of atomic risks can only be obtained either up to a limited amount or at prohibitive prices. While countries like the United States have enacted provisions establishing the amounts for which the operator of a nuclear installation is responsible and, consequently, required to take insurance, and, furthermore, providing for state responsibility for damages exceeding this amount, on the Continent, private enterprises cannot insure a risk that is in no way foreseeable or limited. But as all nuclear installations in Europe were, until recently, state-owned and the risks, therefore, covered by a state responsibility, the problem was not too urgent. The establishment of Euratom, the aim of which was precisely the development of nuclear industries, however, made the solution of this problem indispensable.

The present situation is, indeed, most unsatisfactory and socially unacceptable—unsatisfactory because private enterprise is seriously handicapped in its efforts toward rapid development, and unacceptable because the eventual victims of a nuclear mishap might be deprived of adequate compensation in the absence of state guarantee or sufficient coverage. As the Commission pointed out,[23] the geographical

[22] TROISIÈME RAPPORT GÉNÉRAL 59.
[23] *Id.* at 61.

situation of Europe is such that a nuclear accident can cause damage beyond the borders of the country where the accident occurs. It is, therefore, necessary that all the eventual victims receive compensation according to identical principles and without discrimination based on nationality.

The solution envisaged to resolve these various problems is an international convention. Nearly three years ago, negotiations were initiated within the Organization for European Economic Cooperation (O.E.E.C.), but the task of defining principles acceptable to the eighteen member countries appears to be extremely difficult. Furthermore, the resulting convention will not cover the whole field, and, therefore, the Member States of Euratom have already foreseen and drafted an additional convention that will be open to all countries and will supplement the provisions of the O.E.E.C. Convention.

The principles of the O.E.E.C. Convention are as follows:

1. The operator of a nuclear installation is, irrespective of his fault, responsible for all damages caused by his installation; this is the so-called "objective responsibility."

2. The operator alone is responsible for damages caused to third parties.

3. The responsibility is limited to $15 million; however, this amount may be reduced to $5 million.

4. Appeals against the operator must be filed within a ten-year period.

As can be noted, the convention does not provide for legal responsibility beyond a certain amount; this amount, furthermore, must be considered as insufficient. The additional convention referred to above would, therefore, establish a second "layer" of state responsibility of between $15 million and $50 million, and a third one up to $100 million. The latter would be covered jointly by all the signatories of the additional convention.

It is not an exaggeration to state that the development of nuclear industry depends in great part upon the solution of this problem. It is, therefore, alarming to ascertain that little progress has been made in this field since negotiations were initiated four years ago.

V

Safety Control and Property Rights

These two subjects are examined together because the Community's right of ownership is limited to the special nuclear materials that are subject to Euratom's control.[24] This control has a threefold purpose; the Commission must determine that in the Member States (1) ores and materials are not diverted from the destination for which they were intended, (2) the provisions concerning supply are observed, and (3) special undertakings entered into by the Community in international agreements are respected. It can, therefore, be said that Euratom's control is mainly

[24] Euratom Treaty art. 86.

a "conformity-control"—*i.e.*, conformity of the use with declared destination and with the Treaty provisions regarding supply.

The control-system of Euratom has characteristics that differentiate it from other existing systems. In the first place, it is actually the only working system that applies to more than one country. Secondly, it is compulsory for all the Member States and applies automatically to all ores, source materials, and special nuclear materials—the control of the International Atomic Energy Agency in Vienna and of the O.E.E.C. only applies to materials and equipment received through these organizations or to countries that voluntarily submit to their control. Finally, Euratom's control is not solely intended to prevent materials from being used for nonpeaceful purposes, but also to enforce the provisions concerning supplies.

Euratom's control is based on information, which is obtained through the compulsory communications to the Commission[25] and by inspection, which the Commission is empowered to carry out in all installations within the Community.[26]

It is important to note that the United States,[27] Great Britain,[28] and Canada[29] have formally recognized Euratom's control system by admitting that, as an exception to their usual policy, the materials and equipment supplied by them will be subject to the sole control of Euratom.

The Commission was endowed with large powers in order to ensure compliance with the control measures. The Euratom Treaty provides the Community with the authority to impose directly binding sanctions on any person or enterprise, private or public, that does not fulfill its obligation. The penalties that can be imposed by the Commission range from a simple warning to the complete withdrawal of source materials or special nuclear materials.[30] Decisions of the Commission concerning withdrawal of materials may be enforced within the territories of the Member States in accordance with the provisions of article 164 of the Treaty. After verification of the authenticity of the Commission's writ of execution by a national authority, the Commission may, in accordance with municipal law, proceed with forced execution by applying directly to the competent national bodies.

Euratom's control system became effective in June 1959; as of that date, installations within the Community report each month to the Commission on the stocks and movements of materials. Moreover, the first inspections were carried out at the beginning of 1960. The only limitation imposed on the implementation of the security control—see article eighty-four of the Euratom Treaty—results from the fact that control may not cover materials intended for "the purposes of defense which

[25] Regulations No. 7 and No. 8, [1959] JOURNAL OFFICIEL 298, 651, based respectively on articles 73 and 79 of the Euratom Treaty.
[26] Euratom Treaty art. 81.
[27] Agreement of Cooperation Between the Government of the United States of America and the European Atomic Energy Community (Euratom) Concerning Peaceful Uses of Atomic Energy, Nov. 8, 1958, art. XII, [1959] JOURNAL OFFICIEL 312, [1958] 9 U.S.T. & O.I.A. 1116, T.I.A.S. No. 4091.
[28] Agreement Between the United Kingdom and Euratom, Feb. 4, 1959, art. XIII, § 2, [1959] JOURNAL OFFICIEL 331.
[29] Agreement Between Canada and Euratom, Oct. 6, 1959, art. IX, [1959] JOURNAL OFFICIEL 1169.
[30] Euratom Treaty art. 83.

are in the course of being specially prepared for such purposes or which, after being so prepared, are, in accordance with an operational plan, installed or stocked in a military establishment."

This limitation of the Community's control brings us back to an earlier statement—namely, that Euratom's property rights end with its power to control. What, exactly, are these property rights?

Although article eighty-six of the Euratom Treaty states that "special nuclear material shall be the property of the Community," article eighty-seven qualifies this statement by adding that "Member States, persons or enterprises shall have the widest rights of use and consumption of special nuclear materials legally in their possession, subject to their obligations resulting from the provisions of this Treaty . . . ." One might wonder, therefore, what the meaning is of the Community's property right, when all the attributes of property belong to others. Politically, this right finds its explanation in the fact that private ownership of nuclear material seemed unacceptable at the time of the drafting of the Treaty. Furthermore, in all other countries, even in the United States, special nuclear materials are, in fact, the property of the government.

It is difficult to determine with precision what rights result for the Community from its ownership. The most important consequence is obviously that holders cannot alienate materials belonging to Euratom; and in case of unauthorized transfer outside the Community, Euratom could reclaim these materials on the ground of its ownership. In this regard, ownership reinforces Euratom's legal monopoly in the sale of special nuclear material. Another consequence is that these materials may not be the subject of any administrative or legal measure of constraint without the authorization of the Court of Justice.[31]

Euratom's right of property cannot be compared without qualifications with the right of property recognized by civil law. Articles eighty-eight and eighty-nine of the Euratom Treaty provide that the Supply Agency shall keep, on behalf of the Community, a so-called "Financial Account of Special Nuclear Materials" in which the value of materials put at the disposal of Member States, persons, or enterprises is credited to the Community and debited to that Member State, person, or enterprise, and where produced or imported materials that become Euratom's property are debited to the Community and credited to the producer or importer. Upon the request of the creditor, balances shall be payable immediately. It may, therefore, be said that the Community's property rights are, essentially, of an administrative nature.

One important conclusion is that Euratom's property rights are not incompatible with the ownership of a third party over the same materials. It was first thought that the wording of article eighty-six of the Euratom Treaty ("special nuclear materials shall be the property of the Community") prevented Euratom from importing materials on a lease basis, as the rights of ownership of the lessor would be

---

[31] Protocol on the Privileges and Immunities, art. 1.

an obstacle to the Community's acquiring property rights. The Community would, therefore, be forced to purchase. The financial consequences of such a situation would have been disadvantageous, as, at the present time, purchase entails heavier expenditures than lease. One must admit that such a consequence could not have been intended by the drafters of the Treaty, and the theory of administrative ownership compatible with property rights of a third party appears as a legal and economically satisfactory solution.

VI

Supply

One of the most important tasks entrusted to the Community is to "ensure a regular and equitable supply of ores and nuclear fuels to all users in the Community."[32]

The Euratom Treaty provides that (1) all practices designed to ensure a privileged position for certain users shall be prohibited; and (2) that an Agency shall be constituted having (a) an option right on all ores and materials produced within the Community and (b) the exclusive right to conclude contracts pertaining to the supply of ores and materials, whatever their origin. The Statutes of the Agency were laid down by the Council in July 1958,[33] and the Agency assumed its functions on June 1, 1960.[34] The Commission decided, however, to suspend the authority of the Agency with regard to ores and source material until December 1, 1960. Up to that moment, the conclusion or renewal of agreements for the supply of ores, source materials, and special fissionable materials needed the prior approval of the Commission.[35] Since that date the Agency exercises its exclusive right to conclude all supply contracts, with the exception of ores and source material over which the Agency had no authority prior to December 1, 1960.

Thus, at the present time, all supply contracts must be concluded by the Agency. Does this mean that the Agency necessarily becomes a party to such contracts? This would involve unnecessary delays; furthermore, formal contracts are not concluded for each transfer. Therefore the following system was set up by the Commission: In case of overproduction of a certain product—as is the case for practically all products—the Agency will lay down general conditions that will apply to all contracts; these contracts are then negotiated directly between the producer and the consumer and communicated to the Agency. If the Agency formulates no objections within a time limit of eight days, the contract is considered to have been "concluded by the Agency."[36]

This system, which is certainly in conformity with the spirit of the Euratom Treaty, simplifies the procedures imposed upon the consumer, and at the same time

---
[32] Euratom Treaty art. 2(d).
[33] [1958] JOURNAL OFFICIEL 534.
[34] [1960] *id.* at 776.
[35] Euratom Treaty art. 222.
[36] Regulations of the Agency art. 5, [1960] JOURNAL OFFICIEL 778.

gives the Agency all the information it needs to accomplish its task—*i.e.*, to follow the evolution of the general market situation, the fluctuation of prices, and the conditions prevailing for transactions involving nuclear materials. This information is essential if the Agency wants to improve the supply situation of the Community.

VII

EXTERNAL RELATIONS OF THE COMMUNITY

One of the tasks of the Community is to "establish with other countries and with international organizations all contacts likely to promote progress in the peaceful uses of nuclear energy."[37]

Articles 101 and 102 of the Euratom Treaty establish the principle that the Community may enter into obligations by concluding agreements with third countries, international organizations, or nationals of third countries (external competence of the Community); they also provide internal rules of procedure for the conclusion of such agreements.

Articles 103 and 104 of the Euratom Treaty impose certain obligations on Member States and enterprises that conclude agreements with third parties that in some way or other concern the field of application of the Treaty. Member States must submit the draft of the agreement to the Commission, which can raise objections in case the agreement contains clauses impeding the application of the Treaty. Member States may not conclude the agreement before the objections have been removed. Persons and enterprises, on the other hand, may not invoke such agreements to evade obligations imposed by the Treaty. There are two exceptions to this procedure.

1. When the purpose of the agreement is the exchange of scientific or industrial information[38] and requires on either side the signature of a State exercising its sovereignty, the agreement must be concluded by the Commission, which, however, can also authorize the Member State, person or enterprise to conclude it directly.

2. When the agreement contains provisions relating to the delivery of products coming within the authority of the Agency, the prior consent of the Commission is required.[39]

Articles 105 and 106 of the Euratom Treaty contain provisions regarding agreements with third countries entered into by Member States, persons, or enterprises, their nationals and international organizations, before the entry into force of the Treaty (January 1, 1958). Article 105 restates a general principal of law—namely, that existing rights and obligations resulting from an agreement cannot be voided by a subsequent convention. Article 106 provides that these rights and obligations must be assumed by the Community as far as possible.

This over-all picture reveals a coherent system according to which the Community has the exclusive right to establish with third countries all contacts likely

[37] Euratom Treaty art. 2.
[38] *Id*. art. 29.
[39] *Id*. art. 73.

to promote progress in the peaceful uses of nuclear energy. In matters of international cooperation in the nuclear field, the Member States have joined their forces in order to present a united and, therefore, stronger front in negotiation with third countries.

As, on the other hand, large powers were conferred upon the Community, the logical consequence is that the Member States are not only to abstain from establishing further direct contacts in matters that concern the application of the Euratom Treaty, but they must discontinue the existing contacts by transferring to the Community the rights and obligations resulting from their bilateral arrangements. This last obligation is clearly stated in article 106 of the Treaty. And what would be the meaning of such a transfer, if Member States were later to conclude new nuclear agreements? The underlying philosophy of chapter ten of the Treaty seems clear: All existing bilateral agreements between the Member States and third countries are to be transferred to the Community, which becomes the exclusive channel for all the external relations of the Community in the field of peaceful uses of atomic energy. However, a strict separation between nuclear and other questions is not always possible; and as the creation of Euratom does not affect the external relations of Member States in general, the flexible procedure provided for by article 103 respects both the rights of Euratom and the sovereignty of the Member States.

As for the agreements with the principal nuclear powers of the western world, which were mentioned above, they were concluded on the basis of the provisions of article 101 of the Treaty.

Of particular importance is the agreement for cooperation between the United States of America and the Community, which provides for a joint reactor program and a joint research and development program. The purpose of the first program is to bring into operation within the Community large-scale power plants using nuclear reactors of types that have reached an advanced stage of development in the United States, having a total capacity of approximately one million kilowatts of electricity under conditions that would approach the competitive range of conventional energy costs in Europe. Partly because the premises on which the agreement was based—shortage of conventional fuels—have changed and also because some of the conditions imposed on participating facilities did not appear attractive enough, only one reactor, instead of the expected five, will be in operation by December 31, 1963, while there are reasonable expectations for two more to be in operation by the end of 1965. The research and development program, which met with great successes, was discussed above.

The agreements concluded with Great Britain, with the Government of Canada and with the Atomic Energy of Canada, Ltd., provide the legal bases for further international cooperation in the peaceful uses of atomic energy.

Other contacts were established with international organizations such as the O.E.E.C., the Council of Europe, the International Agency for Atomic Energy (I.A.A.E.) and the International Labor Organization (I.L.O.). Furthermore, several third countries[40] have sent diplomatic representations to the Community, which through all these contacts participates in the international cooperation in the field of peaceful uses of atomic energy.

Conclusion

As was said in the beginning, Euratom cannot be examined separately from the E.E.C. and the E.C.S.C. Together they constitute the joint effort of the European countries to transform the face of the old continent. This close union created by the establishment of the three European Regional Communities is indispensable for a common economic policy. It is true that—as was seen for Euratom—this construction creates many problems, but it makes it possible to find solutions to economic and other difficulties that are beyond the capacities of the Member States when acting by themselves.

Many problems remain to be solved; as the Commission states: "[i]f some real progress was made, it is too limited, it is too slow, compared to the task imposed upon the Community."[41] Nevertheless, Euratom is fulfilling its task by stimulating the development of nuclear industry and contributing to the economic and political unification of Europe. This double achievement constitutes an important contribution to the maintenance and development of world peace.

[40] In chronological order: United States of America, United Kingdom, Israel, Norway, Sweden, Denmark, Switzerland, Austria, Canada, and Japan. By virtue of the Protocol on the Privileges and Immunities art. 16, these missions have been granted the customary diplomatic immunities.
[41] TROISIÈME RAPPORT GÉNÉRAL 7.

THE CONCEPT OF ENTERPRISE UNDER THE EUROPEAN COMMUNITIES: LEGAL EFFECTS OF PARTIAL INTEGRATION*

GERHARD BEBR†

INTRODUCTION

The operation of the European Coal and Steel Community (E.C.S.C.), the European Atomic Energy Community (Euratom), and the European Economic Community (E.E.C.)—established by France, the Federal Republic of Germany, Italy, Belgium, the Netherlands, and Luxembourg—undoubtedly affects enterprises located within the territories of these Communities. This raises the question to what extent enterprises and establishments, partly or totally owned by "foreign" corporations—*i.e.*, corporations outside the Communities—may come under Community jurisdiction. The concept of enterprise is to be examined from this aspect—a problem closely related to the question of competence of the Communities[1] and of the jurisdiction of the Community Court.[2] The primary problem centers around the question of competence of the quasi-legislative and administrative powers of the Communities. The present exposition attempts to analyze some features of this complex and somewhat unexplored question. It will, however, merely touch on the jurisdiction of the Community Court and the parties that may invoke its protection,[3] since this question appears reasonably clear. Moreover, the judicial control as invoked by a party's appeal for annulment or against inaction represents a broader question whose discussion would greatly exceed the scope of this paper.

Member States as well as private parties under Community jurisdiction may appeal before the Community Court allegedly illegal acts of a Community organ or its failure to act.[4] The Treaties, of course, differentiate between appeals of Member States and of private parties, and grant to States a more extensive right of appeal. In specific instances, even third parties outside Community jurisdiction may appeal.[5] The Communities exercise some powers directly over the enterprises, and it is, there-

---

* This article is part of a book, *The Judicial Control of the European Communities*, to be published shortly by Stevens & Sons, London.

The views expressed herein are those of the writer and do not necessarily reflect the opinions of the European Communities.

Due to difficulties in correspondence, certain minor editorial changes in the final draft of Dr. Bebr's article were not passed upon by the writer.

† J.U.D. 1946, Charles University; LL.M. 1948, J.S.D. 1951, Yale University.

[1] E.C.S.C. Treaty art. 80; Euratom Treaty art. 196. Because of the general competence of the E.E.C., its Treaty contains no such similar provision.

[2] E.C.S.C. Treaty arts. 33, 35; Euratom Treaty arts. 146, 148; E.E.C. Treaty arts. 173, 175.

[3] For a general discussion of this problem, see, *e.g.*, Bebr, *Protection of Private Parties Under the European Coal and Steel Community*, 42 VA. L. REV. 879 (1956).

[4] E.C.S.C. Treaty arts. 33, 35; E.E.C. Treaty arts. 173, 175; Euratom Treaty arts. 146, 148.

[5] E.C.S.C. Treaty arts. 63(2b); 66(5), para. 2; 80.

fore, proper and in accord with the political structure if they are allowed to appeal in their own right, independently of their Member States.

The qualification of a Member State as an appellant hardly needs to be elaborated. The qualification of a private party to appeal appears equally simple. As none of the Community Treaties defines the meaning of enterprise, one may quickly conclude that in the context of standing to appeal, the term "enterprise" is to be viewed as a legal concept. As a result of a partial integration as provided for by the E.C.S.C. and Euratom Treaties, the legal and economic aspects of an enterprise need not necessarily coincide.[6] Its economic aspect delimits the competence of the quasi-legislative and regulatory powers of the E.C.S.C. and Euratom in relation to national economies that remain under the Member States' jurisdiction. The legal concept of enterprise, on the other hand, points to the legal person that may act on behalf of this economic unit before the Community Court. At first, such a splitting of the concept of enterprise in its economic and legal aspects may seem arbitrary. The following discussion may show that this "split" concept is but the unavoidable consequence of a partial economic integration.

To view an enterprise in its economic and legal aspects is by no means unique to the Community law. Similar examples may also be found in municipal public laws, which pursue a great variety of public objectives in the fiscal, economic, social, and labor fields. These laws require and develop their own concept of enterprise, a concept that is not always identical with its legal form as formulated by civil or commercial law.[7] This analogy with municipal public laws may be carried even further. Even though they develop their own concept of enterprise suitable to the goals they pursue, when it comes to the question of ability to sue or be sued, they necessarily resort to the traditional legal concept. A similar interplay and interrelation may be found in the E.C.S.C. and Euratom Treaties between the economic concept of enterprise and the legal person to represent and protect it.

I

THE ECONOMIC CONCEPT OF ENTERPRISE

A. The European Coal and Steel Community

According to article eighty of the Treaty, all enterprises that engage within the European territories of the Member States in the production of coal and steel, as technically defined by the Treaty and its annexes, or reclaim iron and steel scrap, are subject to the Community. This production activity establishes the competence of

---

[6] CHARLES DE VISSCHER, LE DROIT PUBLIC DE LA COMMUNAUTÉ EUROPÉENNE DU CHARBON ET DE L'ACIER 51-52 (1956).

[7] See Gieseke, *Der Rechtsbegriff des Unternehmens und seine Folgen,* in E. WOLFF (ED.), BEITRAEGE ZUM HANDELS-UND WIRTSCHAFTSRECHT 606 (1950), who emphasizes that even without a statute, the concept of enterprise is changing, depending on the various purposes of its provisions; EUGEN LANGE, KOMMENTAR ZUM KARTELLGESETZ 55-56 (1957); HANS VON MULLER-HENNEBERG & GUSTAV SCHWARTZ, GESETZ GEGEN WETTBEWERBSBESCHAENKUNGEN 151 (1958), who rightly stress the production and business activity of an enterprise for the application of the law against restraining competition; Ballerstedt, *Unternehmen und Wirtschaftsverfassung,* 6 JURISTENZEITUNG 486, 487-88 (1951). See also GEORGES RIPERT, ASPECTS JURIDIQUES DU CAPITALISME MODERNE 261, 274 (2d ed. 1951).

the Community and forms the underlying concept of enterprise within the meaning of the Treaty.[8] As a result of this narrow competence, an enterprise may only partly come under the Community jurisdiction—only in so far as it produces coal or steel or reclaims scrap within the Community territory.[9] The Treaty evidently bases the concept of enterprise on its specific economic activity: its legal form is irrelevant.[10] Although coal and steel consumers are outside the Community competence, a steel enterprise within the meaning of article eighty of the Treaty is also subject to the Community with regard to its coal or scrap consumption.[11] An enterprise remains under the Community jurisdiction even if it does not produce in its own name. The so-called processing agreements according to which an enterprise carries out only a part of the production process is also an activity subject to the Community.[12]

Regulation of economic affairs must be concerned more with economic activities and their effects than with their legal forms. If the competence of the E.C.S.C. were exclusively based on a formal, legal concept of enterprise, skillful manipulation of this concept could frustrate and paralyze any effort to maintain and administer a common and competitive market. This "playing down" of the legal concept of enterprise has far-reaching consequences. Thus, a coal- or steel-producing enterprise, not legally independent but located within the Community, by whomever owned or controlled and wherefrom directed or administered, is under the jurisdiction of the Community.[13] Neither the "nationality" of such an enterprise nor the domicile or seat of administration of a corporation to which it belongs is relevant.[14]

The economic concept of enterprise is by no means uniform through the Treaty.[15] There are two main reasons for such a flexibility. First, its changing concept results from the recognition that a Community competence may hardly rest only on the narrow nature of this specific production activity. This is particularly true of borderline situations in which such a narrow Community competence would

[8] RÉPUBLIQUE FRANCAISE, MINISTÈRE DES AFFAIRES ÉTRANGÈRES, RAPPORT DE LA DÉLÉGATION FRANCAISE SUR LE TRAITÉ INSTITUANT LA COMMUNAUTÉ EUROPÉENNE DU CHARBON ET DE L'ACIER 78-79 (1951) [hereinafter cited as RAPPORT]; see also ENTWURF EINES GESETZES UEBER DIE GRUENDUNG DER EUROPAEISCHEN GEMEINSCHAFT FUER KOHLE UND STAHL VOM 18. APRIL 1951, BEGRUENDUNG DES VERTRAGSWERKES (Anlage 3) . . . DRUCKSACHE NO. 2401, DEUTSCHER BUNDESTAG I. WAHLPERIODE 1949, at 23.
[9] Macchiorlatti Dalmas e Figli v. Haute Autorité, Cour de Justice des Communautés Europeennes, 5 Recueil de la Jurisprudence de la Cour 415, 424 (1958-59) [hereinafter cited as REC.].
[10] MICHEL DESPAX, L' ENTERPRISE ET LE DROIT 172 (1957); ROLF KIESEWETTER, DAS WIRTSCHAFTSRECHT DES SCHUMAN-PLANS UNTER BESONDERER BERUCKSICHTIGUNG DES PREISRECHTS 45-46 (1954).
[11] Groupement des Industries Siderurgiques Luxembourgeoises v. Haute Autorité, 2 REC. 53, 86 (1955-56), Société des Fonderies de Pont-à-Mousson v. Haute Autorité, 5 REC. 447, 472 (1958-59).
[12] Information of the High Authority, March 23, 1960, [1960] JOURNAL OFFICIEL DES COMMUNAUTÉS EUROPÉENNES 569 [hereinafter cited as JOURNAL OFFICIEL].
[13] See the Decision of the High Authority No. 2/52, as revised, art. 4(3) of which provides for the imposition of annual levies on establishments that belong to enterprises located in a third State. [1959] JOURNAL OFFICIEL 213. See further, Drucksache No. 2401, at 23; see 2 ROBERT KRAWIELICKI, DAS MONOPOLVERBOT IM SCHUMAN-PLAN (1952).
[14] Ibid. KURT BALLERSTEDT, UEBERNATIONALE UND NATIONALE MARKTORDNUNG 13 (1955); Grassetti, Les entreprises en tant que destinataires des regles du droit de la Communauté, in 4 CENTRO ITALIANO DI STUDI GUIRIDICI, ACTES OFFICIELS 11, 34 (1958) [hereinafter cited as ACTES OFFICIELS].
[15] Some support for this view may be found in the conclusions of the Avocat Général Lagrange in Phoenix Rheinrohr v. Haute Autorité, 5 REC. 165, 183, 194 (1958-59).

permit a by-passing of the Treaty provisions. The scope of application of articles sixty-five and sixty-six of the Treaty to the production of coal and steel as well as to their distribution makes this especially evident. Secondly, the different purposes of the various, specific Treaty provisions determine also the changing concept of enterprise. These two questions will be examined at some length in the following discussion.

1. *Counterbalance to Pitfalls of Partial Integration*

A sharp, clear-cut separation of the coal and steel industries from the "rest" of the national economy is economically artificial. A Community competence rigidly limited to these industries would fly directly against economic realities. The Treaty recognizes this shortcoming of a partial integration; it attempts to alleviate it by extending the Community competence in specific instances to first-hand dealers or organizations distributing coal or steel. Thus, article sixty-five, which prohibits "all agreements . . . all decisions of associations of enterprises, and all concerted practices, tending directly or indirectly, to prevent, restrict or impede the normal operation of competition within the common market," is binding on first-hand dealers and organizations as well. Similarly, article sixty-six applies to their participation in an illegal economic concentration with other coal or steel enterprises. The very nature of concentration requires, moreover, that the Community competence be explicitly extended to vertical integration. In this instance, any legal or natural person, even though outside coal or steel production and their distribution, comes under the competence of the Community.[16] Motivated by a similar consideration, the Treaty is also applicable to buyers systematically discriminating among coal or steel enterprises.[17] To prevent such a violation, the Community may require the enterprises of the E.C.S.C. to boycott such a buyer.[18]

A gradual *rapprochement* of the first-hand dealers to the status of coal- and steel-producing enterprises is dictated by the close economic ties existing between production and distribution. The need for viewing this link primarily in terms of its economic effects is apparent. A strict legal view would scrupulously respect a sales agency as an independent legal entity, even though it is entirely directed and owned by and composed of the coal-producing enterprises. Following this "dreamy" legal approach, such a sales agency would be classified as a distributing organization within the meaning of article eighty and subject only to the provisions of articles sixty-five and sixty-six. This example vividly demonstrates the need for an economic concept of enterprise. If the Community is to operate at all, it must disregard the hollow, legal mask of a formally independent enterprise and examine the actual economic link existing between the coal-producing enterprises and the sales organization. The economic ties are in this instance so close and tight that the producers and the sales agency actually represent one economic unit. The sales agency is

[16] E.S.S.C. Treaty art. 66(1).
[17] *Id.* art. 63(1).
[18] *Id.* art. 63(2b).

nothing else but the "distributive arm" of the enterprises, it is part of them. Consequently, the sales agency would be subject to all Treaty provisions, and not only to articles sixty-five and sixty-six.[19] If this were not so, the coal or steel enterprises could easily escape the price and discrimination provisions of the Treaty by establishing their own legally independent sales agency. While the more or less formal and fictitious sales from the enterprises to the agency would be scrupulously correct, the subsequent sales by their sales agency, being practically outside the Community jurisdiction, could disregard the Treaty provisions. This would be an utterly untenable position because it would enable the enterprises to by-pass the Treaty provisions by establishing an independent legal person. Why should the High Authority or the Court respect such a farce intended to avoid the Treaty provisions? Every conceivable reason speaks against such a maneuver.

In this light may be understood an interesting dictum of the Court in *Geitling*.[20] In this case, the Court examined, among other charges, the restrictive effects on competition of a questioned clause according to which dealers, in order to qualify as first-hand dealers with a sales agency, had to draw a certain total amount of coal.[21] As part of this prescribed amount, these dealers could include coal drawn from the other two Ruhr sales agencies—a provision that the High Authority struck down when approving the agreement for establishing these agencies. Examining this disputed clause, the Court placed the sales organization on the same level with the coal producers. "On the basis of the disputed clause," observed the Court, "the appellants included in the deliveries of the first-hand dealers also those that they obtained from the other two sales organizations although they [*i.e.*, the appellants] should be competing with them as with other *producers* of the Community whose deliveries the appellants do not want to include in the total annual amount . . . ."[22]

Even in a reverse situation, the Court does consider the organic link between production and distribution somewhat artificially disrupted by the partial integration. The Court is inclined to protect the first-hand dealers not only when articles sixty-five and sixty-six are directly applied to them, but also when the application of these articles aggrieves their interests.[23]

The economic concept of enterprise permeates, in various degrees, the E.C.S.C. Treaty and loosens and even disregards its legal concept. The controversy between these two concepts and their relative meaning flared up in the recent scrap-iron cases. To subsidize higher priced imports of scrap iron to the Community and prevent price increases of "Community" scrap, the High Authority established a compensation scheme that imposed a surcharge on the consumption of scrap iron by the enter-

---

[19] KIESEWETTER, *op. cit. supra* note 10, at 46-47; see also L'INSTITUT DES RELATIONS INTERNATIONALES, LA COMMUNAUTÉ EUROPÉENNE DU CHARBON ET DE L'ACIER 170 (1953).
[20] Geitling v. Haute Autorité, 3 REC. 11 (1957).
[21] *Id.* at 30-31.
[22] *Id.* at 44-45. (Writer's translation; emphasis added.)
[23] Nold v. Haute Autorité, 3 REC. 235, 240-41 (1957-58), and the conclusions of the Avocat Général Roemer. *Id.* at 245, 251-52. See also Stork v. Haute Autorité, 5 REC. 45, 61-62 (1958-59).

prises.[24] From this surcharge the Authority exempted only the consumption of scrap iron reclaimed by the enterprises during their own steel production (so-called "own" scrap iron).[25] Consequently, the Authority considered the consumption of the so-called "concern" scrap—*i.e.,* scrap of a group of legally independent enterprises that are closely tied together by financial, economic, and administrative links—to be subject to this surcharge. A concrete example may serve as an illustration: A French steel mill, legally independent, but owned by Régie Renault up to 99.77 per cent, receives a large amount of scrap from Renault.[26] Because of this ownership by Renault, the French steel mill tried to claim the scrap iron coming from the holding company as the enterprise's own scrap, free of any surcharge.[27] Following the *legal* concept of enterprise, the Authority refused to extend the concept of "own" scrap iron beyond its formal ownership. "Only that scrap may be considered as the enterprise's own," stated the Authority, "which is reclaimed in its own steel mill managed under the same firm; on the other hand, scrap that comes from mills of other firms must then be considered as purchased scrap iron even if there are close financial or organizational ties between the supplier and the consumer."[28]

Several German and French enterprises appealed this refusal, arguing that the economic concept of enterprise was the underlying principle of the Treaty.[29] They referred to the economic unit that these legally independent enterprises form and to the close financial and economic ties that exist among them. Consequently, argued the appellants, even the scrap iron transferred from one of these enterprises to another should be considered as "own" scrap free of any surcharge. In its defense, the Authority insisted on the ownership of scrap as determining the exemption.[30] Being aware of the dangerous limitation inherent in applying a legal concept of enterprise, the Authority wisely added a caveat that such a criterion was used in this particular instance only. It wished so to forestall a risky, almost fatal, precedent-courting disaster as to the application of articles sixty-five and sixty-six. In this particular instance, the Court followed the legal concept as advanced by the Authority. But it did so only after having satisfied itself that the application of this criterion was compatible with the economic and financial objectives of the compensation scheme. To exempt from the surcharge also "concern" scrap, as the "own" scrap is exempted, would, in the Court's words, "... exceed the meaning and purpose of this exemption and, moreover, constitute an advantage discriminating

---

[24] Decisions of the High Authority Nos. 22/54, [1954] JOURNAL OFFICIEL 286; 14/55, [1955] *id.* at 685; and 2/57, [1957] *id.* at 61.
[25] Letter from the High Authority to the Joint Bureau of Scrap Consumers, Dec. 18, 1957, [1958] *id.* at 45.
[26] S.N.U.P.A.T. v. Haute Autorité, 5 REC. 277, 286 (1958-59).
[27] *Ibid.*
[28] S.A.F.E. v. Haute Autorité, 5 REC. 383, 404 (1958-59). (Writer's translation.)
[29] S.N.U.P.A.T. v. Haute Autorité, 5 REC. 277, 291 (1958-59); S.A.F.E. v. Haute Autorité, 5 REC. 383, 394-95 (1958-59).
[30] Phoenix-Rheinrohr v. Haute Autorité, 5 REC. 165, 174 (1958-59); S.N.U.P.A.T. v. Haute Autorité, 5 REC. 277, 292 (1958-59); S.A.F.E. v. Haute Autorité, 5 REC. 383, 396 (1958-59).

against third enterprises"[31]—*i.e.*, enterprises outside the concern. Had the Court found the legal concept of enterprise inadequate and hindering the achievement of these objectives, it would have most likely set aside this criterion and searched for an economic one better fitted to pursue these objectives. The Court seemed to recognize the predominance of the economic goals of the Treaty and their strong bearing on the concept of enterprise. "It would be evidently contrary to the Treaty requirement," held the Court, "if a measure of the High Authority would make the production cost of steel, entirely or partly produced out of scrap iron, dependent on the legal, organizational, or financial structure of an industrial concern."[32]

2. *Changing Concept of Enterprise*

Brief references may be made to some more typical Treaty provisions that reflect the changing concept of enterprise. Significantly, the provisions concerning the annual levy to be borne by enterprises is to be assessed according to the average production level of the various products under the Community jurisdiction.[33] Similar references to production mark articles 58 (2) dealing with production quotas, and article 59 (2) concerning consumption priorities. But the economic concept is not always so clearly discernible. As a result of an unfavorable opinion rendered by the High Authority on an investment project pursuant to article 54 (5), the enterprise concerned may only use "its own funds to carry out such a project." The question of what is to be understood by an enterprise's "own funds" raises a number of almost insurmountable problems. In this context, the economic concept of enterprise discloses fully its relative, changing character. The situation of a legally and economically independent enterprise exclusively engaged in coal or steel production would hardly present difficulties. But economic and financial relations and situations are everything but simple and clear. Assume that an enterprise is active in several industrial fields and only partly produces coal or steel—as, for example, a shipyard owning a steel mill or a chemical enterprise owning a coal mine. Under these circumstances, which funds are really this enterprise's "own funds?" It seems difficult, if not impossible, to separate the funds of an enterprise in a proportion corresponding to its coal or steel production. On the other hand, to permit this enterprise to utilize for its project all the funds at its disposal derived from other activities would undermine, if not defeat, the purpose of this provision. Even if an enterprise exclusively producing coal or steel and legally independent were restricted to using only its funds, such a restriction could hardly be effective if the enterprise were an organic part of a large holding company located in or outside the Community that might pour its

---

[31] S.N.U.P.A.T. v. Haute Autorité, 5 REC. 277, 306 (1958-59); S.A.F.E. v. Haute Autorité, 5 REC. 383, 407 (1958-59). (Writer's translation.)

[32] S.N.U.P.A.T. v. Haute Autorité, 5 REC. 277, 307 (1958-59); S.A.F.E. v. Haute Autorité, 5 REC. 385, 407 (1958-59). In his conclusions, the Avocat Général Lagrange also justifies the legal concept of enterprise by the economic considerations of the objectives pursued by the compensation scheme. Phoenix-Rheinrohr v. Haute Autorité, 5 REC. 165, 183, 200-01 (1958-59). In the Avocat Général's view, a very extensive interpretation of the "concern" scrap might have weakened the joint effort, based on economic solidarity, to assure imports of scrap iron at the Community price level.

[33] E.C.S.C. Treaty art. 50(2).

funds into this enterprise's proposed investment project. These remarks spotlight the complex problem the Authority encounters when influencing the flow of investment according to article fifty-four. They also reveal the variable economic concept of an enterprise, a concept that is to assist the Authority in determining the proper extent of its "own funds" available to the enterprise concerned. This extent should correspond to the objectives of article fifty-four—*i.e.*, to the establishment of a well-integrated coal and steel industry within the Community with the maximum use of available investment.

The economic considerations—and thus the economic concept of enterprise—rule supreme, of course, over the provisions of articles sixty-five and sixty-six governing the competition within the common coal and steel market of the Community. To permit a clear, unhindered look at economic realities, the legal concept of enterprises must be penetrated.

These observations suggest that the E.C.S.C. Treaty knows no uniform concept of an enterprise, as it is sometimes assumed. For example, a contrast of the concept of enterprise within the meaning of article 54 (4) with that of article sixty-six quickly dispels such an assumption. This should not be disturbing, because even public municipal law knows no uniform concept of an enterprise. Its changing economic concept underlying the different Treaty provisions may be justified by the different purposes these provisions pursue. The changing emphasis of the Treaty objectives—as reflected, for example, in the provisions dealing with discrimination or competition—color and shape the economic concept of enterprise.

B. The European Atomic Energy Community

The Euratom Treaty also bases its competence on the activity of a natural or legal person engaging in a highly technical production, as defined by the Treaty.[34] As under the E.C.S.C. Treaty, an enterprise may only partly come under the competence of Euratom; its legal form is thus equally irrelevant.[35] Article eighty-one particularly points to an economic concept of enterprise. According to this article, the Commission has extensive powers of control to assure that ores, special fissionable material, and other source material are not diverted by the user from their professed use. The economic concept of enterprise on which the competence of the Community rests is also strongly underscored by the provisions of article eighty-six, according to which Euratom is the exclusive owner of plutonium and uranium, whether imported or produced within the Community. This facilitates the Commission's control over enterprises utilizing or processing this special fissionable material.

C. The European Economic Community

The E.E.C. competence extends over the entire national economy of the Member States. It encounters, therefore, much less need for developing a special concept

---

[34] Euratom Treaty art. 196.
[35] See Euratom Commission Reg. No. 1, art. 2, [1958] JOURNAL OFFICIEL 511; see also HANS SÜNNER & KLAUS PFANNER, DER GEWERBLICHE RECHTSSCHUTZ IM EURATOMVERTRAG 32 (1959).

of enterprise, than is necessary under the E.C.S.C. and Euratom Treaties. The only exception may be the general Treaty provisions of articles eighty-five and eighty-six regulating competition, to be later implemented by Community regulations or directives. The nature of the matters to be regulated will undoubtedly again strongly emphasize the economic concept of enterprise in disregard of its legal form.

II

THE LEGAL CONCEPT OF ENTERPRISE

When the Treaty provisions are to be executed and enforced or the right of appeal to be exercised, the economic concept of enterprise loses its usefulness and justification. The economic concept of enterprise is in this instance merely the basis for exercising the right of appeal by the legal entity entitled to represent it. Defining enterprises subject to its competence, the Euratom Treaty speaks of ". . . any enterprise or institution wholly or partly engaged in activities" as determined by the appropriate chapters of the Treaty.[36] But it is worth noting that when the Euratom Treaty deals with the right of appeal, it significantly states "any natural or *legal* person."[37] The replacement of the expression "enterprise" by the notion of a "legal person" clearly points to a differentiation between an enterprise as an economic notion and its legal form.[38]

Although that much is clear, still the question remains as to the law under which the legal personality of an appealing enterprise should be examined. The Community Treaties know no legal concept of enterprise independent of the municipal law of the Member States. Examining the capacity to appeal, the Court constantly resorts to the municipal law concerned.[39] But even this practice may not always determine the proper law that may govern the forms, rights, and duties of a corporation or of an enterprise if it is incorporated in one Member State but maintains its actual seat of administration in another. Generally, according to the Continental law and practice, the place of incorporation alone is inadequate for establishing the proper law of corporation. As a rule, the place of incorporation as well as the actual seat of administration in the Member State is required.[40] Conflicts are likely to arise as soon as these two elements do not coincide. An even more complex problem is presented in those instances in which a foreign corporation,

---

[36] Euratom Treaty art. 196.
[37] *Id.* arts. 146(2), 148(3).
[38] It may be observed that the E.C.S.C. Treaty arts. 33 and 80 do not differentiate so clearly.
[39] The provisions of the Rules of Procedure art. 38 § 5, [1959] JOURNAL OFFICIEL 349, which require legal persons recognized by private law to attach to their appeals a copy of the statute giving them legal personality, clearly indicate that in this instance, reference is made to the proper municipal law of the Member State. This is particularly clearly stated in Nold v. Haute Autorité, 5 REC. 91, 110 (1958-59); Fedechar v. Haute Autorité, 2 REC. 201, 206 (1955-56). The avocat généraux share this view. *E.g.*, Roemer in Nold v. Haute Autorité, 5 REC. 91, 119, 123-25, 133 (1958-59); Lagrange in Macchiorlatti Dalmas e Figli v. Haute Autorité, 5 REC. 415, 431, 433 (1958-59).
[40] 2 ERNST RABEL, THE CONFLICT OF LAWS 38 (1947); Audinet, *The Right of Establishment in the European Economic Community*, 86 JOURNAL DU DROIT INTERNATIONAL 983, 1017 (France 1959); Thibièrge, *Le Statut des sociétés etrangeres*, in 75TH CONGRÈS DES NOTAIRES DE FRANCE, LE STATUT DE L'ETRANGER ET LE MARCHÉ COMMUN 239, 303-04 (1959).

for one reason or another, maintains an establishment or a legally dependent enterprise in one of the Member States. The situation would be similar if, for example, an American corporation, incorporated in Delaware, were to maintain its seat in Belgium and operate an establishment in Germany or France. Without going into any details, it may be safely assumed that such a corporation would not enjoy a legal personality according to the European law. Only a treaty of friendship, commerce, and trade concluded between the United States and a Member State, which usually contains a special reciprocity clause as to the mutual recognition of the legal personality of corporations, could uphold the right of such a corporation to sue before a municipal court of the other State, even though it is not "domesticated" there.[41] If such a treaty were concluded between a Member State and a third State, the Community Court would undoubtedly recognize its legal consequences and uphold the right of such a corporation to appeal—assuming, of course, that this corporation maintained within the Community an enterprise on whose behalf it appealed.

[41] See, *e.g.*, the Treaty of Friendship, Commerce, and Navigation, with the Federal Republic of Germany, Oct. 29, 1954, [1956] 2 Bundesgesetzblatt (Ger. Fed. Rep.) 487; [1956] 7 U.S.T. & O.I.A. 1839, T.I.A.S. No. 3593, art. VI(1): "Nationals and companies . . . shall be accorded national treatment with respect to access to the courts of justice and to administrative tribunals and agencies within the territories of the other Party, in all degrees of jurisdiction, both in pursuit and in defence of their rights. It is understood that companies of either Party not engaged in activities within the territories of the other Party, shall enjoy such access therein without any requirement of registration or domestication." See also art. XXV(5): "Companies constituted under the applicable laws and regulations within the territories of either Party shall . . . have their juridical status recognized within the territories of the other Party."

RULES GOVERNING COMPETITION WITHIN THE EUROPEAN REGIONAL COMMUNITIES*

JOCHEN THIESING†

INTRODUCTION

It is necessary to refer to the European Communities in the plural because the six European countries (Belgium, the Federal Republic of Germany, France, Italy, Luxembourg, and the Netherlands) that have united in these Communities have, by three separate Treaties, established three Communities, each of which is endowed with its own legal personality.[1] The six Member States took the first step in 1951, when they established the European Coal and Steel Community (E.C.S.C.).[2] They proceeded further by concluding the Treaties establishing the European Economic Community (E.E.C.)[3] and the European Atomic Energy Community (Euratom)[4] in 1957.

Though the three Communities are three separate legal entities, they are, nonetheless, linked to one another in various ways, both legally and in practice. Under the Convention on the Joint Institutions of the European Communities,[5] which came into force simultaneously with the Treaties on January 1, 1958, the powers of the Parliament and the competence of the Court of Justice—for which provision is made in the three Treaties—are exercised by a single European Parliamentary Assembly and a single Court of Justice, which has its seat in Luxembourg. Moreover, a single Economic and Social Committee, composed of representatives from the various

---

* Translated from the German by R. Lederer. The views expressed in this article are those of the writer and do not necessarily reflect those of the Commission of the European Economic Community.

† Attorney in Berlin, Germany, since 1939. Chief of bureau in Federal Ministry of Economics, Bonn, for matters of deconcentration since 1950, and legal problems of the European Coal and Steel Community since 1954. Legal Adviser, Commission of the European Economic Community, Brussels, since 1958.

[1] E.C.S.C. Treaty art. 6; E.E.C. Treaty art. 210; Euratom Treaty art. 184.

[2] The E.C.S.C. Treaty of April 18, 1951, came into force on July 23, 1952; only the French text of the Treaty is authentic E.C.S.C. Treaty art. 100. See generally PAUL REUTER, LA COMMUNAUTÉ EUROPÉENNE DU CHARBON ET DE L'ACIER (1953); FRANZ JERUSALEM, DAS RECHT DER MONTANUNION (1954); WILLIAM DIEBOLD, THE SCHUMAN PLAN: A STUDY IN ECONOMIC COOPERATION 1950-59 (1959).

[3] The Treaty of March 25, 1957, came into force on Jan. 1, 1958. Like the Euratom Treaty, it was drawn up in the four official languages of the Community (German, French, Italian, and Dutch), all four texts being equally authentic. E.E.C. Treaty art. 248; Euratom Treaty art. 225. The texts of the two Treaties were published in the four official languages in [1957] 2 Bundesgesetzblatt 753 (Ger. Fed. Rep.). The Secretariat of the Interim Committee for the Common Market and Euratom has published an unofficial English translation. See generally NICOLA CATALANO, LA COMMUNITÀ ECONOMICA EUROPA E EURATOM (2d ed. 1959); HANS VON DER GROEBEN & HANS VON BOECKH (EDS)., HANDBUCH FÜR EUROPÄISCHE WIRTSCHAFT (1958, 1960); ERNST WOHLFARTH ET AL., DIE EUROPÄISCHE WIRTSCHAFTSGEMEINSCHAFT (1960); 1 and 2 ERIC STEIN & THOMAS L. NICHOLSON (EDS.), AMERICAN ENTERPRISE IN THE EUROPEAN COMMON MARKET: A LEGAL PROFILE (1960).

[4] The Treaty of March 25, 1957, came into force on Jan. 1, 1958. For further details, see *supra* note 3; see also JACQUES ERRERA ET AL., EURATOM, ANALYSE ET COMMENTAIRES DU TRAITÉ (1958).

[5] Of March 25, 1957. [1957] 2 Bundesgesetzblatt 1156 (Ger. Fed. Rep.)

spheres of economic and social life,[6] advises both the Commission of E.E.C. and that of Euratom. The three Communities have a joint Legal Service, a joint Statistical Office, and a joint Press and Information Service.

The Council, which in all three Communities consists of representatives of the Governments of the Member States,[7] is frequently composed of the same persons for the three Communities, responsible as members of their Government for the various affairs of the Communities. Further, the Commissions of the E.E.C. and of Euratom and the High Authority, the executive organ of the E.C.S.C., have in 1958 and 1959 set up interexecutive groups of the three Communities to deal with the following issues: external relations, energy policy, social affairs, transport problems, press and information, statistics, and interexecutive co-operation.[8] The scope of this paper does not require any detailed examination of the provisions of the Euratom Treaty. It is the function of Euratom to contribute to raising the standard of living in the Member States and to develop relations with other States by creating the conditions necessary for the speedy establishment and evolution of nuclear industries.[9] In particular, the supply of all Member States with ores, basic materials, and fissionable materials is to be ensured on the principle of equal access to resources by means of a common supply policy.[10] Apart from this broad principle, the Euratom Treaty does not contain any real rules on competition.

The E.C.S.C. Treaty's rules on competition are laid down in its articles sixty-five[11] and sixty-six.[12] These provisions apply only to coal- and steel-producing enter-

[6] E.E.C. Treaty art. 193; Euratom Treaty art. 165.
[7] E.C.S.C. Treaty art. 27; E.E.C. Treaty art. 146; Euratom Treaty art. 116.
[8] *Cf.* EURATOM COMMISSION, THIRD GENERAL REPORT 145 (German version) and 115 (French version) (1960). Even wider proposals on the cooperation between the three executives are under consideration.
[9] Euratom Treaty art. 1.
[10] *Id.* art. 52.
[11] Art. 65:
1. There are hereby forbidden all agreements among enterprises, all decisions of associations of enterprises, and all concerted practices, which would tend, directly or indirectly, to prevent, restrict or distort the normal operation of competition within the common market, and in particular:
(a) to fix or influence prices;
(b) to restrict or control production, technical development or investments;
(c) to allocate markets, products, customers or sources of supply.
2. However, the High Authority will authorize enterprises to agree among themselves to specialize in the production of, or to engage in joint buying or selling of specified products, if the High Authority finds:
(a) that such specialization or such joint buying or selling will contribute to a substantial improvement in the production or marketing of the products in question; and
(b) that the agreement in question is essential to achieve such effects, and does not impose any restriction not necessary for that purpose; and
(c) that it is not susceptible of giving the interested enterprises the power to influence prices, or to control or limit production or marketing of an appreciable part of the products in question within the common market, or of protecting them from effective competition by other enterprises within the common market.
If the High Authority should recognize that certain agreements are strictly analogous in their nature and effects to the agreements mentioned above, taking into account the application of the present section to distributing enterprises, it will authorize such agreements if it further recognizes that they satisfy the same conditions.
An authorization may be made subject to specified conditions and may be limited in time. If so

limited, the High Authority will renew it once or several times if it finds that at the time of renewal the conditions stated in paragraph (a) to (c) above are still fulfilled.

The High Authority will revoke or modify the authorization if it finds that as a result of changes in circumstances the agreement no longer fulfills the conditions set forth above, or that the actual effects of the agreement or of the operations under it are contrary to the conditions required for its approval.

The decisions granting, modifying, refusing or revoking an authorization shall be published along with their justification; the limitations contained in the second paragraph of Article 47 shall not be applicable to such publication.

3. The High Authority may obtain, in accordance with the provisions of Article 47, any information necessary to the application of the present article, either by a special request addressed to the interested parties or by a regulation defining the nature of the agreements, decisions or practices which must be communicated to it.

4. Any agreement or decision which is prohibited by virtue of Section 1 of the present article shall be automatically void and may not be invoked before any court or tribunal of the member States.

The High Authority has exclusive competence, subject to appeals to the Court, to rule on the conformity of such agreements or decisions with the provisions of the present article.

5. The High Authority may pronounce against enterprises:

which have concluded an agreement which is automatically void;

which have complied with, enforced or attempted to enforce by arbitration, forfeiture, boycott or any other means, an agreement or decision which is automatically void or an agreement for which approval has been refused or revoked;

which shall have obtained an authorization by means of knowingly false or misleading information; or

which engage in practices contrary to the provisions of Section 1, fines and daily penalty payments not to exceed double the turnover actually realized on the products which have been the subject of the agreement, decision or practice contrary to the provisions of the present article; if the object of the agreement is to restrict production, technical development or investments, this maximum may be raised to 10 percent of the annual turnover of the enterprises in question, in the case of fines, and 20 percent of the daily turnover in the case of daily penalty payments.

See ROBERT KRAWIELICKI, DAS MONOPOLVERBOT IM SCHUMAN-PLAN (1952); HANS-WOLFRAM DAIG, VERBOT UND GENEHMIGUNG FÜR KARTELLE NACH ART. 65 DES MONTAN-VERTRAGS (1957).

[12] Art. 66:

1. Except as provided in paragraph 3 below, any transaction which would have in itself the direct or indirect effect of bringing about a concentration, within the territories mentioned in the first paragraph of Article 79, involving enterprises at least one of which falls under the application of Article 80, shall be submitted to a prior authorization of the High Authority. This obligation shall be effective whether the operation in question is carried out by a person or an enterprise, or a group of persons or enterprises, whether it concerns a single product or different products, whether it is effected by merger, acquisition of shares or assets, loan, contract, or any other means of control. For the application of the above provisions, the High Authority will define by a regulation, established after consultation with the Council, what constitutes control of an enterprise.

2. The High Authority will grant the authorization referred to in the preceding paragraph if it finds that the transaction in question will not give to the interested persons or enterprises, as concerns those of the products in question which are subject to its jurisdiction, the power:

—to influence prices, to control or restrain production or marketing, or to impair the maintenance of effective competition in a substantial part of the market for such products; or

—to evade the rules of competition resulting from the application of the present Treaty, particularly by establishing an artificially privileged position involving a material advantage in access to supplies or markets.

In this appreciation, and in accordance with the principle of non-discrimination set forth in subparagraph (b) of Article 4, the High Authority will take account of the size of enterprises of the same nature existing in the Community, to the extent it deems justified to avoid or correct the disadvantages resulting from an inequality in the conditions of competition.

The High Authority may subject such an authorization to any conditions which it deems appropriate for the purposes of the present section.

Before taking action on a transaction concerning enterprises of which at least one is not subject to the application of Article 80, the High Authority will request the observations of the interested government.

3. The High Authority will exempt from the requirement of prior authorization those classes of transactions which, by the size of the assets or enterprises which they affect taken together with the nature of the concentration they bring about, must in its opinion be held to conform to the conditions

Rules Governing Competition

required by Section 2. The regulation established for this purpose with the concurrence of the Council will also fix the conditions to which such exemption is to be subject.

4. Without limiting the applicability of the provisions of Article 47 to enterprises subject to its jurisdiction, the High Authority may obtain from physical or juridical persons who have acquired or regrouped or might acquire or regroup the rights or assets in question, any information necessary to the application of the present article concerning operations which might produce the effect mentioned in Section 1; it may do this either by a regulation established after consultation with the Council which defines the nature of the operations which must be communicated to it, or by a special demand addressed to the interested parties within the framework of such regulation.

5. If a concentration should occur, which the High Authority finds has been effected contrary to the provisions of Section 1 but which it finds nevertheless satisfies the conditions provided in Section 2, it will subject the approval of this concentration to the payment, by the persons who have acquired or regrouped the rights or assets in question, of the fine provided in the second sub-paragraph of Section 6; such payment shall not be less than half of the maximum provided in the said sub-paragraph in any case where it is clear that the authorization should have been requested. In the absence of this payment, the High Authority will apply the measures provided hereafter for concentrations found to be illegal.

If a concentration should occur which the High Authority recognizes cannot satisfy the general or special conditions to which an authorization under Section 2 would be subject, it will establish the illegal character of this concentration by a decision accompanied by a justification; after having allowed the interested parties to present their observations, the High Authority shall order the separation of the enterprises or assets wrongly concentrated or the cessation of common control, as well as any other action which it deems appropriate to re-establish the independent operation of the enterprises or assets in question and to restore normal conditions of competition. Any person directly interested may take an appeal against such decisions under the conditions provided in Article 33. Notwithstanding the provisions of that article, the Court shall be fully competent to judge whether the operation effected is a concentration within the meaning of Section 1 of the present article and of the regulations issued in application of that section. This appeal shall be suspensive. It may not be taken until the measures provided above have been ordered, unless the High Authority should agree to the taking of a separate appeal against the decision declaring the transaction illegal.

The High Authority may at any time, subject to the possible application of the provisions of the third paragraph of Article 39, take or cause to be taken such measures as it may deem necessary to safeguard the interests of competing enterprises and of third parties, and to prevent any action which might impede the execution of its decisions. Unless the Court decides otherwise, appeals shall not suspend the application of such precautionary measures.

The High Authority will grant to the interested parties a reasonable period in which to execute its decisions, at the expiration of which it may begin to impose daily penalty payments not to exceed one tenth of one percent of the value of the rights or assets in question.

Furthermore, if the interested parties fail to fulfill their obligations, the High Authority shall itself take measures of execution and in particular may: suspend the exercise, in enterprises subject to its jurisdiction, of the rights attached to the assets illegally acquired; bring about the designation by judicial authorities of a receiver-administrator for these assets; organize the forced sale of such assets in conditions preserving the legitimate interests of their proprietors; annul, with respect to physical or juridical persons who have acquired the rights or assets in question by the effect of illegal transaction, the acts, decisions, resolutions, or deliberations of the directing organs of enterprises subject to a control which has been irregularly established.

The High Authority is also empowered to address to the interested member States the recommendations necessary to obtain, within the framework of national legislation, the execution of the measures provided for in the preceding paragraphs.

In the exercise of its powers, the High Authority shall take account of the rights of third persons which have been acquired in good faith.

6. The High Authority may impose fines not to exceed:

—3 percent of the value of the assets acquired or regrouped or to be acquired or regrouped, against physical or juridical persons who shall have violated the obligations provided for in Section 4;

—10 percent of the value of the assets acquired or regrouped, against physical or juridical persons which shall have violated the obligation provided for in Section 1; after the end of the twelfth month following the transaction, this maximum shall be raised by one-twenty-fourth per month which elapses until the High Authority establishes the existence of the violation;

—10 percent of the value of the assets acquired or regrouped or to be acquired or regrouped, against physical or juridical persons which shall have obtained or attempted to obtain the benefit of the provisions of Section 2 by means of false or misleading information;

prises within the European territories of the Member States, as well as to enterprises or organizations regularly engaged in distribution of products of the coal and steel industries other than sale for domestic consumers or to craft industries.[13] The terms "coal" and "steel" are defined in annex one to the E.C.S.C. Treaty. The E.E.C. Treaty explicitly specifies[14] that the provisions of the E.C.S.C. Treaty—especially those concerning the rights and obligations of the Member States, the powers of the institutions of the E.C.S..C., and the functions of the Common Market for coal and steel—shall not be affected by it.

The rules on competition in the E.E.C. Treaty apply to all enterprises that do not fall within the terms of reference of the E.C.S.C. These rules are composed of provisions applicable to enterprises,[15] provisions on the prohibition of state aids or aids granted by means of state resources that distort or threaten to distort competition by favoring certain enterprises or certain productions, to the extent to which they adversely affect trade between Member States,[16] and provisions on the prohibition of dumping practices within the Common Market.[17]

Only the provisions concerning enterprises will be considered in detail in this article.

The E.E.C. Treaty stipulates that the Council, acting on a proposal of the Commission and after the Assembly has been consulted, shall lay down any appropriate regulations[18] or directives,[19] with a view to the application of the principles set out in articles eighty-five[20] and eighty-six.[21] This provision has led to considerable differ-

---

—15 percent of the value of the assets acquired or regrouped, against enterprises subject to its jurisdiction which shall have participated in or lent themselves to the realization of transactions contrary to the provisions of the present article.

Persons who are the object of sanctions provided for in the present paragraph may appeal before the Court under the conditions provided for in Article 36.

7. To the extent necessary, the High Authority is empowered to address to public or private enterprises which, in law or in fact, have or acquire on the market for one of the products subject to its jurisdiction a dominant position which protects them from effective competition in a substantial part of the common market, any recommendations required to prevent the use of such position for purposes contrary to those of the present Treaty. If such recommendations are not fulfilled satisfactorily within a reasonable period, the High Authority will, by decisions taken in consultation with the interested government and under the sanctions provided for in Articles 58, 59 and 64, fix the prices and conditions of sale to be applied by the enterprise in question, or establish manufacturing or delivery programs to be executed by it.

See KRAWIELICKI, *op. cit. supra* note 11; PETER KERN, DAS RECHT DER UNTERNEHMENSZUSAMMENSCHLÜSSE IN DER MONTANUNION (1955); Thiesing, *Zusammenschlüsse von Unternehmen nach dem Montan-Vertrag*, [1954] BETRIEBS-BERATER 449 [hereinafter cited as BB].

[13] E.C.S.C. Treaty art. 80.
[14] E.E.C. Treaty art. 232.
[15] *Id.* arts. 85-90.
[16] *Id.* arts. 92-94.
[17] *Id.* art. 91.
[18] Under art. 189, E.E.C. regulations are binding in every respect and directly applicable in each Member State.
[19] Under art. 189, E.E.C. directives shall bind any Member State to which they are addressed as to the result to be achieved, while leaving to domestic agencies a competence as to form and means.
[20] Art. 85:

1. The following shall be deemed to be incompatible with the Common Market and shall hereby be prohibited: any agreements between enterprises, any decisions by associations of enterprises and any

ences of opinion as to whether the prohibitions contained in these articles already constitute effective law or not. It is unfortunately not possible within the scope of this article to go into the details of the various views and arguments adduced to support one opinion or the other.[22] The main arguments presented in defense of the view that the prohibitions of articles eighty-five and eighty-six cannot be applied until after the entry into effect of the regulations to be issued under article eighty-seven consist of the assertion that the content of articles eighty-five and eighty-six is too vague and needs supplementation through implementing regulations; and further, that the immediate application of the prohibition provisions would be incompatible with general principles of law, as these provisions would thereby be given retroactive effect.

Neither of these arguments is convincing. The two articles under review express the prohibitions more concisely than does the text of the two basic articles of the

---

concerted practices which are likely to affect trade between Member States and which have as their object or result the prevention, restriction or distortion of competition within the Common Market, in particular those consisting in:
  (a) The direct or indirect fixing of purchase or selling prices or of any other trading conditions;
  (b) the limitation or control of production, markets, technical development or investment;
  (c) market-sharing or the sharing of sources of supply;
  (d) the application to parties to transactions of unequal terms in respect of equivalent supplies, thereby placing them at a competitive disadvantage; or
  (e) the subjecting of the conclusion of a contract to the acceptance by a party of additional supplies which, either by their nature or according to commercial usage, have no connection with the subject of such contract.
  2. Any agreements or decisions prohibited pursuant to this Article shall be null and void.
  3. Nevertheless, the provisions of paragraph 1 may be declared inapplicable in the case of:
  —any agreements or classes of agreements between enterprises,
  —any decisions or classes of decisions by asociations of enterprises, and
  —any concerted practices or classes of concerted practices which contribute to the improvement of the production or distribution of goods or to the promotion of technical or economic progress while reserving to users an equitable share in the profit resulting therefrom, and which:
  (a) neither impose on the enterprises concerned any restrictions not indispensable to the attainment of the above objectives;
  (b) nor enable such enterprises to eliminate competition in respect of a substantial proportion of the goods concerned.
For the extensive literature on this article, see Ernst Wohlfarth et al., *op. cit. supra* note 3, *Introductory Remark No. 9 on Articles 85 et seq.*; see also George Nebolsine, The European Common Market Rules Governing Competition (1960).

[21] Art. 86:
To the extent to which trade between any Member States may be affected thereby, action by one or more enterprises to take improper advantage of a dominant position within the Common Market or within a substantial part of it shall be deemed to be incompatible with the Common Market and shall hereby be prohibited.
  Such improper practices may, in particular, consist in:
  (a) the direct or indirect imposition of any inequitable purchase or selling prices or of any other inequitable trading conditions;
  (b) the limitation of production, markets or technical development to the prejudice of consumers;
  (c) the application to parties to transactions of unequal terms in respect of equivalent supplies, thereby placing them at a competitive disadvantage; or
  (d) the subjecting of the conclusion of a contract to the acceptance, by a party, of additional supplies which, either by their nature or according to commercial usage, have no connection with the subject of such contract.

[22] *Cf.* von der Groeben & von Boeckh, *op. cit. supra* note 3, *Introductory Remarks 10-12 on Articles 85 et seq.*; see also, *Nebolsine, op. cit. supra* note 20, at 7, 8.

Sherman Act,[22a] which has given American administrators and courts a sufficient basis for the practical application and development of American antitrust legislation. Also, it is wrong to maintain that the prohibitions would be given retroactive effect; this could be the case only if the prohibition had been expressed in respect of a period prior to the entry into force of the Treaty. There is nothing unusual in certain conduct being forbidden as from the entry into effect of a law. It is, however, frequently desirable in such cases to introduce some transitional arrangement in order to avoid difficulties. Such an arrangement has been made in the E.C.S.C. Treaty. The E.E.C. Treaty does not contain any explicit transition provisions, though these could be introduced by way of implementing regulations under article eighty-seven,[23] to which reference has already been made.[23a]

So far as the practical application of the Treaty is concerned, it is right to proceed from the assumption that the prohibition provisions in articles eighty-five and eighty-six have, with the entry into force of the Treaty, become immediately applicable law in the Member States. The Commission has repeatedly and officially upheld this view[24] which has, moreover, found the approval of the government experts of the Member States.[25]

I

PROHIBITION OF CARTELS

The prohibition provisions in article sixty-five of the E.C.S.C. Treaty and in articles eighty-five and eighty-six of the E.E.C. Treaty largely coincide as to content.

[22a] 26 Stat. 209 (1890), as amended, 15 U.S.C. §§ 1, 2 (1958).

[23] Art. 87:
Within a period of three years after the date of the entry into force of this Treaty, the Council, acting by means of a unanimous vote on a proposal of the Commission and after the Assembly has been consulted, shall lay down any appropriate regulations or directives with a view to the application of the principles set out in Articles 85 and 86.
If such provisions have not been adopted within the above-mentioned time-limit, they shall be laid down by the Council acting by means of a qualified majority vote on a proposal of the Commission and after the Assembly has been consulted.
2. The provisions referred to in paragraph 1 shall be designed, in particular:
(a) to ensure observance, by the institution of fines or penalties, of the prohibitions referred to in Article 85, paragraph 1, and in Article 86;
(b) to determine the particulars of the application of Article 85, paragraph 3, taking due account of the need, on the one hand, of ensuring effective supervision and, on the other hand, of simplifying administrative control to the greatest possible extent;
(c) to specify, where necessary, the scope of application in the various economic sectors of the provisions contained in Articles 85 and 86;
(d) to define the respective responsibilities of the Commission and of the Court of Justice in the application of the provisions referred to in this paragraph; and
(e) to define the relations between, on the one hand, municipal law and, on the other hand, the provisions contained in this Section or adopted in application of this Article.

[23a] The draft of the first implementing regulation which since January, 1961, has been in committee of the European Parliament (E.E.C. Treaty art. 137), contains transition provisions in its arts. 5 and 6. *Cf.* German text, [1960] WIRTSCHAFT UND WETTBEWERB 856 [hereinafter cited as WuW], French Text [1961] REVUE DU MARCHÉ COMMUN 16.

[24] *Cf.* E.E.C. COMMISSION, FIRST GENERAL REPORT § 84 (1958), SECOND GENERAL REPORT § 115 (1959).

[25] *Cf. ibid.*; FEDERAL CARTEL OFFICE, REPORT 55 (1959) (German Bundestag Paper No. 1795, 1960).

Both forbid any agreement between enterprises, any decisions by associations of enterprises, and any concerted practices that have as their object the prevention, restriction, or distortion of competition within the Common Market. In prohibiting concerted actions, both Treaties follow the example of American antitrust legislation. This term, so far unknown to European lawyers, is interpreted to mean that the prohibition is intended to cover any joint action by several enterprises in distortion of competition, such action being influenced by one enterprise or an association of enterprises, without, however, those concerned entering into legal engagements or commitments.[26] The interpretation and application of this concept will probably give rise to as much dispute in European practice as it has in America.

The essential difference between the provisions in the two Treaties lies in the fact that the E.E.C. Treaty forbids cartel practices only to the extent that they are likely to impede trade between Member States. The prohibition in the E.C.S.C. Treaty, on the other hand, applies also to cartels of which the activities are limited to one Member State. The E.E.C. Treaty, which applies to all trade and industry with the exception of coal and steel products, leaves it to the Member States to decide how far they wish to go in combatting cartel arrangements that are of no importance to trade between Member States.

The (unofficial) English version of article eighty-five says "which are likely to affect"; this agrees with the official French text, which says *"sont susceptibles d'affecter."* The equally authentic texts in the three other official languages of the Community[27] contain words that, in English, would have to be rendered by "harmfully affect."[28] This narrower interpretation would seem to be more in line with the purpose behind the prohibitive clauses.[29] In its comments on a cartel arrangement between German coal and fuel oil producers, the Commission has interpreted the provision in that sense by not objecting to a licence issued under German law[30] because the arrangement concerned would not have any disadvantageous effect on trade between Member States.[31]

Moreover, it is to be assumed that the limitation of the prohibition to cases in which trade between Member States is jeopardized will lose much of its importance

---

[26] WOHLFARHT ET AL., *op. cit. supra* note 3, art. 85 n.3; VON DER GROEBEN & VON BOECKH, *op. cit. supra* note 3, art. 85 n.2.
[27] E.E.C. Treaty art. 248.
[28] German text:
"zu beeinträchtigen geeignet sind"
Italian text:
"che possano pregiudicare"
Dutch text:
"ongunstig kunnen beinvloeden"
[29] But see WOHLFARHT ET AL., *op. cit. supra* note 3, art. 85 n.4.
[30] The licence was based on the Restriction of Competition (Prevention) Act (GWB) § 8, July 27, 1957, [1957] 1 Bundesgesetzblatt 1081 (Ger. Fed. Rep.), under which the Federal Minister of Economics may authorize a cartel if, by way of an exception, the restriction of competition is necessary for predominant economic and general reasons. [1959] WuW 385. This cartel has since then dissolved itself.
[31] VERLOREN VAN THEMAAT, SOME PROBLEMS OF COMPETITION IN THE COMMON MARKET (1959), quoted by NEBOLSINE, *op. cit. supra* note 20, at 19.

as the Common Market progresses. During the transition period, customs duties and quantitative restrictions continue amongst the Member States in respect of many goods; they will, however, be completely eliminated by the end of the transition period,[32] so that trade between the Member States will increase—which is the very objective of the Treaty.

In those fields in which the E.C.S.C. Treaty applies, especially in the coal market, conditions of competition differ substantially from those obtaining in the remainder of the Common Market.[33] These differences are reflected in several provisions in the E.C.S.C. Treaty that have a certain influence on the rules of competition. For instance, the institutions of the E.C.S.C. are to ensure that the Common Market is regularly supplied, while taking into account the needs of third countries;[34] they are also to assure to all consumers in comparable positions within the Common Market equal access to the sources of production.[35] The E.C.S.C. Treaty then goes on to prohibit measures or practices discriminating among producers, among buyers or among consumers, especially as concerns prices and delivery terms.[36] Finally, the E.C.S.C. Treaty contains explicit rules on the introduction of production quotas should the Community be faced with a serious shortage of certain products.[37]

These provisions reflect the anxieties that were felt on the subject of coal shortage when the Treaty was being worked out in 1951. It is now nearly three years since the situation in the energy market has undergone a fundamental change, because while coal production has risen, coal has been facing keen competition from fuel oil. The High Authority has been compelled to make use of a safeguard provision in the Treaty[38] in order to restrict coal imports from other Member States to Belgium.[39] Apart from this, competition in the Common Market for coal is limited by the fact that imports into France are handled by a state agency.[40]

[32] Under E.E.C. Treaty art. 8(1), the transition period covers 12 years from the entry into effect of the Treaty (Jan. 1, 1958). In accordance with the provisions of art. 8, it can be extended or shortened. Under the decisions of the Council dated May 12, 1960, on bringing forward the dates for the abolition of customs duties and quantitative restrictions within the Community, [1960] JOURNAL OFFICIEL DES COMMUNANTES EUROPEENNES 1217 [hereinafter referred to as JOURNAL OFFICIEL], it is to be expected that the second and third stages of the transition period will be reduced in accordance with art. 8(5).

[33] See Heinrich Kronstein in his lecture *Die Bedeutung der Wettbewerbsregeln im Gesamtrahmen des Montan-Vertrags und des Vertrags über die Europäische Wirtschaftsgemeinschaft*, to the International Conference on Cartel Law, in Frankfurt/Main, on June 8, 1960.

[34] E.C.S.C. Treaty art. 3a.
[35] *Id.* art. 3b.
[36] *Id.* arts. 4b, 60.
[37] *Id.* art. 59.
[38] *Id.* art. 37(1).
[39] Decision of the High Authority No. 46/59, Dec. 23, 1959, [1959] JOURNAL OFFICIEL 1327, as amended by Dec. No. 1/60, Jan. 18, 1960, [1960] JOURNAL OFFICIEL 103, No. 24/60, Dec. 7, 1960 [1960] JOURNAL OFFICIEL 1534, and No. 25/60, Dec. 20, 1960 [1960] JOURNAL OFFICIEL 1915. Two German coal-mining enterprises have, under E.C.S.C. Treaty art. 33, brought a suit of nullity against the first decision before the Court of Justice. *Cf.* [1960] JOURNAL OFFICIEL 546.

[40] Association Technique de l'Importation Charbonnière. The High Authority regarded this institution as a restriction, inadmissible under the Treaty, of the access of French dealers to the coal producers of other Community countries. The French Government which had appealed against the relevant Decision of

On the other hand, the rules of competition laid down in the E.E.C. Treaty have the unrestricted objective to set up a system that will protect competition within the Common Market from distortion.[41] For this reason, the E.E.C. Treaty contains neither any provisions to meet conditions of shortage, nor any general prohibition of discrimination.

The E.E.C. Treaty lists a number of agreements, decisions, and concerted practices as being prohibited.[42] This enumeration is not exhaustive and is merely intended to furnish examples of particularly flagrant types of distortion of competition. Therefore, if the prohibition provision is to be applied, the general conditions set for the prohibition must be fulfilled (likelihood of trade between Member States being impaired, or the prevention, restriction, or distortion of competition within the Common Market).

In the first place, the direct or indirect fixing of purchase or selling prices, or of any other trading conditions is forbidden. Clearly, any concerted fixing of prices will prevent competition in a particularly important field. Not only the so-called "horizontal price agreements" are forbidden—*i.e.,* amongst manufacturers of the same type of goods—but also the so-called "vertical" price fixing agreements—*e.g.,* between producers and distributors of a commodity.[43]

Secondly, the limitation or control of production, markets, technical development, or investment is forbidden. Agreements of this nature not only impede competition, but are also incompatible with the Treaty objective, which is to bring about expansion of trade and a speedy increase in standards of living.

Market sharing or the sharing of sources of supply is also a danger to the above-mentioned Treaty objective and is likewise prohibited. The beneficial effects on trade between the Member States to be obtained from the removal of customs duties and quantitative restrictions would be undone if enterprises in the various States were to conclude market-sharing agreements.

The application, to parties to transactions, of unequal terms in respect of equivalent supplies is prohibited under article eighty-five of the E.E.C. Treaty only to the extent that such parties are thereby placed at a competitive disadvantage. This so-called prohibition of discrimination, therefore, does not go so far as that of the E.C.S.C. Treaty, which quite generally prohibits any discrimination.[44] Under article eighty-five, a producer is not prevented from applying unequal terms to customers who are not in competition with one another.

---

the High Authority of Dec. 18, 1957, has finally accepted such modifications of that institution as to render it compatible with the Treaty. The case has therefore been settled without trial. See [1961] JOURNAL OFFICIEL 575.

[41] E.E.C. Treaty art. 3f. The chapter on rules governing competition is applicable to the production of and trade in agricultural products only to the extent determined by the Council, however, due account being taken of the objectives mentioned in art. 39. *Id.* arts. 39 and 42.

[42] *Id.* art. 85(1)(a)-(e); *cf. supra* note 20.

[43] WOHLFARHT ET AL., *op. cit. supra* note 3, art. 85 n.6; Guenther, [1957] WuW 280, Oberlandesgericht Düsseldorf, [1958] BB 1110.

[44] E.C.S.C. Treaty art. 4b. Under art. 7, only any discrimination *on the grounds of nationality* is prohibited within the field of application of the Treaty and without prejudice to the special provisions menioned therein.

The last example of prohibited measures listed in article eighty-five is the subjecting of the conclusion of a contract to the acceptance, by a party, of additional supplies that, either by their nature or according to commercial usage, have no connection with the subject of such contract. In other words, the manufacturers of, say, some new kind of textile machine would not be permitted to conclude a contract under which they would supply this new type of machine on condition only that their customers at the same time purchase a certain other machine, the performance of which was in no way connected with the former.

Naturally, the assessment of such cases depends largely on the individual circumstances and on conditions obtaining in the various industries, so that it will hardly be possible to lay down any exact rules.

II

Exemption

The strict prohibition contained in article eighty-five is mitigated in that under certain conditions it may be declared inapplicable in the case of otherwise prohibited agreements, decisions or concerted practices.

However, the conditions under which exemption may be granted are strict. In the first place, it is necessary that any such agreement must contribute to the production or to the distribution of goods, or to the promotion of technical or economic progress while reserving to users an equitable share in the profit resulting therefrom. It will, however, have to be assumed that the benefits from which consumers are to profit need not necessarily be expressed in terms of money, but could also consist in the improvement of service.[45] In addition to these two positive conditions of exemption, the Treaty also sets two negative conditions by laying down that no restrictions not indispensable to the attainment of these objectives must be imposed on the enterprises—that is to say no restrictions not indispensable to the improvement of supply or the promotion of technical or economic progress. Nor must enterprises be enabled to eliminate competition in respect of a substantial proportion of the goods concerned. In practice, this will give rise to many problems, which are likely to play a part when the regulation laying down details for the implementation of article 85(3) is issued in accordance with article eighty-seven.

On the whole, the conditions set under article 85(3) for the exemption of the so-called "good" cartels are more stringent than the provisions applicable in any one of the six Member States.

The E.C.S.C. Treaty, too, contains an authorization provision for certain cartel agreements.[46] These must be agreements to specialize in the production of or to engage in the joint buying or selling of specified products, or agreements strictly analogous to those in their nature or effects. Agreements of another kind—as,

---

[45] Guenther, [1957] WuW 281.
[46] E.C.S.C. Treaty art. 65(2); *cf. supra* note 11.

for instance, an agreed sharing of sales markets or quantities of supply—cannot be authorized. For the rest, the conditions of authorization are similar to those of the E.E.C. Treaty.[47]

Under the E.E.C. Treaty, the authorities of the Member States shall, until the entry into force of the provisions adopted in application of article eighty-seven, rule upon the admissibility of agreements, decisions, and concerted practices under article 85(3) of the Treaty.[48] At present, therefore, the Commission is not charged with granting exemptions, and so has acquired no practical experience to date with such exemptions.[48a]

In the E.C.S.C., 209 proceedings had been taken under article sixty-five by the beginning of 1960—about half of them upon application, half of them ex officio. In 116 cases, it has been found that article sixty-five was not applicable. Prohibitions were issued in four cases, and in eight, the cartel concerned was dissolved voluntarily; twenty-seven agreements were authorized. The problem of Ruhr-coal sales organizations is of particular importance.[49]

III

Infringements

Agreements or decisions forbidden under article 65(1) of the E.C.S.C. Treaty are null and void; they cannot be pleaded in defense before any court in the Member States.[50]

The E.E.C. Treaty also lays down that agreements or decisions forbidden under its article eighty-five shall be null and void.[51] The wording of this provision indicates that this nullity is a direct consequence of the Treaty, so that a decision by

---

[47] E.E.C. Treaty art. 85(3), which specifies that the provisions of art. 85(1) may be declared inapplicable to classes of agreements, decisions, or concerted practices; cf. supra note 20.
[48] E.E.C. Treaty art. 88.
[48a] The draft of the first implementing regulation (supra note 23a) provides the exclusive authority of the Commission for granting exceptions (art. 2(2)).
[49] This problem has been before the High Authority of the E.C.S.C. for several years. By a Decision of June 22, 1960, the High Authority rejected an application on the part of the Ruhr coal producers for the authorization of a single sales cartel for Ruhr coal, at the same time permitting them to continue, for the time being, with the present system based on Decision No. 17/59 of Dec. 18, 1959, authorizing sales by three sales companies and the maintenance of one joint office by these companies. [1959] Journal Officiel 279. Without the Decision of June 22, 1960, this permit would have expired on June 30, 1960. In the opinion of the High Authority, the sales cartel could not be authorized because it would have enabled the producers to determine prices on a substantial section of the coal market. According to the calculations of the High Authority, the share of Ruhr coal in the Common Market. is more than 33% (49,500,000 tons out of a total consumption of 146,000,000 tons). Bodol Boerner, Die Marktbeherrschung im Kartellrecht der Montanunion und die Ruhr-kohle 27-29 (1960), however, calculates that the Ruhr coal producers planning to join the sales cartel supply no more than 11.37% of the primary energy consumed in the Common Market. In his calculation, however, Boerner includes all other sources of energy (lignite, liquid fuels, natural gas, water-power). The question, answered in the negative by the High Authority, whether the significance of other sources of energy can be taken into account when calculating the market share in accordance with E.C.S.C. Treaty art. 65(a), is the subject of a suit that the Ruhr coal-producers have brought against the High Authority and which in May, 1961, was still pending before the Court of Justice (Affair No. 13/60).
[50] E.C.S.C. Treaty art. 65(4).
[51] E.E.C. Treaty art. 85(2).

an authority in one of the Member States would be of no more than a declaratory nature. According to another school of thought, article 85(2) is to be interpreted as meaning that nullity would result only from the authority having found that an infringement of article 85(1) had occurred.[52] The Commission has refrained from commenting upon this problem, because a decision on it is not essential for the evolution and implementation of the cartel policy of the Communities. The determination of the date from which onward the agreements or decisions prohibited under the Treaty become null and void is of importance mainly for the interrelation of the parties to any such cartel agreement, but not for any outsiders with whom the members of the cartel have entered into transactions. The Commission believes that the decision in this matter should be left to the competent courts, all the more since the Commission itself would not be able to make a binding declaration one way or the other.[53]

IV

Market-Dominating Positions and Monopolies

Whereas the cartel prohibition rules in the two Treaties coincide on many points, their provisions on monopolies differ in essence.[54]

Under the E.C.S.C. Treaty, any concentration of enterprises of which at least one is engaged in production in the field of coal and steel within the meaning of article eighty[55] is subject to prior authorization by the High Authority. Where a concentration has been concluded that has not been authorized and that cannot be authorized retrospectively, the High Authority will exercise its powers to ensure the separation of the enterprises thus concentrated and to restore their independence.

The complicated procedure laid down in article 66(5) shows the difference between the criteria for article sixty-five and article sixty-six: a concentration cannot simply be "revoked" or regarded as "null and void."

Articles sixty-five and sixty-six differ further in that article sixty-six is concerned with "transactions" and not with agreements intended to have continuing operative effect. Therefore, article sixty-six applies only to transactions that occur after the entry into force of the Treaty. Any prior concentrations—and also enterprises that obtain a market-dominating position without having entered into any transaction that is subject to authorization—are merely placed under supervision intended to prevent any abuse of their power in the market.[56]

All transactions leading to the concentration of several enterprises are subject to

---

[52] The Netherlands Regulation under the E.E.C. Treaty art. 88, Dec. 5, 1957, [1957] NETHERLANDS OFFICIAL GAZETTE 1070, is based on this view.

[53] Cf. E.E.C. COMMISSION, SECOND GENERAL REPORT 87 (German version) (1959); FEDERAL CARTEL OFFICE, op. cit. supra note 25, at 56. But see, for divergent opinion, WOHLFARHT ET AL., op. cit. supra note 3, art. 88 n.4c.

[54] E.C.S.C. Treaty art. 66; cf. supra note 12; E.E.C. Treaty, art. 86; cf. supra note 21.

[55] Cf. supra note 13 and accompanying text.

[56] E.C.S.C. Treaty art. 66(7).

authorization. "Concentration" is to be understood as meaning not only fusion, but any condition in which several enterprises come under a unified control. Article sixty-six quotes several examples of such transactions, amongst them the acquisition of shares or assets, contracts, or any other means of control. The concept of control, which thus is of decisive importance for the criteria governing concentration—the condition brought about as a result of the transaction—has been defined in greater detail by an ordinance of the High Authority.[57]

The concept covers horizontal concentrations—*i.e.*, concentrations of enterprises on the same level of production and in the same economic category—as well as vertical concentrations in which the end product of one enterprise is the basic product of another. As stated above, it is sufficient if one of the enterprises involved falls within the definition given in the Treaty; therefore, a concentration between a steelworks and a shipping line or a finance company is subject to authorization.

Nor does it make any difference whether a concentration is brought about directly or indirectly. If an enterprise *A* already controls enterprises *B* and *C*, and enterprise *X* already controls enterprises *Y* and *Z*, a concentration of *A* and *X* is a concentration of *all* the enterprises named, so that the market position of the whole complex of enterprises must be considered.

The requirement of prior authorization is to give the High Authority control over all cases of concentration and to enable it to prevent any too far-reaching concentration of economic power, which would considerably impede competition within the Common Market. Under an authorization contained in the Treaty,[58] the High Authority has, with the approval of the Council of Ministers, listed in an ordinance[59] a number of concentrations not requiring authorization, since they are not likely to give rise to a major distortion of competition within the Common Market.

Where a concentration has occurred without prior authorization having been obtained, the High Authority can grant such authorization retrospectively, but makes this subject to the payment of a fine.[60] Where a concentration has occurred that is not eligible for authorization, the High Authority, in rendering a decision denouncing this concentration as illegal, orders the above mentioned deconcentration procedure to be initiated.[61]

In the field of concentrations, the High Authority has so far dealt with 136 cases (seventy-four upon application and sixty-two ex officio). In fifty-five cases, it was found that no concentration within the meaning of article sixty-six had occurred; in twelve cases, the concentrations had already existed before the entry into force of the Treaty, so that article sixty-six does not apply; four cases fell within the

---

[57] Ordinance of the High Authority, No. 24/54, May 6, 1954, [1954] Journal Officiel 345; *cf.* *supra* note 12 (at the end).
[58] E.C.S.C. Treaty art. 66(3).
[59] Ordinance of the High Authority No. 25/54, May 6, 1954, [1954] Journal Officiel 346, in the version of Decision of the High Authority No. 28/54, May 26, 1954, *id.* at 381.
[60] E.C.S.C. Treaty art. 66(6).
[61] *Id.* art. 66(5).

exemption ordinance;[62] thirty-eight concentrations were authorized, one in retrospect. The remaining cases are still under consideration.[63]

In addition to the prior control of concentration, the E.C.S.C. Treaty also provides for the control of market-dominating enterprises. One or several enterprises will have to be regarded as dominating the market[64] if they are not subject to genuine competition—at least in respect of certain goods or services. Such a position can come about:

a. as a result of a concentration already in effect when the E.C.S.C. Treaty came into force;
b. through the evolution of a concentration of enterprises authorized by the High Authority; or
c. through an enterprise growing and acquiring unusual importance—perhaps because of some exceptional technical achievement.

If the High Authority finds that such a market-dominating enterprise uses its position for purposes incompatible with the Treaty, it will address the appropriate recommendations to such enterprise.[65] If these recommendations are not satisfactorily complied with within a reasonable period, the High Authority is empowered to take very far-reaching measures[66] after consultation with the Government concerned.

The E.E.C. Treaty does not provide any prior control of concentrations, but only prohibits the abuse of a dominant position within the Common Market, or within a substantial part of it, by one or more enterprises to the extent to which trade between Member States may be impaired thereby.

Like the cartel prohibition in article eighty-five, the prohibition of the abuse of a dominant position within the Common Market applies only to the extent that such

---

[62] *Cf. supra* note 59.

[63] It should be noted that within the E.C.S.C. 35 enterprises account for 80% of steel production, the largest of these enterprises being responsible for 6%; whereas in the United States, no more than 10 enterprises share 80% of steel production, two of them accounting for 45%. If the High Authority had authorized the merger between August-Thyssen-Huette-AG. and the Phoenix-Rheinrohr-AG. planned at the beginning of 1960 (the applicants have withdrawn their request because they were not prepared to accept certain conditions set by the High Authority), the new enterprise resulting from this fusion would, with an annual capacity of more than 5,000,000 tons, have become by far the largest within the E.C.S.C. By American standards, an enterprise of that magnitude is, however, in no way remarkable. *Cf.* Peter Bart, *Control Dispute Halts Bonn Steel Merger,* N.Y. Times, May 8, 1960, § 3, p. 1, cols. 1-4, p. 13, cols. 2-3.

[64] *Cf.* Restriction of Competition (Prevention) Act (GWB) § 22(1), July 27, 1957, [1957] 1 Bundesgesetzblatt 1081 (Ger. Fed. Rep.). Under the Belgian Law on Protection Against the Abuse of Economic Power § 1, May 27, 1960, [1960] Moniteur Belge 4674, economic power is the ability of a natural person or a body corporate, or a group of such persons acting in concert, to exert, by means of industrial, commercial, agricultural, or financial activities, a preponderant influence on supplies to the commodity or capital market, or on the price or the quality of a commodity or a service.

[65] E.C.S.C. Treaty art. 66(7). Under E.C.S.C. Treaty art. 14(3), recommendations by the High Authority shall be binding with respect to the objectives that they specify, but shall leave to those to whom they are directed the choice of appropriate means for attaining these objectives. They are, therefore, similar to the directives issued under E.E.C. Treaty art. 189, which, however, can be addressed to Member States only. *Cf. supra* note 19. Recommendations issued under the E.E.C. Treaty are not binding. E.E.C. Treaty art. 189(5).

[66] *Cf.* E.C.S.C. Treaty art. 66(7) (for full text, see *supra* note 12). The High Authority has not, so far, availed itself of these powers.

abuse may impair the trade between Member States. The Treaty, therefore, is not concerned with monopolies of only local effect and, accordingly, leaves it to the Member States whether or not they wish to tolerate such monopolies.

As article eighty-five does in the case of the prohibition of cartels, so article eighty-six recites a number of particularly characteristic examples of improper advantages taken of a dominant position. They include the direct or indirect imposition of any inequitable purchase or selling prices or any other inequitable trading conditions; the limitation of production, markets, or technical development to the prejudice of consumers; the application to parties to transactions of unequal terms in respect of equivalent supplies—as in the case of the cartel prohibition, to the extent that thereby such parties are placed at a competitive disadvantage; and finally, the subjecting of the conclusion of a contract to the acceptance, by a party, of additional supplies that, either by their nature or according to commercial usage, have no connection with the subject of such contract. This latter example represents a particularly characteristic and, at the same time, dangerous type of the abuse of monopoly power.

In principle, the prohibition provisions of both Treaties apply to all enterprises, irrespective of whether they are privately or publicly owned. In the E.E.C. Treaty, however, account had to be taken of the fact that it covers enterprises charged with the management of services of general economic interest, and that in some Member States, there exist fiscal monopolies that, by the sale of commodities, provide revenue for the State.[67]

Such enterprises are subject to the Treaty rules on competition to the extent only that the application thereof does not obstruct the *de jure* or *de facto* fulfillment of the specific tasks entrusted to them.[68] The public utilities will have to be regarded as the main enterprises charged with the management of services of general economic interest, since—by concession—they supply the population with essential commodities, such as power, gas, and water. In the case of such enterprises, market sharing, for instance, is a regular necessity, because it would be technically and economically unreasonable if, say, several electrical power companies were to endeavor to supply consumers in the same area. In granting enterprises of this nature exemption from the rule, the criterion is not whether they are privately or publicly owned, but solely that they must be charged with the management of services of general economic interest.

The same exemption holds good for fiscal monopolies to the extent that the application of the rules of competition would prevent them from fulfilling their special function. Article eighty-six, therefore, does not provide any basis for charging the French and Italian tobacco monopolies with imposing inequitable selling prices, because it is is the very function of these monopolies, by fixing their prices, to obtain a high surplus for the benefit of the national budget. The exception made

---

[67] Fiscal monopolies exist in the Federal Republic of Germany (for spirits and matches) and in France and Italy. The tobacco monopolies in the latter two countries are of outstanding importance.
[68] E.E.C. Treaty arts. 85-94. *Cf. supra* notes 15-17.

by the Treaty in favor of enterprises charged with the management of services of general economic interest and of enterprises having the character of a fiscal monopoly is restricted by the stipulation that development of trade must not be affected to such a degree as would be contrary to the interests of the Community. Under this provision, it would not be proper for the tobacco monopolies to refuse to acquire and sell tobacco goods from other Member States, because they can well fulfill their function of providing national revenue through their monopoly by selling, at the appropriate prices, tobacco goods produced in other Member States. On the other hand, these monopoly administrations, which run their own factories, can hardly be expected to close these down in order to purchase and sell produce from the other Member States. The problems connected with the implementation of this provision are at present the subject of negotiations between the Commission and the Governments concerned.

The existing national trading monopolies must be gradually so modified by the Member States that at the end of the transition period,[69] all discrimination in the conditions governing supplies and sales between the nationals of the Member States will have been abolished.

V

Competence

Under the E.C.S.C. Treaty, the High Authority is exclusively competent for the implementation of the rules on competition; in certain circumstances only, must it consult the Governments of the Member States.[70]

Under the E.E.C. Treaty, on the other hand, there exists concurrent competence between the Commission and the authorities of the Member States—at least until the implementing regulations under article eighty-seven are issued.[71] The Treaty provides that until the entry into force of the implementing regulations, the authorities of the Member States shall, in accordance with their respective municipal law and with the provisions of articles eighty-five and eighty-six, rule upon the admissibility of agreements, decisions, and concerted practices and upon any improper advantage taken of a dominant position in the Common Market.[72]

To the extent, therefore, that lacunae will exist until the implementing regulations under article eighty-seven have been issued, the Treaty refers to the municipal law of the Member States.[73] This applies, in the first place, to questions of pro-

---

[69] E.E.C. Treaty art. 8. *Cf. supra* note 32.
[70] E.C.S.C. Treaty arts. 65(4)2 and 66(1).
[71] Under art. 66(2)4, the High Authority must ask for the observations of the interested Government in the case of concentrations in which at least one of the enterprises concerned is not subject to the application of E.C.S.C. Treaty art. 80. *Cf. supra* note 13.
[72] E.E.C. Treaty art. 88.
[73] The following provisions are at present in force in the various Member States:
Belgium—Lois sur la Protection contre l'Abus de la Puissance Economique, May 27, 1960.
Federal Republic of Germany—Gesetz gegen Wettbewerbsbeschränkungen, July 27, 1957.
France—Ordinance No. 53-704, Aug. 9, 1953, supplemented by Ordinances Nos. 58-545, June 24, 1958, and 59-1004, Aug. 17, 1959.

cedure, but also to the settlement of matters such as the formalities governing the conclusion of agreements within the meaning of article eighty-five, the question of whether agreements or decisions are to be notified and registered, under what conditions those concerned can withdraw from cartel arrangements, and so on.

The authorities of the Member States are to apply their municipal law in accordance with articles eighty-five and eighty-six. Since these articles apply only in cases where the prohibited agreements or decisions or the abuse of a dominant position are likely to impair trade between the Member States, no problem arises where these conditions, on which the application of these articles depends, are not fulfilled. In consequence, the authorities of the Member States have to apply only their own municipal provisions to agreements that do not affect trade between the Member States. To the extent that trade between the Member States is impaired—which is likely to be the case with increasing frequency as the establishment of the Common Market progresses—the authorities of the Member States will also apply their municipal law until the implementing regulations under article eighty-seven shall have entered into force. But in doing so, they must, at the same time, take into account the principles contained in articles eighty-five and eighty-six. Where, for instance, the municipal anticartel provisions allow an exception in favor of export cartels, the authorities of the Member States may no longer grant this exception if such an export cartel is likely to impair the trade between the Member States. The provision in municipal law allowing export cartels is based on the consideration that it is of no concern to the internal market if producers of certain goods agree on the fixing of prices or the sharing of markets when exporting their produce to other countries. Since the entry into force of the E.E.C. Treaty, this point of view is no longer fully justified, since the interest of the Community is affected if an export cartel in one Member State fixes prices for exports into other Member States or if the markets in the other Member States are allocated. The authorities of the Member States may, therefore, under article eighty-eight only continue to apply their municipal provisions on the admissibility of export cartels in accordance with article eighty-five, and they may only tolerate export cartels if they export their goods into nonmember countries.[74]

From the inception of its work, the Commission has been charged with the function to ensure that the principles laid down in articles eighty-five and eighty-six are translated into practice.[75] In fulfillment of this function, the Commission, acting either upon the request of a Member State or ex officio—*e.g.*, on a complaint received from an enterprise aggrieved by cartel agreements or by the abuse of a dominant position—examines all those cases in which an infringement of articles eighty-five

---

The Netherlands—Wet Economische Mededing, July 16, 1958.
In Italy and Luxembourg, no cartel legislation proper has yet been introduced. The Italian Government submitted a draft antimonopoly law to Parliament on Nov. 28, 1959. A Luxembourg draft is being prepared.

[74] WOHLFARHT ET AL., *op. cit. supra* note 3, art. 88 n.6.
[75] E.E.C. Treaty art. 89.

and eighty-six is suspected. The Commission carries out such examinations in cooperation with the competent authorities of the Member States, which are obliged to assist it. At present, the Commission is investigating a number of cases brought to its knowledge by complaints. Should the Commission find that the principles of articles eighty-five and eighty-six have been infringed, it proposes the appropriate steps to remedy the situation. As a rule, the Commission will have to address these recommendations to the enterprises concerned in the agreement. Under article eighty-nine, the Commission is not empowered to compel those concerned to cease the infringement.[75a] If the infringement is continued, the Commission will issue a reasoned decision, declaring such an infringement to exist. The Commission can, moreover, publish its decision and authorize the Member States to carry out the necessary remedies, the conditions and details of which it lays down. It is to be assumed that the publication of a Commission decision declaring that articles eighty-five and eighty-six have been infringed would have a considerable moral effect.

It is important to note that the competence vested in the Commission under article eighty-nine, in contrast to the competence of the authorities of the Member States under article eighty-eight, is not restricted to the period until the entry into effect of the implementing regulations under article eighty-seven of the Treaty. Even if these implementing regulations were completely to transfer the application of articles eighty-five and eighty-six to the authorities of the Member States, the Commission would still retain its function of ensuring that the principles contained in articles eighty-five and eighty-six are translated into practice; to this end, the Commission would continue to initiate its own investigations.

VI

Appeals

The Court of Justice of the Communities[76] ensures observance of law and justice in the interpretation and application of the Treaties.[77] Under article thirty-three of the E.C.S.C. Treaty, enterprises may plead for the annulment of individual decisions and recommendations affecting them, or of general decisions and recommendations that they deem to involve an abuse of power affecting them, on the grounds of lack of legal competence, major violations of procedure, violation of the Treaty or of any rule of law relating to its application, or abuse of power. However, the Court may not review the High Authority's evaluation of the situation, based on economic facts and circumstances, that led to such decisions or recommendations, except where the High Authority is alleged to have abused its powers or to have clearly misinterpreted the provisions of the Treaty or of a rule of law relating to its application.[78] An appeal to the general jurisdiction of the Court may be lodged against

---

[75a] The draft of the first implementing regulation provides for a power in the Commission to issue decisions against enterprises or associations of enterprises (art. 8).
[76] See *supra* note 5.
[77] E.C.S.C. Treaty art. 31; E.E.C. Treaty art. 164; Euratom Treaty art. 136.
[78] E.C.S.C. Treaty art. 33.

the pecuniary sanctions and daily penalty payments imposed under the provisions of the Treaty. The petitioners may contest the legality of the decisions and recommendations that they are charged with violating.[79]

The provisions of the E.E.C. Treaty concerning appeals to the Court against Commission decisions are similar to the corresponding provisions in the E.C.S.C. Treaty.[80] The E.E.C. Treaty, however, does not provide any restrictions of the Court's review so far as the evaluation of the situation based on economic facts and circumstances is concerned.

So far as the authorities of the Member States are called upon to implement the rules of competition laid down in the Treaty,[81] appeals against their decisions must, under article eighty-eight, be lodged in accordance with the municipal law of the individual Member State. So far as the competent courts in the Member States must, in so doing, take action predicated on an interpretation of the rules of competition laid down in the Treaty, the Court of Justice of the Communities is competent to make preliminary decisions. Under article 177, any court in one of the Member States may place any doubt about the interpretation of the Treaty before the Court of Justice, if it considers that its judgment depends on a preliminary decision on this question. Where any such question is raised in a case pending before a domestic court from whose decisions no appeal lies under municipal law, such court is obliged to refer the matter to the Court of Justice.[82] Article 177 thus ensures uniform interpretation of the Treaty and prevents differences in the conditions of competition from existing in the various Member States as a result of varying interpretations by the authorities or courts in them.

Summary

Both the E.C.S.C. Treaty and the E.E.C. Treaty contain rules of competition in respect of enterprises. Both Treaties prohibit agreements among enterprises, decisions by associations of enterprises, and any concerted practices leading to a prevention, restriction, or distortion of competition within the Common Market.

The prohibition contained in the E.C.S.C. Treaty applies to all agreements, decisions, and concerted practices of enterprises engaged in the production or distribution in the field of coal and steel (with the exception of sales to domestic consumers or craft industries). The E.E.C. Treaty, which applies to all other branches of the economy, prohibits cartel practices only to the extent that they are likely to impede trade among the Member States.

Both Treaties provide that agreements, decisions, or concerted practices may be authorized under relatively strict conditions.

[79] *Id* art. 36(3).
[80] E.E.C. Treaty arts. 172 and 173; Euratom Treaty arts. 144 and 146.
[81] E.E.C. Treaty art. 88. *Cf. supra* note 72 and accompanying text.
[82] A somewhat similar procedure is foreseen by the Basic Law of the Federal Republic of Germany, art. 100(1), May 23, 1949, [1949] 1 Bundesgesetzblatt 1 (Ger. Fed. Rep.). This provision obliges the courts to ask for a preliminary decision of the Federal Constitutional Court when they have doubt as to the compatibility of a Federal or State law with the Basic Law and when their judgment depends on the validity of such a law.

The E.C.S.C. Treaty makes concentrations of enterprises subject to prior approval by the High Authority if at least one of the enterprises concerned is a coal and steel enterprise. The E.E.C. Treaty, on the other hand, prescribes no prior control of concentrations, but merely prohibits the abuse of a dominant position in the Common Market, and that only if it is likely to impede trade among the Member States.

Under the E.C.S.C. Treaty, the High Authority is exclusively competent for the implementation of the rules of competition. Under the E.E.C. Treaty, these are exclusively applicable by the authorities of the Member States until implementing regulations are issued; nevertheless, the Commission is already charged with ensuring that these rules are translated into practice. The implementing regulations to be issued can confer unto the Commission a further reaching competence in the application of the rules on competition laid down in the Treaty.

THE RULES OF COMPETITION WITHIN THE EUROPEAN COMMON MARKET*

FERNAND SPAAK[†] AND JEAN N. JAEGER[‡]

Although this article deals with two different Treaties, concluded at different periods and for different products, it actually refers to the Common Market of one single European Community. Furthermore, the Common Market is not the simple juxtaposition or the simple addition of the national markets of Germany, Belgium, France, Italy, Luxembourg, and the Netherlands; the implementation of the European Treaties aims at the integration of these separate markets, the European Common Market being the basis of a new economic unit, the European Community.

This unity is already reflected at the institutional level in the existence of a single Court of Justice and a single Parliament for the Community.[1] Furthermore, the Council of Ministers consisting of one member from each of the six Governments, is likewise a common institution of the three Communities, although the Ministers meeting for the European Economic Community (E.E.C.) or the European Coal and Steel Community (E.C.S.C.) are not the same in each case, nor are the powers conferred on the Council the same under each of the two Treaties.

The rules of competition illustrate clearly the unity of the Common Market, based as they are on the same principles of economic policy. The fact that, in practice, these rules are applied by different institutions—for the E.C.S.C., High Authority, and for the E.E.C., the national authorities, the Commission, and the Council of Ministers—cannot disrupt this unity because, on the one hand, the parliamentary control and, accordingly, the political impulse lie within the jurisdiction of one and the same Parliamentary Assembly; and because, on the other hand, the

---

* The writers have, over the last few years, been intimately associated with the implementation of the rules of competition within the European Common Market. Their professional work has enabled them to observe very closely the gradual development of a corpus of legal precedents, administrative and juridical. To avoid the risk of their account being regarded as an official interpretation and to enable them to express their opinion as freely as possible, they have chosen to write this article entirely on their personal responsibility.

† Docteur en droit 1948, University of Brussels; B.A. 1950, Cambridge University. Director, Cartels and Concentrations Division, High Authority of the European Coal and Steel Community; Director-General, Supply Agency, European Atomic Energy Community. Secretary, Economic Division, High Authority of the European Coal and Steel Community, 1952-54; Executive Assistant to the President, 1954-58; Deputy Director, Cartels and Concentrations Division, 1958-60.

‡ Ingénieur Commercial 1951, University of Brussels. Principal Officer, Cartels and Concentrations Division, High Authority of the European Coal and Steel Community.

[1] Although the Treaty instituting Euratom provides for the establishment of a Common Market, it contains no rules of competition applicable to the enterprises, and this for the following reasons:
   (1) The nuclear industry is only being created, and this creation requires a very close cooperation from the scientific, industrial, and financial point of view.
   (2) The supply of fissionable materials, under equal conditions, is assured by the supply agency as directed by the Euratom Commission.
   (3) The use of the materials is under control; Euratom assures the coordination of research and promotes the creation of common enterprises.

jurisprudence must, of necessity, be unified by the judgments of a single Court of Justice.

In order to demonstrate the unity of the Common Market more effectively, the writers will describe the rules of competition of the two Treaties not separately, but side by side, thereby underlining their identity and the points on which, for technical and economic reasons, a differentiation has, nevertheless, been unavoidable.

In contrast to the national laws on competition, the rules of competition of the Common Market are directed at the behavior of the States as well as at the behavior of the enterprises. The intention of the authors of the Treaty having been to create a genuine Common Market, it would, indeed, have been vain to subject enterprises to rules while allowing state monopolies or laws and government measures—such as subsidies or restrictions on trade—to persist. The Treaties provide for the amendment or prohibition of government measures which prevent the integration of the national markets as effectively as practices of the enterprises. In order not to exceed the scope of this article, however, the writers will confine themselves to the rules of competition as they apply to the enterprises.

I

The Principles of Competition within the Common Market

There is a fundamental difference between the basic principles of the rules of competition instituted under national laws and those laid down in a treaty establishing a common market. National laws are laid down after the national market has been in existence for some considerable time. National laws have exclusively the purpose of protecting the consumer and the general interest. They are founded either upon economic principles or upon ethical grounds of equality and liberty, in line with the aspirations and the way of life of the inhabitants of the country. Competition thus becomes an end in itself, and the laws serve to attain this end.

Where it is proposed to introduce a common market, however, the process is completely reversed. Rules of competition are laid down in advance—*i.e.*, before the common market has come into being. To introduce a common market among several countries, it is not enough to abolish customs duties and quotas, to harmonize economic and currency policies, and to achieve a harmonized transport policy, if enterprises continue to be confined within their former national borders, out of tradition, habit, or simply intertia. There can obviously be no question of compelling the enterprises to act against their own will, but it is necessary to lay down rules of behavior that will allow enterprises and consumers to respond freely and on equal terms to the new economic incentives offered by the common market. These rules are designed to make it impossible to circumvent the measures establishing the common market and, in particular, to restore impediments to trade by practices restricting or distorting competition.

With the establishment of a common market as the objective, competition is, therefore, not an end in itself, but one of the main instruments of an economic policy aiming at the integration of the markets. Competition has been chosen as the motive force of the economic revolution that is to promote the interpenetration of several national economies, prisoners for centuries of their different structures, different traditions and habits, and merge them in a new economic entity, the European Common Market.

The main consequence of the subordination of competition to the purpose of establishing a common market is that the rules of the Treaties do not aim at introducing or maintaining any kind of competition. It is not a question of competition at any price, but of creating the degree of competition required to attain the objectives of the Treaties. Excessive competition leading to fundamental disequilibria or to disturbances in the economy of the Member States, especially in the social field, must be prevented.

This limitation placed on the concept of competition, which deprives it of its dogmatic character, is defined in article two of both Treaties setting forth the objectives to be attained. According to the E.C.S.C. Treaty, the Community must "progressively establish conditions which will in themselves assure the most rational distribution of production at the highest possible level of productivity, while safeguarding the continuity of employment and avoiding the creation of fundamental and persistent disturbances in the economies of the member States." Under the E.E.C. Treaty, the aim is "to promote throughout the Community a harmonious development of economic activities, an accelerated raising of the standard of living and closer relations between its Member States."

Thus, while the conception of competition is similar in both cases, the formulation is not identical in the two Treaties. It is, therefore, necessary to pinpoint the differences existing between the rules of competition in the two Treaties and to explain why these rules are more detailed, more precise, and more extensive in the E.C.S.C. Treaty than they are in the E.E.C. Treaty.

II

The Fundamental Differences between the Two Treaties

The outstanding difference, which logically involves all the other differentiations, stems from the fact that the E.C.S.C. Treaty establishes a Community for two basic industries only, coal and steel, while the E.E.C. Treaty establishes a Community comprising all the other sectors of economic activity.

Though limited to two industries, the economic integration provided for in the E.C.S.C. Treaty affects the basic sector of the economy. In its endeavor to create, by the integration of these two industries, at the European level a common basis for industrial expansion and further economic integration, the E.C.S.C. establishes a "pool" of coal and steel production. It is the pooling of production into a single whole that explains why the Treaty gives the High Authority definite powers in the field of production, investment, and prices.

This notion of "pool" of production could no longer apply when it came to the integration of the entire economy of the six countries. It was no longer a question of partial integration, limited to basic industries. In fact, it would not have been possible to transfer to an executive organ such wide powers over the whole economy of the six countries while leaving to the Governments of the States the political responsibility involved. The political unification of Europe has not as yet reached the stage where full political responsibility for economic policy can be vested in a single European Executive.

This difference explains the wording of the above-mentioned passage of article two of the E.C.S.C. Treaty, "the most rational distribution of production," which does not figure in the corresponding article of the E.E.C. Treaty.

The notion of a "pool" also explains why article three of the E.C.S.C. Treaty assigns to the institutions certain tasks that are not equally clearly defined in the E.E.C. Treaty. These tasks are worth quoting, since they show the scope and limitations of competition under the E.C.S.C. Treaty. According to this article, the institutions of the Community shall:

a) ensure that the common market is regularly supplied, while taking into account the needs of third countries;
b) assure to all consumers in comparable positions within the common market equal access to the sources of production;
c) seek the establishment of the lowest possible prices without involving any corresponding rise either in the prices charged by the same enterprises in other transactions or in the price-level as a whole in another period, while at the same time permitting necessary amortization and providing the possibility of normal returns on invested capital;
d) ensure that conditions are maintained which will encourage enterprises to expand and improve their ability to produce and to promote a policy of rational development of national resources, while avoiding undue exhaustion of such resources;
e) promote the improvement of the living and working conditions of the labor force in each of the industries under its jurisdiction so as to harmonize those conditions in an upward direction;
f) foster the development of international trade and ensure that equitable limits are observed in prices charged in foreign markets;
g) promote the regular expansion and the modernization of production as well as the improvement of quality, under conditions which preclude any protection against competing industries except where justified by illegitimate action on the part of such industries or in their favor.

If these tasks were carried out separately and independently of one another, conflicting results would be produced. The institutions must, therefore, do their utmost to combine them in order to achieve in the Member States the highest possible level of employment, the highest rate of economic expansion, and the highest standard of living. Therein lies the scope of their economic policy. The need for this constant conciliation of apparently contradictory objectives shows that no one of them can be regarded as sufficient by itself. Therefore, competition among enterprises is not a dogma in the Treaty. It is not to be introduced for its own sake.

For instance, to ensure the accomplishment of the tasks set forth in article three of the E.C.S.C. Treaty, the institutions are empowered, in exceptional circumstances of "manifest crisis" or shortage, to fix maximum or minimum prices, to institute financial arrangements, and to fix production quotas by countries and by enterprises.

It can thus be seen that the institutions of the Community can reduce, and even abolish, competition in serious circumstances and for definite periods. The intention has been to create a solidarity within the Community, freeing the enterprises from the major risks of competition, which would endanger the welfare of the workers and the very existence of the Community.

In return, contrary to certain national laws that enable the enterprises to conclude cartel agreements in times of serious cyclical or structural recession, the E.C.S.C. Treaty does not allow the enterprises themselves to restrict competition simply for the purpose of coping with such situations.

In the E.E.C. Treaty, apart from the quoted passage of article two, the fundamental provisions do not stipulate more detailed limits to the principles of competition. As we shall see, however, the rules of competition as laid down in that Treaty contain yet another limitation that does not exist in the E.C.S.C. Treaty: restrictions on competition are prohibited only in so far as they affect trade between the Member States.

This difference is likewise explained by the different nature of the economic activities that fall under the two Treaties. In the heavy industries of coal and steel, where the great majority of the enterprises are located within the triangle formed by the Ruhr, Lorraine, Northern France and Belgium, practically any action restricting competition directly or indirectly affects the trade between Member States. This explains why the rules of competition are more extensive in the E.C.S.C. Treaty than they are in the E.E.C. Treaty. On the other hand, numerous practices or actions restricting competition in the other sectors of economic activity have a purely local effect, without in any way affecting the establishment or the functioning of the Common Market. In both Treaties, the principle remains the same: they regulate competition only in so far as this is necessary to the Common Market.

Like the E.C.S.C. Treaty, the E.E.C. Treaty does not provide for the possibility of coping with situations of glut or shortage by means of agreements between enterprises. The Governments have retained the requisite powers in regard to prices, while the Treaty embodies safeguards for dealing with exceptional economic or financial difficulties.[2]

Another major consequence of this difference between partial integration based on the pooling of productions and a broader integration with no such pooling, is the different allocation of powers among the institutions responsible for the implementation of the rules of competition. In the E.C.S.C. Treaty, the High Authority alone has the requisite executive power. Under the E.E.C. Treaty, which is more concerned

---

[2] The Treaty provides for permanent action designed to produce a common economic policy. Precautionary measures and government action cannot, therefore, go beyond what is strictly necessary and must be confined to the needs of the Community in line with the procedures laid down in the Treaty.

with the framing of a common economic policy for the entire economy of the six countries, the executive power is normally shared by the Commission and the Council of Ministers; but in regard to matters concerning competition, several other bodies also have jurisdiction, as, for instance, the national authorities[3] and the Court of Justice (whose powers in this sphere remain to be defined). The rules of competition of the E.E.C. Treaty cover restrictions on competition only in so far as they affect trade between Member States. The Governments have, however, retained the power to regulate competition within their respective territories. Conflicts of law between the rules of the Treaty and the national legislation might occur. For this reason, and to ensure a nondiscriminatory application of the rules throughout the Community, the Treaty provides for close collaboration between the national and supranational authorities in matters concerning competition.[4]

III

The Fundamental Rules of Competition

A distinction has to be made in both Treaties between the fundamental articles setting forth the principles and representing, as it were, the Constitution of the Community, and the other articles, which are nothing more than the development and codification of the principles laid down in the fundamental articles.

The fundamental rules of competition are laid down very clearly in article four of the E.C.S.C. Treaty, which says:

The following are recognized to be incompatible with the Common Market for coal and steel, and are, therefore, abolished and prohibited within the Community in the manner set forth by this Treaty:

. . . .

b) by measures or practices discriminating among producers, among buyers and among consumers, especially as concerns prices, delivery terms and transport rates, as well as measures or practices which hamper the buyer in the free choice of his supplier;

. . . .

d) restrictive practices tending towards the division or the exploitation of the markets.

Article five of the E.C.S.C. Treaty lists the means the Community is to employ in the execution of its tasks and specifies that it shall "assure the establishment, the maintenance and the observance of normal conditions of competition."

In the E.E.C. Treaty, the principles underlying the rules of competition are much less elaborate. According to article 3(f), the activities of the Community shall include "the establishment of a system ensuring that competition shall not be distorted in the common market."

---

[3] The authority of the national authorities is provided for by the E.E.C. Treaty only until the rules that shall be laid down on the basis of art. 87 come into force. The question as to whether and how far the national authorities shall keep this authority has been left open in the E.E.C. Treaty, although it is rather certain that a centralization of the powers has been anticipated.

[4] Independently of the coordination needed in regard to the application of the rules of competition of the Treaty, harmonization of national laws may be arrived at under art. 100 of the E.E.C. Treaty, should this prove necessary to the establishment or functioning of the Common Market. See Grisoli, *The Impact of the European Economic Community on the Movement of the Unification of Law, supra,* at 418.

Rules of Competition

All the rules of competition of both Treaties are based on these principles. They are grouped here in four categories, according to the type of conduct they regulate—namely, (1) discrimination, unfair competition, and prices; (2) cartels; (3) concentrations; and (4) abuses of power.

A. Discrimination, Unfair Competition, and Prices

1. *Discrimination*

For the establishment and the functioning of a common market, the notion of discrimination is of much greater importance than it is in connection with a law designed to safeguard competition in one country only. There are two aspects to this notion. First, the aspect of restraint of competition, which can be found in certain laws, more especially in the legislation of the United States. Secondly, there is a more general and more important aspect that superimposes itself on the first: equal treatment of all consumers whatever their nationalities.

For the Common Market to develop into a new economic unit, it is necessary that differences in nationality should be disregarded and should no longer involve different treatment in industrial or commercial activities. The principle of nondiscrimination on these lines is important. Regardless of the effect this principle may have on competition, national prejudices and habits, deep-rooted for centuries in the different countries, must be overcome so as to enable everyone to enjoy on an equal footing the advantages of the new Common Market.

From this angle, the rule of nondiscrimination is no longer a rule of competition, but an absolute principle of equality, by which the enterprises as well as the Governments must be compelled to abide.

This dual conception of discrimination in a common market established between six different countries is clearly underlined in the E.E.C. Treaty. Article seven prohibits "any discrimination on the grounds of nationality." But article seven is not a rule of competition. It is one of the fundamental articles in the first part of the Treaty, entitled "Principles." Nondiscrimination on grounds of nationality is, therefore, a constitutional principle that applies to the Member States and to the institutions of the Community as much as it does to the enterprises.[5]

Independently of and over this general prohibition of discrimination on grounds of nationality, the prohibition of discrimination also figures in the rules of competition. In so far as the trade between the Member States is affected, the E.E.C. Treaty prohibits discrimination only if it is the result of an agreement or a concerted practice

---

[5] As regards the E.C.S.C. Treaty, the judgments of the Court of Justice have underlined the fact that the High Authority is required to comply with the fundamental articles of the Treaty (arts. 2-5), including the principle of nondiscrimination. *Cf.* Gouvernement de la République Française v. Haute Autorité, Cour de Justice de la C.E.C.A., Dec. No. 1-54, 1 Recueil de la jurisprudence de la Cour 13 (1954-55) [hereinafter cited as Rec]; Groupement des Industries Sidérurgiques Luxembourgeoises v. Haute Autorité, Cour de Justice de la C.E.C.A., Dec. No. 7-54, 2 *id.* 53 (1955-56); Groupement des Hauts-Fourneaux et Aciéries Belges v. Haute Autorité, Cour de Justice de la C.E.C.A., Dec. No. 8-57, 4 *id.* 230 (1957-58).

between enterprises[6] or if it is caused by an enterprise occupying a dominant position in the market.[7]

The E.E.C. Treaty thus does not contain a rule of competition amounting to a general prohibition of discriminatory practices by individual enterprises. It is not opposed to differentiations in prices and conditions of sale.

The position is quite different under the E.C.S.C. Treaty. No distinction is made between the general prohibition of discrimination on grounds of nationality (which should be a superior principle independent of the rules of competition) and the necessity of prohibiting discriminations where these affect competition. The confusion between these two types of discrimination, plus the fact that the non-discrimination rule has been linked with those concerning unfair competition and prices, have prompted a strict general prohibition that has since proved an obstacle to the establishment of the type of competition envisaged by the Treaty.

In chapter five, containing provisions on prices, article sixty of the E.C.S.C. Treaty develops the principle of nondiscrimination introduced by article four, as follows:

Pricing practices contrary to the provisions of Articles 2, 3 and 4 are prohibited, and in particular:
. . . .
—discriminatory practices involving within the common market the application by a seller of unequal conditions to comparable transactions, especially according to the nationality of the buyer.

This shows how the two types of discrimination have been merged. Although it defines the notion of discrimination, this article does not enumerate discriminatory practices. This is left to the High Authority, which, after consulting the Consultative Committee and the Council, can define these practices. We shall see what use has been made of this power and how the prohibition of the discriminations is enforced when we come to deal with the rules on prices.

It should be noted that prohibition of discrimination is also provided for in article seventy of the E.C.S.C. Treaty, concerning the transport of goods between the territories of the Community countries. This article deals with discriminations according to the country of origin or destination of the goods so transported. Similar provisions concerning transport are contained in article seventy-four of the E.E.C. Treaty.

2. *Unfair competition*

Apart from the prohibition of agreements imposing tying-clauses in business transactions,[8] and the prohibition of dumping practices,[9] which the Commission can bring to an end by issuing recommendations to the parties concerned or by authorizing the injured Member State to take protective measures, the E.E.C. Treaty does not lay down any specific rule concerning unfair competitive practices.

[6] E.E.C. Treaty art. 85.
[7] *Id.* art. 86.
[8] *Id.* art. 85(1)e.
[9] *Id.* art. 91.

In the E.C.S.C. Treaty, article sixty, concerning prices and discriminations, prohibits unfair competitive practices. As an example of unfair practice, this article mentions purely temporary or purely local price reductions, the purpose of which is to acquire a monopoly within the Common Market. These practices, however, are not defined, this being left, as in the case of discriminatory practices, to the High Authority.

3. *Prices*

The E.E.C. Treaty does not lay down any regulations concerning prices when fixed by enterprises individually. Only where prices are fixed by means of agreements or by concerted practices, or where such price-fixing constitutes an abuse of a dominant position, do the provisions of article eighty-five and eighty-six restrict the freedom of action of the enterprises in so far as trade between the Member States may be affected by their action.

In the E.C.S.C. Treaty as it has been seen, both the prohibition of discriminations and of unfair competitive practices introduce an element of rigidity into pricing. This rigidity is further increased by the rules of publicity laid down in article 60(2).

While allowing a basing point for establishing a choice of prices, article 60(2) makes it obligatory for all enterprises to publish, to the extent and in the form prescribed by the High Authority, their price-lists and conditions of sale.

The main concern in laying down these rules was not so much to ensure competition as such, as to secure perfect market transparency in order to assure equal access to the sources of production to all consumers,[10] in particular to consumers of a nationality different from that of the producer; and to make any discrimination and unfair practices, if not impossible, at least very difficult. This absolute principle of nondiscrimination, a vital necessity for abolishing differences of nationality in a common market, has thus been incorporated into the rules of competition.

The choice of basing points was introduced to make allowance for those enterprises that have insufficient local sales possibilities on account of the smallness of their national market. It was thought that the basing points would make it easier for them to penetrate into the Common Market. Probably it was also felt that in view of the fact that most of the enterprises in the Community are concentrated within a relatively small area, a system of basing points did not present any major drawback.

The prices are made less rigid by the fact that article sixty allows enterprises to align their quotations, by means of reductions, with those of competing enterprises whose price-list is established on another basing point. This alignment may be only partial where the discount allowed is smaller than the price-difference between the two competitors, but it cannot be greater than this difference. Consequently, price-competition can only take place either by changing the price-list or by alignment with pricies based on another basing point.[11] The High Authority, however, can

---

[10] E.C.S.C. Treaty art. 3b.
[11] A communication, published in [1954] Journal Officiel de la Communauté Européenne du Charbon et de L'Acier 221 [hereinafter referred to as Journal Officiel], sets out the details of the rules with which the enterprise must comply in regard to price-alignment for sales of steel.

limit or prohibit these alignment practices when this proves necessary in order to avoid disturbances or disequilibria within the market.

Furthermore, the enterprises can align their prices with quotations from enterprises outside the Community. In this case, too, the High Authority, to which such alignments must be reported may limit or prohibit these in case of abuse.

This set of rules has produced a definite pattern of competition. Owing to the close propinquity of the various plants, and because the enterprises are obliged to adhere to their published prices and conditions of sale, the result of these rules has been a rather limited number of basing points, the enterprises in a particular area having generally chosen the same basing point, and a standardization of prices by areas of the Common Market. Competition by alignment discounts, therefore, is essentially competition between industries of different areas, though it also has certain effects on competition among enterprises within the same area.

Generally speaking, the E.C.S.C. Treaty is applicable only to producers, except in the case of the rules concerning agreements and concentrations that also apply to dealers. Notwithstanding this principle, all the provisions of article sixty can be extended to the dealers, although only indirectly. Under article sixty-three, the High Authority may require that the producers oblige their dealers to respect their published price-lists and that the producers be held responsible for any violation. Furthermore, the High Authority may temporarily deprive the producers of the right to do business with an offending dealer.

This extension was necessary in order to prevent producers from getting around the provisions of article sixty through their direct dealers. The High Authority may also, to the same end, address to the Member States any recommendation necessary to ensure that the dealers comply with the rules of nondiscrimination and the prohibition of unfair competitive practices.

Fines of up to twice the value of the irregular sales may be imposed by the High Authority on the enterprises that do not comply with the rules of article sixty or with decisions taken in implementation of this article. The decisions of the High Authority imposing pecuniary sanctions are legally enforceable throughout the whole territory of the Common Market.

In its Decisions Nos. 4/53 and 31/53,[12] the High Authority had laid down very detailed rules concerning the publication of price-schedules and conditions of sale. According to these rules, only the prices and conditions in respect of socalled unusual transactions—*i.e.*, isolated transactions of a special nature—need not be published. Apart from this, any price difference, such as quantity discounts, fidelity rebates or trade discounts, must be shown in the price-lists. The High Authority has made it obligatory for the producers, by these decisions, to compel their direct dealers to respect the prices and conditions published in the schedules.

Side by side with the rules on publicity, the High Authority introduced certain measures concerning alignments and defined the practices prohibited under article 60(1) of the E.C.S.C. Treaty.

[12] [1953] JOURNAL OFFICIEL 3, 111.

Since the structure of the coal-mining industry and, in particular, the marked differences between the production costs of the different coalfields did not allow a competition by alignment without serious disturbances—especially of social nature—the High Authority, by its Decision No. 3/53,[13] in accordance with section twenty-four of the Convention containing the Transitional Provisions, prohibited price alignments in respect of sales of coal during the transitional period, except where specially authorized by it. Subsequently, the High Authority allowed the introduction of zone prices.

By Decision No. 30/53,[14] the High Authority gave a definition of the forbidden discriminatory practices, the basic definition being that any price difference that is not published in the price-schedule constitutes a discrimination. Both rules—that of publicity and that of nondiscrimination—are thus combined.

This set of rules very soon proved to be too rigid, as it left no flexibility of action to the enterprises and impeded the play of competition within the Common Market. This excessive rigidity made itself felt first in the steel market, and much later, raised problems, difficult to solve, in the coal market.

The High Authority first made its basic definition of discriminatory practices more flexible by separating the rule of nondiscrimination from that of publicity. According to Decision No. 1/54,[15] a deviation from the price-list constitutes a discrimination only where the seller cannot prove that the transaction in question falls outside the conditions specified in the price-list or where the seller cannot prove that the price-differences granted are extended equally to all comparable transactions. This greater flexibility does not affect the obligation to publish all price-differences for comparable transactions.

At the same time, the High Authority sought to give more latitude for price-variations, in order to facilitate a speedier and more flexible adaptation to the prevailing market situation: it amended the publicity rules in respect of the prices of steel products. Under Decision No. 2/54,[16] the enterprises were no longer required to publish price differences up and down not exceeding an average of 2.5 per cent of the published price, these deviations being permitted only for a period not exceeding sixty days. Only where the average price difference exceeded 2.5 per cent, or where these differences were granted over a period exceeding two months, did the enterprise concerned have to alter its price-schedule in order to keep published prices in line with the prices actually charged in the market.

The enterprises made extensive use of this latitude. The French Government, however, appealed against Decision No. 2/54 before the Court of Justice, as it considered that such relaxation of the publicity rules was incompatible with the

[13] Id. at 3.
[14] Id. at 109.
[15] [1954] Journal Officiel 217.
[16] Id. at 218.

Treaty. The Court found for the French Government, and Decision No. 2/54 was reversed.[17]

In 1958, the situation in the coal market deteriorated, since the enterprises were no longer able to sell their entire production. Owing to the differences in the structure of the various coal fields of the Community and between production costs, the price of coal was not the same throughout the whole Common Market. This situation was liable to cause serious disturbances: enterprises with low production costs, finding their sales within their own particular area diminishing, tended to step up their sales to the areas where prices were higher, thereby increasing the difficulties in the areas already seriously affected by the shrinkage of the markets. To avoid these difficulties, the High Authority limited the right of alignment with the lowest competing prices to a certain proportion of the tonnage sold within the area in question during a given reference period,[18] alignment thus becoming a defensive measure.

These alignment rules regulate price competition among the producers of the Community, and the last paragraph of article 60(2) of the E.C.S.C. Treaty, which permits alignments with quotations from producers outside the Community, makes it possible to meet competition from imported coal. It does not, however, regulate competition with the other sources of energy, and in particular with fuel oil. In the structural crisis through which the European coal industry is now going, competition from fuel oil is growing. The E.C.S.C. Treaty does not contain any rule governing competition with substitute products, and the E.E.C. Treaty, which covers fuel oil, contains no rules governing prices.

The difference between the two Treaties in regard to rules of competition thus creates a difficult situation, owing to the fact that the competing products and producers are subject to different régimes—almost complete freedom for fuel oil and very strict regulations for coal.

In conjunction with the coordination of the energy policies of the Community, endeavors are being made to deal with this problem. These endeavors may follow one of two main lines: either to apply to fuel oil the pricing system of the E.C.S.C. Treaty, or to make these rules less rigid, to begin with, and extend them to fuel oil later on. The first course is rather difficult, owing to the size and the international character of the oil companies. The alternative course comes up against legal and technical difficulties.

The principal legal obstacle is the position taken by the Court, which has already once opposed the relaxation of the publicity rules and, in a more recent case, found that the main purpose of price publicity is to attain "the fundamental objectives of the Treaty."

The technical difficulties stem largely from the limits imposed by the E.C.S.C. Treaty on the "right of information and investigation" of the institutions. The criticism expressed in regard to the rigidity of certain rules of competiton of the

---

[17] *Cf.* Gouvernement de la République Française v. Haute Autorité, Cour de Justice de la C.E.C.A., Dec. No. 1-54, 1 REC. 13 (1954-55).
[18] *Cf.* High Authority decision No. 3-58, [1958] JOURNAL OFFICIEL 157.

Treaty generally overlooks this aspect. The scope of this right is of paramount importance for the efficient implementation of the rules of competition within the European Common Market and should be examined before we go on to deal with agreements.

a. *The right of information and the rules of competition.* The broader the scope of the right of information and investigation of the authority responsible for the implementation of the rules of competition, the more flexible these rules can be made without loss of efficacy.

This may be regarded as going too far, since the essential thing is to deal with the outstanding violations that are most harmful to competition. It must be remembered that there is a great difference between the national administrative authorities and the institutions of the Community. In most cases, as in the United States, the national authorities can select the cases to be dealt with, as they may deem advisable. This freedom of action is enhanced by the fact that national authorities are not compelled to take a definite position in regard to all complaints. The freedom of choice is more restricted for the institutions of the Community. Political sensitivity in a Community that is still young requires that the institutions take great care and avoid being accused of discriminations according to nationality in selecting only the most important cases. Therefore, the institutions have to examine all complaints, even those of minor importance. According to the E.C.S.C. Treaty, when an enterprise makes a complaint and this complaint is not dealt with by a decision of the High Authority, an appeal may be lodged before the Court, in accordance with article thirty-five of the Treaty, against the tacit negative decision. A similar provision also exists in article 175 of the E.E.C. Treaty. Consequently, the institutions of the Community can be obliged to take action according to the principle of legality, to the detriment of the principle of opportunity.

Article forty-seven of the E.C.S.C. Treaty forms the basis of the High Authority's right of information and investigation. This right is very extensive, and the High Authority may impose fines and daily penalty payments upon those who refuse to supply information or knowingly furnish false information. The High Authority may proceed with the most extensive investigations. Its officials enjoy, according to article eighy-six, the same rights and powers as are granted by the national laws to officials of the member countries' own tax services.

These powers, however, are often inadequate. In the first place, article five of the E.C.S.C. Treaty requires of the institutions of the Community that they carry out their activities "with as small an administrative machinery as possible." The administrative means are thus too limited for carrying out extensive investigation. Secondly, the powers of control may be exercised only on enterprises producing or selling products covered by the Treaty. This limitation, a direct consequence of partial integration, is a great weakness of the Treaty.

The effects of this limitation are felt most noticeably when ensuring compliance with the rules of competition concerning prices and nondiscrimination. Checking which cannot be carried farther than the first, or even the second stage in distribution —*i.e.,* which cannot be followed up through all stages including the end-consumer— would have been ineffectual, unless the rules were such as to simplify these checks. Therefore rules and published price-lists were to be rigid.

This underlines the technical difficulty referred to earlier as regards any relaxation of the rules of competition. If the publicity-requirements were relaxed and the concept of discrimination broadened, abuses would be all the more difficult to check.

In spite of the fact that article 65(3) of the E.C.S.C. Treaty empowers the High Authority, in accordance with article forty-seven, to "obtain any information necessary, either by a special request addressed to the interested parties or by a general regulation for that purpose," the limitation of the power of investigation may also prove an obstacle to the implementation of the rules concerning agreements, since this power does not extend to natural persons, enterprises, and associations not subject to the E.C.S.C. Treaty.

For the implementation of the rules of article sixty-six of the E.C.S.C. Treaty regarding concentrations, the High Authority's right to obtain information is, however, much more extensive, since paragraph four of this article extends it without restriction to all natural and legal persons. This extension was indispensable, owing to the fact that a concentration between enterprises can be effected by persons, with the enterprises themselves taking only a passive part in the operation. In its Decision No. 26/54,[19] the High Authority has defined the type of information any natural or legal person who has acquired or regrouped the rights or assets of Community enterprises must automatically communicate to the High Authority.

Nevertheless, difficulties still arise, since the High Authority has no means of obtaining, from consumer enterprises, information often necessary to the assessment of a vertical concentration.

In the E.E.C. Treaty, the right of information of the institutions is not yet defined. Under article eighty-seven of the E.E.C. Treaty, the Council must, on the proposal of the Commission, lay down "any appropriate regulations or directives with a view to the application of the principles set out in Articles 85 and 86." Paragraph two of this article specifies that the particulars for the application of this article must be determined by "taking due account of the need, on the one hand, of ensuring effective supervision and, on the other hand, of simplifying administrative control to the greatest possible extent." This constitutes a first restriction on the right of information.

Even before the regulations defining the powers and competences of the institutions are laid down, the Commission has a right of information by virtue of article eighty-nine of the E.E.C. Treaty, which provides that "it shall, at the request of a member State or ex officio, investigate . . . any alleged infringement . . . [of the rules of Articles 85 and 86]." Such investigations must, however, be carried out "in conjunction with the competent authorities of the member States, which shall lend it

---

[19] [1954] JOURNAL OFFICIEL 350.

their assistance . . . ." According to the meaning given, in practice, to the wording "in conjunction with . . . ," the powers and means of action of the Commission will be either considerable or, on the contrary, restricted.

It is obvious that within this very vast and complex sphere of the over-all economy of the six countries of the Community, the Commission cannot, by itself, have the means of investigation required for the implementation of the rules of competition. It is desirable—indeed, essential—that it should be able to rely on the cooperation of the national administrations. This need is all the greater because, for as long as the regulations referred to in article eighty-seven of the E.E.C. Treaty have not been laid down, the Commission has no means of compelling the enterprises to supply information. The national authorities, however, have these powers and, moreover, have an intimate knowledge of the economic sectors involved.

This cooperation must, however, take the form of coordination, not subordination. The Commission must retain its independence and its own powers. It must be in a position to deal with the enterprises directly "in conjunction with the national authorities," but the latter must not have the possibility of shielding the enterprises from the Commission. Where checks prove necessary, the Commission must have the right of taking an active part in the investigations. It should, for instance, not be up to national authorities alone to decide as to the nature and scope of information required by the Commission, and still less so, should they be able to withhold such information from the Commission on grounds of trade secrecy.

The cooperation to be established between the Commission and the national authorities must be the crucible in which a genuine common policy concerning competition in the European Common Market will gradually evolve. But this indispensable cooperation must not be allowed to provide grounds for depriving the Commission of the right of information and direct action. The independence and the powers of the Commission are important not only from the psychological point of view—producers and dealers must be made aware of the existence of a Community with its own institutions—but also to ensure that the Commission will be in position to act as an impartial arbitrator in the competitive system created by the Treaty.

Technical reasons also have to be taken into consideration. Agreements affecting trade between Member States most directly are those that are concluded between enterprises of different countries. Where investigations have to be carried out in different countries, only direct action by the Commission, in cooperation with the national authorities, can ensure a uniform procedure and a homogeneous implementation of the rules in all the countries involved. Besides, if the Commission were deprived of the right of initiative and of its powers of investigation, it would have to rely entirely on the national authorities for detecting agreements and practices contrary to the rules of competition of the Treaty. Yet, only the institutions of the Community will have the required over-all view of the Common Market to judge whether an agreement does or does not restrict trade between Member States. Thus, if it were left exclusively to the national authorities to uncover violations of the rules, these might easily be implemented in different ways in the different Community countries, and imperfectly so.

B. Cartels

A perfect parallelism exists between articles sixty-five of the E.C.S.C. Treaty and eighty-five of the E.E.C. Treaty concerning cartels. The word "cartel" does not figure in either of these articles. Both prohibit "all agreements among enterprises, all decisions of associations of enterprises and all concerted practices" that, in the E.C.S.C. Treaty, would tend "directly or indirectly, to prevent, restrict or distort the normal operation of competition," and, in the E.E.C. Treaty, "are likely to affect trade between the member States, and which have as their object or result the prevention, restriction or distortion of competition within the Common Market."

The principle of economic policy is the same in both Treaties, but the differences in nature, number, and importance of the respective economic sectors have been taken into account.

In both Treaties, the general principle of prohibition is followed by a non-exhaustive enumeration of instances of prohibited agreements: price fixing (since it has no rules concerning individually fixed prices, the E.E.C. Treaty is more precise: direct or indirect fixing of purchase or selling prices or of any other trading conditions); limitation or control of production, technical development, or investment (the E.E.C. Treaty adds the limitation or control of the markets); and market-sharing or the sharing of the sources of supply (the E.C.S.C. Treaty adds the sharing of products and customers).

To this list, the E.E.C. Treaty, which contains no other specific rules on discrimination, adds two types of cartel—those establishing discriminations and those establishing unfair practices in the form of tying-clauses.

In both Treaties, the prohibited agreements are null and void.[20]

Like any legislation on agreements, the Treaties provide for the possibility of derogating from the general prohibition if the disadvantages due to the restraint of competition are largely offset by positive effects which could not be attained by other means within an economy based on free enterprise.

Under the E.C.S.C. Treaty, this waiver operates in favor of specific types of cartels. The High Authority authorizes "agreements to engage in joint buying or selling of specified products," or "agreements strictly analogous in their nature and effects." (E.C.S.C. Treaty art. 65(2).) Under the E.E.C. Treaty, however, which covers a great variety of economic sectors in which very different types of agreement may be found, exemption may be granted in respect of any type of agreement. This more flexible approach allows the granting of exemptions for entire economic sectors. Certain activities might possibly be exempted if, by their nature, they involve very close relations beyond the frontiers, and if, furthermore, the public control to which they are subject in each country excludes all risk of abuse. This particularly could be the case in the insurance and banking business.

[20] E.C.S.C. Treaty art. 65(4); E.E.C. Treaty art. 85(2).

Rules of Competition

Exemption can be granted where the conditions set forth in the Treaties are fulfilled. These conditions are practically identical in both Treaties, with the usual slight difference: more detailed and precise conditions in the E.C.S.C. Treaty, and a broader formulation, easier to adapt to a greater variety of cases, in the E.E.C. Treaty. The agreements must contribute in a positive manner to "an improvement ["substantial" in the E.C.S.C. Treaty] in the production or distribution of the products in question"; the E.E.C. Treaty provides a broader alternative by adding "or to the promotion of technical or economic progress," but subjects these positive elements to an important condition: the agreements must "reserve to users an equitable share in the profit resulting therefrom." It is not sufficient, however, for the agreements to present these advantages. According to the E.C.S.C. Treaty, they must, furthermore, be essential to attain these results, and, according to both Treaties, they must not impose on the enterprises concerned any restrictions greater than necessary for the purpose of the agreement. Finally, a third condition concerns the size and power of the enterprises, and is designed to prevent agreements among enterprises that are too powerful or among too large a number of enterprises.

Although the formulation in the E.C.S.C. Treaty is more precise and detailed, the implementation of these rules can be quite flexible in view of the powers vested in the High Authority. It is alone qualified to decide, without prejudice to the right of appeal to the Court, whether an agreement is or is not subject to article sixty-five of the E.C.S.C. Treaty. It can authorize an agreement for a limited period and extend it a number of times, or revoke it, if it finds that the agreement no longer fulfills the requisite conditions. Furthermore, the High Authority can make its authorization subject to specified conditions. It thus possesses the means necessary for the progressive adaptation of its policy in the field of cartels to the requirements of the Common Market, with due regard to the interests of the consumers.

The decisions taken under article sixty-five of the E.C.S.C. Treaty must be published in the *Journal Officiel* by the High Authority with all the grounds on which its decisions are based.

Where the rules regarding cartels and the decisions taken for their implementation are not observed, article sixty-five of the E.C.S.C. Treaty provides for the most severe pecuniary sanctions of the whole Treaty.

In the E.E.C. Treaty, the regulations for implementing articles eighty-five and eighty-six are not yet defined. In an extensive and complex field such as this, in which it is necessary to take into account also the existence of the national laws, it was intended merely to define principles and provide a general framework, while leaving scope for adapting the implementation of the provisions to the special problems experience would reveal.

For this reason, article eighty-seven of the E.E.C. Treaty provides that, at a later stage, appropriate regulations will have to be laid down to ensure compliance with the provisions of articles eighty-five and eighty-six by the institution of pecuniary sanctions, to define the respective responsibilities of the Commisson and of the

Court of Justice and the relations between national laws and the relevant provisions of the Treaty.

So long as the above-mentioned measures are not taken, two separate bodies are responsible for the implementation of the rules laid down in articles eighty-five and eighty-six of the E.E.C. Treaty. On the one hand, under article eighty-eight, the national authorities can rule on the compatibility of any agreement with the Treaty and upon any improper advantage taken of a dominant position in the Common Market "in accordance with their respective municipal laws" and with the provisions of the E.E.C. Treaty. On the other hand, under article eighty-nine, the Commission has to ensure the application of the principles concerning agreements and abuses of power, investigate any alleged infringement, and propose appropriate means for bringing it to an end. If the proposal is not complied with, the Commission may confirm the existence of the infringement by issuing a reasoned decision and authorize the Member States to take the necessary remedial measures, of which it will determine the conditions and particulars.

The responsibilities thus assigned to the national authorities by article eighty-eight of the E.E.C. Treaty and the fact that the Commission depends on the latter for the investigation of cases of infringement made it necessary that all Member States should appoint the authorities in question. In three countries, however, Belgium, Italy, and Luxembourg, there existed no special laws on competition. The first concern of the Commission was, therefore, to cause such laws to be drawn up in these countries. This was done in Belgium; a bill was also drafted in Italy; and preparations for such a law are in progress in Luxembourg. The laws of the different countries are anything but similar. Since article eighty-eight provides that the authorities must give their opinion "in accordance with their respective municipal law," the risk of arriving at six different interpretations of the rules of the E.E.C. Treaty was very great. To avoid this risk, the Commission called a meeting of representatives of the six national administrations, with the object of jointly working out a uniform interpretation of these rules.

In both Treaties, the problem existed whether the general prohibition on cartels was to come into operation forthwith, making a clean sweep of all the cartels in existence at the time the Treaties came into force, or whether transitional arrangements might not be necessary in order to avoid serious economic disturbances.

The problem was settled in the E.C.S.C. Treaty by section twelve of the Convention containing the Transitional Provisions, which—apart from the measure the High Authority must take in the event of a dissolution of the cartels to protect the interests of the workers and to preserve the productive capacity needed by the Community—stipulates that the High Authority must fix a reasonable time-limit for the coming into effect of the prohibitions laid down in article sixty-five of the E.C.S.C. Treaty. By its Decision No. 37/53,[21] the High Authority fixed this limit at August 31, 1953. All cartels that had applied for authorization before this date

[21] [1953] JOURNAL OFFICIEL 153.

were allowed to carry on their activities until a decision was taken by the High Authority in respect of each case. All other cartels were prohibited and declared unlawful.

As regards the E.E.C. Treaty, the Commission, with the support of the six Governments, declared that the rules of competition must be applied from the day the Treaty came into force. The Commission has not, however, taken a decision whether the prohibitions and declarations of invalidity would take effect *ex nunc*—i.e., only from the day on which the national authorities and the Commission took a decision as to the permissibility, or otherwise, of a cartel—or *ex tunc*, respectively from the date on which the Treaty came into force. This question will have to be settled by the Court of Justice. The Commission merely wanted to ensure that no powerful cartels would arise and delay the introduction of the Common Market before the rules provided for by article eighty-seven of the E.E.C. Treaty had been laid down.

C. Concentrations

The expansion of enterprises by concentration is a particularly characteristic feature of the basic industries, where mass production, technical development, and rationalization call for large production units. Concentrations, however, frequently involve companies that are already very big in themselves, so that concentrations can alter the competitive conditions very suddenly. For this reason, the coal and steel industries are subjected by the E.C.S.C. Treaty to certain rules regarding concentration, while the E.E.C. Treaty, which covers all other economic sectors, contains no provisions to that effect.

While in regard to agreements (cartels) the general principle of the E.C.S.C. Treaty is prohibition (authorization being granted only where advantages in the general interest will result), the reverse is the case where concentrations are concerned: if article sixty-six of the E.C.S.C. Treaty requires prior authorization, it can be refused only when certain conditions are not satisfied.

Any transaction which in itself—*i.e.*, irrespective of the intentions of the parties involved—would have the direct or indirect effect of bringing about a concentration, requires prior authorization, even if the transaction concerns enterprises only one of which falls under the jurisdiction of the E.C.S.C. Treaty.

Like the rules concerning agreements, article sixty-six of the E.C.S.C. Treaty also covers dealers (distributors), but in addition applies to transactions carried out by a person or an enterprise, or a group of persons or enterprises not falling under the E.C.S.C. Treaty. The article does not, however, define what is meant by a group. The High Authority itself will assess, in accordance with the position *de facto* and *de jure*, whether several enterprises or persons do or do not form a group within the meaning of this article.

The transaction itself must be carried out within the Community. Article 66(1), of the E.C.S.C. Treaty does not give a definition of a concentration operation, but enumerates the means whereby such a transaction can be carried through—namely, "by merger, acquisition of shares or assets, loan, contract or any other means of control." It can thus be seen that the transaction referred to in article sixty-six is the transaction through which a Community enterprise loses its independence (either in relation to other Community enterprises or in relation to enterprises not falling under the Treaty), or a transaction that enables an enterprise of the Community to acquire, within the Common Market, directly or indirectly, the control over enterprises that are not subject to the rules of the E.C.S.C. Treaty.

The intention was to establish control over both horizontal concentrations—*i.e.*, those affecting the size of the enterprises—and vertical concentrations—*i.e.*, those altering the competitive conditions through the acquisition of too powerful a position in regard to sources of supply or markets.

By its Decision No. 24/54,[22] the High Authority defined the business relations, financial tie-ups, and interlocking directorships which after taking into account all circumstances, in fact and in law, constitute the control of an enterprise.

For authorization to be granted, it must be shown that the group of enterprises under one and the same control will not occupy a position in the market giving them the power "to determine the prices, to control or restrict production or distribution, or to prevent the maintenance of effective competition in a substantial part of the market or to evade the rules of competition as they result from the execution of the Treaty, in particular by establishing an artificially privileged position involving a substantial advantage in access to supplies or markets."

The conditions laid down in article 66(2) of the E.C.S.C. Treaty do not have to be satisfied merely in relation to the situation prevailing at the time of submitting an application for authorization. The article says clearly: "The High Authority shall grant the authorization . . . if it finds that the transaction in question will not give to the interested persons or enterprises . . . the power." Accordingly, the High Authority must take into account the development of the market and the expected increase in production capacities (which it knows from the declarations of investment projects in accordance with article fifty-four), and it must estimate the possible future effects of the concentration in order to determine whether these conditions will still be fulfilled after a reasonable length of time.

It is necessary to ensure a balanced growth of all the Community enterprises, if the Common Market is to operate satisfactorily. The Treaty makes a distinction, however, between internal growth of enterprises, and external growth through concentration. It considers internal growth as the normal and desirable result of the efficiency of the enterprises under the competitive system provided for by the Treaty.

Article sixty-six of the E.C.S.C. Treaty applies only to concentrations carried through after the coming into force of the Treaty and does not affect concentrations that already existed before. This is an essential difference between articles sixty-five and sixty-six, since this distinction is not made in regard to cartels. In assessing the

[22] [1954] JOURNAL OFFICIEL 345-46.

effects of a transaction involving a concentration, the High Authority, therefore, has to take into account the size of enterprises already existing in the Common Market.

As in the case of cartels, the High Authority can make the authorization of a concentration subject to certain conditions. In this respect, however, it does not have the same latitude as in the case of cartels. The conditions must be in line with the criteria laid down in article 66(2), of the E.C.S.C. Treaty. This means that conditions can only be imposed when the High Authority can prove that but for these conditions, the concentration in question could not be authorized at all.

Because of the size and importance of the interests involved in concentration, the authorization, once granted, cannot be altered or revoked. Therein lies a fundamental difference between the rules of the E.C.S.C. Treaty and the antitrust legislation in the United States, where the authorities can step in both before and after a concentration has been effected, without being tied down by time limits. They can thus catch up with a concentration, which the High Authority cannot.

To affect the competitive conditions in the Common Market, a concentration has to be of certain size. This is why, according to article 66(3) of the E.C.S.C. Treaty, the transactions bringing about concentrations of minor importance may be exempted from the requirement of prior authorization. In its Decision No. 25/54,[23] the High Authority defined the types and size of enterprises for which prior authorization is not required. This exemption is never made in cases of concentrations between producers and dealers, in order to avoid any petrification of the Community's channels of distribution.

Where a concentration has been effected without prior authorization, but, nevertheless, satisfies the conditions of authorization, the High Authority will grant the authorization, but may, in accordance with article 66(5) of the E.C.S.C. Treaty, impose a fine on the parties concerned. If the concentration does not satisfy the conditions, the High Authority is empowered to denounce it as illegal and to order the separation of the enterprises or assets involved. In that case, however, the parties concerned may lodge an appeal with the Court of Justice, which, notwithstanding the provisions of article thirty-three, according to which the Court may not review the High Authority's evaluation of economic facts, has full competence for deciding whether the transaction in question is or is not a concentration within the meaning of article 66(1).

D. Abuses of Power

The E.C.S.C. Treaty endeavors, as we have seen, to restrain the establishment of dominant positions in the market through concentrations, but it does not abolish the dominant positions that existed before the Common Market was introduced, and it cannot prevent the creation of new dominant positions as a result of the internal growth of the enterprises. The E.E.C. Treaty does not even attempt to restrain concentrations, still less to prevent the creation of dominant positions.

[23] *Id.* at 346-49.

This deficiency in the Treaties can be explained chiefly by the fact that the rules of competition were laid down before the Common Market was actually introduced. The very purpose of a common market is to raise the standard of living, to expand sales outlets, and to increase trade. These objectives imply continued expansion of production and a corresponding growth of the enterprises. It must not be overlooked that European enterprises have remained of a size in keeping with the limitations of their national markets. The Common Market is an attempt to bring about their adaptation to the production conditions of today and in particular to the requirements of a larger market. It is, therefore, understandable that this development was not to be hampered by restrictions where these were not essential to the introduction and operation of the Common Market. This applies particularly to the E.E.C. Treaty, which covers a variety of economic sectors, comprising in many cases new industries in full development. It would have been difficult, and even dangerous, to lay down a rule designed to prevent the acquisition of a dominant position.

Nevertheless, where enterprises occupy or acquire a dominant position, this may present a danger for the Community. These enterprises often have the requisite power to disregard the rules of competition and even act in a manner that prevents or delays the attainment of the objectives of the Communities. In both Treaties, this danger has been warded off by almost identical means—*i.e.*, by granting the institutions the right to put an end to abuses of power.

According to article 66(7) of the E.C.S.C. Treaty, where a public or private enterprise has or acquires "a dominant position in the Common Market which protects it from effective competition in a substantial part of this market and this enterprise makes use of such position for purposes contrary to those of the Treaty," the High Authority may put a stop to these practices by means of recommendations. If such recommendations are not carried out, "the High Authority will, after consulting the interested Government, fix the prices and conditions of sale to be applied by the enterprise in question, or draw up a production or delivery program."

In the E.E.C. Treaty, the wording of article eighty-six is more severe and more precise. It forbids the abusive exploitation of a dominant position "to the extent to which it influences trade between member States." These improper practices are enumerated in a non-restrictive manner—namely, direct or indirect imposition of any inequitable trading conditions; limitation of production, markets or technical development to the prejudice of consumers; and discriminatory practices and unfair practices (tying-clauses).

The authority of the various institutions of E.E.C. in regard to the implementation of article eighty-six has not yet been decided, nor have the details of the manner in which these provisions are to be implemented. These will be dealt with in appropriate regulations and directives to be laid down in accordance with article eighty-seven.

Article 66(7) of the E.C.S.C. Treaty also mentions "public enterprises." This refers particularly to nationalized industries the size of which generally exceeds that of private enterprises, and which may, therefore, easily acquire a dominant position. This does not imply that the other rules of competition do not apply to public enterprises: the rules are applicable to all enterprises, whatever their legal status.

The position in this respect is the same under the E.E.C. Treaty: article ninety, referring to public enterprises, forbids Member States to enact or to maintain in force any measure contrary to the rules contained in the Treaty, in particular to those rules provided for in article seven and in articles eighty-five to ninety-four inclusive.

Conclusion

The rules of competition that have been described are not based upon any dogmatic conception of competition. They are one of the main instruments of economic policy for the establishment of the European Common Market and the foundation of the common economic policy to be worked out by the institutions of the Community. However pragmatic the approach to the problems of competition may have been, the rules of competition laid down in the Treaties of Paris and Rome have the merit of having created a new spirit in Europe by preparing public opinion for a competitive system in countries where international and national cartels have been flourishing.

With the object of greater efficiency and greater unity, efforts are in progress for the unification of the institutions set up under the European Treaties. In a first stage, it is to be hoped that the rules of competition, enforced under the E.E.C. and the E.C.S.C. Treaties, will not be affected. They are, indeed, justified in both Treaties by the nature and structure of the industries to which they have to be applied. Rather than an artificial harmonization on political or even legal grounds, the aim should be to take into account economic considerations and to apply the same rules to economic sectors having comparable characteristics. In other words, rules that were deemed necessary for the heavy industries, which by historical accident fall under the E.C.S.C. Treaty, should become applicable also to industries of a similar type that subsequently came under the jurisdiction of the E.E.C. Treaty.

Such transformations involve political choices and are, therefore, outside the province of those entrusted with day-to-day implementation of the rules. The writers would, therefore, merely express the hope that the statesmen responsible for formulating new rules in the field of competition which affects the political freedom and economic welfare of the peoples of Europe will bear in mind that, as Montesquieu wrote in *L'Esprit des Lois*:

It is sometimes necessary to change certain laws. But this happens rarely; when it does, they must only be touched with a trembling hand; so many solemnities must be observed and so many precautions taken, that the people naturally conclude that the laws are well made, since it requires so many formalities to abrogate them.

CAPITAL MOVEMENTS AND INVESTMENT IN THE EUROPEAN COMMUNITIES

Hermann J. Abs[*]

Introduction

So far, it has been difficult to obtain an exact idea of international capital movements within the European Economic Community (E.E.C.) owing to the lack of accurate statistics permitting comparisons among the various countries. It is, therefore, impracticable to furnish reliable information on the extent to which the organization of the E.E.C. has had had an effect on the capital imports and exports of the partners to the Treaty of Rome, and to forecast what the future will hold in store. However, it may be taken for granted that any intensification of capital transactions within the E.E.C. will conform to the degree in which the functioning of a Common Market in the fullest sense of the word is accomplished, meaning a market characterized by generous freedom of movement in all transactions relating to persons, money, goods, and capital, and by close coordination of national economic and financial policies capable of functioning satisfactorily in difficult situations.

Nobody seems to be able to tell exactly to what degree it will be possible to realize this ideal, although past experiences inspire a fair measure of confidence. During the last few years, financial stability has been consolidated even in those countries of the E.E.C. that a few years previously, from the viewpoint of financial policy and capital transactions, had to some extent still been "problem children." Quite generally, considerable progress has been made in removing impediments to competition.

In the event that the realization of the Treaty of Rome—in accordance with the spirit as much as the letter—is really accomplished along liberal lines of thought, it should be possible to anticipate a favorable development of the contribution that the countries bound together in the E.E.C. can make towards world-wide capital transactions. Freedom of movement between the E.E.C. and third-party countries must, in the writer's personal view, be looked upon as an essential sequel to a liberal nonprotectionist order within the E.E.C.; it should, in fact, be a matter of course. Again, the fact that the regional structure of foreign trade among the E.E.C. countries, especially in the Federal Republic of Germany and the Benelux countries, is characterized by world-wide interramification—a trend that it is important not merely to maintain, but to strengthen—affords ground for expectations that the progressive interlocking of capital within the Six will not proceed along exclusive lines. There is all the less reason to be apprehensive of the contrary result, since the European Monetary Agreement—in which, in addition to the E.E.C. coun-

---

[*] Vice-President of Board of Directors, Reconstruction Loan Corporation, Frankfurt (Main); Member, Board of Management, Deutsche Bank Aktiengesellschaft, Frankfurt (Main).

tries, the United Kingdom, the Scandinavian countries, Switzerland, and other nations are partners—and the convertibility of currencies in general have proved a success. There thus exists a very effective link as regards currencies and capital transactions among almost all countries of western Europe and with the dollar-bloc countries.

The Commission of the E.E.C. has, in the meantime, issued directives designed to accelerate the liberalization of capital transactions among the E.E.C. The success of these measures remains to be seen. In any case, they are in line with the conception communicated beforehand. This also implies that they will certainly not create fresh impediments to capital transactions between the Six and the other countries.

I

Private Capital Transactions within the E.E.C.

In endeavoring to convey a general idea of capital transactions within the E.E.C., the writer feels that one ought to start out with private capital exports and imports—and not only because in terms of quantity they are first in significance. If we are determined to maintain and to promote along sound lines an order founded on the notion of private property—which includes means of production—and the principle of fair competition on a national and international scale, we shall have to admit that if commercial capital transactions are to stand any real chance, they must be accorded priority over those accomplished by the government. The fact that, as things stand today, foreign investments cannot be organized entirely on a commercial basis, especially in the so-called development countries and areas, is a different matter, with which we are not immediately concerned at this juncture.

A. Increasing Share of E.E.C. Countries in German Private Capital Exports

As has already been observed, there are, so far, no accurate figures at hand regarding the development of capital transactions as a whole within the E.E.C. However, it may be of interest to analyze the capital movements relating to the E.E.C. for an individual member country for which some records are available—for example, the Federal Republic of Germany. Of German private long-term net capital investments abroad, totalling DM 1,400,000,000 in 1960, DM 526,000,000, or somewhat more than one-third, went to E.E.C. countries; in 1958, the corresponding figure had been roughly twenty per cent. The European Free Trade Area (E.F.T.A.) in 1960 took up twenty-five per cent of private long-term capital investments abroad, against twenty-nine per cent in 1958.

Now, it would obviously be unwise to deduce too much for the long run from the experiences of a few years. Nevertheless, the fact stands out that cooperation between interested German quarters and foreign bourses and banks within the E.E.C. area, has developed in a particularly impressive manner. In recent years, a very large part of the capital investments of German citizens in foreign paper related to securities domiciled in other E.E.C. countries. On an over-all view, private long-term net capital exports in 1958 comprised just under one-quarter of portfolio investments; in 1960, this share had reached slightly less than fifty per cent. Last year, over one-half of all foreign securities bought concerned issues in E.E.C. countries, while between eleven and twenty-four per cent concerned issues in the United States and the E.F.T.A. countries respectively. In part—particularly as far as issues of the E.E.C. are concerned—this may be due to foreign securities being acquired by firms seeking interests in other countries, but there is no doubt that the bulk is accounted for by the purchase of foreign paper by individual German investors. Due to currency speculation and changes in the international structure of interest rates, the long-term net capital exports of the Federal Republic of Germany—which in 1959 had amounted to almost DM 4,000,000,000—were in the past year reduced to DM 480,000,000 (excluding donations, restitution payments, etc.). Only to an insignificant degree was this decline the result of diminished German transfers to foreign countries; on the other hand, the extraordinary increase of foreign capital investment in the Federal Republic was of unusually great importance.

B. Direct Investments within the Community

As far as the writer can see, it is unlikely that any decisive regional shifts have taken place in direct investments on the part of business enterprises in recent years. Actually, there is, on the face of it, for many business enterprises within the Common Market little reason to establish production plants of their own in other E.E.C. countries. After all, the reduction of customs duties and the removal of other trade impediments offer ample opportunities to supply the entire E.E.C. from each national production base without any fear of discriminating restrictions on competition. Exceptions may apply in cases where the cost of transport is relatively great by comparison with the value of the product. Also, it will probably frequently be necessary to set up individual sales organizations throughout the E.E.C.

However that may be in individual instances, financial interramification between the national economies of E.E.C. is steadily on the rise. We must also envisage an increasing exchange of licences, patents, and the like, which likewise entail financial consequences. Incidentally, international investment trusts have achieved considerable popularity both in Germany and other E.E.C. countries, the securities of the latter countries being accorded preference by the trusts.

II

Government-controlled Capital Transactions in E.E.C.

Government-controlled capital transactions within E.E.C. are primarily governed by customary international principles. In this connection, mention must be made in particular of government contributions towards export financing. In the Federal Republic of Germany, as in other countries, this consists principally in the granting of government guarantees and assurances in favor of medium-term export credits. As a general principle, the writer is inclined to think that the policy of the

E.E.C. should be as prudent as in other matters—meaning that, under all circumstances, a revival of unsound competition among governments in granting financial assistance to regular exports of durable goods to be financed over medium and longer terms must be avoided.

Special institutions serving government-controlled capital transactions within the E.E.C. are, in particular, the European Investment Bank and the E.E.C. Development Fund.

A. European Investment Bank

It is the purpose of the European Investment Bank primarily to contribute towards the opening-up of less-developed areas within the Common Market. In addition, its tasks include the financing of production change-over projects, which may become necessary in the course of the continuing realization of the E.E.C., and participation in other projects of common interest where financing requirements exceed the capacities of the various member countries. The Bank was set up with a capital of $1,000,000,000, of which twenty-five per cent had to be paid in initially in installments. The balance is considered guarantee capital, to be called up when required. The various E.E.C. countries share in the capital of the Investment Bank in the following proportions:

Germany	$300,000,000
France	300,000,000
Italy	240,000,000
Belgium	86,500,000
Netherlands	71,500,000
Luxembourg	2,000,000

In addition to responding to requests for special loans on the part of the member countries, the Bank is also authorized to make loans on the international capital markets. It is explicitly provided that in its financing principles, the Bank is to model its activities on those of the World Bank, with which it proposes to cooperate closely.

In certain respects, it has become apparent during the past few years that there is less dependence on the Bank than had been generally anticipated before the conclusion of the Treaty of Rome. Whenever investment projects within the E.E.C. failed to obtain the necessary financing by commercial credits or by the aid of the respective national government, international syndicates, and also occasionally the World Bank, have offered favorable financing possibilities.

So far, the granting of loans by the Bank has been kept within comparatively narrow limits. During the first three business years, it authorized a total of twelve loans in the aggregate amount of $93,500,000 of which $61,000,000 related to projects in Italy and just under $26,000,000 to projects in France. Although as much as $250,000,000 had been paid in on the capital by the end of last year, the payments actually made to loan recipients amounted to a total of $33,000,000. The facilities offered by the Bank are thus at present far from being fully utilized.

Nevertheless, it seems possible that in the long run, the Bank should do more business than it has to date. Quite apart from the fact that every credit institution requires time to set up in business on a sound basis, it seems likely that as the Treaty of Rome comes nearer to realization, there will be an increasing demand for investments to permit better structural adjustment of specific industries and regions. The extent, however, to which this will involve a greater demand for public funds will presumably be largely dependent upon the development of international business activities and the capital markets.

B. E.E.C. Development Fund

The E.E.C. Development Fund was formed to contribute towards furthering the social and economic development of those overseas countries and territories that are associated with the Common Market. Under the terms of article 131 of the E.E.C. Treaty, they include such non-European countries and territories as maintain particular relations with Belgium, France, Italy, and the Netherlands. The general tendency is to afford an opportunity of association to those overseas countries that are no longer by international law linked with one of the European partners of E.E.C. This would seem to apply in particular to the African territories that have now become politically independent. By the end of 1962, the E.E.C. partners will have paid $581,000,000 into the Fund, of which $200,000,000 will come each from France and the Federal Republic of Germany. The Fund, like the Investment Bank, could at first make final decisions on comparatively few projects. At the end of summer, 1961, financing contracts for only seventeen projects in the amount of around $10,000,000 had been firmly agreed upon. In the meantime, however, the Fund has received higher capital allotments. At the end of April 1961, the approved financial appropriations amounted to $148,000,000.

The projects to be financed out of the Fund are not, as a general rule, scheduled to produce any yield, although their promotion is to be in the interest of the overseas territories and of the members of the E.E.C. Only "genuine economic assistance matters" are envisaged. Doubtlessly, the success of financial aid granted out of the Fund will essentially depend upon whether efforts to establish the necessary political and economic conditions for a steady, progressive opening-up of the regions in question are successful. If the Fund is forced to rely on its own resources—*i.e.*, if its grants are not supplemented by capital invested on a commerical basis—the results can hardly be expected to prove adequate nor to have any lasting effect.

In recent decades, private capital exports from the Federal Republic of Germany to Africa have been negligible. During the years following 1950, the total was no more than DM 180,000,000, which is slightly over six per cent of the over-all foreign investments of German enterprises (direct investments). This low share reflects the fact that since World War I, German trade and industry has taken comparatively little interest in Africa and, indeed, was not very often offered opportunities to do so. At the same time, it is indicative of the fact that German businessmen capable of investing money abroad and willing to do so have hitherto considered activities in other parts of the world to be more rewarding.

III

Investments of Non-Member Countries within the E.E.C.

The formation of a Common Market on the European continent naturally has a great attraction for foreign capital. By the aid of its own production plants and sales agencies within the Market, or by acquiring participations there, even an enterprise domiciled outside the E.E.C. may enjoy the advantages that accrue from association with that economic area. For Americans, the still comparatively low labor costs form a supplementary incentive. The noticeable lack of skilled labor in the European industrial centers is, however, often an obstacle in the way of commissioning new manufacturing plants that is not always easy to surmount.

Capital coming in from non-member countries is today enabled to operate in the E.E.C. area under practically the same conditions as domestic capital, although there are still differences within the various countries. The Federal Republic of Germany is among those countries where foreign-exchange control to all intents and purposes no longer exists. In view of the favorable balance-of-payments situation with all E.E.C. countries, whose currency reserves from 1957 to 1959 rose by $3,300,000,000, it seems fair to anticipate a further improvement of the chances for investments by foreigners even in the countries that in recent years still had to put up with foreign-exchange difficulties.

Until a short time ago, the United Kingdom absorbed the bulk of the United States capital flowing to Europe, but since the beginning of 1959, the countries of the Common Market have been gaining in popularity as an objective of American investments. In the Federal Republic of Germany, too, foreign enterprises have, during the past two years, acquired interests in considerably greater measure than in the past. Here, again, it is American firms that account for the principal share. It is a noteworthy fact that United States capital no longer concentrates in the same measure as in former times on specific industrial fields (such as the mineral oil industry and processing industry), but has been turning its attention to a wider range of activities, including chemistry, agricultural machinery, the rubber-processing industry, the paper industry, the foodstuffs industry, and others. Aside from the fact that West Germany will increase her capital exports—above all, in consideration of the capital requirements of development countries—she should remain a relatively significant capital importing nation.

A most important question for any investor, whether German or foreign, is whether in the foreseeable future there will be an amalgamation of some kind between the E.E.C. and E.F.T.A. Producers and exporters anxious to safeguard their sales in one or both of the two regions will, if they are sceptical as regards chances of a merger, tend to establish production plants or branches or to seek participations in both. But double-investment projects of this kind may turn out to be misdirected in the event that an effective economic association embracing the whole of western Europe does come about. The fact that this is looked upon by the West German business community and public opinion in general as a task to be realized at the earliest possible date is something that should be stressed, although at the same time, it should be emphasized that European economic integration is far from being envisaged as a means to insure segregation from other continents. On the contrary, it is seen as a contribution to the progressive intensification of goods and capital transactions on a world-wide scale.

Whatever the future may have in store for us, the writer is firmly convinced that the European, and more particularly the West German, contribution to international capital transactions will remain characterized by a world-embracing outlook and that the share of a number of non-European countries in capital exports from Europe will become even greater.

THE STRUCTURE AND FINANCIAL ACTIVITIES OF THE EUROPEAN REGIONAL COMMUNITIES*

GIANDOMENICO SERTOLI[†]

The three Communities—European Coal and Steel Community (E.C.S.C.), European Atomic Energy Community (Euratom), and the European Economic Community (E.E.C.)—have, without doubt, a common origin: namely, the will of the six member countries to establish the foundations of an ever closer union between the European peoples. In addition, they exhibit, at least at first sight, the same institutional structure. Each of the Communities is composed of an Executive (the High Authority in E.C.S.C., the Commission in Euratom and E.E.C.), a Council of Ministers, a Parliamentary Assembly, and a Court of Justice. The last three institutions, moreover, are unique and common to the three Communities. Finally, in the sphere of administration of the Executives, certain common staffs have been established.

Although the analogies and common interests between the Communities are numerous and important and although one can foresee, and at the same time hope for, ultimate progress in the direction of unification, it must be admitted that, in the present state of affairs, the three Communities differ appreciably among themselves so far as their structure and their means of action are concerned. These differences are due primarily to the diversity of the objectives which they seek to attain. Two of them, E.C.S.C. and Euratom, are, in fact, specialized Communities with limited powers over a determined sector of production. The third, E.E.C., has, on the contrary, wider tasks—its final object being to fuse the economic systems of the member countries into a single economic entity spreading over all sectors of production and trade. Also these differences are due to the diversity of the political situations existing in the member countries at the time when the treaties setting up these Communities were negotiated and signed, this diversity being reflected alike in their structure and in the means placed at their disposal.

I

THE EUROPEAN COAL AND STEEL COMMUNITY

A. Its Tasks

The E.C.S.C. was instituted by the Treaty of April 18, 1951, and saw the light of day a few years after the end of the war, when the European economic system was experiencing a marked slow-down in very large sectors. In spite of the efforts

* The author's treatment and analysis of the subject of this article is dependent on factual developments prior to March 1961, and does not account for developments since then.

† Dr. iur. 1945, University of Padua (Italy). Manager of the Finance and Treasury Department of the European Investment Bank. Author, LA BANCA EUROPEA PER GLI INVESTIMENTI (1957).

made for reconstruction, investment appeared clearly inadequate. Thus, in 1952, per capita investment (stated in dollars) was $126 for the six Community countries as a whole, whereas in the same year in the United States it was $314. This deficiency was particularly felt in the basic industry sectors, which were affected more than the others by wartime destruction and the aging of installations. Independently even of the creation of a common market for the products of the coal and steel industry, an energetic policy of investment was from that time necessary in order to improve productivity. This effort to obtain new investment became even more indispensable with the creation of a common market for coal and steel, which implied increased competition and, therefore, an added need to modernize equipment, specialize activities, and concentrate production in order to reduce costs.

If accelerated investment was avowedly indispensable for E.C.S.C. enterprises, it was still necessary to make this investment possible by providing adequate financial means. Furthermore, it was indispensable that this adaptation to the new and more stringent competitive conditions created by the common market not be realized at the expense of the workers through reduction of employment and a worsening of working conditions.

The arduous task thus given to E.C.S.C. was to ensure the most rational allocation of production at the highest level of productivity, and at the same time, to safeguard continuity of employment and avoid the creation of fundamental and persistent disturbances in the economic systems of the member countries. Accomplishment of this task required efficacious intervention at the Community level in the promotion of investment and of technical and economic research, as well as in assistance to workers affected by the progressive establishment of the common market.

B. Field and Means of Action

The field of action which the Treaty establishing the E.C.S.C. has laid down for its executive, the High Authority, is vast and covers the Community's whole sphere of action. With respect to financing activity, in the true sense, the High Authority may grant loans or guarantees:

(a) to facilitate the financing of industrial investments in the coal and steel industries;

(b) to facilitate the financing of the construction of housing for the workers in these industries;

(c) to facilitate the financing of investments which do not relate to Community enterprises, on the condition that they help directly and essentially to increase production, lower production costs, or facilitate the disposal of products subject to the jurisdiction of the High Authority;

(d) to facilitate the financing of the creation of new jobs for the benefit of workers set free by technical progress or by the consequences of the establishment of the common market.

Furthermore, the High Authority may give grants or loans:
- (a) to facilitate the "readaptation" of workers set free by the establishment of the common market, by technical development in the coal or steel industry, or as a result of structural modifications in the marketing conditions in those industries;
- (b) to encourage technical or economic research relating to the production of coal and steel and the development of their use, as well as to the security of workers in those industries.

This is the field of action of the High Authority. The financial means at its disposal on venturing into this field arise principally from two sources—its own taxing power and borrowed funds. Of course, these two categories of resources are not interchangeable. Money borrowed by the Authority can, in fact, only be utilized in granting loans—and not to meet administrative expenses or to grant monetary assistance which is not reimbursable. The resources arising from the Authority's taxing power can be used only within the Treaty's definite limits, which do not include the grant of loans to enterprises. Finally, the High Authority has certain other incidental revenues derived from interest on bank deposits and from other sources, including monetary fines and penalties imposed on enterprises for violation of the E.C.S.C. Treaty or of the High Authority's decisions.

C. The Taxing Power of the High Authority

The treaty creating the E.C.S.C. recognizes the right of the High Authority to impose on the enterprises subject to its jurisdiction a levy calculated on the value of the production of coal and steel in the six countries of the Community. This levy is paid monthly by the enterprises on the production realized by them and is calculated at a rate which may not exceed one per cent of the average value of that production. If necessary, and subject to the authorization of the Council of Ministers of the E.C.S.C., the rate could even be fixed above one per cent. We see here the first example of a European tax which the High Authority, by virtue of its own decision and without soliciting any specific authorization either from the Member States or from the other Community institutions, can levy to meet its needs.

To give an idea of the dimensions of the High Authority's taxing power by virtue of this levy, it suffices to say that the value of all Community products subject to the levy totaled about $8.9 billions[1] in the fiscal year ended June 30, 1960. Thus, the taxing power of the High Authority amounts at the present time to nearly $89,000,000 a year. In fact, the High Authority has never applied the ceiling rate of one per cent; and at present the rate in force is 0.35 per cent, which is well below

[1] Except as otherwise specified, all amounts in this article are expressed in American dollars and represent either American dollars or their equivalent in the national currency of one or more member countries or in Swiss francs, at the following exchange rates: One American dollar equals 50 Belgian francs, 4.93706 French francs, 4.20 West German marks, 50 Luxembourg francs, 3.80 Dutch guilders, 625 Italian lire, and 4.29 Swiss francs.

the ceiling. The proceeds of the levy were approximately $31,000,000 during the fiscal year ended June 30, 1960.

In accordance with the Treaty, the proceeds of the levy are intended to cover:
(a) the administrative expenses of the institutions of the Community;
(b) grants or loans which the E.C.S.C. may make for "readaptation" of workers and for technical and economic research, as mentioned above;
(c) any part of the interest and principal payments due on funds borrowed by the High Authority which are not covered by repayments received by the High Authority on the loans which it makes to the enterprises, and any payments required to be made by the High Authority under any guaranties which it may grant for loans obtained directly by the enterprises.

Thus, it is not unreasonable to assert that the taxing power of the High Authority constitutes the primary basis of its credit.

D. The Guarantee Fund

From the outset of its activity the High Authority decided to put a large portion of its taxing power to immediate use by setting up a guarantee fund destined to cover eventual defaults or delays of payment in the loan and guarantee operations of the Community. It may well be questioned whether the establishment of this guarantee fund was really necessary since the High Authority can, at any moment and by its sole decision, increase the rate of the levy in order to face up to its obligations to its lenders and since, in addition, the mere decision of the High Authority to create a guarantee fund confers no privilege whatsoever on those lenders as to the fund thus reserved. If, however, the financial structure of the High Authority is closely examined, the opportuneness of the creation of this fund appears evident. In fact, it has a double objective since:

(a) the existence of this provision is the best assurance of the punctuality of the High Authority in servicing its borrowings for, if the Authority had to wait for defects in payment to appear in order to increase the rate of the levy, the punctuality essential to its credit would risk being compromised; and
(b) The High Authority thus avoids the necessity of having recourse to a sudden increase in the rate of levy to meet important losses in the servicing of loans. (Such a sudden increase would be inopportune for, if such losses were to occur, it would probably be by reason of a general crisis in the coal and steel industry, at which time greater difficulty would arise in paying the surcharge.)

The total of the guarantee fund amounts at present to the equivalent of $100,000,000; and the High Authority has declared that it does not contemplate for the moment any increase in the fund. In any case it is the policy of the High Authority to maintain a reasonable relationship between the total of the guarantee fund and that of its outstanding obligations, so that the fund should always be in a position to protect lenders against every foreseeable interruption in the servicing of loans made or guaranteed by the Authority. The guarantee fund is thus the second basis of the credit of the High Authority.

E. The Act of Pledge

Following upon the first loan contracted in 1954, the High Authority in the same year concluded with the Bank of International Settlements an agreement (better known as "the Act of Pledge") which is accepted by all the lenders to the High Authority and cannot be modified without their consent. Pursuant to this agreement, the credits of the High Authority and the concomitant securities arising from the loans granted by the Authority out of the monies it has borrowed are included in a separate portfolio placed as a pledge in the hands of the Bank of International Settlements for the benefit of all the lenders to the Authority.

It would take too long to enumerate in detail the provisions of this Act of Pledge, which constitute for Europe a somewhat original formula. For the objects of the present study, it is sufficient to indicate the more important consequences of this common pledge. First of all, the pledging of the credits held by the High Authority has the effect of placing its lenders in a privileged position in relation to all the other creditors of the Authority. Furthermore, by reason of this common pledge none of the lenders has, nor can have, any private rights over any category whatsoever of the credits representing loans granted by the Authority, whatever the currency of those loans. The combined group of lenders has as a guarantee the combined group of credits of the High Authority arising from loans made to enterprises by the Authority. Finally, it is the Bank of International Settlements which, on the instructions of the High Authority and after having assured itself that these instructions comply with the provisions of the Act of Pledge, receives the funds borrowed and pays out the sums loaned. The Bank also receives, as they fall due, the annual payments owed to the Authority by the borrowing enterprises and pays out, as they fall due, the sums due from the Authority to its lenders.

This security accorded to lenders, which is added to the assurances implicit in the taxing power of the High Authority and in the existence of an important guarantee fund, is not so superfluous as it might at first sight appear. In fact, it must not be forgotten that the High Authority is neither a bank nor an institution whose sole activity consists in the grant of credits. It is a complex institution with numerous characteristics of governmental power; and its field of action is vast, entailing the use of its resources for very differing ends. Furthermore, if it is true that its taxing power is very wide, it is also true that such power is not unlimited and could, at least theoretically, be reduced by modifications of the Treaty. Finally, the duration of the Treaty creating E.C.S.C. was fixed for a period of fifty years. Again, theoretically, the possibility arises that at the end of this period the member countries may decide to dissolve the Community or, at least, radically change it. Therefore, the creation of a separate portfolio as to which lenders to the High Authority will have a privileged right for the satisfaction of their loan represents not merely a superfluity but, on the contrary, a third essential foundation for the credit of the High Authority.

F. Loans for Industrial Investments

It has been seen that the treaty establishing the E.C.S.C. outlines only in very general terms the objects for which the High Authority may grant loans. Hence, since the annual investment needs of the Community's coal and steel industries far exceed the funds which the High Authority could hope to place at their disposal by its borrowing policy, the High Authority has been confronted with the problem of establishing criteria for the selection of the projects to be financed. Such criteria could evidently not be purely financial. In fact, the very nature and purpose of the Community were opposed to any choice made solely on the basis of the best risk, the E.C.S.C. being a supranational public institution charged with the duty of fostering the balanced development of these basic industries. The High Authority, moreover, had among its numerous tasks that of periodically defining and publicizing general objectives for the development of the coal and steel industries to ensure that the requirements for the Community in future years will be met and for the modernization of production facilities, enlargement of capacity, and increase in efficiency of operations. It is in these general objectives that the High Authority finds criteria for the selection of projects to be financed.

For loans granted up to now, the High Authority has recognized a claim for priority in the following categories of capital investments:

(a) modernization and mechanization of coal mining installations, including coking plants;
(b) expansion of pithead power stations for consumption of low grade coal;
(c) expansion of facilities for the production and dressing of iron ore;
(d) increase in production of pig iron and coke in order to lessen consumption of scrap;
(e) construction of new manufacturing facilities and other projects providing productive employment for workers unemployed because of the coal crisis.

After a first selection of projects has been made pursuant to these criteria, the final decision of the High Authority is based on financial criteria; and the only projects eventually retained are those exhibiting the desired characteristics of profitability, the borrowers giving every guarantee of solvency. The principal conditions of the loan contracts are these:

(a) The rate of interest is fixed in relation to the cost to the High Authority of the corresponding money borrowed, with the sole addition of the expenses and commissions involved in the administration of the Act of Pledge. The High Authority, which has no profit goal in view, has renounced the seeking of any marginal profit on its loans, although the treaty gives it that option. The rate of interest is the same for all loans granted out of any particular sum borrowed, whatever the nationality of the borrower or the nature of the project.

(b) The period of repayment of the loan is fixed in relation to the time for repayment which the High Authority itself obtained for the corresponding sum borrowed.

(c) The security demanded varies in each case according to the nature of the project and the situation of the borrower and in conformity with banking custom.

(d) Finally, the loan is made and is reimbursable in the same currency as that which applies to the corresponding sum borrowed. Thus it is the beneficiaries of the loans who bear any subsequent exchange risks.

G. Loans for Financing the Construction of Workers' Homes

From the commencement of its activity, the High Authority has realized the importance of housing workers with a view to the amelioration of their conditions of life and work. It has, therefore, decided to provide substantial means of financing for the realization of programs of construction of houses destined for coal and steel workers.

For such financing it was impossible to place the burden of exchange risks on the borrowers, and it was, therefore, necessary to grant loans in the respective national currencies. Furthermore, account had to be taken of the fact that the profitability of workers' houses in the Community countries was generally too limited to remunerate capital at the high interest rate applicable in most of the national financial markets. Faced with these difficulties which threatened the effectiveness of its financial aid, the High Authority decided to allocate to the financing of housing a special reserve supported by the resources arising out of any net profit derived from investment of the levy funds. By adding to these resources, lent at reduced rates of interest, other capital obtained or mobilized in accordance with market conditions, the High Authority has been able to place credits at the disposal of the borrowers at the rates usually in force in each of the Community countries for the financing of workers' houses.

H. The Financial Results of the Activity of the High Authority

Although the Treaty setting up E.C.S.C. came into force in July 1952, it was the year 1954 which marked the real commencement of the High Authority's financial activity. In the spring of that year, in fact, the United States Government signed a contract with the High Authority whereunder, with the Export-Import Bank as intermediary, a credit of $100,000,000 was accorded to the High Authority.

The liability for loans thereafter contracted by the High Authority amounted on December 31, 1960, to about $250,000,000. Of this amount, $120,000,000 arose from three public issues in the United States market and about $11,600,000 (50,000,000 Swiss francs) from a public issue offered in Switzerland in 1956. On the other hand, no public issue has been made in Community countries. The balance arises from the loan by the United States and from other loans arranged with specialized organizations in Community countries and allocated to financing workers' houses. The breakdown of these borrowings is shown in detail in the following table:

Country	Year of Issue	Original Amount of Loan	Original Amount (U.S. Dollars)	Outstanding December 31, 1960
U. S. A.	1954	$ 100,000,000	100,000,000	90,800,000
Germany	1955	DM 50,000,000	11,904,762	10,627,452
Belgium	1955	FB 200,000,000	4,000,000	3,688,000
Luxembourg	1955	Flux 5,000,000	100,000	—
		FB 20,000,000	400,000	368,800
Germany (Saar)	1956	DM 2,977,450*	708,923	638,734
Switzerland	1956	FS 50,000,000	11,655,012	11,655,012
U. S. A.	1957	$ 35,000,000	35,000,000	31,700,000
Luxembourg	1957	Flux 100,000,000	2,000,000	2,000,000
U. S. A.	1958	$ 50,000,000	50,000,000	50,000,000
U. S. A.	1960	$ 35,000,000	35,000,000	35,000,000
		Total	250,768,697	236,477,998

* Upon the economic integration of the Saar with the Federal Republic of Germany in July 1959, the outstanding amount of such loan was converted at the then official rate from French francs to Deutschmarks.

Also as of December 31, 1960, the High Authority had granted loans out of borrowed funds and prepayments on loans in a total amount of about $260,790,000. In addition, it had granted out of its own funds loans totaling about $30,000,000. The division of the loans granted according to the capital investments financed and among borrowers in the various member countries is shown in the following table, the figures being in millions of dollars.

Division of Loans	Loans from Borrowed Funds	Loans from Funds not Borrowed	Total
A. By capital investments financed			
Coal mines (including coking plants)	88.14	—	88.14
Pithead power stations	46.31	—	46.31
Production and dressing of iron ore	22.25	—	22.25
Steel industry	83.98	—	83.98
Housing for workers	20.11	21.68	41.79
Readaptation	—	5.40	5.40
Research	—	2.88	2.88
Miscellaneous	—	0.72	0.72
	260.79	30.68	291.47
B. By locations of Borrowers			
Germany	135.98	22.06	158.04
Belgium	27.20	1.06	28.26
France	55.86	4.13	59.99
Italy	40.45	1.14	41.59
Luxembourg	1.30	1.01	2.31
Netherlands	—	1.28	1.28
	260.79	30.68	291.47

FINANCIAL ACTIVITIES

The outstanding loans at the same date amounted to $238,200,000. In addition, the High Authority guaranteed loans contracted by enterprises up to a total of about $10,000,000.

To this report of more strictly financial activity must be added some information relating to assistance granted by the High Authority in connection with "readaptation" and technical and economic research. Up to December 31, 1960, the aggregate commitments that had been contracted by the High Authority for "readaptation" amounted to the equivalent of $52,500,000. A total of $29,500,000 having already been paid out, the net commitments as of that date were about $23,000,000. The commitments contracted by the High Authority in connection with research amounted at the same date to the equivalent of $28,000,000. A total of about $13,000,000 having been paid out, the net commitments amounted to $15,000,000.

These few figures should suffice to demonstrate the importance of the financial activities of E.C.S.C. The High Authority started its activities at a time when the industries placed under its jurisdiction suffered from a penury of long-term capital and the capital markets of nearly all the Community countries offered only limited sources of capital and at particularly high rates. There is no doubt that the High Authority has effectively contributed to making possible the necessary capital investment which, without its action, would not have been realized or would have been realized later. The High Authority is a recently-created juridical entity, new and complex in form, whose constitution, powers, functions, and financial situation were first almost unknown to the public; but it has rapidly succeeded in obtaining access to the international capital markets, and notably to that of the United States—markets which had been very cool to foreign borrowers due to past unfortunate experiences of the lenders. Finally, the happy results attained by the Authority in the sphere of assistance for readaptation and research have not failed to furnish particularly useful experience for the analogous mechanisms brought into action in the two new European Communities.

II

THE EUROPEAN COMMUNITY OF ATOMIC ENERGY

A. Its Tasks

The Treaty setting up the European Atomic Energy Community, better known as Euratom, indicates that its mission is, by establishment of the conditions necessary for the formation and rapid growth of the nuclear industry, to contribute to raising the standard of life in the member countries and to the development of exchanges with other countries. Nuclear energy presents itself as an essential resource in the future for the development and maintenance of production and for industrial progress of peaceful enterprises; a new technical revolution is awaited as to the use of this new source of energy. Hence comes the urgency for the Community countries to overcome their backwardness in this sphere, in order to assure that their role in these developments is not seriously compromised.

However, the necessary means are no longer available to the separate European countries; therefore, Euratom proposes to unite the resources of the Member States in a common effort to permit a production of nuclear energy which each of them working alone would have found it difficult to realize. The common use of the resources, scientific as well as technical and economic, in existence in the six countries was really the only way to achieve that aim and avoid dispersion and waste of energy in enterprises competing among themselves and often superfluous.

Euratom is a specialized Community and represents in the sphere of nuclear energy what E.C.S.C. represents for the coal and steel industry. But E.C.S.C., as the first of the European Communities to see light—and solely because of its earlier appearance on the scene—was equipped with fairly wide powers even in fields (such as labor problems) which are outside the scope of the basic industries. On the other hand, Euratom, born at the same time as E.E.C., finds its powers more strictly limited.

Among the tasks allotted to Euratom, the following seem susceptible of involving financial activity:

(a) developing research;
(b) facilitating investments and ensuring, particularly by encouraging business enterprise, the construction of the basic facilities required for the development of nuclear energy within the Community;
(c) ensuring a regular and equitable supply to all Community users of ores and nuclear fuels.

B. Field and Means of Action

Article four of the Euratom treaty allocates to the Euratom Commission the task of promoting and facilitating nuclear research in Member States and carrying it to completion by the execution of a program of research in the Community. To carry out this task the Commission:

(a) is to create a common center of nuclear research;
(b) may entrust third parties with the implementation of certain parts of the Community's research program;
(c) may encourage research programs undertaken by third parties by giving financial support in the form of loans, by supplying or providing—either for payment or free of charge—raw materials or fissionable substances, as well as installations, equipment or expert assistance.

As regards action in the investment sphere, the Commission may either grant loans or participate directly in the financing of enterprises which it recognizes as having outstanding importance for the development of nuclear energy in the Community and which, for this reason, may be constituted as Joint Enterprises in accord with article forty-five of the Euratom Treaty.

Finally, as regards the supply of ores and nuclear fuels, the Treaty has provided

FINANCIAL ACTIVITIES

for the creation of a Supply Agency having a right of option on all ores, raw materials and special fissionable substances produced in the territories of the Member States, and having, furthermore, the exclusive right of concluding contracts relating to the supply of these same materials issuing from within or without the Community.

C. Its Resources

In examining the resources at the disposal of Euratom to meet its obligations, distinction must be made between expenditure for operation and research, the financing of research and investment, and the activity of the Supply Agency. The costs of operation and of research are a charge on the Member States of the Community and are based on the budget prepared each year by the Council of Ministers according to the following scale of division:

Country	Operational Budget	Research and Investment Budget
Belgium	7.9%	9.9%
Germany	28	30
France	28	30
Italy	28	23
Luxembourg	0.2	0.2
Netherlands	7.9	6.9

In contrast to E.C.S.C., Euratom does not enjoy financial autonomy. It is true that article 173 of the Treaty leaves the door open for the establishment of a levy which Euratom would collect in the Community, the proceeds of which would be destined to replace in whole or in part the financial contributions of the Member States. However, the establishment of such a levy is only a possibility, since the Member States are by no means committed to taking any such action. Therefore, at least in the present state of the Treaty, the autonomy of resources which constitutes the primary basis of E.C.S.C. credit does not exist in the case of Euratom.

For the financing of research and investment, the Treaty endows Euratom with borrowing powers, but here again a difference can be seen between the provisions which govern the borrowing activity of E.C.S.C. and those laid down for Euratom. In fact, the High Authority of E.C.S.C. is alone competent to undertake borrowing, as well as to grant loans. On the contrary, for Euratom the power of decision in borrowing matters resides in the Council of Ministers on the basis of proposals from the Commission. This concentration of the powers of decision on financial matters in the hands of the Council of Ministers, which consists of representatives of the Member States, is the logical consequence of the financial structure of Euratom. In fact, since Euratom has no resources of its own, the Member States are the ones who finally would have to face up to its obligations in case the financing arrangements made by Euratom proved insufficient to meet its debts. Hence, it appears natural that the Member States should have reserved the right to decide on the exercise of borrowing powers. It may, however, be questioned whether the somewhat intricate procedure resulting from the necessity of a Council decision is the most appropriate one for an institution like Euratom which is supposed to procure part of its resources by floating loans on the capital markets.

This financial autonomy, which Euratom lacks, exists, on the other hand, in the case of the Supply Agency (which is likewise endowed with juridical personality) although the Agency is subject to the control of the Euratom Commission, which has, notably, a right of veto over Agency decisions. The Agency capital is equivalent to $2,400,000 and has been subscribed by all Member States except Luxembourg. Of this total, ten per cent has been paid up, and the balance may be called in as necessary to meet the obligations of the Agency. Moreover, the Agency may levy a charge on the transactions within its jurisdiction—a charge which can serve only to defray its operating expenses. In fact, the Agency has so far avoided recourse to levying this charge, and its expenses have been financed by the Community's budget of operations. Finally, the Agency may resort to borrowing in order to procure the resources necessary for the accomplishment of its tasks. These borrowings, which are guaranteed by Euratom, may not, however, be undertaken without the consent of the Commission and of the Council of Ministers.

D. Its Activity

The time gone by since the dates of entry into force of the Euratom Treaty and of the establishment of that Community's institutions is surely too short to permit an evaluation of the results of its activity in the financial sphere, a sphere wherein somewhat prolonged preparation is natural before operations can begin. However, attention may be drawn with satisfaction to one early financial operation of wide scope already undertaken by Euratom in the second year of its activity and whose realization will be spread out over several years. In the framework of a cooperation agreement between Euratom and the United States, the latter, through the Export-Import Bank, has placed funds at the disposal of Euratom, by opening a credit of $135,000,000, which Euratom may use in order to make a contribution to the financing of the construction, on Community territory, of nuclear centers. These centers are to be of the same types as those in which research and development have been pushed to an advanced stage in the United States. They will have a total installed capacity of about 1,000,000 kilowatts.

The situation which has arisen in the energy market in the last few years makes nuclear energy more costly than classic energy and has had the effect of slowing down the final approval of projects for centers capable of being financed within the framework of the agreement with the United States. For that reason, no loan has yet been made by Euratom, although projects are now being studied. This delay, however, in no way detracts from the importance of the agreement—which demonstrates once more the active interest the United States takes in the progress of European unification and, at the same time, its confidence in this new Community.

As regards the field of research, the creation of a Joint Research Center was delayed due to complex negotiations between Euratom and the Member States. Nonetheless, it can be estimated that effective commitments by Euratom within the framework of the Community's first five year program of research will reach at the end of 1961 the total amount of $104,000,000 and that disbursement on these commitments will reach at the same time the amount of $78,000,000.

Finally, as regards the Supply Agency, neither a shortage of ores and raw materials has so far been encountered nor a change in the good prospects for obtaining special fissionable substances necessary for Euratom. Thus, the Agency's task has momentarily been reduced to guaranteeing good supply conditions, without involving any financial operations in this respect. But the activity of the Agency will be quickly developed in the future with the extension of the research programs and the construction of nuclear centers.

III

The European Economic Community

A. Its Tasks

Of the three existing Communities, the European Economic Community is undoubtedly the one which has the greatest task to accomplish. Its objective is to build up a common European market—and so to call into life a vast zone of common economic policy, constituting a powerful unit of production and permitting continuous expansion, increased stability, accelerated elevation of the standard of life, and the development of harmonious relations between the component states.

The mere list of these objectives is sufficient to understand the amplitude of the tasks of the E.E.C., whose powers extend from the free circulation of goods to the establishment of a common agricultural policy; from the free circulation of persons, resources and capital, to the means of transport and rules of competition; from the coordination of the economic, financial and commercial policies of the member states, to social policy, and last but not least, to assistance to underdeveloped countries.

B. Field and Means of Action

In spite of the amplitude of its tasks and responsibilities, the E.E.C. is, of the three European Communities, the one whose financial activities are the most limited. In fact, although the problem of the investment policy in the Community figures among those calling particularly for attention by the E.E.C., its role in this sphere comprises tasks of coordination, supervision, orientation, and sometimes even of promotion of projects; but it does not include either the financial activity or responsibility of the Community organs.

The task of lending financial aid to investments, the accomplishment of which is recognized to be of importance for the balanced development of the common market, has been entrusted to another organization, the European Investment Bank. Although originating in the same Treaty of Rome which created the E.E.C. and working in close cooperation with that Community, the Bank is endowed with its own juridical personality and with complete autonomy vis-à-vis the E.E.C. as to both decisions and resources. Analysis of the structure and activities of the Bank will form the subject of a separate section in this article, wherein at the same time the role played in this sphere by the E.E.C. Commission will be examined. There remain, however, to be examined here two other areas in which the E.E.C. engages in direct financial activity—namely, the "readaptation" of workers and assistance to overseas countries.

Article 123 of the Treaty of Rome provided for the creation of a European Social Fund, having as its mission the promotion of employment opportunities within the Community and of workers' mobility, both geographic and occupational. This Fund is administered and directed by the E.E.C. Commission, assisted in this task by a committee formed of representatives of Member States and unions or workers and employers. The fundamental objective of the Fund is to prevent prejudicial consequences to labor as a result of the progressive establishment of the common market; however, the Fund is not supposed to intervene in cases where only unemployment is a consequence of the common market. This is a substantial difference from the mechanism of "readaptation" provided for by the E.C.S.C. Treaty; and this difference needs to be underlined because it involves considerably extended tasks for the Fund.

The Fund is in fact called upon to cover fifty per cent of the expenses incurred by a Member State or by a body under public law in the three following cases—professional reeducation of unemployed workers, relocation of those workers, and maintenance of the same wage level for workers affected by conversion of their enterprise to other production. As the Social Fund enjoys neither juridical nor fiscal autonomy vis-à-vis the E.E.C., its expenses are a charge on the E.E.C.

A Convention annexed to the E.E.C. Treaty relating to the Association with the Community of the Overseas Countries and Territories implemented the constitution of the Development Fund for the overseas countries and territories which formerly were colonies or possessions of Member States. The aim of this Fund is to have the Member States participate in measures designed to achieve the social and economic development of these countries in an effort exceeding the one of their responsible authorities. The limits of activity of the Development Fund are clearly fixed, and in that respect it differs from the Social Fund. Both are limited, however, to nonreimbursable assistance. The Development Fund is to be supported by contributions that the Member States have undertaken to make during a period of five years. The amount of this contribution is divided up as follows: $70,000,000 from Belgium; $200,000,000 from Germany; $200,000,000 from France; $40,000,000 from Italy; $1,250,000 from Luxembourg, and $70,000,000 from the Netherlands.

The funds available must be utilized in financing projects in the overseas countries and territories, former colonies, or possessions of the Member States according to the following scale: Belgium, $30,000,000; France, $511,250,000; Italy, $5,000,000; the

Financial Activities

Netherlands, $35,000,000. It falls to the Council of Ministers to fix each year the amount destined to finance social institutions (schools, hospitals, etc.) or economic investments (mainly infrastructural projects). It falls to the Commission to choose the individual projects to be financed. However, as regards economic investments, each Member State has the right of insisting that individual projects be submitted to the Council of Ministers.

C. Its Resources

Like Euratom, E.E.C. has no resources of its own and its expenses are covered by contributions which the Member States make each year on the basis of the budget fixed by the Council of Ministers. The E.E.C. Treaty contains, however, a provision analogous to that found in the Euratom Treaty, by virtue of which the Commission is charged with studying the conditions under which the contributions of Member States could be replaced by other sources of funds—notably by receipts arising from the common customs tariff when such a tariff has been definitely established. However, the powers of the Commission in this field are limited to the submission of proposals to the Council of Ministers; and it is only by unanimous vote that the Council, after consultation with the Assembly, could eventually formulate proposals which it would recommend that the Member States adopt in accord with their respective constitutional rules.

Although the problem of endowing the Communities with their own financial resources is always important—notably because of the influence that autonomy of resources can have in the relations between the Executives of the Communities and the Member States—nevertheless, from the strictly financial point of view this need to possess its own resources is less evident in the case of E.E.C., which, since it does not have to borrow, is not confronted with a need to establish a sound basis for obtaining credit.

Division of the financial contributions required from the Member States differs according to whether the contributions are for operational expenses or for the Social Fund.

Country	Operational Expenses	European Social Fund
Belgium	7.9%	8.8%
Germany	28	32
France	28	32
Italy	28	20
Luxembourg	0.2	0.2
Holland	7.9	7

D. Its Activity

The institutions of the E.E.C. were set up only at the beginning of 1958—at the same time as those of Euratom. Despite that, their early years of activity in the progressive establishment of the common market were distinguished by results largely outstripping the most optimistic forecasts. On the other hand, progress was necessarily slower with respect to the Social Fund and the Development Fund in view of the need to establish at the outset, with the consent of the Member States, the details of the rules and procedures to govern their activity.

Thus, the regulations for the European Social Fund were not adopted by the Council of Ministers until May 11, 1960; and, mainly for this reason, no expenditure has yet been made. The activity of the European Overseas Development Fund, on the other hand, developed more rapidly. By December 31, 1960, the Commission had received proposals involving an over-all request for financing equalling $666,000,000, allocable, according to their objects, as follows: studies and researches, $14,000,000; economic investments, $499,000,000; social investments, $153,000,000. By the same date the amounts granted for these projects amounted world-wide to $113,000,000, divided as follows: studies and research, $8,500,000; economic investments, $65,500,000; social investments, $39,000,000.

IV

THE EUROPEAN INVESTMENT BANK

From the commencement of negotiations between the Member States for the establishment of the European Economic Community, the creation of an investment institution endowed with assured financial resources, and at the same time capable of introducing itself on the capital market as a first-class borrower, has been considered indispensable to assure conditions for a balanced and smooth development of the common market. It is not true, as has been abundantly proved by the experiences of Italy after its unification in 1860 and of the United States after the Civil War, that when regions of unequal economic development are suddenly brought into communication, the lower cost of labor and the greater productivity of investments automatically ensure more rapid progress in the region less favored initially, and thus a general levelling up. On the contrary, the gap may increase cumulatively, if the basic conditions for a universal development of production are not at the outset created by public means and if, besides other facilities accorded by the government, important means of financing are not placed at the disposal of the enterprises desirous of settling themselves in these less-developed regions.

On the other hand, economic reconversion constitutes an essential element of the policy of the common market. It is not enough to consider the enlargement of outlets and of competition as a sufficient incentive to enhance the reorientation of industrial activities and the modification of production methods. In addition, it is necessary that the enterprises, forced to modify methods by the progressive disappearance of protectionism, should be able to find financing for these changes; thus, the need to lend financial help is obvious. Industrial reconversion and the opening of new activities capable of providing employment for workers, figure among the tasks which are of the greatest social and economic utility. Their benefits cannot be measured solely by their direct effects nor by the existing facilities which they manage to use or save, but rather by the climate of progress and transformation which they help to create.

Finally, the establishment of the common market embraces the realization of projects, which by reason of their scope, or even simply their very nature, do not qualify easily for the various sources of capital available in each of the different member countries. The most typical projects of this kind will occur in the field of communications and the production or transport of energy. From the moment that European interest is attested by the number of countries concerned with a project or associated with it, a Community source normally should be provided for its financing.

Article 130 of the Treaty establishing the European Economic Community has confided to the European Investment Bank the mission of granting loans or financial guarantees for projects to develop underdeveloped regions, modernize enterprise, or create new activities called for by the progressive establishment of the common market. The same applies to projects of common interest to several of the member countries, but which cannot be financed by means available in each country.

In order to achieve these aims, two solutions can be envisaged: creation of a financial institution of bank character or the setting up of an assistance fund. Two different categories of development loans correspond with these two solutions. In the first category stand loans which offer to the borrower more favorable conditions than those of the financial markets in regard to rate of interest, term of the loan, and other accessory matters. Such loans, called "soft loans," are necessary in the case of investments which—while constituting a sort of first step on the road to economic development or being indispensable to the launching of a process of cumulative development—do not offer the desired financial profitability. Thus, the financial servicing of these loans by the borrower cannot be secured unless their rate of interest is fixed considerably below the market rate. These loans cannot be granted by bank-type institutions but fall, by contrast, within the scope of financial assistance funds, which have their resources more or less directly in the contributions of the participating States. Examples of institutions of this kind can be found in the Development Loan Fund, the International Development Association, and—on the European scale—in the Development Fund for Overseas Countries and Territories.

In the other category are loans of the banking type. These loans are suitable for self-liquidating investments, which offer the desired financial profitability and thus offer secured financial servicing in accordance with normal market conditions. These loans come within the scope of financial institutions of the banking type, which draw the essential bulk of their resources from the financial market, and for which the quality of these investments constitutes one of the principal bases of their own credit. Examples of similar financial institutions on the international scale are the International Bank for Reconstruction and Development and the International Finance Corporation. Under this same heading can also be included the financial activity of E.C.S.C.—although this body not only grants "self-liquidating" loans for industrial investments, but also others to finance workers' houses, which then have the characteristics of "soft loans." The European Investment Bank also comes within the category of financing institutions of the banking type. Moreover, simply by reading its statute, which forms an integral part of the Treaty setting up E.E.C., it is evident that the Investment Bank has all the characteristics of that category.

A. Its Structure

The European Investment Bank, as has been seen, was created within the framework of the E.E.C.; but it has its own juridical personality, its own means of financial action, and its own organs of operation. This autonomy and independence of the Bank are inherent in its nature as a banking institution called upon to obtain essential means of action from the financial markets; and these factors constitute the best guarantee to lenders of the Bank's capability to act as a real credit institution—without being conditioned by political considerations and yet being inspired by the economic policy and goals of the Community.

The capital of the Bank amounts to a billion units of account; and this unit has a value of 0.88867088 grams of pure gold, which is the par in gold of the American dollar. The breakdown of the capital according to the Member States is as follows: Germany, 300 millions; France, 300 millions; Italy, 240 millions; Belgium, 86.5 millions; Holland, 71.5 millions; and Luxembourg, 2 millions. Of this total of one billion, 250 millions have actually been paid in by the Member States. The balance of 750 millions has the character of guarantee capital, which can be called in if necessary to meet the Bank's obligations to its lenders. In other words, the Member States are guarantors of the Bank's liabilities up to the limit of their share in the total capital subscribed but not paid up.

Provisions analogous to those governing the International Bank for Reconstruction and Development aim at ensuring the maintenance of the original value of the paid-up capital, in case of modification in the par value of the currencies of the Member States, by a system of adjustments between the Bank and the Member States in question. These provisions fulfill the double objective of assuring (a) that the devaluation of the currency of a Member State will not unbalance the agreed contributions of the Member States to the Bank capital and (b) that the Bank will not sustain unjustified losses.

However, the support given by Member States to the Bank does not stop at that point. In fact, the Bank may approach the Member States in order to obtain special loans, if the market situation would not allow it to procure the necessary resources under convenient conditions. These loans may be demanded in 1961 and thereafter, and may not exceed altogether a total of 400 million units of account or 100 millions in any one year. These special loans are to be granted by Member States in proportion to their subscription to the Bank's capital.

Finally, the Bank will procure the resources necessary for its activity by floating loans on the financial markets within the Community as well as outside. It can be pointed out in this connection that the loan and guarantee capacity of the Bank has been fixed by statute at 250 per cent of the subscribed capital—at the present time 2,500,000,000 units of account. Compared with the paid-up capital, this figure implies a large recourse to sources of outside capital.

The Bank is an institution which does not aim at profit and does not remunerate its capital. All of its net revenues are devoted to creating reserves and provisions. The organs of the Bank are the Board of Governors, the Board of Directors, and the Management Committee. The Board of Governors, composed of ministers designated by the Member States, has functions similar to those exercised by the shareholders at the annual meeting of a private corporation. It is notably this body which defines the general directives for the Bank's credit policy. The Board of Directors, whose members are nominated by the Board of Governors on the recommendation of the Member States and the E.E.C. Commission, is alone authorized to decide on the grant of loans and guarantees and on borrowing by the Bank itself. In addition, it has control of the ordinary administration of the Bank.

The Management Committee, which is composed of the President and two Vice Presidents, is the veritable center of the activity of the Bank. In effect, independent of its statutory powers—the management of current affairs, the preparation of the decisions of the Board of Directors, and their execution—this is the organ in which is vested full power of initiative.

B. Principles of Action

The provisions of its statute define certain principles to be followed by the Bank in granting loans and guarantees. These principles may be summed up as follows:

(a) the financial aid of the Bank can be sought by the Member States as well as by any enterprise or institution, public or private, operating in any sector whatever of the economy. Requests for financing may be made direct to the Bank, or through a Member State or the E.E.C. Commission;

(b) the Bank may finance only investment projects which contribute to the increase of economic productivity in general and favor the establishment of the common market; the financial soundness of the project must be assured by the earnings when the enterprise to be aided is in the sector of production, and for other projects the interest and amortization of the loan must be guaranteed by an obligation of the State in which the project is carried out or by any other means;

(c) the projects to be financed normally must be situated in the territory of the Member States, but under special procedures the Bank may also finance projects in third party countries;

(d) the Bank grants financial aid in so far as other sources are not available on reasonable terms; and, so far as possible, the granting of its loans is subject to employment of other means of finance. Thus, instead of competing with the existing banking system, it complements that system;

(e) unlike the International Bank for Reconstruction and Development, the European Investment Bank is not obliged to make the grant of a loan subject to a guarantee from a Member State; it has the right to choose the required guarantees in conformity with banking custom. It must, in any case, include in its loan contracts appropriate protection against exchange risks;
(f) the rate of interest on loans granted by the Bank must be adapted to the conditions prevailing in the capital market and no reduction in rate of interest may be allowed; but if the case so requires, a rebate may be granted the Member State concerned or a third party on the condition that it is compatible with the E.E.C. Treaty.

A detailed procedure is laid down for the approval of requests for loans and guarantees. As to each application for loan or guarantee, after having received the opinion of the Member State interested and of the E.E.C. Commission, the Management Committee submits its own views to the Board of Directors. In practice, the latter cannot grant loans or guarantees for projects as to which either the Management Committee or the Commission of the E.E.C. have made a negative decision. These provisions not only allow a reconciliation between the autonomy of the Bank and the desired parallelism of its policy with that of the E.E.C., but, at the same time, constitute an efficient guarantee against the possibility that exterior pressure might persuade the Bank to grant credits incompatible with its banking character.

C. Its Activities

The European Investment Bank was created on January 1, 1958, the date of the coming into force of the Treaty establishing the E.E.C., and is now in the fourth year of its existence. In fact, the first year was devoted to its organization; and only in 1959 did its real activity commence. The very uniqueness of the new institution imposed upon it the task of resolving a number of new problems before entering upon the active phase.

The Bank has been confronted with many projects, among which it had to make an especially careful selection, since it could accept only those which conformed to the conditions for giving financial aid as prescribed in the statute of the Bank. Out of the projects submitted to it, the Bank had approved by December 31, 1960, twelve loans for a total amount equivalent to $93,500,000. The total cost of the projects financed is estimated at about $689,000,000; the Bank's share in their financing has averaged about fourteen per cent and varies between eight per cent and fifty-seven per cent according to the nature and size of the projects. Three new loans were approved in February 1961, bringing the total amount of loans granted to the equivalent of $120,500,000.

The loans have been granted for projects located in the following countries:

Italy	$82,400,000
France	$31,700,000

Luxembourg	$ 4,000,000
Germany	$ 2,400,000

The largest share of the money loaned goes to the less developed regions of the Community.

The loans are distributed by economic sector as follows:

Sector	Number of Projects	E.I.B. Loans
Energy	5	$37,600,000
Transport	2	25,000,000
Iron and Steel	1	24,000,000
Chemicals	4	19,000,000
Agriculture	1	9,500,000
Processing industries	2	5,400,000
Total	15	$120,500,000

With regard to the conditions attached to these loans, the Bank follows the banking practice common to the six member countries for comparable operations. The term of the loans is established according to the nature of the projects financed; it has varied from twelve to twenty years for the loans granted up to the present.

Since it has resources in different currencies and since its borrowers are situated in different countries, the Bank had to consider with particular attention the problem of how to apply to the loans granted by it at any particular time the same rate of interest—no matter what the borrower's nationality may be—and how at the same time to place its borrowers in conditions of substantial equality in relation to exchange risks. At present, the Bank gives its clients the choice between two formulae. Under the first formula, the borrower receives the currencies drawn by the Bank—which may even include currencies of third party countries, but not his own national currency, and he repays in the same ones that he received. Under the second formula, the borrower receives the currency of whichever of the six member countries he chooses, but then the Bank has the right to decide in which currency of the member countries each instalment has to be repaid. These repayments have to be made according to the par values existing at the time the loan was paid out. The rate of interest varies according to the market situation and depends solely on the monetary formula chosen by the beneficiary. For the loans granted up to the present, the rate of interest has been $5\frac{5}{8}$ per cent for the first formula, and $5\frac{1}{4}$ per cent for the second.

It has not been considered opportune to resort to borrowing during the first period of activity, the fraction of subscribed capital paid in having been large enough to meet all the requirements of loans granted up to now. Moreover, payments on loans are spread over the whole period of implementation of projects financed. But the expansion of loans and commitments made by the Bank is bringing nearer the time that it will have to turn to the capital markets for the funds it needs; and doubtlessly the first borrowings by the Bank will take place in 1961.

D. Perspectives

The European Investment Bank is a new institution, and, although in different ways it bears resemblance to the International Bank of Reconstruction and Development, it is not a reproduction of that Bank on a European scale. Its sphere is certainly less extensive, both from a geographical standpoint and in respect to the nature of the projects to be financed. In addition, at least up to the present time, it has been called upon to operate in countries where the capital market has been relatively normal for many years and where the introduction of foreign currencies is not the essential aspect of financing operations.

Certain criticisms have been made with regard to the Bank's activity, which is considered by some people to have been too limited in terms of loans granted up to the present time. The Bank could easily have avoided such criticisms. Had its executives been anxious to indulge in "window-dressing," they could simply have made a less severe selection among the projects submitted to them. Such a policy would certainly have been popular; but it would scarcely have been wise.

Up to the present the Bank has granted almost all its loans to projects situated in underdeveloped regions. This priority conforms with good judgment and with the directives of its Board of Governors. In these regions, the Bank has chosen, in particular, projects concerning energy and the chemical industry—fields which, from the viewpoint of common economic policy, raise no major problems. The Bank has a mission to accomplish—namely, facilitating European integration within the Community edifice of which it is a part. In order to succeed in this mission, it must harmonize its credit policy with the economic policy of the E.E.C. However, the formulation of that policy is very complex, and time and experience are required to develop precise ideas concerning the action to be taken in several different sectors, such as agriculture and transport. That is the reason why the first loans in these two sectors have been granted by the Bank only in the last few months. Had the Bank financed projects in those sectors before even knowing the general lines of the investment policy desired for the establishment of the common market, it would have failed in its mission by deferring to a facile popularity. Undoubtedly, the prudence with which the Bank has chosen to act will be properly appreciated by those who constitute the real judges of the activity of an investment bank—*i.e.*, the financial markets to which it will have to resort in order to obtain capital and for which the quality of the loans granted will constitute a fundamental basis for evaluating its credit.

The Bank has not yet made any loans in one of its three spheres of action—for modernization or reconversion of enterprises or the creation of new activities called for by the progressive realization of the common market. But that realization has only just started. Although progressing with accelerated rhythm, the abolition of tariffs and quantitative restrictions is not yet sufficient to make its effects felt—especially because the member countries are all passing through a very favorable period of growth. The real problems of reconversion are thus attenuated and sometimes masked, although they may very well reappear with full vigor when the first economic reversal occurs. In this sphere also, the prudent inception of the Bank will allow it to summon up its resources more easily when their use really becomes necessary.

After all, the evolution of the European and worldwide situation opens up for the Bank new perspectives which were probably not foreseen by the authors of its statute. In fact, the general reinforcement of the economic and financial structures of the member countries in the course of the last few years coincides with a global situation in which all the underdeveloped countries—and that means a large majority of the world population—call with ever-growing insistency upon the industrial countries to adopt measures, and notably a policy of investment, which will reduce the gap which separates the ones from the others. It is impossible to ascertain at the present if, and to what extent, this new situation will be capable of exercising any influence on the Bank's activity. What is certain is that the means at its disposal will never be in excess of its needs.

V

Conclusion

At the end of this exploration of the institutions of the European Communities and their financial activities, the reader will probably be under the impression that he is coming out of a labyrinth. All these names of institutions with sometimes analogous activities—High Authority of E.C.S.C., Commissions of Euratom and E.E.C., Social Fund, European Investment Bank—will perhaps appear to him as pieces of a very complicated puzzle. He will perhaps consider that, by eliminating some of these pieces, the construction would have gained in efficiency.

To judge thus would be to forget that European construction is not the work of one day, but the result of journeys interspersed with many stopping-places and reached sometimes with difficulty and not without setbacks. This edifice is far from being finished; sometimes the work is slowed down; sometimes the architects change and make new plans; and the time has not yet arrived for hoisting the framework of the roof—namely, political unification. Nevertheless, the construction is making progress; and, since the communal dwelling is already inhabited, there is no question of leaving it incomplete. It would certainly have been preferable to complete the construction in one single operation. It would have gained in unity of style. But it must be realized that it is often too difficult to bring co-proprietors into harmonious agreement.

To revert to the financial sphere, doubtless if there had been one single European Community, the different financial activities would have been concentrated in one single institution. Today, it is probably too late, and at the same time too early, to proceed with this concentration. It is too late because it is always painful and often unwise to disturb institutions whose credit is affirmed. It is too soon because the reality within which these institutions are called to operate is still too fluid. Doubtless, one day the concentration of the Community's financial activities in one central institution will be a necessity. Meanwhile the best results will be obtained by the ever closer collaboration between the existing different institutions. The problems to be resolved are so vast and the resources so limited that this cooperation will be a natural consequence—cooperation between the High Authority and the Bank for financing basic industries and operations of reconversion; between Euratom and the Bank for financing nuclear energy; between the Social Fund and the Bank for reconversion; between the Development Fund and the Bank for aid to underdeveloped countries. All these institutions have one task in common, namely, the construction of a united Europe as an element of peace and progress in the world.

TARIFFS AND TRADE IN THE COMMON MARKET*

Hans W. Gerhardt†

I

The Rome Treaty establishing the European Economic Community (E.E.C.) provides for a number of measures designed to establish an economic union between the signatory countries and make possible a more economic allocation of resources within the Community. This, in turn, would, it was hoped, increase the over-all productivity within the region comprised by the six participating countries—including certain overseas areas. The establishment of a customs union was envisaged as only one of the measures to be employed for these purposes; but, so far,[1] this is the only task of "harmonization" that has reached the first stages of realization. On January 1, 1961, tariffs on a large group of imports from member countries were reduced by a further ten per cent, after two previous reductions of the same proportion. At the same time a first step towards a common external tariff went into effect—*i.e.*, each one of the four customs areas of the union[1a] began to apply on imports from nonmember countries a tariff which is thirty per cent closer to the common tariff provided for in the Rome Treaty.

This change in the tariff structure of the world's most intensive trading area is often regarded as an event which will have the most direct and obvious effect upon the relationship between the E.E.C. and the rest of the world. Any prediction as to the scope of this effect, however, is based largely on static models—*i.e.*, on the analysis of cost-price-quantity relationships under extremely limiting assumptions as to market structure and income changes. Therefore, whatever tendencies or effects such models may indicate are meaningful only in the context of an extremely special case. At best, they give an indication of the direction of change to be expected from changes in tariffs; but the "tendencies" revealed by static models lack the significance of those which in reality connect different stages of economic processes over a period of time. In short, these models have only logical, rather than real-time dimensions.

Apart from the problem of prediction, one might wonder at the comparative ease with which the treaty countries have found agreement on the bulk of tariff items. If it could be argued that the establishment of the customs union was easier than the implementation of other features of economic union, one might well suggest that apparently less powerful economic obstacles were encountered in its course. Turning this argument around, this would suggest that the economic effects of

* Discussion and critique of this paper by Professors Fred Joerg, Thomas Keller, and especially Robert S. Smith, all of Duke University, are gratefully acknowledged as major aids in its preparation.

† Dr. rer. pol. 1958, Tübingen University (Germany). Assistant Professor, Department of Economics, Duke University.

[1] Winter 1960-61.

[1a] Benelux (Belgium, Luxembourg, and the Netherlands) enters as one customs area.

customs union were expected to bear relatively less on the distribution of economic gains among members than either of the other harmonization measures—*i.e.*, common fiscal or common monetary policy. This inference seems to find some support in the general (static) theory of the economic effect of customs union.

Subject to all the limitations stemming from reliance on static models, the following conditions might be taken as a summary statement of a preliminary general theory:[2]

The over-all welfare effects of a customs union are the more likely to be beneficial:

A. The greater the gains from production expansion and trade creation; in turn, such gains are the more likely to accrue in varying proportion to—
   (1) The economic importance of the area to which the tariff agreement applies. (The larger the area's share in world production, consumption, and trade, with geographic size itself an important factor in this regard, the greater will be the scope for such improvements as are generally associated with and expected from higher degrees of international specialization and reallocation of factor uses);
   (2) The scope there is for "internal" economies of large scale production in such industries as may expand their production as a result of the tariff change;
   (3) The difference in cost of production between the same industries in the different member countries, where they were protected by tariffs prior to the customs union arrangement;
   (4) The level of the protective tariffs which are subjected either to preferential reduction or complete elimination;
   (5) The competition between member countries with respect to industries enjoying high tariff protection, and the potential scope for developing complementary industries after protection is removed from the industries previously competing in the production of close substitutes; and

B. The smaller the losses from trade diversion; such losses being minimized in varying proportion to—
   (1) The dependence among the member countries and their lack of dependence on the "outside" world. (If each member country is the main supplier of exports to the other member countries and is the main market

---

[2] See especially J. VINER, THE CUSTOMS UNION ISSUE 54 (1950); J. E. MEADE, THE THEORY OF CUSTOMS UNION 107 (1955); J. E. MEADE, THE THEORY OF INTERNATIONAL ECONOMIC POLICY, II: TRADE AND WELFARE (1955). For a convenient summary, see R. SANNWALD & J. STOHLER, ECONOMIC INTEGRATION (1959). By introducing the concepts of "trade creation" and "trade diversion," Viner showed that the effects of customs union as an arrangement for regional free trade need not point in the same direction as the effects of universal free trade. If the customs union leads to shifts in imports from low cost nonmember countries to imports from high cost member countries, the efficiency of resource allocation will decline. To the extent that resource efficiency via product maximization enters the index of universal economic welfare the effect of trade diversion through customs union reduces rather than increases world economic welfare. For a prediction of the welfare effects of a customs union, then, it is necessary to predict the relative strengths of the forces causing trade creation and trade diversion. See Lipsey & Lancaster, *The General Theory of Second Best*, 24 REV. ECON. STUD. 11 (1956).

for exports of the other members, there is relatively little scope for damage to third countries);

(2) The insensitivity to price changes of the supply from outsiders to the member countries, and/or the insensitivity to price changes of the demand by the member countries for imports from outsiders;

(3) A low level of tariffs both of the member countries and of third countries in the lines of trade subject to the preferential tariff treatment. (In this case there has never been very much scope for distortions of the patterns of trade and production, so that the economic gains from a "correction" are correspondingly slight);

(4) The extent to which trade restrictions consist of quantitative restrictions—quotas. (Only as against either free trade or ineffective quotas can a tariff be said to have any distorting effect at all.)

II

Although only two of the model conditions just recited are directly concerned with the tariff as such, it is in each case the tariff which provides the frame of reference. Tariff rates, or rather the differences in tariff rates, serve as criteria for the grouping of countries as "members" and "third countries"—as "insiders" and "outsiders." It is as between these groupings that gains or losses are to be accounted for. Therefore, the first inquiry will be concerned with the absolute and relative level of tariffs under the provisions of the Rome Treaty.

This, of course, is not an area void of previous arrangements and still valid commitments on the part of member countries vis-à-vis the larger number of third countries. On the contrary, bilateral obligations, sometimes of long standing, and more recent commitments under the auspices of the General Agreement on Tariffs and Trade (G.A.T.T.) precondition and limit the perimeter of action. Indeed, it is still questionable whether the implementation of the Rome Treaty will be allowed to follow the presently intended design. In particular, the question of compatibility of the treaty with G.A.T.T. commitments remains under scrutiny, even if its resolution can be postponed.

While any prediction of the outcome of continued negotiation remains speculative, it is assumed that, in the absence of important shifts in power and leadership within G.A.T.T., the present attitude of general acceptance of E.E.C. by the contracting parties of G.A.T.T. will prevail long enough to allow the Common Market to consolidate on the basis of some form of preferential tariff arrangements. It is not, however, taken for granted that the final position of complete customs union envisaged by the Rome Treaty will be reached;[3] instead, consolidation may be found, somewhere short of this goal.

Besides the possibility—and, indeed likelihood—of increasing pressures from third

[3] Complete customs union exists when internal tariffs are reduced to zero and uniform external tariffs are established for all member countries. The revenues accruing from the common external tariff are pooled.

countries, which might stop the E.E.C. short of its goal, the case for the customs union itself must weaken during the transitional period. The additional economic gains resulting from each step of internal tariff reduction will likely decrease, whereas the losses to third countries will likely increase absolutely and/or relatively.

It is at this point that economic reasoning and wishful thinking most obviously diverge. Too much in current thought, it would seem, has come to depend upon the prediction of a mysteriously operating "internal dynamisme," sometimes more urbanely dressed in expectations of supposedly inevitable "spill-over" effects. Partly as an antidote to such exaggerated optimism, attention here is focused on the problems created—on the braking forces, rather than on the self-acceleration, of the development towards customs union.[4]

As far as the tariffs of the member countries on imports from each other are concerned, there is a reasonable presumption that the proposed timetable and the zero tariff target can be realized. However, even in this basically internal sphere a few snags remain—*e.g.*, the problems of nonliberalized agricultural imports and the problem of granting largely unilateral tariff concessions of the same magnitude to the overseas territories. The timetable and the final level of the common external tariff remain much more uncertain. The recent acceleration of the first stage in aligning the outside tariffs of the four customs areas within the E.E.C. toward the common external tariff and the conditional character of the over-all reduction of this tariff by twenty per cent of its originally computed level are cases in point. These uncertainties are emphasized still more by the fact that the common external tariff has not been completed for all items traded. According to the report of the E.E.C. Commission, seventy-two items, "representing less than three per cent of the tariff lines," had not been agreed upon as of the reporting date. This report does not indicate, however, how heavily these items weigh in the total imports of the E.E.C. or in the total imports from individual nonmember countries. Without such information, the eventual over-all incidence of the common external tariff cannot be assessed.[5]

Apart from possible changes in policy as to time schedule and the "official" target level of the common external tariff, there remain formidable statistical problems, which make extremely hazardous any estimate of the likely effects of the common external tariff on trade with third countries. These problems result largely from the method chosen to compute the tariff. The present common external tariff is the arithmetical average of the tariffs in each of the four customs areas on January 1, 1957. This method, which gives equal weight to the tariffs in each area, has invoked much criticism. An alternative method, frequently suggested, would weight the average tariff by the relative amount of imports into the different customs areas.[6]

[4] For examples of this argumentation in support of the treaty provisions, see R. SANNWALD & J. STOHLER, ECONOMIC INTEGRATION (1959). For a discussion of the "spill over effects," see ERNST B. HAAS, THE UNITING OF EUROPE (1958).
[5] EUROPEAN ECONOMIC COMMUNITY COMM'N, THIRD GENERAL REPORT ON THE ACTIVITIES OF THE COMMUNITY 237 (1960). The common tariff, so far, has 2,893 lines.
[6] Still other methods, of course, could have been employed with different weights and differing

Unfortunately, no reliable method of measuring, and, *a fortiori,* of predicting, the effects of a tariff is available. Thus, even if it is agreed that there should be no increase, and, if possible, a reduction in the over-all incidence of the tariff, there remains some scope for differing opinions over the preferable method.

In defense of the method of computation employed, the E.E.C. Commission rejects the criticism that the common external tariff violates the G.A.T.T. rules, which, in addition to other conditions, permit customs unions only to the extent that the common tariff resulting therefrom is not, in its effect, more restrictive than were the national tariffs before the customs union was formed. The Commission reports in fact that the level reached is[7]

on the whole moderate. The weighted average rate resulting from its application to all the imports of the Community in 1958 amounts to 7.4 per cent. From this it follows that the calculation of the tariff on the arithmetical average proved more favorable to non-member countries than the weighted average would have done; though many people favored this latter method, the resulting level would have worked out at 9.1 per cent.

Statistical problems of exact measurements aside, this level would compare with an average level of 8.1 per cent if the separate national tariffs, as applicable on January 1, 1957, were computed for the same (1958) volume of imports. In this case the common tariff would, indeed, appear as "moderate" and compatible with G.A.T.T. rules. If the twenty per cent over-all reduction were actually to come into effect, the common tariff—weighted again in terms of 1958 imports—would amount to 6.1 per cent.[8]

Not all trading partners of the E.E.C. countries find this method of comparing the average incidence of the tariff to be acceptable as a measure of changes in the tariff's economic impact. It is true that E.E.C. imports in 1958 had declined from their 1957 volume, so that the statistics on average incidence, on the whole, overstate, rather than understate, the restrictive effect of the tariff. However, even during this year there were a number of cases—particularly cases involving nonmember countries other than the United States—where exports to E.E.C. countries increased. Since then, moreover, total imports have resumed their previous trend of substantial annual increases. The average incidence, when computed in terms of the comparatively low 1958 imports, tends in these cases to understate the change in the restrictive effect of the tariff.

A more basic criticism of the E.E.C. Commission's calculation of the external tariff's incidence originated in the West German Ministry of Economic Affairs

---

degrees of economic reasonableness. For instance, instead of designating the Benelux countries as one customs area, these countries might have gone into the average as three different areas; and since they had the lowest over-all tariff level, this would have given them relatively more weight, thus turning the average of the common tariff downwards. It perhaps would have been more reasonable to weight the average according to the population within each area. Using this method, the weight given the Benelux levels would have been half that given by employing the straight arithmetical method. Consequently, the average tariff would have turned upwards.

[7] E.E.C. COMM'N, THIRD GENERAL REPORT, *op. cit. supra* note 5, at 238. The later publication from the statistical office of the E.E.C. quotes a weighted average rate of 7.6%. E.E.C. INFORMATIONS STATISTIQUES 244 (1960).

[8] E.E.C. INFORMATIONS STATISTIQUES 244 (1960).

and was adopted by the Berliner Bank A.G. and by other important business groups in Germany and outside the Community. It is argued that the Commission's calculations are distorted in their economic significance because they fail to distinguish between protective tariffs on manufactures, tariffs on agricultural products, and fiscal (revenue) tariffs. Only the first type, it is contended, can properly be considered in determining the actual restrictiveness of the tariff on imports. On this basis, a seemingly persuasive case can be made that an increase is likely in the effective incidence of the common tariff on imports from nonmember countries. For German imports, which in 1959 accounted for approximately forty per cent of all E.E.C. imports from nonmember countries, it is estimated by the Ministry of Economic Affairs that, with due weight given to commodity composition, the average incidence of the tariff on imports from nonmember countries will increase by 117.4 per cent. According to this method of calculation and taking into account imports both from member and nonmember countries, the net increase in the tariff incidence on manufactured goods imported to Germany will be around twenty-six per cent.

This result depends primarily on the decision to exclude revenue and agricultural tariffs from the computation.[9] In fact, a few more tariff items were excluded, so that approximately seventy per cent of manufactured imports actually remained under consideration. Of course, for individual tariff items the rates are sufficiently fixed and—within the limits of general uncertainties mentioned earlier in this article—predictable for each stage of the transitory period. And, for the export-import firm, while the overall tariff incidence problem cannot be said to be irrelevant, it certainly does not add anything basically different to the normal decision-making process. The economist, however, faces a problem qualitatively different when he is called upon to estimate the overall effect of tariff changes. The abstract character of the averages involved is at the core of this problem; and, in the context of the controversy mentioned here, the different possibilities for evaluating fiscal (revenue) tariffs serve to highlight this point. It is by no means clear that their exclusion from the overall estimate made by the German Ministry of Economic Affairs is more meaningful economically than their summary inclusion in the E.E.C. Commission's reports. And yet, at least in the case of Germany, one's judgment on this point is the pivotal factor. In 1958, for instance, imports of crude petroleum brought customs revenues of DM 450 million, as compared to DM 518 million of customs revenues from imports of manufactures. Under the common tariff, the former imports will be entirely free from duties; and so the average tariff rate as applied to all imports could go down even if substantial increases of protective tariffs on manufactured imports went into effect.[10] The economic effects which really matter—the

[9] Commodities covered by the E.C.S.C. and by Euratom were considered as independent from the newly constituted tariff. This would seem acceptable enough if one were to take the realistic view that only such changes can be attributed to the new tariff as actually are determined by it. On the other hand, E.C.S.C. and Euratom are parts of the same general project and should, therefore, be allowed to enter into the evaluation of the final effects of the Common Market.

[10] Even if the 20% reduction in the common tariff is taken into account there will be a number of

restriction of that category of imports which tends to grow most vigorously—would be covered up under the E.E.C. Commission's method of computation.[11]

Although the question of the proper treatment of revenue tariffs may be quite ambiguous and deceiving in the short run, there is good enough reason to include such tariffs in any long run analysis. The distinction between protective tariffs and revenue tariffs is anything but rigid; given sufficient time, a revenue tariff may well develop into a *de facto* protective tariff. This possibility will, of course, be modified with respect to different commodities. A given country's endowment with highly specialized production factors may well prevent a fiscal tariff from becoming, in effect, protective. In general, however, there probably would be much wider scope in E.E.C. for substitution of production factors—especially capital for labor— and hence, for just such a transformation in the economic effects of a tariff. With respect to the time required for such a substitution of factors, it is significant that the length of the transitional period has been chosen specifically with a view to allowing adjustments to fairly substantial (it is hoped!) changes in the industrial structure of the member countries. If chosen adequately for this purpose, surely it will also prove adequate for such adjustments as may be necessary to exploit protective possibilities of revenue tariffs, where they are found to exist. An example would be provided by a tobacco tariff declared to be fiscal rather than protective by a country with marginal production of tobacco; this country may, in terms of pro-

---

fairly substantial increases in individual tariff rates, especially in the countries of the low tariff areas, Germany and Benelux. Based on Der Deutsche Gebrauchstarif 1959 and computed from a list published by Berliner Bank A.G. Mitteilungen für den Aussenhandel 12. Jg.Nr. 3, 1960, the following cases are quoted as examples. No attempt at weighting these cases for their relative importance in the total imports has been made; the importance of individual items, therefore, varies considerably.

Item	German tariff rates in effect 1959	German tariff rates in the common tariff reduced by 20%
Automobiles (passenger cars)	13%	23%
Radio appliances, receivers, and TV	11	17.6
Electr. household appliances	7	16
Machine tools	0-4	3.2- 9.6
Textile machinery	0-4	8.8-11.4
Printing machinery	0-4	8.8-12.8
Dairy machinery	4	8.8
Refrigerators	2-4	11.6
Leather footwear	8-13	16

According to Berliner Bank A.G., Mitteilungen, Nr. 9/10, 1960, p. 5, the list of tariff positions increased under the common external tariff contains about 10,000 items. Most of these items refer to increases in the tariff on imports into Benelux and Germany.

[11] Not even the E.E.C. Statistical Office claims that no such increases in effective rates and incidence of the German tariff will result from the common tariff. In fact, it allows for an increase from 5.1% to 7.2% in the tariff incidence on German capital goods imports. This office does claim, however, that the overall effect of the common tariff as applied to German imports as a whole will be a reduction from (1957) 9.5% to 4.9% at the end of the transition period. E.E.C. INFORMATIONS STATISTIQUES 247 (1960).

ductive factor proportions available, be "unsuited" for tobacco production, if one were to take as criteria for being suited the specific factor proportions employed in the typical tobacco-growing countries. A tariff in this case might make it possible to produce tobacco in this country, since different factor proportions might then become feasible.

Even in the short run, protective and fiscal tariffs may be quite indistinguishable in their economic effects. Market responses to price changes may be induced equally well by either type of tariff and, to the extent that the rates of revenue tariffs applied to commodities are similar to those which prevail for protected commodities, the consumption contraction effect of a tariff increase and the consumption expansion effect of a tariff reduction will be similar.

In addition to the general problems of computing a common tariff and ascertaining its effects, some specific complications influence the overall level and effect of the E.E.C.'s common external tariff. For one thing, the common tariff is not computed exclusively by the averaging method. Indeed, modifications have been introduced, some of which tend to lower and some to raise, the level of the tariff. The Rome Treaty has seven lists (A-G) attached containing groups of commodities subject to special arrangements. These fall into one or the other of two categories: those where entirely new tariffs were fixed, and those where tariffs other than the ones actually in effect on January 1, 1957, were taken as points of reference for computing the average.

List A contains commodities for which the French tariff actually levied on January 1, 1957, did not correspond to the tariffs then "on the books." The tariff in these cases had been temporarily suspended or relaxed, and quantitative restrictions for the time being controlled imports of the commodities in question. List A represents what appears to be an economically, rather than legally, convincing solution; if the restrictive effect of the tariff provides the criterion in formulating a common external tariff, then it is quite reasonable to look for a tariff with a "restriction equivalent" to the quantitative measures being employed. However, since in no other case have attempts been made to translate quantitative restrictions into corresponding "tariff equivalents," the tariff rates fixed in list A seem rather arbitrary.[12] The result is, of course, a higher level of the common tariff than would have resulted from a "legalistic" approach. With an average tariff of about twenty per cent for the seventy-three items on List A (the tariff rates ranging from six to eighty per cent),

---

[12] In general, the E.E.C. Commission has taken the view that de facto rather than de jure tariffs are to be used as bases for the averaging computation. But, in this regard, there may be some doubt as to the correct interpretation of the treaty itself. Articles 19-23—as translated into English—refer to duties "applicable" or "applied" by the member nations. (The corresponding term in the German text is "anwendbar.") Compliance with G.A.T.T. rules could be more easily demonstrated by the E.E.C. Commission, the higher the base tariffs for the averaging could be shown to have been. Thus, the interpretation of the Treaty which is utilized may substantially affect the ease with which compliance with G.A.T.T. can be shown. Because of the divergence between de jure tariffs and actual restrictions on imports, it is not surprising that compromises such as List A were reached. *Cf.* Jacobi, *Der kommende gemeinsame Zolltarif der EWG*, 15 AUSSENWIRTSCHAFT 49 (1960).

the corrected increase in the common tariff has been estimated at five per cent of the tariff base, namely, the value of the imports.[13]

Lists B, C, and D, on the other hand, seem to indicate downward modifications of the results of simple averaging. These lists contain groups of commodities for which tariff maxima have been fixed, which in some important cases remain below the tariffs previously applied to the imports of such commodities into the individual member countries. List E, modifying the result upwards again, contains fictitious tariff bases for chemicals to "correct" for the fact that Benelux, having no protective interest in these industries, in 1957, levied very low import duties on imports, or none at all. Covering fifty-three items, this list is estimated to increase the common tariff by two to three per cent of the tariff base.

More important modifications of the common tariff result from special treatment of the groups of commodities in lists F and G. Here no attempt has been made to apply simple arithmetical formulae; instead, these lists reflect negotiations and policy decisions. List F contains commodities on which agreement among the member countries actually had been reached when the Rome Treaty went into effect, while list G contains those items which were then still under negotiation. The former includes eighty-seven positions, with tariffs ranging from zero to eighty per cent (eighty per cent for sugar imports), and covering mostly raw materials. To the extent that previously applied tariffs are exceeded, the common tariff tends to be raised, but there are sufficiently great individual reductions to leave unchanged the general incidence on commodities in this group. There still remain seventy positions on list G, which represent 15.6 per cent of total E.E.C. imports from non-member countries in 1957. Raw materials account for two-thirds of these imports, while the rest consists of foodstuffs and manufactured goods. "When these products were studied," the E.E.C. Commission reports, "it appeared that the fixing of duties gave rise to very serious difficulties because of their social and economic repercussions. In addition to these difficulties, there were the divergent interests of producer and consumer countries, which explains why some of the solutions arrived at are of a mixed type."[14] Furthermore, this is not a final list, as article twenty of the E.E.C. Treaty provides for the adding of items to list G—with a limit of two per cent of the total value of 1956 imports from third countries to the E.E.C. member which requests the addition. Additions of this type have since been requested by several member countries.[15]

With respect to several of the matters discussed, the situation will remain fluid, pending the outcome of negotiations scheduled for the spring of 1961 among the contracting parties of G.A.T.T. Until then an assessment of the effect of the special treatment of commodities on the seven lists cannot be attempted. However,

---

[13] Giersch, *Einige Probleme der Kleineuropäischen Zollunion,* 113 ZEITSCHRIFT FÜR DIE GESAMTE STAATSWISSENCHAFT 602-31 (1957). Giersch also calculates that similar distortions in the common tariff, resulting from disregarding Italian tariff reductions or suspensions in force on Jan. 1, 1957, have increased the tariff base 2.75%.

[14] E.E.C. COMM'N, THIRD GENERAL REPORT, *op. cit. supra* note 5, at 238.

[15] So-called "lists G2."

it does seem clear that the overall level of the common external tariff of the E.E.C., as it is submitted to the G.A.T.T. parties, will be higher than an unbending application of the averaging method would have led one to expect. This is not, however, to say that the same is likely to be true for the common tariff as it will ultimately emerge from the G.A.T.T. negotiations. In fact, a proposal for a twenty per cent reduction of the common external tariff is already on the table. This proposal, made by the E.E.C. Commission in connection with the acceleration of its time schedule, remains provisional for the present, and subject to the condition of reciprocity on the part of third countries. In effect, however, it is most likely that this reduction will remain largely unilateral, since in many cases tariff agreements between at least one of the member countries and third countries exist with respect to the commodities in question. Compliance with article twenty-four, section six, of G.A.T.T. will, then, substantially mitigate any such increases as may be implied in the common external tariff. Under this provision, third countries are entitled to compensation in any such case where rates on individual tariff items are increased. Compliance with article twenty-four, section six, on the part of the E.E.C. seems beyond doubt, even if at the beginning of negotiations the Community emphasizes that it will enter such negotiations from a position of strength.[16]

III

The problems mentioned here should make it sufficiently clear that—quite apart from the uncertainties in the target rate and the target date of the common external tariff—the computation of average rates of incidence remains somewhat academic. This is not to say that the concept cannot be refined so as to gain real economic meaning; but that such refinement could be achieved only after considerable disaggregation of present data. To make an exact static analysis of the price-quantity effects of tariff changes and of tariff differentials, one would need a statistical device which, first, would measure both the regional (or country) and the commodity concentration of trade flows and which, secondly, would combine these measures in an index to show the degree of commodity specialization in regionally concentrated trade.

This rather formidable task of statistical analysis cannot be undertaken here, nor is it certain that at present the necessary statistical information can be obtained in suitable form.[17] However, since relationships of this kind tie in directly with the general conditions determining the effects of the E.E.C. customs union on trade

---

[16] The Commission makes this sufficiently clear in its Third Report, *op. cit. supra* note 5, at 385. No automatic compensation is here envisaged for each binding touched by the common tariff. "The Commission will state in respect to each binding whether it considers it subject for negotiation. In many cases, the increase of duties in certain tariffs are compensated by reductions in others; frequently this internal compensation exceeds the compensation required, and in such cases the Community must be given a credit to be set off in the negotiations on headings where the increases in duties outweigh the reductions."

[17] For the systematic problems involved in designing such an index of concentration, and for some empirically derived concentration coefficients, both with respect to commodity and country concentration, see Michaely, *The Shares of Countries in World Trade*, 42 REV. ECON. & STATISTICS 307 (1960).

and economic welfare, it seems appropriate to point to some of the more obvious instances of trade concentration—instances that will display important features in the pattern of trade relationships between the E.E.C. and the rest of the world.

Considered together, the E.E.C. countries form the most important trading bloc of the free world. With roughly one third of the United States Gross National Product, they receive approximately twenty-two per cent of total world imports, as compared with not quite nineteen per cent for countries of the European Free Trade Association (E.F.T.A.) and approximately fifteen per cent for the United States. At the same time, the E.E.C. countries account for more than twenty-four per cent of world exports, compared with seventeen per cent for the United States and just below seventeen per cent for the E.F.T.A.[18]

The E.E.C. countries' importance as a world trading area increased strongly during the 1950's and continues to increase at present. From 1950 to 1959 the value of imports into this area increased by 117 per cent, while total world imports expanded slightly more than seventy-two per cent and imports into E.F.T.A. countries sixty-nine per cent. More pronounced still was the gain in trade for E.E.C. exports, which rose by a remarkable 171 per cent, with world totals increasing just under seventy-one per cent and E.F.T.A. exports slightly more than seventy-one per cent. These figures, of course, must be modified to reflect the share of intra-E.E.C. trade.

Once the alignment to the common external tariff is under way, the "intra-trade" among E.E.C. nations can no longer be regarded as "foreign" in assessing the position of the E.E.C. as a whole vis-à-vis the rest of the world. In 1959, intra-trade of the E.E.C. countries accounted for about thirty-nine per cent of their total trade; this reduces and alters the trade position of the E.E.C., both in terms of absolute trade volume and in terms of shares in total world trade. In terms of actual "external" trade, the E.E.C. ranks second in exports (although the difference between the three trading areas—United States, E.E.C., and E.F.T.A.—is narrow) and third in imports behind E.F.T.A. (first) and the United States. Even then, E.E.C. imports from "outside" accounted, in 1959, for about one-sixth of the value of imports originating in the rest of the world (*i.e.,* total world imports minus intra-E.E.C. trade). E.E.C. exports to nonmember countries accounted for more than one-fifth of world exports. The pronounced increase in the ratio of intra-E.E.C. trade to world trade provides, of course, the crucial gauge for measuring both the integrative forces of regional free trade within E.E.C. and the disruptive forces brought to bear upon the trade between E.E.C. and the rest of the world.

The E.E.C. countries have a much higher ratio of intra-trade to world trade than do the countries associated under the Stockholm Convention in the E.F.T.A.[19] This difference is fundamental since it indicates that E.E.C. is relatively less dependent than E.F.T.A. on imports from nonmembers. In light of the general

---

[18] The Soviet Area countries and Chinese Mainland are not included in "world" totals for lack of sufficiently comparable statistics.

[19] 1959: E.E.C. intra-trade, 39% of world exports; E.F.T.A. intra-trade, 18% for exports and 16% for imports. E.E.C. INFORMATIONS STATISTIQUES 250, 253 (1960).

theory posited earlier, this justifies an optimistic view toward minimizing losses from trade diversion and damage to third countries. However, when the total external trade figures are itemized to show their regional and commodity composition, it becomes clear that there is room for severe damage in some cases. Such damage is especially likely to occur in trade between E.E.C. and E.F.T.A.

For an adequate comparison of the economic status of these two trading groups, it is not enough to compare population, geographical size, total production, consumption, and the like. In terms of such comparisons the E.F.T.A. is certainly the smaller of the two groupings; yet, in a per capita comparison, E.F.T.A. exceeds the E.E.C. in output, consumption, and foreign trade. It may well be that these latter magnitudes play a decisive part in determining the potential for further economic growth and for the expansion of trade.

The scope for damage to the trade between E.E.C. and E.F.T.A. resulting from implementation of the customs union provisions in the Rome Treaty appears considerable when present—and traditional—patterns of market interpenetration between the two areas are brought into focus. At least two countries (Germany and the Netherlands) within the E.E.C.'s "low tariff areas" have substantial export surpluses vis-à-vis E.F.T.A. countries. Moreover, in 1958, more than twenty-seven per cent of German exports, twenty-five per cent of Dutch exports, twenty-one per cent of Italian exports, and thirteen per cent of French exports went to E.F.T.A. countries.[20]

The importance of E.E.C. countries as markets for E.F.T.A. exports is even more pronounced. In 1959, the ratios between exports to E.E.C. and exports to other E.F.T.A. countries were these: Austria, 49.6:10.4 (this high ratio emphasizes the political character of Austria's decision to join the E.F.T.A. and remain uncommitted as to the political implications of E.E.C.); Switzerland, 39.0:15.4; Denmark, 31.7:40.3; Sweden, 31.0:35.0; Norway, 27.3:37.6; Portugal (not including overseas territories) 24:17.2; the United Kingdom, 13.1:10.0.[21] Changes in this pattern would seem inevitable under the provisions of both the Rome Treaty and the Stockholm Convention. Indeed, developments since 1953 indicate general shifts in trading patterns already under way. While trade among Western European countries increased on the whole by sixty-three per cent during this period, intra-E.E.C. trade rose 110 per cent, and intra-E.F.T.A. trade, thirty per cent. Significantly, although intra-E.F.T.A. trade increased at a faster rate than E.F.T.A. export trade to the E.E.C., it increased at a slower rate than E.E.C. export trade to E.F.T.A.[22]

While these statistics forebode losses to the participants in trade between E.E.C. and E.F.T.A., they also indicate incentives for a "bridging of the gap" between these two highly interdependent markets. Since the deficit country—or the group of deficit countries—typically holds the stronger bargaining position vis-à-vis a trade

[20] Source: O.E.E.C. STATISTICAL BULLETIN, Ser. I (April 1959).
[21] Source: O.E.E.C. STATISTICAL BULLETIN, Ser. I (April 1959), and Berliner Bank A.G., Mitteilungen für den Aussenhandel No. 6/59 (1959).
[22] G.A.T.T., INTERNATIONAL TRADE 1959, at 148-51 (1960).

partner vitally interested in preserving his export markets, the E.F.T.A., by reason of its trade position, may be in a good position to negotiate a solution of some of the problems created by the present customs union.

Two special features of the present situation make the prospects for successful bargaining appear favorable. In the first place, the present arrangement is meeting with increasing dissatisfaction in the United Kingdom.[23] A review of the economic effects of imperial preferences on Commonwealth trade and a reappraisal of the question of compatibility between British membership in E.E.C. and Commonwealth ties might well alter British attitudes towards the customs union.[24] In a period of vigorously expanding world trade, and even more vigorously expanding E.E.C. trade, the gains to be foregone by the United Kingdom as a result of nonparticipation in the Common Market may well appear an excessive price for the preservation of Britain's special Commonwealth position.[25]

Secondly, the prospect of losing important E.F.T.A. export markets has given rise to misgivings in the Federal Republic of Germany. (German opposition to the method used in calculating the common external tariff has already been mentioned.) Although Germany in terms of size and total output does not occupy the position of economic dominance within the E.E.C. that the United Kingdom holds within the E.F.T.A., it is not clear that this is the pivotal measure in assessing the weight

[23] The United Kingdom is singled out because of its general interest in the E.E.C. market. This is not to suggest that other E.F.T.A. countries may not have similar or stronger interests in bridging the gap. The ratios of their exports to E.E.C. countries to their exports to other E.F.T.A. countries should make this abundantly clear. If individual commodity groups of exports are considered, different industries in the E.F.T.A. countries have, of course, much more to lose than such over-all export ratios might suggest. Sweden, in 1957, exported 44% of its pulp and paper exports to E.E.C. countries, as compared to 35% to E.F.T.A. countries (and as compared to a reverse ratio of total exports, *i.e.*, 31%: 35%). Danish meat and egg exports figures illustrate this even more vividly.

[24] A change in the British attitude towards customs unions would require rather strong motives. It would mean, in the case of the United Kingdom, a reversal of firmly established conventions and principles. It should be recalled, in this connection, that Great Britain in the past has been the firmest supporter of the notion that customs unions are incompatible with the most-favored-nations principle. *Cf.* J. VINER, THE CUSTOMS UNION ISSUE 12 (1950). However, as Professor Viner has pointed out, there is no question that majority opinion and historical precedent favor arrangements whereby customs unions are exempted from the most-favored-nations obligations.

Actually, one might assign a less important role to the most-favored-nations principle than does Professor Viner. "The realization of a steady rate of growth, as little disturbed by cyclical fluctuations as possible, and of other important goals of economic policy, is incompatible with an unlimited application of the most-favored-nations principle." Pütz, *Meistbegünstigung*, I HANDWÖRTERBUCH DER SOZIALWISSENSCHAFTEN 288 (1960). [Writer's translation.]

With regard to Commonwealth trade and Imperial Preferences, compare THE ECONOMIST INTELLIGENCE UNIT, THE COMMONWEALTH AND EUROPE (1960). The share of Commonwealth trade on which preferential treatment makes for a substantial margin is comparatively small—approximately two-fifths of total Commonwealth exports. United Kingdom exports to Commonwealth countries, on the other hand, actually benefit more.

[25] A comparison of recent economic development in the United Kingdom and E.E.C. countries provides a good basis for the expectations herein expressed.

Based on figures for the first half of 1960, British exports increased by 10% in 1959-1960, while the index of change for E.E.C. countries was as follows: Benelux, 18%; Germany, 21%; France 34%; Italy, 41%.

British industrial production rose by 10%; Benelux, 12%; Germany, 15%; Italy, 18%.

The United Kingdom during the year September 1959 to September 1960, lost 5% of her gold and foreign exchange reserves, while the E.E.C. countries together increased such reserves by 24%.

of German influence.[26] Rather the measure may depend on the share in trade of the area as a whole. In this latter respect, Germany's position in the E.E.C. is similar to the position held by the United Kingdom in the E.F.T.A. Moreover, Germany's export surpluses with the smaller E.F.T.A. countries account almost exclusively for the E.E.C.'s net creditor position vis-à-vis the E.F.T.A.

In light of the German and British trading interests at stake, these factors may create a bargaining atmosphere more conducive to compromise than could be expected with a more symmetric pattern of intra-European trade. So far, it has been the policy of the E.E.C. Commission to offer "negotiations" with the United Kingdom on the condition that the provisions of the Rome Treaty are to be fully accepted by any country joining the union. This position is likely to prove untenable; after all, each of the treaty provisions is the result of lengthy negotiations between the signatory countries. It would seem quite unreasonable to expect the United Kingdom to join—if she so desired—without substantial bargaining and renegotiating of at least parts of the treaty.

In trade with third countries—*i.e.*, with countries which are neither E.E.C. nor E.F.T.A. members—similar concentration patterns are evident. Although a further breakdown according to the regional concentration of E.E.C. trade or the shares therein of individual third countries cannot be attempted here, at least a general indication of the commodity composition of such trade may be given.[27] The special features of E.E.C. trade emerge best from a comparison with E.F.T.A. countries' trade with third countries.

E.E.C. imports from third countries in 1959 exceeded corresponding E.F.T.A. imports by slightly more than one billion dollars. Foodstuffs and manufactures, however, weighed more heavily in E.F.T.A. imports and actually exceeded E.E.C. imports in value. The larger E.E.C. total, then, is wholly accounted for by the larger pro-

---

[26] At least one opinion should be quoted as not in concurrence with this quantitatively conceived statement. E. STRAUSS, COMMON SENSE ABOUT THE COMMON MARKET (1958), sees "the true motive forces behind the Rome treaty, in German interests. The unmistakable power centre of the new block is the German Federal Republic directed by the rulers of German industry, which has successfully harnessed the urges and aspirations of the dominant social forces and the hopes and fears of many people in Western Europe to the service of a combination promising to be of great benefit to Western Germany in general and to its business interests in particular." *Id.* at 7. After an excursion into the history of the common market idea in German thought, the author concludes: "By committing the future of European economic integration to the care of Western Germany, the signatories of the treaty . . . have embarked on an unjustifiable gamble." *Id.* at 127.

For a more structured view of German industrial interests in the "integration," compare ERNST B. HAAS, THE UNITING OF EUROPE 162-76 (1958).

Also, the more recent opposition of influential industrial groups in Germany against some of the implications of E.E.C. tariff policy indicates a much looser connection between German interests and E.E.C. than the political history of the treaty negotiations might suggest.

[27] For a detailed analysis of trade between E.E.C. and a number of individual third countries, see P. ERDMANN & P. ROGGE, DIE EUROPÄISCHE WIRTSCHAFTSGEMEINSCHAFT UND DIE DRITTLÄNDER (1960).

For E.E.C. trade with the United States, see Kreinin, *European Integration and American Trade*, 49 AM. ECON. REV. 615 (1959). See also Comm. on Foreign Affairs, *Report of the Special Study Mission to Europe*, H.R. REP. No. 1226, 86th Cong., 2d Sess. (1960), and *Hearings Before the Joint Economic Committee on Employment, Growth, and Price Levels* pt. 5, *International Influences on the American Economy*, 86th Cong., 1st Sess. (1959).

portion of crude materials imports.[28] With the exception of manufactures, imports from third countries accounted for more than half of all commodity imports into both the E.E.C. and the E.F.T.A. In short, only in manufactured goods is trade between the E.E.C. and E.F.T.A. the predominant element, while for imports of foodstuffs and crude materials both areas depend heavily on third countries. This dependence is more pronounced in the case of the E.F.T.A. than of the E.E.C. However, with respect to imports from the United States, the E.E.C. accounts for a larger absolute value and a larger share. This is partly explained by the predominance of crude materials imports among total E.E.C. imports, and also by the much larger E.E.C. imports of American manufactures.[29]

These figures must, of course, be seen against the background of changing trade relations between western Europe as a whole and the United States. What otherwise might appear as trade diversion resulting from E.E.C. tariff policy may, after all, represent nothing but a continuation of trends well under way before the Common Market and for quite different reasons. With as much as forty per cent of total American exports going to western Europe in 1928 and as little as seventeen per cent in 1953, there is, indeed, a strong case for holding the latter view. Obviously, with the disruption of trade in the world depression and during World War II, there is little hope of uncovering the purely commercial "causes" underlying such changes. At any rate, in 1959, western Europe (the Organization of European Economic Cooperation (O.E.E.C.) countries) received just under twenty-five per cent of exports from the United States.

Only a breakdown of commodity composition will lead to some insight into the prospective effects of the Common Market on trade with the United States. The most important commodity group comprises foodstuffs, of which the O.E.E.C. countries received forty-one per cent of the United States exports. In so far as American exports of crude materials and manufactures were concerned, the O.E.E.C. countries accounted for thirty-five and fifteen per cent respectively. Since agricultural production in Common Market countries is expected to grow at approximately four times the rate of population growth, a declining E.E.C. share in total American agricultural exports is easily foreseen. Even if the outcome of agricultural integration in the E.E.C. remains uncertain and even if the development of Common Market policies towards the overseas territories is regarded with some scepticism, overproduction in grain seems most likely. Moreover, self-sufficiency in most other

---

[28] Imports from third countries (in billions of dollars and percentage of total imports):

	E.E.C.		E.F.T.A.	
Foodstuffs	3.87	32%	4.41	40%
Crude Materials	6.53	54	4.73	43
Manufactures	1.62	13	1.71	16

Source: O.E.E.C. FOREIGN TRADE BULLETIN Ser. B and C (1960).

[29] E.E.C. countries in 1959 imported more than twice the value of E.F.T.A. imports from the United States in this category. In all three categories together, E.E.C. imports from the United States account for 22% of the total commodity imports as compared to 17% in the case of E.F.T.A. In manufactures, E.E.C. imports 14% more from the United States than E.F.T.A. O.E.E.C. FOREIGN TRADE BULLETIN Ser. B and C (1960).

agricultural products of the temperate zones (other than raw materials) seems well within the realm of possibility.[30]

Quantitatively more important to the United States are the prospects for exports of crude materials to the E.E.C. In 1959, the E.E.C. accounted for twenty-five per cent of American exports in this category, as compared to twenty per cent of foodstuffs exports.[31] In this commodity group, there seems to be relatively little room for tariff discrimination, since the major portion will enter the Common Market duty free. However, in some cases, such as coal and crude petroleum, special regulation by the High Authority of the European Coal and Steel Community may effectively limit the quantities allowed to enter the Common Market area. There is also a tariff, ranging from two to five per cent, on vegetable oils and fats, products for which the E.E.C. provides the largest United States export market, but the restrictive effect is likely to remain negligible.[32] The only severe case of discrimination is aluminum, with a tariff rate of ten per cent.[33]

Decisively bleaker is the outlook for American exports of manufactured goods, which by far provided the strongest tie in United States-E.E.C. trade as of 1959. However, the E.E.C. market accounts for only about ten per cent of total United States exports in this category.

Were it not for the fact that American foreign economic policy remains committed to a program involving heavy unilateral spending abroad, one could certainly conclude that "the impact of European integration on aggregate American production is not likely to be significant, because foreign trade plays a relatively unimportant role in the American economy."[34] As it is, discrimination in manufac-

---

[30] *Cf.* Fritz Baade, Die deutsche Landwirtschaft im Gemeinsamen Markt (1958). For production possibilities and market conditions of grains, especially with regard to France and Tunisia, and for a survey of E.E.C. grain policy proposals, see F. C. Fabre, La politique céréalière en Europe au seuil de l'Unification (Aspects Européens No. 3) (1960).

[31] In 1928, this category accounted for 40% of United States exports as against 20% in 1959. From 1957 to 1959, United States exports of crude materials decreased by 44%. Not all of this decrease can be explained by a change in the relative availability of the products in this category. Part of the explanation must be seen in the fluctuation of economic activity in Europe. It is in this respect that the much cited dependence of Europe on cyclical fluctuations in the United States might well be reversed in the future, if, indeed, such reversals might not already be observable. In 1958-59, the decline of crude material exports from the United States coincided with a 6% increase in imports. The outstanding feature in that period was, of course, the decline of 64% in iron and steel exports in consequence of the steel strike. The relatively mild increase in iron and steel imports (20%) points to structural rather than cyclical factors ("excess-capacity").

[32] The rates of 2 to 5% apply to inedible fats and oils, which are practically all the United States exports to E.E.C. in this category. Higher rates apply to edible fats.

[33] The value of aluminum exports in 1959 was approximately $20,000,000.

[34] Kreinin, *supra* note 27, at 626. The estimates offered by this author place the share of total United States exports likely to be injured by the E.E.C. at 5%. Mr. S. Stewart, of the British Board of Trade, in an unpublished paper, estimates that 20 to 30% of total United States exports are likely to be affected. This drastically different estimate occurs because this author gives more weight to the fact that, in 1959, of total imports of engineering products into the O.E.E.C. countries from third countries, 73% originated in the United States. Furthermore, since the low tariff areas of the E.E.C. accounted for more than half of these imports, the tariff increases must be expected to have especially strong impact. As Germany accounts for as much engineering production as the rest of the E.E.C. countries together, the internal tariff elimination will also be more likely to have stronger effects upon trade in this commodity group with the United States.

tures—the very category of exports in which the United States has shown the most promise for production and trade expansion[35]—may come to bear more heavily on the American economy than would be suggested by the relatively small role exports play in creating United States national income. The result will depend largely upon the possibility of expanding American exports to other countries, as the United States has already done with some of its manufactured goods. On the whole, a comparison of American export performance with that of Western Europe tends to be prejudiced by the large share of western European exports accounted for by Germany. The special factors underlying West German economic growth, and particularly the special stimuli provided for German exports by an export-conscious governmental policy, do not justify any prima facie conclusions concerning the commercial competitiveness of United States exports.

Any attempt at forecasting the long-run effects of E.E.C. integration must place the present pattern and any short-run changes in trade relationships between E.E.C. and the rest of the world into the context of past developments and the potential for economic growth. Such a task is formidable, because potential growth in E.E.C. economies may depend markedly on the effects of integration itself; indeed, the rationale of the whole venture is to achieve such integration effects. At best, from the forecaster's point of view, hitherto observable trends will continue along established paths, and the "integration effect" will come into play only with the "official" beginning of the step-by-step integration schedule. At worst, the E.E.C. provides an altogether unique case, with patterns of development determined by the special features of the participating countries and with the "integration effect" largely preempted by anticipatory adjustments of economic activity within the Community and in third countries.

Many factors point to the latter possibility—the rather unique structure of E.E.C. trade and the strong influx of foreign capital into the Common Market providing the more obvious illustrations. Accordingly, the various forecasts on rates of economic growth within the E.E.C. differ widely: most estimates concur, however, in placing the minimum average annual growth rate at 3.1 per cent.[36] If due consideration is

---

[35] Exports in metal manufactures and railway vehicles to markets other than Western Europe or Canada increased between 1953 and 1958. Exports of chemicals, aircraft, and paper increased even in western European markets. See U.N. ECONOMIC COMM'N FOR EUROPE, ECONOMIC SURVEY OF EUROPE IN 1959, 13-15 (E/ECE/383) (U.N. Pub. Sales No.: 60.II.E.1). U.S. DEP'T OF COMMERCE, SURVEY OF CURRENT BUSINESS 11 (Dec. 1960), reports a steep increase in the over-all merchandise trade surplus during the third quarter of 1960. Steel, cotton, and aircraft exports accounted for almost two-fifths of the expansion in exports. Passenger cars, copper, and aluminum contributed an additional one-fourth of the total improvement in the United States balance of merchandise trade.

[36] The G.A.T.T. Secretariat forecasts an increase in GNP by 90% over the period 1953-55–1973-75 for the E.E.C.; see *The Possible Impact of the European Economic Community*, TRADE INTELLIGENCE PAPER No. 6 (1957). The average annual growth rate, in this case, would be 3.3%. This estimate was amended to take into account a special integration effect on growth. The total GNP increase over the same period was placed at a minimum of 120% and a maximum of 150%, with average annual rates of 4.0% and 4.7%.

The List Gesellschaft, Research Department (Basle), in a more recent estimate, gives a figure of 113% for the total increase in GNP from 1955 to 1975, and an average annual rate of 3.8%. This forecast places the prospective annual rate for the period 1955-65 at 4.3%, and for the period 1965-75 at 3.4%.

given to the special factors determining the growth leaders of recent years and to the fact that growth leadership shifts from country to country,[37] this conservative estimate appears quite acceptable.

When even the minimum projected E.E.C. growth rate is compared with such rates in nonmember countries, substantial differentials are likely to appear,[38] which, however, need not adversely affect trade. Rising national incomes and reversals in the terms of trade may well result in nonmember countries receiving a bigger share of trade gains. However, such optimistic results will come about only under special conditions in the world trade structure, which recent developments in international trade indicate do not exist. In the first place, the unusually high rate of annual increases in the volume of world trade (six to eight per cent over the 1948-1958 period) cannot be expected to continue very long. Secondly, the danger of trade diversion damage is aggravated by the long-run tendency for trade between industrial countries and nonindustrial countries to decline relative to total world trade.[39] Thirdly, the long-run tendency towards regionalization may well continue to prevent an optimal pattern of trade between the E.E.C. and other industrialized countries, including the United States.[40]

[36] P. ERDMANN & P. ROGGE, DIE EUROPÄISCHE WIRTSCHAFTSGEMEINSCHAFT UND DIE DRITTLÄNDER 133 (1960). (These authors also list and analyze forecasts given by other official and private institutions.) As to the more immediate prospects, Mr. Robert Marjolin, Vice President of the European Economic Community, in a speech on Jan. 19, 1961, predicted a rate of 4 to 5% in real GNP for 1961, which compares to a rate of almost 7% realized in 1960. European Community, Information Service, Washington, D.C., Jan. 23, 1961.

[37] At present, the shift appears to be from Germany to Italy and France. See note 25 *supra*. For the problems encountered in analyzing the factors determining economic growth in Germany, see Sohmen, *Competition and Growth: The Lesson of West Germany*, 49 AM. ECON. REV. 986 (1959), and the comments on this article, especially by Roskamp, 50 *id*. at 1015 (1960).

[38] G.A.T.T. estimates an average annual growth rate of 2.6% for the European countries outside E.E.C. See *The Possible Impact of the European Economic Community*, *supra* note 36.

[39] *Cf.* P.L. YATES, FORTY YEARS OF FOREIGN TRADE 56 (1959).

[40] ERIK THORBECKE, THE TENDENCY TOWARDS REGIONALIZATION IN INTERNATIONAL TRADE, 1928-1956 (1960) argues that monetary and political forces, rather than tariff barriers, have brought about an increasing degree of regionalization in international trade. Three regions examined by Thorbecke are the O.E.E.C., the Sterling Area, and the Dollar bloc. Intra-regional trade as a ratio of total trade of these areas is found to have increased from 48.8% in 1928 to 57.8% in 1956 for exports, and from 41.6% to 51.4% for imports. As a ratio of total world trade, intra-regional trade increased from 15.6% to 18.8% for exports, and from 15.0% to 19.0% for imports. The author concludes "that the rise in intraregional trade which took place between 1938 and 1956 within the smaller European countries reflects to a large extent a more efficient use of the existing natural complementarity, which was made possible by significant changes in the over-all state of technology." *Id.* at 126. It is largely on the basis of technological considerations that Thorbecke gives a rather optimistic outlook on the effects of the E.E.C. He assumes a rather substantial scope for economies of scale and the concomitant improvements in resource productivity. Other authors are much more skeptical with respect to foreseeable economies of scale. *Cf.* Johnson, *The Economic Gains from Freer Trade with Europe*, The Tree Banks Review, Sept. 1958, p. 9, and P. ERDMANN & P. ROGGE, DIE EUROPÄISCHE WIRTSCHAFTSGEMEINSCHAFT UND DIE DRITTLÄNDER 35 (1960).

This asymmetrical pattern of world trade expansion was repeated in European trade; and with the resumption in 1959 of a high rate of economic growth, western European trade continued to expand vigorously. While intra-European trade accounted, on the whole, for the biggest share, the less industrialized western European countries were "hardly touched" by this trade expansion. "Increase countries," on the other hand, accounted for 73% of the intra-European imports, and for nearly 80% of the increase in such exports. U.N. ECONOMIC COMM'N FOR EUROPE, ECONOMIC SURVEY OF EUROPE IN 1959, at 7 (E/ECE/383) (U.N. Pub. Sales No.: 60.II.E.1).

Here again, the impact of the E.E.C. upon trade with nonmember countries cannot be judged by aggregate statistics, for the effects on the group of nonindustrialized or less industrialized countries as a whole do not determine the results for individual countries in the group. Growth rate differentials within the group may worsen the trade position of individual countries. As to the commodity compositions of these countries' trade, there exist, of course, as many terms of trade as there are pairs of commodities traded.[41]

Even if sufficiently specific information can be obtained about the effective rates under the E.E.C. common external tariff, and if the structure of trade between the Common Market countries and outsiders is sufficiently analyzed, the likely effects of the E.E.C. tariff remain uncertain. Price effects are directly proportional to tariff changes only in the case of perfectly competitive markets in trade participating countries. If imperfections exist, tariff changes are much less likely to be transmitted to prices. Both lack of sensitivity to price changes on the side of demand and the ability to engage in some measure of "price policy" on the side of supply would account for such possibilities. In either case the theoretically possible price effects would be of different magnitudes for changes within different price ranges. On the other hand, tariff changes are likely to have stronger price effects than the general theory would suggest, since customs evaluation practices, as a rule, are such as to reinforce the price effects of tariff changes.[42]

With respect to the "welfare effects" resulting from a comparison of "trade-creating" and "trade-diverting" effects of the E.E.C. customs union, there is some room for doubt whether the preferential tariff arrangement of this customs union will disturb the optimal economic pattern of world trade. Particularly with respect to the postwar period and in light of some fairly obvious disparities in foreign exchange rates, there is little to suggest that trade flows actually correspond to any such optimal pattern, either in the direction or in the commodity composition of trade. Of course, as was shown above, this statement does not mean that serious

---

[41] The "terms of trade" concept, as usually employed in analyses of changes in a country's trade position, is a highly aggregative statistical device involving index numbers. It does not directly measure gains or losses from trade. These are measured only by changes in net income. *Cf.* Flexner, *An Analysis of the Nature of Aggregates at Constant Prices*, 41 REV. ECON. AND STATISTICS 400 (1959).

Terms of trade have been found to favor developed countries as against underdeveloped countries in the long run. The empirical record does not, however, show that terms of trade moved at the same time in favor of manufactures and against primary products, as might have been expected. *Cf.* C. P. KINDLEBERGER, THE TERMS OF TRADE: A EUROPEAN CASE STUDY 253 (1956). This, too, would suggest extreme caution with respect to generalizations on the basis of aggregative terms of trade concepts.

See also G.A.T.T., INTERNATIONAL TRADE 1959, at 36 (1960): "Changes in terms of trade gave North America and Western Europe an increase in real national income which can (for the period 1953-58) be roughly estimated at about $2,800 million at 1953 prices. At the same time, however, the changes in terms of trade decreased the import capacity, and probably also the imports, of the non-industrial areas by about $1,700 million, resulting in a net gain from improved terms of trade for the industrial areas of about $1,000 million."

[42] This is especially true for the treatment of discount, rebate, and certain tax compensations upon crossing a customs barrier. The customs duty is in such cases usually added to the "custom value" on the basis of which it has been computed. The compensation is then charged as against this higher "base value," and has, therefore, a cumulative effect on price. *Cf.* Jürgensen, *Die Wirtschaftsgemeinschaft im Freihandelsraum*, I JAHRBUCH FÜR SOZIALWISSENSCHAFT 53 (1959).

damage is unlikely to occur in individual (industry or country) cases. It is suggested, however, that such damage often occurs only because industries or countries have adapted themselves to patterns of trade which are far from optimal and, therefore, basically unstable.

Also, it must not be assumed that tariffs always have been the major factors in distorting international trade. Indeed, quantitative restrictions and exchange controls during the post-depression period may well have been the more important instruments in restricting and rechanneling international trade.[43] In this connection it is significant that the E.E.C. treaty does not contain any direct provisions for the removal of quota restrictions on trade with nonmember countries. Although the treaty provides for lifting quotas in intra-E.E.C. trade along with the step-by-step elimination of tariffs, nonmember countries must rely for relief on the general commitment of the E.E.C. Commission to the principles of a "liberal" commercial policy.[44]

There remains, then, an important reservation: whatever the structure of trade between E.E.C. and nonmember countries, and whatever the final rates of the E.E.C. external tariff, the establishment of a customs union among the six countries of the European Economic Community is no substitute for other tasks of common economic policy.

[43] The assumption that the effective rates of tariffs just "fit" the relative cost situation of trade competing industries, and therefore give a correct measure of protection and trade restriction, would imply a presumed economic rationality in the use of the tariff, and in the fixing of its rates, which neither the normal administrative procedures nor the actions of interest groups promoting a tariff seems to warrant.

[44] Certain quota concessions were made by the E.E.C. to G.A.T.T.-member countries in 1959. At present, a complaint by Australia against the agricultural quota set by the Federal Republic of Germany is pending under G.A.T.T. procedure. See Die Welt, Feb. 25, 1961, p. 7.

THE EUROPEAN COMMON MARKET AND THE GENERAL AGREEMENT ON TARIFFS AND TRADE: A STUDY IN COMPATIBILITY

JAMES JAY ALLEN[*]

When the European Common Market[1] first came into existence, it attracted world-wide publicity. Amid praise from all sides, and particularly from the United States, came an increasing flood of apprehension concerning the effect this new Community might have on patterns of world trade. As the first transitional steps provided for by the Rome Treaty were put into effect, the anxiety increased. That the formation of the European Economic Community (E.E.C.) would eventually produce significant economic and political changes seemed evident: some are already observable. The formation of the European Free Trade Area (E.F.T.A.) was a direct result of the putting into effect of the Rome Treaty. This grouping, brought into being more as a bargaining counter to the Common Market than as a serious attempt to construct a free-trade area, will seek progressively closer identification with the E.E.C. Greece has already joined the Common Market and Great Britain is now giving favorable consideration to doing so; many consider her membership only a matter of time. Such a step would have far-reaching ramifications for the British Commonwealth. Other members of the E.F.T.A. and the Organization for Economic Cooperation and Development (O.E.C.D.) can be expected to follow suit. In addition, plans for customs unions and free-trade areas are blossoming forth around the globe. How such groupings will relate to the General Agreement on Tariffs and Trade (G.A.T.T.), which makes provision for customs unions and free-trade areas under certain conditions, will also have widespread repercussions, especially with regard to the world's newly developed countries.

The General Agreement on Tariffs and Trade[2] is a multilateral trade agreement whose members, called "contracting parties," include all of the free world's major trading nations.[3] The agreement consists of a schedule of tariff commitments, a group of common rules of trade, and an organization to promote negotiations, to

---

[*] B.A. 1953, Cornell University; LL.B., LL.M. 1958, Georgetown University. Attorney, Office of the Assistant General Counsel for International Affairs, Department of Defense. Member of the District of Columbia bar. Author, THE EUROPEAN COMMON MARKET AND GATT (1961), on which the present article is, in part, based.

The views expressed in this article are those of the writer, and do not purport to be those of the Department of Defense.

[1] The Treaty establishing the European Economic Community and connected documents are found in a publication of that title published by the Secretariat of the Interim Committee for the Common Market and European Atomic Energy Community (Euratom), Brussels in 1957.

[2] This multilateral agreement was signed on October 30, 1947. For the text of the agreement, see 61 Stat. pt. 5, at 6 et seq. (1947); T.I.A.S. No. 1700, as renewed, id. No. 2886.

[3] These nations jointly account for over 80% of world trade.

settle disputes, and to administer the provisions of the G.A.T.T.[4] The code of conduct set forth in the general trade provisions of the G.A.T.T. was created to protect the value of tariff concessions made, to reduce trade restrictions and controls other than tariffs, and to secure the largest possible observance of the principle of nondiscrimination in trade matters.[5] Prior to the Fall of 1960, three rounds of tariff negotiations[6] between the contracting parties resulted in the reduction or binding of the tariffs on over 59,000 items, affecting well over half the total of world trade.[7]

One of the chief underlying principles of the General Agreement on Tariffs and Trade is the most-favored-nation doctrine. Under article one, a contracting party must unconditionally extend to all contracting parties the tariff and other trade concessions granted to any country. However, article twenty-four expressly permits a customs union to exist and grants an exception to the most-favored-nation rule as long as certain requirements are fulfilled. This derogation[8] of article one was provided because the G.A.T.T. signatories believed that the propensity of customs unions to liberalize trade, both within the customs area and eventually for the whole trading world, outweighed the initial disadvantage of depriving the other contracting parties of the benefit of the trade reductions made between the members of the union. With regard to the contracting parties of the G.A.T.T., therefore, it is of material importance that the Common Market adhere closely to the conditions set out in article twenty-four. The purpose of this paper is to analyze in legal terms the compatibility of the E.E.C. Treaty with the provisions of the G.A.T.T.[9]

Article XXIV(7) of the G.A.T.T. lays down the procedure by which the compatibility of an aspiring customs union is to be tested and approved.[10] Countries seeking to form such a union shall, states this paragraph, promptly notify the contracting parties and make available such information as will enable them to decide whether the proposed argreement is "likely to result in the formation of a customs union or of a free-trade area within the period contemplated by the parties to agreement or that such period is . . . a reasonable one." If these results are not likely, the parties to such an agreement are forbidden from putting it into force, or main-

[4] For a detailed and thorough analysis of G.A.T.T., see SEYID MUHAMMAD, THE LEGAL FRAMEWORK OF WORLD TRADE (1958).
[5] For a very readable, but less exhaustive account of G.A.T.T. organization and operation, see UNITED STATES COUNCIL, INTERNATIONAL CHAMBER OF COMMERCE, G.A.T.T.: AN ANALYSIS OF THE GENERAL AGREEMENT ON TARIFFS AND TRADE (1955).
[6] These negotiations were held at Geneva in 1947, Annecy in 1949, and Torquay in 1950-1951.
[7] UNITED STATES COUNCIL, op. cit. supra note 5, at 17.
[8] Since article twenty-four does represent a derogation of the general principles embodied in article one, it "should be interpreted strictly and construed according to its wording to obtain its clear intent and purpose." G.A.T.T., BASIC INSTRUMENTS AND SELECTED DOCUMENTS 104, Appendix A (Note submitted by the Delegation of Ceylon) (6th Supp. 1958) [hereinafter cited as G.A.T.T., B.I.S.D.].
[9] No attempt is made here to analyze the effects of the E.E.C. in economic terms.
[10] All of the members of the E.E.C.—Belgium, France, the Federal Republic of Germany, Italy, Luxembourg, and the Netherlands—are also contracting parties to G.A.T.T. Of course, if all members were not also members of G.A.T.T., they could form customs unions, free-trade areas, or even preferential systems with no interference from the G.A.T.T. contracting parties. If only some of the prospective members of the grouping were G.A.T.T. members, as is the case with the Rome Treaty Overseas Territories, a special situation would arise which would require different treatment. With respect to this problem, see MUHAMMAD, op. cit. supra note 4, at 249-50.

taining it in effect, as the case may be, unless they are prepared to modify it in accordance with recommendations made by the contracting parties.

The contracting parties first dealt with the E.E.C. Treaty at G.A.T.T.'s eleventh Session late in 1956, when the Community was still in the negotiating stages.[11] Between the eleventh and twelfth Sessions, an intersessional committee was appointed by the contracting parties to meet at Geneva with the express purpose of exploring the European Economic Community agreement.[12] As a result of the preparatory work completed at this conference, the contracting parties launched into a full scale discussion of legal compatibility at G.A.T.T.'s twelfth Session. However, because the transitional provisions of the E.E.C. Treaty tend to paint purposes and objectives in broad, sweeping strokes, yet leaving the details of implementation for future action, it was not possible to reach a definitive decision until such implementing action was taken. Most of the members of the G.A.T.T. Sub-Group felt that the Rome Treaty plan for the elimination of internal trade barriers was fairly detailed and complete.[13] On the other hand, the contracting parties were not in a position to judge the consistency of the E.E.C. external tariff with the General Agreement, because the common level of duties had not yet been published.[14] And, although not satisfied that the Rome Treaty provisions might not entail action inconsistent with the General Agreement, the Sub-Group noted that the provisions with respect to quantitative retrictions at least were not mandatory in the external sphere and imposed on Community members no obligation to take action incompatible with the G.A.T.T. However, since some uncertainties in the implementation of these provisions existed, the Sub-Group believed that the six E.E.C. Member States should be subject to consultation procedures as would any other G.A.T.T. member.[15]

The contracting parties were equally indecisive in the area of agriculture. Due to the large area of discretion left to the institutions of the Member States and the lack of a sufficiently precise plan showing how the agricultural provisions of the Rome Treaty would be applied, both in regard to the trade of third countries with members of the Community, and in regard to the removal of trade barriers between the Member States, the majority of the G.A.T.T. Sub-Group "decided that it was not able to determine either that the agricultural provisions of the Rome Treaty or their implementation would be consistent with the provisions of the General Agreement."[16] Thus, although "the particular measures envisaged under the Treaty carried a strong presumption of increased external barriers and a substitution of new internal barriers in place of existing tariffs and other measures,"[17] it was considered

---

[11] See *European Customs Union and Free Trade Area*, 35 DEP'T STATE BULL. 896 (1956).
[12] See Corse, *The Common Market and the GATT*, 36 id. 863.
[13] G.A.T.T., B.I.S.D. at 81.
[14] Id. at 76. The rates of the products on List F were determined by negotiation and not by application of the arithmetical average, and were, therefore, not then available for inspection. E.E.C. Treaty art. 19(4).
[15] G.A.T.T., B.I.S.D. at 81.
[16] Id. at 88.
[17] Ibid.

proper to take action under article XXIV(7) of the G.A.T.T. at a later stage.[18] In the meantime, it was recommended that the Committee set up suitable machinery "to follow and consider together with the Six the measures to be taken in the course of establishing the common agricultural policy and organization and the relationship of these measures with the provisions of the General Agreement."[19]

No definite conclusions were reached with regard to the Association of the Overseas Territories and its compatibility with the General Agreement. Upon the request of a number of delegations who wanted to examine the practical problems of the arrangement and its external effects on a product-by-product basis, the G.A.T.T. Sub-Group recommended an investigation dealing with individual products.[20]

One hopeful indication that the United States and other non-Common Market countries might be able to avoid the trade-diverting effects of the Community external common tariff, is set out in E.E.C. Treaty article eighteen, where the Member States[21]

declare their willingness to contribute to the development of international commerce and the reduction of barriers to trade by entering into reciprocal and mutually advantageous arrangements directed to the reduction of customs duties below the general level which they could claim as a result of the establishment of a customs union between themselves.

There can be little doubt that tariff concessions agreed upon as a result of such negotiations would ease the adjustment which the United States and all countries would be compelled to make as the internal trade barriers of the common market were gradually removed and the outer duties—remolded into a common customs tariff—remained approximately the same. However, this method would avail the United States nothing if the executive department of the American Government were not authorized by legislation to enter into reciprocal tariff negotiations.[22] In gaining the extension of the Trade Agreements Act[23] for the eleventh time since 1934,[24] this time for an unprecedented four years (June 30, 1958, through June 30, 1962), it is interesting to note that the Department of State, in presenting its case, wielded the club of possible Common Market discrimination against the United States to good advantage in easing the renewal of the Act through a reluctant Congress.[25]

[18] This paragraph lays down certain requirements that an incipient customs union must fulfill, and the contracting parties must oversee, before the grouping is regularized with respect to the G.A.T.T.
[19] G.A.T.T., B.I.S.D. at 88.
[20] *Id.* at 102.
[21] The representative of the E.E.C. at the twelfth Session of the G.A.T.T. confirmed this intention. G.A.T.T., B.I.S.D. at 74.
[22] Such authorizing legislation is necessary because under the United States Constitution, the Congress "shall have the power to regulate commerce with foreign nations." U.S. CONST. art. 1, § 8, cl. 3.
[23] 46 Stat. 696 (1930), as added by 48 Stat. 943 (1934), as amended, 19 U.S.C. § 1351 (1958).
[24] The task of extending the reciprocal trade agreements legislation has never been easy, principally because local interests, exerting powerful pressure through their elected representatives, are loath to permit a volume of imports that would compete to their disadvantage on the home market. Even the latest extension (1958), states that the Act shall not be construed as either approval or disapproval of the G.A.T.T. 72 Stat. 680, 19 U.S.C. § 1351(a)(1)(A) (1958).
[25] See, *e.g.*, Secretary of State Dulles' statement before the Senate Committee on Finance, *Vital*

Under article twenty-four another step is available to non-Common Market members who are contracting parties of the G.A.T.T. to ameliorate the effect of the Community's common external tariff. If a duty, raised by a member of the customs union in order to conform to the common level of external tariffs of the Community, should be inconsistent with article two[26] of the General Agreement (that is, a duty previously "bound" or reduced in tariff negotiations already held by the G.A.T.T.), the injured contracting parties can seek compensatory adjustment under G.A.T.T. article twenty-eight. If such negotiations fail to achieve a satisfactory adjustment, the contracting party is entitled to withdraw or modify the concession originally given. Such negotiations under article XXIV(6) have been under way since the fall of 1960. The fourth general round of tariff negotiations began in the fall of 1960. Still to come—and of material significance to G.A.T.T. members—are negotiations with the Common Market as a whole to seek reductions of the common external tariff on products of importance to non-members of the the Community. After this negotiation, the contracting parties will be in a position to take up the various aspects of compatibility of the Rome Treaty to the General Agreement pursuant to article XXIV(7).

In discussing the question of compatibility, five major and pertinent areas of the E.E.C. Treaty must be examined: the internal characteristics of the common market, the common external tariff, quantitative restrictions, the agricultural provisions, and finally, the Association of the Overseas Territories.

I

Internal Operations of the European Common Market

Incompatibility must be based either on a Treaty provision of the customs union which absolutely requires certain action to be taken that would violate the G.A.T.T., or on a course of action taken under a permissive provision of the Treaty but which is inconsistent with provisions of the General Agreement. The transition period for the progressive establishment of the Common Market is twelve years, divided into three stages of four years each.[27] All stages of the transition period may be extended by a "decision of the Council acting by means of a unanimous vote on a proposal of

---

Importance of Extension of the Trade Agreement Act, 39 Dep't State Bull. 34 (1958); Undersecretary Dillon's remarks, *Extending the Reciprocal Trade Agreements Legislation*, 38 Dep't State Bull. 629 (1958). The approach employed was to suggest that during the next five years the E.E.C., under the Rome Treaty provisions, would be making long-term decisions concerning the level of the European common external tariffs and the commercial policies which the Community would adopt. Therefore, argued the State Department spokesmen, the trade agreements program must be renewed for five years so the United States would have the authority to enter into negotiations with the E.E.C. and thereby mitigate the adverse effects these anticipated actions were expected to produce. This approach was then taken up by the legislation's supporters in Congress. See, *e.g.*, 104 Cong. Rec. 1499 (1958) (remarks of Senator Douglas).

[26] The concessions made in the general tariff negotiations are incorporated in schedules of tariff rates, which article two makes an integral part of the Agreement. This article also contains various provisions designed to prevent impairment of the value of the concessions.

[27] E.E.C. Treaty art. 8(1).

the Commission,"[28] but in no case shall such provisions prolong the transition period beyond a total of fifteen years.[29] At that time all quantitative restrictions and tariff duties must have been abolished.[30] Of course, if for any reason the internal duties and quotas on agricultural products are not eliminated during the transition period, there is little doubt that the Community will not have complied with G.A.T.T. article XXIV(5)(a), which requires that such barriers be removed from substantially all the trade between the constituent member countries. A published decision of the Council of Ministers of May 12, 1960,[31] indicates that the Community had only partially complied with the Treaty provisions up to that time.

There are, to be sure, several escape clauses interspersed throughout the E.E.C. Treaty provisions.[32] But these provisions, even if employed, will not extend the transitional period beyond fifteen years or preclude the elimination of tariff duties and quotas. In fact, in a *Declaration of Intention Concerning Internal Acceleration* attached to the decision of May 12, 1960, the Council of Ministers confirmed plans to proceed as rapidly as possible with the acceleration of economic integration in all sectors.[33] Therefore, the internal market provided in the E.E.C. Treaty appears by its terms to provide for the elimination of barriers to substantially all the trade between the constituent territories[34] and ensure its formation within the period contemplated by the parties,[35] as required by article twenty-four of the General Agreement.

II

The Common External Customs Tariff

The basic relationship of a customs union to the General Agreement has already been mentioned. The heart of the G.A.T.T. Agreement is the most-favored-nation clause. However, the customs union need not extend to the other contracting parties the trade reductions granted to each other, provided that "the duties and other regulations of commerce ... shall not on the whole be higher or more restrictive than the general incidence of the duties and regulations of commerce applicable in the constituent territories prior to the formation of such union."[36] This provision does not require that the common tariff on each product be subjected to the specifications of this requirement. It is sufficient that the common tariff duties of the customs union comply as a whole.

Article nineteen of the Rome Treaty lays down the general rule that the outer tariff for each product be computed by means of an arithmetical average. It was

---

[28] *Id.* art. 8(6).
[29] *Ibid.*
[30] *Id.* arts. 33, 14, respectively.
[31] Press Release, Office for the European Communities, Washington, D.C. (May 13, 1960).
[32] E.E.C. Treaty arts. 8(3), 8(5), 8(6), 14(7), 107 (1, 2).
[33] Press Release, *supra* note 31.
[34] G.A.T.T. art. 24(8)(a)(i).
[35] *Id.* art. 24(7)(b).
[36] *Id.* art. 24(5)(a).

at first feared that such a method would not meet the requirements of the General Agreement because it fails to take into account the volume of trade of the constituent member countries. For example, in a case where the Benelux import duty on plate glass was sixteen per cent and the Italian tariff on the same commodity thirty-one per cent,[37] the arithmetical average would be approximately twenty-four per cent. However, since Benelux accounts for 31.3 per cent of the imports of the six Common Market countries and Italy only 14.2 per cent,[38] it is obvious that almost twice as many foreign exporters are suffering from the tariff increase in Benelux as are benefiting from its decrease in Italy.[39] It was partially a situation of this type that led the contracting parties to declare that "an automatic application of a formula, whether arithmetic average or otherwise, could not be accepted . . . [T]he matter should be approached by examining individual commodities on a country by country basis."[40] However, this assertion would appear to be in error. Article XXIV(5)(a), if it is to have any meaning at all, requires a certain standard to be observed for the outer tariff duties of the customs union as a whole. Before reaching a finding with respect to compatibility, the contracting parties must determine what that standard is and then apply it to the external common tariff of the E.E.C.

If all the external tariffs of the Community were computed by means of an arithmetical average, there would certainly be considerable doubt whether the General Agreement would be complied with. However, this is not the case. Specifically provided exceptions to the rule are contained in a series of "lists" lettered from A to G which are computed by various formulae or, in the case of products on List F, are fixed by the mutual agreement of the parties.[41] All such outer tariff duties towards which the Member States will adjust their individual duties according to a transition schedule have already been published.[42] Although no finding has been made in this respect, it appears that the over-all level of external tariff duties will be well below the level that would exist if an arithmetical average were used in combination with a weighted system to take into account the volume of trade. The chances for compatibility with the General Agreement, therefore, appear reasonably good.

III

QUANTITATIVE RESTRICTIONS

Even if tariff barriers of the Common Market are placed at sufficiently low levels, little trade would result if the volume of imports into the Community area

---

[37] The figures given are the correct duties for the respective countries for the year 1956. U.N. ECONOMIC COMM'N FOR EUROPE, ECONOMIC SURVEY OF EUROPE IN 1957 ch. 4, at 12, U.N. Doc. No. E/ECE/283, (1958) [hereinafter referred to as E.C.E. REPORT 1957].
[38] EMIL STRAUSS, COMMON SENSE ABOUT THE COMMON MARKET 94 (1959).
[39] This might not be the case for plate glass, since these figures refer to trade as a whole.
[40] G.A.T.T., B.I.S.D. at 72.
[41] E.E.C. Treaty art. 19. For a detailed treatment of the tariff structure of the E.E.C., see Gerhard, *Tariffs and Trade in the Common Market, supra*, at 539.
[42] *Id.* art. 23.

was restricted by quotas on a substantial number of commodities. Generally speaking, G.A.T.T. places two requirements on quantitative restrictions: one dealing with internal restrictions, and the other concerning quotas placed on imports from third countries. Under the first requirement the customs union must eliminate such quotas from substantially all the trade between the constituent territories of the union.[43] In addition, the customs union must be formed "within the period contemplated by the parties to the agreement" or within a reasonable time.[44] The compliance of the Rome Treaty provisions with these requirements has been discussed in a previous section.[45]

With respect to quantitative restrictions placed on imports from third countries, the first question is whether a customs union may maintain a common level of quotas against nonmembers pursuant to article XXIV(5)(a). It appears that the phrase contained in this paragraph, "duties and other regulations of commerce," excludes this interpretation in view of the fact that paragraph 8(a)-(i) of this article, concerning the reduction of internal trade barriers, uses the language, "duties and other restrictive regulations of commerce." The latter phrase by the use of the word "restrictive" clearly applies to import quotas. Paragraph 5(a), however, omits this word, and thereby excludes quantitative restrictions from the operation of this provision. Thus, the normal G.A.T.T. requirements would govern.[46]

The conclusion that a customs union may not establish an external common level of quantitative restrictions is far-reaching. The Community members are obligated generally to extend to other contracting parties the reductions in import quotas made as to each other under E.E.C. Treaty article thirty-three. This is so because quantitative restrictions are prohibited by the G.A.T.T. unless pursuant to specifically provided exceptions and, moreover, are subject to the operation of the most-favored-nation clause.[47] Although it is true that the Common Market countries eliminated, through the *Code of Liberalization of the Organization for European Economic Cooperation,* more than eighty-five per cent of their quantitative restrictions, there is considerable doubt that they will be willing to extend to nonmembers the remaining few, but crucial, quotas that they grant to each other.[48] If they choose not to do so, and assuming that these restrictions cannot be justified under balance of payments or other legitimate G.A.T.T. exceptions, the Member States will have violated the General Agreement and will require a waiver under G.A.T.T. article XXV(5)(a).[49]

[43] G.A.T.T. art. 24(8)(a)(i).
[44] *Id.* art. 24(7)(9b).
[45] See pp. 563-64 *supra.*
[46] See generally, G.A.T.T. arts. 11-14.
[47] MUHAMMAD, *op. cit. supra* note 4, at 212.
[48] It is important to remember that the liberalization of import restrictions will not automatically benefit United States exports to Europe, since such goods must still compete with similar products produced either there or in other third countries.
[49] G.A.T.T. art. 24 could be employed here. It is provided in that paragraph that the "[C]ontracting Parties may, by a two-thirds majority, approve proposals which do not fully comply with the requirements of paragraphs 5 to 9 inclusive, provided that such proposals lead to the formation of a customs union or a free-trade area in the sense of this Article."

The Rome Treaty abolishes all internal quotas by the end of the transition period.[50] However, Member States are under few restraints in setting quantitative restrictions for nonmember countries. Although article III(5), states that Member States shall aim at securing uniformity between themselves at as high a level as possible in respect to their quota liberalization lists regarding third countries,[51] the only machinery available to oversee this obligation consists of appropriate recommendations by the Commission to the Member States. Then, if Member States do "abolish or reduce quantitative restrictions in regard to third countries, they shall inform the Commission beforehand and shall accord identical treatment to the other Member States."[52] However, as the G.A.T.T. Sub-Group noted, the E.E.C. Treaty provisions in the external sphere are not mandatory and impose on Member States no obligation to take action which would be inconsistent with G.A.T.T. Articles.[53]

IV

AGRICULTURAL PROVISIONS

The criteria for judging the compatibility of the agricultural provisions are those standards laid down for a customs union's internal market, the external common customs tariff, and quantitative restrictions. The Common Market's agricultural provisions[54] do not appear to prevent the internal progressive elimination of tariff duties and quantitative restrictions. Instead, these provisions superimpose a massive combination of cartel-like competences and a Community economic complex over the common market for agricultural products to allow the internal reduction of barriers to take place with as little discomfort to the member countries as possible. It appears doubtful that tariff duties and import quotas will be eliminated between the trade of the Rome Treaty members to the extent necessary so that the reduction of trade barriers on the products of the Common Market as a whole will meet the requirements of G.A.T.T. article XXIV(8)(a)-(i). The decision of the Council of Ministers of May 12, 1960,[55] clearly shows what is already evident from the Treaty provisions themselves—that the Community has a difficult path ahead in attempting to bring the agricultural sector to a parallel status with the free market for non-agricultural products.

Two devices for easing the transition of member countries to a common market for agricultural products are "minimum prices" and "long term contracts." Article

---

[50] E.E.C. Treaty art. 30.

[51] The United States has advocated that quantitative restrictions for balance-of-payments purposes should be justified on an individual country basis. "This does not, in the mean time, rule out the possibility of a common liberalization list, but we believe that any such list should represent a floor rather than a ceiling on liberalization. In short, each member of the Community should continue to liberalize over and above any such common list as rapidly as the balance-of-payments position of that member warrants." 36 DEP'T STATE BULL. 928-9 (1957).

[52] E.E.C. Treaty art. 111(5).

[53] However, since uncertainties in the implementation of these provisions existed, the Sub-Group believed that the Six should be subject to consultation procedures as would any other G.A.T.T. member. G.A.T.T., B.I.S.D. at 80-81.

[54] E.E.C. Treaty arts. 38-47.

[55] Press Release, *supra* note 31.

forty-four of the E.E.C. Treaty provides that Member States are permitted, during the transitional period, to apply a system of minimum prices below which imports may either be temporarily suspended, or reduced, or made conditional on the import prices being above the minimum price fixed.[56] Although this article requires that such minimum prices must be applied "in a nondiscriminatory manner,"[57] this relates only to the trade among the Member States and does not imply a similar commitment as to imports from third countries.[58] Assuming that the application of this system leads to a displacement of the trade with outside countries, would such a result be illegal under the General Agreement? It is the view of this writer that they would not. Since the General Agreement allows a period specified by the parties or a reasonable time for the formation of a customs union, a system of "minimum prices" designed to assist such formation by facilitating the internal reduction of trade barriers[59] would not be incompatible with the G.A.T.T. provided such a system was imposed only during the Common Market transitional period.[60]

Article forty-five of the E.E.C. Treaty permits the development of exchanges in regard to certain products[61] to "be pursued by the conclusion of long-term agreements or contracts between exporting and importing Member States."[62] Such contracts shall be concluded during the first stage of the progressive development of the Common Market and shall be allowed until the substitution for the national organizations of the common agricultural organization. Although due account must be taken of "traditional trade currents,"[63] the effect of the long-term contracts would seem to be the diversion of trade from third countries to within the Common Market. If this occurs, would such a consequence be illegal under the General Agreement? Subject to certain limitations, no illegality is perceived. The purpose of long-term contracts is to facilitate the abolition of quantitative restrictions and import duties in cases where the E.E.C. Treaty provisions conflict with national regulations.[64] Since these contracts would only be applied to a limited number of

[56] The Treaty states that the system of minimum prices "shall be permitted to apply to certain products." E.E.C. Treaty art. 44(1).
[57] Ibid.
[58] G.A.T.T., B.I.S.D. at 83.
[59] Such non-discrimination is required by G.A.T.T. art. 24(8)(a)(i).
[60] This would even be true if the minimum prices were deemed to be restrictive in character as quantitative restrictions, or protective like customs duties, since G.A.T.T. art. 24(8)(a)(i), in requiring that barriers be reduced from substantially all trade does not prescribe the schedule that should be followed in achieving this goal. However, minimum prices acting in this way could be taken into account to discern whether, at any particular moment, a liberalization as to "substantially all the trade" was in effect.
[61] "[F]or which there exist in certain Member States . . . provisions designed to guarantee to national producers a sale of their production, and . . . a need of imports . . . ." E.E.C. Treaty art. 45(1).
[62] Ibid.
[63] The United States delegate at G.A.T.T.'s Twelfth Session declared that if this provision were followed, the Community would further G.A.T.T.'s objective of expanding multilateral trade. "In our view policies and programs which take into account the interests of other countries will also be those most likely to contribute to the Community's agricultural objectives." Frank, *United States Statement on the European Economic Community*, 38 DEP'T STATE BULL. 926, 929 (1958).
[64] E.E.C. Treaty art. 45(1).

products,[65] and until such time as the national organizations are replaced by a common agricultural organization (possibly in the second stage),[66] and because the General Agreement grants a reasonable time (or a time period specified by the parties which is considered reasonable) for the formation of a customs union which, by G.A.T.T.'s definition, must eliminate the duties and quantitative restrictions from substantially all internal trade,[67] it appears doubtful that such contracts are incompatible with the General Agreement.

V

THE ASSOCIATION OF OVERSEAS TERRITORIES

The E.E.C. Overseas Territories provisions, in that they look to the economic and social development of the countries and territories of the constituent members, closely parallel the aims and purposes of the General Agreement, as set out in its preamble. However, no section of the Treaty establishing the European Economic Community has caused greater concern than has this one. Not only does this section appear plainly incompatible with G.A.T.T. provisions with respect to preferences not accorded nonmembers, but the unparalleled opportunity for trade diversion, especially at the expense of the newly developed countries, makes this system a primary target for regulation and control by the contracting parties. The Association reflects the desire both to allow the Common Market countries to share in the benefits of the dependent overseas territories—held by and large by France—and to further "the interests and prosperity of the inhabitants of these countries and territories in such a manner as to lead them to the economic, social and cultural development which they expect."[68]

The main charge leveled at the Association of Overseas Territories is that it represents a preference arrangement forbidden by the General Agreement. Article 1(2) of the G.A.T.T. permits certain listed existing preferences to continue, so long as the margin of preference meets G.A.T.T. requirements.[69] An extension of preferences not permitted by the G.A.T.T. can come about in two ways. First, the G.A.T.T.-prescribed level for existing preferences[70] could be altered; second, the preferential arrangement could be extended to new territories or countries. Both courses of action are prohibited by the General Agreement. Under article 133 of the E.E.C. Treaty, imports from the overseas territories are to benefit by the progressive and total abolition of customs duties scheduled to take place in conformity with the Treaty provisions,[71] while at the same time the overseas countries and territories

---

[65] To be the subject of a long-term contract, the products must fulfill two requirements under the E.E.C. Treaty: (1) they must appear on List II of the Annex to the Treaty and (2) they must fit into the classes of national legislation described in article 45(1).
[66] *Id.* art. 45(1).
[67] G.A.T.T. art. 24(8)(a)(i).
[68] E.E.C. Treaty art. 131.
[69] G.A.T.T. art. 1(4).
[70] *Ibid.*
[71] E.E.C. Treaty art. 133(1).

are permitted to levy tariffs "which correspond to the needs of their development and to the requirements of their industrialization or which, being of a fiscal nature, have the object of contributing to their budgets."[72] This would seem to demonstrate an extension of tariff preferences violative per se of the General Agreement; the reduction of duties by the countries maintaining the preferences and unlimited use of tariff duties by the territories.[73]

The problem, however, cannot be reduced to such simple terms. The General Agreement makes specific provision for the creation of a free-trade area, which the Overseas Territories purport to be.[74] It requires that such a grouping reduce substantially all trade barriers within a reasonable period of time. Therefore, if it can be shown that the overseas territories as a whole will comply with paragraph 8(b) of article twenty-four,[75] a charge that preferences were created or extended could not at the same time be put forward. It would be illogical and inconsistent to assert that a free-trade area meeting G.A.T.T. requirements for the reduction of internal barriers in a reasonable time, would simultaneously be violating article one of the General Agreement by extending preferential arrangements. However, until a definition of the term "substantially all the trade" has been formulated and the statistical criteria selected to be measured against the definition adopted, no finding could be reached regarding compliance with the "substantially all the trade" requirement, or, subsequently, that the overseas territories represented an extension of preferences. Even if an unpermissible increment of protective trade barriers was determined to exist after the application of a definition of "substantially all the trade" and selected statistical criteria, such duties could still be justified if permitted by G.A.T.T. article eighteen, which allows the imposition of import restrictions under certain conditions in order to promote economic development. If not so justified under that article, that portion remaining could truly be said to be violative of paragraph 8(b) of article twenty-four and an extension of preferences forbidden by G.A.T.T. article I(2).

Conclusion

As the previous analysis has indicated, the G.A.T.T. may find some aspects of the Rome Treaty or courses of action taken pursuant to its provisions to be inconsistent with article twenty-four of the General Agreement. However, a narrow

---

[72] *Id.* art. 133(3).
[73] To be sure, the alleged extension of preference could come after the E.E.C. began reducing tariff duties under Treaty provisions if the provisions are permissive. In fact, certain reductions have already been made. However, since the first reductions were also extended to all other contracting parties to the G.A.T.T., it could hardly be claimed that this represented an extension of preferences. However, for reductions not also granted to other G.A.T.T. contracting parties, an extension of preferences might be considered to have taken place.
[74] The chief difference between a customs union and a free-trade area is that the latter does not impose a system of common external tariff duties for each product.
[75] This paragraph provides that "the duties and other regulations of commerce maintained in each of the constituent territories and applicable at the formation of such free-trade areas . . . shall not be higher or more restrictive than the corresponding duties and other regulations of commerce existing in the same constituent territories prior to the formation of the free-trade area . . . ." G.A.T.T. art. 24(8)(b).

and legalistic approach, at least from the standpoint of the United States, would not be in the national interest. If the G.A.T.T. were too juridical in its appraisal and too demanding in its requirements, the Community could conceivably find it more profitable to withdraw from the organization altogether.[76] The United States has the North Atlantic Treaty Organization to bear in mind; the political and strategic interest in a stable and prosperous Europe, able to take its place as a full partner of the West in its continuing struggle with the Communist bloc, more than compensates for any slight amount of discrimination or technical inconsistency with the G.A.T.T. A subsidiary interest, all too often forgotten, is that at long last France and Germany, who thrice in ninety years have involved Europe and the world in turmoil, are finally united in the eminently constructive pursuit of restoring Europe to its rightful place in the power constellation of nations. Moreover, the United States, which for so long has strongly supported the economic integration of Europe, should strongly support a development which promises to bring an even greater degree of European unity in the future. Such a course can and should be pursued by the United States, while at the same time using its vast influence to prevent discrimination and trade diversion with respect to the newly developed countries which it is committed to assist. With regard to Rome Treaty provisions or implementations thereof, which are determined to be contrary to G.A.T.T. article twenty-four, the United States should be prepared, within reason, to regularize the inconsistencies, either by approving Common Market proposals which do not fully comply with the requirements of paragraphs five to nine of that article,[77] or by granting a waiver of the obligations contained in those paragraphs.[78]

[76] *Id.* art. 31, permits any contracting party to withdraw from the Agreement, upon six months notice in writing, any time after January 1, 1951.
[77] See *id.* art. 24(10), which permits such action by a two-thirds vote.
[78] *Id.* art. 25(5)(a), provides that the contracting parties may, by a two-thirds majority vote, grant waivers from its obligations in exceptional circumstances.

LABOR AND THE EUROPEAN COMMUNITIES
Meyer Bernstein[*]

I

The European Coal and Steel Community

The European Coal and Steel Community (E.C.S.C.) was the first—and for labor, up to the present moment, the most favorable—of the regional economic groupings which arose under the impetus to international cooperation given by the Marshall Plan.

A. Labor Background

The Schuman Plan was proposed at a time when social and political conditions made it necessary that labor support be secured in order to assure adoption and successful operation. This was especially so in the three major participating countries: the Western Zones of Germany, France, and Italy. In Germany, the trade unions had acquired a status and strength never before attained. The labor movement, as it were, was a kind of warranty that the Federal Republic was now democratic and denazified. During the early years of the occupation, political and business groups of all shades and descriptions eagerly sought labor's good will. This was particularly true of the coal and steel industries, which were fearful for their existence under allied control and directives. The dominant Christian party joined in this new appreciation of labor, and they all urged that labor be given equal power and influence in the management of these basic industries. This offer or promise was firm and explicit: the spokesmen for management made it in letters to the Unified Labor Organization;[1] and the party, in an official program and in proposals to the state legislature of North Rhine-Westphalia.[2]

The British secured the Ruhr as their occupation zone; and, as soon as production of steel and coal began to get under way again, they put these new ideas of co-

---

[*] A.B. 1936, Cornell University. International Affairs Director of the United Steelworkers of America. Author, The Hundred Largest Steel Companies in the Free World (1956); Steel Wages and Foreign Competition (1959); The 1959 Steel Strike (1961).

[1] The basic letters were sent by Dr. Jarres, chairman of the board of the Kloeckner-Werke A.G., and Reuse and Hilbert of the Gutehoffnungshuette, on Jan. 18, 1947, addressed to the Unified Labor Organization. The Jarres letter contained the following:

". . . We therefore make on behalf of Kloeckner the following proposal:

"The Kloeckner-Werke board of directors shall be reconstituted on the principle of equality of 'Capital and Labor.' The representative of the employees should therewith together with the public receive the majority of the places [on the board] . . . ." The full texts of the letters are given in Erich Potthoff, Der Kampf um die Montan-Mitbestimmung 42-43 (1947). The title means: *The Struggle for Codetermination in the Steel and Coal Industries.*

[2] The so-called Ahlener Program was adopted by the British Zone Conference of the C.D.U. (the Christian party) on Feb. 1-3, 1947, and bills were introduced by the C.D.U. in the session of March 4-6, 1947. One of the sponsors of these codetermination measures was Konrad Adenauer, who later became Chancellor. Potthoff, *op. cit. supra* note 1, at 50-54.

determination into effect on the level below their occupation control agencies. The main steel producers were decartelized into twenty-four so-called unit companies under the direction of a Steel Trustee Association manned by eleven Germans, four of them union men. Each unit company was organized under a board of directors and a board of officers. Each board of directors consisted of eleven men, with either just under or just over half of the board members for the different companies named by the union or the work council. In practice, the president and vice president of the work council (the German substitute for our local union), a member of the executive board or some other high functionary of the metalworkers' union, a member of the executive board or some other high functionary of the German Federation of Trade Unions, plus some man in public life friendly to the union, were named by labor to the board of directors of each company.

The eleven members of the Steel Trustee Association assumed the chairmanship of each of the twenty-four boards of directors. Most members became chairmen of the boards of directors of two companies. This meant, of course, that the four union members were also chairmen of the boards of directors of eight German steel companies, including some of the biggest, like Mannesmann.

The board of officers generally consisted of three persons of equal status: one was business director; the second, production director; and the third, labor director. In each case the labor director was named by the union. For the most part, these labor directors were former union officials, often district directors of the metalworkers' union. The labor director was given much more power than, say, a vice-president in charge of labor relations in the United States. In the first place, he was one of three officers and had equal power with the other two. He had no superior officer, since there was no president as in the United States. And finally, half of the members of the board of directors—and in almost half the companies the chairman of the board as well—were union men nominated by the same union organization which put him in office. Codetermination in the coal industry was somewhat weaker but nevertheless well-anchored.

All of this was introduced by the British and confirmed by the Americans when they assumed part of the responsibility for the iron and steel industry of Germany. Labor participation was also later extended to the government control agencies on which the Germans were represented. The deputy German member of the Ruhr Authority, for example, was selected on nomination of the German Federation of Trade Unions.

While adoption of the Schuman Plan was being discussed, the German labor movement was carrying on a campaign to incorporate the principles of codetermination into German law so that they would continue after the occupation ended. It is true that by this time the ardor of the dominant party and management for codetermination had cooled; nevertheless, the Parliament was ready—under some pressure from the unions and the Socialist Party, plus the union wing of the Christian party—to pass a law establishing codetermination in steel and coal along the same lines as under the occupation. The companies were now independent and had been returned to their previous owners. There no longer was a Steel Trustee Association, but, as before, half the members of the board of directors and one of the members of the board of officers were, in effect, to be named by the union. Today, therefore, the leading officers of the German Federation of Trade Unions and the Metalworkers' Union are members of the boards of directors of the German steel and coal companies. For example, Ludwig Rosenberg, vice president of the German Federation of Trade Unions, is also vice chairman of the board of directors of the Deutsche Edelstahlwerke; Otto Brenner, president of the Metalworkers' Union is vice chairman of the board of directors of the Krupp steel company; Heinrich Deist, the union's chief adviser on codetermination problems during the crucial period (and presently chief economic spokesman for the Social Democratic Party) is chairman of the board of directors of the Gusstahlwerke Bochumer Verein. Also, as before, the labor directors are all union men and have the same powers and prerogatives previously held. The labor directors are full-time officers of the companies, retaining only their union memberships but *not* their former union positions. The union members of the boards of directors remain full-time union functionaries, and only serve the companies at board meetings or other similar occasions.

The pattern for Germany had been set. It was clear, therefore, that if the Schuman Plan, which would cover exactly the same industries, was to be accepted, it had to have similar principles. This was acknowledged at the very outset by the German government's naming an executive board member of the German Federation of Trade Unions to be on the German delegation negotiating the details of the treaty with the other five countries.

In France and Italy labor had received no such recognition; but it was generally agreed that something had to be done there to overcome the Communist Parties and their captive trade unions. The Communists had, of course, denounced the Schuman Plan proposal as a capitalistic-imperialistic-monopolistic plot against the rights of workers. In each of these countries there were also non-Communist unions, either Christian or Socialist or Socialist-influenced. These were all numerically weaker than the Communist organizations, but, nevertheless, important as bulwarks of democracy. If the Schuman Plan was to succeed, these non-Communist unions had to be won over.

Combinations of the two situations—in Germany on the one hand, in France and Italy on the other—existed in the three other member nations: namely, Belgium, Holland, and Luxembourg. It was, therefore, relatively easy to give the European Coal and Steel Community strong pro-labor and even pro-free-union orientation, and, indeed, this is what happened.

B. Treaty Provisions

The E.C.S.C. Treaty itself emphasizes the importance of labor in the Common Market. The first paragraph of article two reads:

The mission of the European Coal and Steel Community is to contribute to the expansion of the economy, the development of employment and the improvement of the standard of living in the participating countries. ...

Title Three is devoted to "Economic and Social Provisions," and here, too, labor is given special consideration. For example, articles forty-six and forty-seven provide for consultation with interested parties. Continuing this theme, article forty-eight states: "The right of enterprises to form associations is not affected by this treaty...." But since employers' associations also participate in the Schuman Plan activities, the question arose as to what share labor has in their deliberations. So, to safeguard against possible lack of objectivity, article forty-eight goes on to stipulate:

The High Authority shall normally call upon producers' associations to obtain information which it requires or to facilitate the fulfillment of its objectives, provided that the associations in question either permit the properly chosen representatives of the workers and consumers to participate in the direction of these associations or in consultative committees attached to them, or in any other way give a satisfactory place in their organization to the expression of the workers' and consumers' interests.

One of the most important implementations of the social purposes of the European Coal and Steel Community is set forth in article fifty-six providing aid to labor displaced by changing conditions in the coal and steel industry. This article was found, however, to be inadequate; accordingly, it was amended in January 1960.

Curiously enough, the German government, which has one of the most widespread programs in the field, objected to strengthening the clause and wished to place a time limit on it. The other five governments overruled the Germans. Following is the new addition to article fifty-six:[3]

Should profound changes in the marketing conditions of the coalmining or of the iron and steel industry, not directly connected with the introduction of the Common Market, make it necessary for certain enterprises permanently to discontinue, curtail or change their activities, the High Authority, at the request of the interested Governments,
(a) may, in accordance with the methods provided for in Article 54, facilitate the financing either in the industries under its jurisdiction or, with the agreement of the Council, in any other industry, of such programs as it may approve for the creation of new and economically sound activities, or for the conversion of enterprises, which are capable of assuring productive re-employment to workers rendered redundant;
(b) may grant non-repayable assistance as a contribution to
—the payment of compensation to tide the workers over until they can obtain new employment,
—the enabling of enterprises, by means of special grants, to pay their personnel during any temporary stand-offs necessitated by the change in their activities,
—the granting of resettlement allowances to the workers,
—the financing of technical retraining for workers who are obliged to change their employment.

[3] E.C.S.C. HIGH AUTHORITY, EIGHTH GENERAL REPORT ON THE ACTIVITIES OF THE COMMUNITY 293 (1960) [hereinafter cited as REPORT].

The High Authority shall make the granting of nonrepayable assistance conditional upon the payment by the interested State of a special contribution at least equal to the amount of such assistance, unless an exception is authorized by a two-thirds majority of the Council.

The Treaty was to bring about profound changes in the industries affected. The end result, of course, was intended to be good, but precautions had to be provided for if the adjustment or transitional period was to be kept under control. The six countries, therefore, adopted a Convention containing the Transitional Provisions wherein chapter one of the General Provisions is entitled "Readaptation" and provides for the kind of aid which the Schuman Plan will make available to workers who are affected by the consequences of the introduction of the common market for coal and steel.

Following is the text of this section:

Chapter 1. GENERAL PROVISIONS. *Readaptation.* Section 23.

1. If the consequences of the establishment of the single market should oblige certain enterprises or parts of enterprises to cease or to modify their activity during the transition period defined in Section 1 of the present Convention, the High Authority, at the request of the interested governments and under the conditions specified below, shall furnish assistance in order to protect the workers from the burdens of readaptation and assure them a productive employment, and may grant non-reimbursable assistance to certain enterprises.

2. At the request of the interested governments and under the conditions defined in Article 46, the High Authority shall participate in a study of the possibilities of reemployment for unemployed workers either in existing enterprises or through the creation of new activities.

3. According to the procedure specified in Article 54, the High Authority shall facilitate the financing of approved programs submitted by the interested governments for the transformation of enterprises or for the creation, either in the industries coming under its jurisdiction or, with the concurrence of the Council, in any other industry, of new, economically sound activities capable of providing a productive employment for workers who have been released. Subject to the concurrence of the government concerned, the High Authority shall give preference in granting such facilities to the programs submitted by enterprises which have been obliged to cease their activity on account of the establishment of the common market.

4. The High Authority shall grant non-reimbursable assistance for the following purposes:

(a) to contribute, in case of total or partial closing of enterprises, to the payment of allowances to tide the workers over until they can find new employment;

(b) to contribute, by means of allotments to enterprises, to assuring the payment of their personnel in case of temporary unemployment necessitated by their change in activity;

(c) to contribute to the payment of allowances to workers for reinstallation expenses;

(d) to contribute to the financing of technical retraining for workers obliged to change employment.

C. The Practical Role of Labor

These Treaty provisions are, of course, substantial, but of equal importance is the manner in which labor participated in the Treaty's administration. This was achieved on several levels and had an immediate and continuing effect. First, two of the nine members of the High Authority have from the very beginning been men supported by labor and enjoying labor's confidence, and another one was added later.

In 1952, in accordance with its labor participation policy, the German government permitted the German Federation of Trade Unions to nominate one of the two German members of the High Authority, the chief executive organ of the Schuman Plan. The union submitted the name of Dr. Heinz Potthoff, who had previously served under its nomination on the Ruhr Authority, which, however, was to be abolished upon the introduction of the Schuman Plan. Dr. Potthoff had also served as chairman of the board of directors of a steel company, again on nomination of the union.

The second member of the High Authority from the labor movement is Paul Finet, who was formerly president of the International Confederation of Free Trade Unions. Finet was actually named not by a participating government but by the other eight members of the High Authority. The choice, however, was made by labor. Mr. Finet served one term as president of the High Authority. The third labor member of the High Authority, Mr. Roger Reynaud, comes from the French Christian union movement.

The High Authority has a staff of several hundred persons, many of whom are from the labor movement and some of whom hold very important posts. For example, the man called to direct the statistical services was Dr. Rolf Wagenfuehr. Dr. Wagenfuehr had formerly been with the Research Institute of the German Federation of Trade Unions. Dr. Potthoff's chief technical assistant, Dr. Willi Schwarz, came from the research department of the Metalworkers' Union of Germany.

Labor, of course, was most heavily concentrated in the division, Problems of Labor, under Mr. Finet; here union people from practically all of the six countries were given important assignments. Labor people, however, were also offered employment in many other divisions and often in key places. There is no quota system or anything of that nature in existence. Nevertheless, labor is highly represented.

Direct representation of labor, as such, is to be found in the Consultative Committee. The Consultative Committee is an organ of the Community whose opinion must be sought by the High Authority on all important decisions. It may on its own initiative institute action. It consists of fifty-one members—seventeen representing management in the Community's industries; seventeen representing consuming industries, such as railroads, metalworking industries and the like; and seventeen representing labor in the Community's industries. In addition, each group is entitled to one observer.

The labor members are chosen by the non-Communist coal and steel unions of the six countries. Although the Communists control the dominant labor organizations in France and Italy and are quite important in Luxembourg, they have been given no recognition whatever under the Schuman Plan. The chairmanship of the Consultative Committee rotates, so that from time to time union men occupy this office. Andre Renard, leader of the recent general strike in Belgium, has been a chairman of the Consultative Committee. So has Fritz Dahlmann, vice president of the German Mine Workers' Union. Of the eighteen union men on the Consultative Committee, thirteen come from the free or Socialist oriented unions, and five from the Christian.

Originally the Common Assembly of the E.C.S.C. consisted of seventy-eight members divided as follows:[4] Germany, eighteen; France, eighteen; Italy, eighteen; Belgium, ten; the Netherlands, ten; and Luxembourg, four. When the Coal and Steel Community was supplemented by Euratom and the E.E.C., this Common Assembly of the Schuman Plan was superseded by a single European Parliament for all three Communities, in which the delegates were allocated as follows:[5] Germany, thirty-six; France, thirty-six; Italy, thirty-six; Belgium, fourteen; the Netherlands, fourteen; and Luxembourg, six. At present delegates are all selected by the respective national parliaments, but provision is made for the preparation of proposals to accomplish election of delegates from each country by direct universal suffrage of its citizens.[6] Among its other powers, the European Parliament is authorized by a two-thirds vote of its members to compel the resignation of the members of the High Authority of the E.C.S.C.[7]

Labor is represented in this supranational parliament through associated or friendly political parties. Moreover, several of the union men who serve in Germany as labor directors or members of boards of directors are members of the European Parliament. Eight functionaries of free or Socialist-oriented unions are currently members of the parliament, along with three or four from Christian-oriented unions. Only exponents of democracy have been named as delegates, and so there are no Communists in the European Parliament.

The Court of Justice, originally established for the E.C.S.C. but with its jurisdiction later extended to include the two other Communities, is another institution on which a labor man has served—however, in this case with only one justice out of seven. The only organ of the Schuman Plan on which labor is not directly repre-

[4] E.C.S.C. Treaty art. 21.
[5] Convention Relating to Certain Institutions Common to the European Communities, arts. 1-2. See also E.E.C. Treaty art. 138.
[6] Convention, *supra* note 5, art. 2. In this same connection, compare article 21 of the E.C.S.C. Treaty with article 138 of the E.E.C. Treaty.
[7] E.C.S.C. Treaty art. 24. A similar power exists to compel the resignation in a body of the members of the Commission of the E.E.C. See E.E.C. Treaty art. 144.

sented is the Council of Ministers, consisting of one cabinet member from each of the six countries.

In this entire context care should be exercised in understanding the meaning of representation. When someone is employed by the High Authority, he owes his allegiance to that body and not to the organization from which he came. Nevertheless, it is foolish to ignore the effects of a person's antecedents or prior environment. Persons with labor background are, if nothing more, at least better able to understand labor's problems and point of view. They need not receive instructions from their former colleagues in order to be effective in protecting labor's interests.

D. Labor Liaison

In the six countries of the E.C.S.C., the unions of the industries covered by the Schuman Plan have organized themselves better to represent and promote labor's position. Both those organizations affiliated with the International Confederation of Free Trade Unions (I.C.F.T.U.) and those affiliated with the International Confederation of Christian Trade Unions have set up liaison bureaus in the High Authority's capital of Luxembourg. The I.C.F.T.U. office was originally called the "Committee of 21," for that was the number of participating organizations: one coal and one steel union from each of the six countries; one from each of the central federations of the six countries; one from the I.C.F.T.U.; and one from each of the international trade secretariats concerned—the International Metalworkers' Federation and the Miners' International Federation.

A permanent secretariat—originally under the direction of a Luxembourg steelworker union official on a part-time basis, then under a Dutch union official on a full-time basis, and now under a German metalworker also on a full-time basis—coordinates the activities of the committee. Meetings are held normally just before a session of the Consultative Committee, to which most of the participants also belong. The secretariat would gather material and help formulate proposals, so that the union members of the Consultative Committee could be well informed with a prepared position. Special meetings were called to discuss important questions as they arose. Normally the top members of each affiliated union, including the president or vice president and generally accompanied by the union research director or economist, were in attendance. Between meetings of the "Committee of 21," the secretariat would be in constant touch with the different agencies of the E.C.S.C. and particularly with the various divisions or departments of the High Authority. This was made easier because of the large number of union men on the staff of the High Authority. Certainly there was no lack of opportunity for labor to make its influence felt within the Schuman Plan, and this is indeed demonstrated by the record.

E. Labor Benefits

There are four major fields in which the European Coal and Steel Community has established policies or programs of direct benefit or interest to labor: (1) readaptation, (2) housing, (3) mobility, and (4) safety, health and hygiene.

1. *Readaptation*

Prior to 1952, many coal mines and steel companies were actually submarginal and remained in operation only because of protection of one form or another from competition across the border. Under a free market, these companies could no longer survive, and the workers would lose their jobs. Therefore, provision was made to aid labor in readaptation to other forms of employment. Section twenty-three of the convention quoted earlier provides authority for such aid to labor.[8]

The following typical program covers over 50,000 German coal miners, many of them in mines belonging to steel companies, and provides for workers who lost their jobs as a result of discontinuance of their mine or department (in Germany, coke works are normally at the mine site):

Discharged Workers[9]

(a) A discharged worker finding himself unemployed is to be entitled to a tide-over allowance for one year, calculated on a descending scale for three periods of four months each, at 90, 80, and 70% respectively of his former monthly wage.

From this will be deducted unemployment and sickness benefit and any earnings totalling more than DM 40* per month from activities exercised on the worker's own account or on that of another party.

(b) A worker undergoing retraining within twelve months from the date of his discharge will be entitled during such retraining to assistance at the first-period tide-over rate.

In addition, he will be refunded all expenses incurred in connection with his attendance at a retraining course approved by the labor exchange.

(c) A worker taking up employment in an industry other than the coal mining industry will be entitled to a differential allowance, making up his new wage for the first six months to 95% of his former wage, and for the following six months to 90%.

Where a worker signed on at another pit is downgraded or put from piece rates to day wage rates, he will be entitled for six months to an allowance making up his new wage to 95% of his former wage.

Other provisions in the agreement

(a) A discharged worker called for interview by a prospective new employer is to be entitled to a refund of his travel expenses.

(b) For twelve months following discharge or transfer to another pit or branch of the enterprise, a worker will be refunded any additional travel expenses incurred as a result of his having to travel a greater distance to reach his work.

(c) Where the distance between a worker's new place of employment and his home is so great that he cannot cover it in both directions daily, he will be entitled to a separation allowance of DM 7.50 a day, and to a refund of the cost of one journey home per month.

(d) A worker compelled to change his residence in order to take up new employment will be refunded his travel expenses and those of his dependents, and his removal expenses; in addition, he will be entitled to a resettlement allowance amounting to two months' wages. The resettlement allowance will be payable only within the twelve months following his discharge or transfer. As regards removal expenses, on the other hand, a

---

[8] See note 5 *supra*.
[9] REPORT 284-85.
* At that time a DM (Deutsche Mark) was worth 4.19 to the dollar.

worker finding new employment within twelve months of his discharge may apply for a refund in respect of a removal up to two years from discharge.

(e) Over and above the tide-over, differential or retraining allowance, workers will receive a specified sum (DM 20 or DM 10 per month, according as they are or are not heads of households) in compensation for the loss of their entitlement to concessionary coal.

In addition, a worker who, having fulfilled the requirements for one or another of the various pension plans, voluntarily decides to retire early so that another worker can be kept on his job, would receive a lump sum of DM 3,000, plus DM 300 for each dependent child, and DM 240 as compensation for his loss of concessionary coal. An amount equal to one month's instalment of his friendly society pension[9a] will be deducted, up to a maximum of DM 500. Payment will be made as follows: one-half of the total sum on the day of departure, one-quarter on the first day of the seventh month and one-quarter on the first day of the tenth month following departure.

The provisions in Italy are somewhat different. There, 2,300 workers in all were discharged from twenty iron and steel enterprises in various parts of the country. The allowance in Italy is eighty-five per cent of the former salary, instead of the descending scale from ninety per cent to seventy per cent; it continues for fifteen months, instead of for one year. Furthermore, in case the worker finds employment, he shall receive the difference between his former wages and his new wages.

In France, a modification of this procedure was put into effect for a company which was in the process of reorganizing a department affecting ninety workers.[10]

... These men will not be discharged, but stood off temporarily, and will be entitled during the stand-off, under section 23(4) of the Convention, to an allowance equal to their former real wage, including bonuses. The reorganization is to take one year. The enterprise undertook not to discharge workers in receipt of the allowance either during the period for which this is payable or during the six months following.

Total credits made available by the High Authority of the European Coal and Steel Community for readaptation reached approximately $42,000,000[11] as of February 10, 1960, and covered 110,000 workers employed in 195 enterprises.

Authority for new programs expired this year, but was extended by the Parliament. As the High Authority's *General Report* states:[12]

The assistance granted by the High Authority, in cooperation with the Governments of the Member States concerned, has made it possible for the adjustments necessitated by the

---

[9a] The "friendly society pensions" referred to are those in the coal industry and are called "Knappschaftsversicherung." This refers to the special system of social security for the industry first established by law in 1923 and amended several times since then. It includes not only pensions but also sickness, childbirth, death, invalidity, and so on. It is financed by joint contributions—the employers paying a total of 26.8% of payroll up to certain limits, and the employees paying 11%.

[10] REPORT 287.

[11] The interested states must make a contribution at least equal to that of the High Authority.

[12] REPORT 288-89.

effects of the Common Market to go through without involving serious social disturbances. The measures taken, which were adapted as far as was at all possible to the special requirements of each case, helped the workers through the difficult period following their discharge, and in most cases made it easier for them to find fresh employment.

It was no doubt in consideration of the results obtained that the European Parliament and the employers' and workers' associations repeatedly expressed the hope that the High Authority would continue its readaptation work after the expiration of Section 23.

The support they gave the High Authority when it submitted its proposals for the revision of Article 56 of the Treaty was a valued encouragement to it.

Under the new article fifty-six of the Treaty, also quoted heretofore,[13] this same kind of general action can now be taken on behalf of workers who lose their jobs as a result of automation or new technology.

2. *Housing*

One of the most urgent needs of labor in all Europe after the war was housing. Practically all European steel companies have housing programs for their employees. Desirable as this may be, there are nevertheless certain objections to living in a company house. The European Coal and Steel Community, therefore, decided to embark upon a housing program of its own.

The E.C.S.C. made a three-fold approach.[14] First, it conducted a survey to ascertain the needs for worker housing. Second, it established a housing design competition to bring out the best possible forms of workers' housing. And, third, it established an intensive housing construction program.

The survey was done on a sample basis involving some 40,000 workers in the six-nation community. After the need was ascertained, the housing design competition was announced. By the closing date, August 1, 1959, plans had been submitted by 250 architects. Patrons of the competition were the housing ministers for the various countries involved. Each minister appointed an expert who, together with the others, settled the rules and conditions of the competition in cooperation with the International Union of Architects.

Plans were displayed at a special exhibition held in Luxembourg from December 7 to 18, 1959, and the winners received their prizes at a ceremony in the same city on December 17. The High Authority is bringing out a brochure on the results of the competition, containing studies by members of the panel of judges.

The housing construction program of the High Authority got under way before the survey and the design competition were completed. Up to January 1, 1960, the High Authority had approved arrangements to finance 44,987 dwellings in all. Of these, 24,851 were already completed; 14,285, under construction; and 5,851, in preparation. The total amount set aside by the High Authority for this purpose up to the same date was 74,600,000 units of account (*i.e.*, American dollars). Of the 44,987 dwellings, 26,563 were intended to be let and 18,424 to be available for ultimate ownership by their occupiers.

[13] See note 3 *supra*.
[14] REPORT 327-36.

This program is part of a cooperative venture involving the High Authority of the Schuman Plan and various public credit institutions or funds of the participating countries. This is to say that the $74,600,000 referred to above represented only a part of the total cost. In each country some other institution, such as a public savings scheme, the social security fund, or the like, would put up the rest of the money. Since these institutions had their own established interest rates, that portion made available by the High Authority would be subject to abnormally low interest in order to reach a more moderate average, and thus offset the higher going rate. For example, in a program in Germany, the social security institutions there made their money available at 5-5½ per cent. The High Authority, therefore, set a rate of 1.25 per cent on its own contribution. The social security share was DM 19.8 million, and the High Authority's share DM 6.6 million. These monies are only a part of the total financing on this project of 3,200 dwellings. The total cost will approximate DM 100,000,000.

Unions are represented on the administration of the social security institutions; and, of course, the unions are also represented on the Coal and Steel Community. Thus, they have at least an equal participation with management in these housing programs. As a matter of fact, the unions' participation is direct, while management's is two or three degrees removed. Therefore, the housing which results from this program cannot be considered company housing. The program is still under way, and new projects are in preparation.

The programs just outlined are intended to provide homes for ordinary workers. In addition, however, there is the special case of workers whose plants or departments have been abolished and who have therefore been resettled on other jobs in other parts of the country. An example of this is the case of the Compagnie de Ateliers et Forges de la Loire, a steel company which transferred its operation from Assailly to St. Etienne. The workers, of course, were provided moving and other expenses, as discussed hereinbefore under the topic of Readaptation. But where were they to live when they reached St. Etienne? The High Authority, therefore, arranged with the French Government for a joint venture involving the French housing program's HLM Office (Habitations a loyer modéré—moderate cost housing program) to construct the 100 necessary units for these workers on the basis of a forty-year loan.

3. *Mobility*

If, as the E.C.S.C. Treaty states, one of the missions of the Community is to harmonize conditions upward, then there must be mobility of labor among the six participating countries. Such free movement of labor is provided for under article sixty-nine of the Treaty:

1. The member States bind themselves to renounce any restriction, based on nationality, on the employment in the coal and steel industries of workers of recognized qualifications for positions in such industries possessing the nationality of one of the member States; this commitment shall be subject to the limitations imposed by the fundamental needs of health and public order.

2. In order to apply these provisions, the member States will work out a common definition of skilled jobs and conditions of qualification, and will decide by common agreement upon the limitations provided for in the preceding paragraph. They will also work out administrative procedures which will permit offers of and demands for employment in the Community as a whole to be brought together.

3. In addition, for the categories of workers not falling within the provisions of the preceding paragraph and where an expansion of production in the coal and steel industries might be hampered by a shortage of suitable labor, they will adapt their immigration regulations as much as may be necessary to eliminate that situation; in particular, they will facilitate the reemployment of workers from the coal and steel industries of other member States.

4. They will prohibit any discrimination in payment and working conditions as between national and foreign workers, without prejudice to special measures concerning frontier workers; in particular, they will work out among themselves any arrangements necessary so that social security measures do not stand in the way of the movement of labor.

5. The High Authority must guide and facilitate the application by the member States of the measures provided for in this article.

6. This article shall not interfere with the international obligations of the member State.

Putting this article into effect involved overcoming enormous complexities. In the first place, it was not enough simply to provide that, for example, a Frenchman could move from Lorraine to the Ruhr. Provision had to be made for the equalization of his social security and other benefits, which he would want to enjoy upon returning home. In consultation with the liaison bureau, the High Authority worked out a draft program which it then presented to the "Committee of 21." As it turned out, the High Authority was more liberal than the national unions; and, as a result, the original proposal had to be watered down considerably to meet the objections of union leaders who feared unwholesome effects upon their own membership at home. The fears turned out to be groundless and now there are thousands of foreigners working in the steel industries of Germany and Luxembourg.

4. *Safety, Health, and Hygiene*

For the first time, a whole multitude of problems affecting labor in the steel and coal industries can now be handled on an international basis with all the advantages of broad scale treatment and comparative study. Among the most important of these is safety,[15] into which significant research is now possible. The High Authority can take advantage of the best available sources or can coordinate the individual projects in the participating countries.

Another field is hygiene and worker psychology, which were previously either neglected or treated on a limited basis. Industrial health and medicine have also been the subject of investigations which promise considerable success. For example, there is a program set up by the industrial health and medicine research committee

---

[15] REPORT 340-46.

which has conducted studies in basic silicosis research, pneumonociosis in the iron and steel industry, carbon monoxide poisoning, work at high temperatures, noise abatement, dust prevention and suppression, and other subjects. These represent but a fraction of the kind of activities undertaken by the High Authority under the Schuman Plan.

F. Shortcomings

Labor, therefore, has reason to be proud of its achievements under the European Coal and Steel Community. Nevertheless, certain shortcomings have appeared. The close collaboration with management, both under national law and the aegis of the Community, has brought about a certain identification of viewpoint between official representatives of the union and management. Under such circumstances the interests of the workers themselves may not always receive the attention they deserve. For example, the writer once visited the scene of a coal disaster and attempted to ascertain the cause. The union leaders whom he interviewed insisted there was not any cause, that the company had done all it could for the safety of the men.

One of the reasons which unions have given for demanding an equal share in management, both on an industry and a supranational basis, was to prevent the kind of cartel building characteristic of the period between the wars. Yet the unions have done comparatively little to prevent a resurgence of the same movement. In fact, some of the union leaders, overconfident of their power to prevent abuse, have played a major role in generating public acceptance of concentration in the basic industries.

If anything, there may be an excess of at least one kind of labor participation. There are endless meetings—all with per diems and travel allowances—with the result that the real purpose of labor participation sometimes tends to become confused.

G. Conclusion

Nevertheless, it is clear that the European Coal and Steel Community has, on balance, brought about tremendous gains for the men and women employed in the basic steel and coal industries of the six countries. At the same time, it has strengthened the role of labor and has given the unions a sense of participation and responsibility never before exercised in a democracy. These objectives have been achieved to a reasonable degree. Most difficulties have been foreseen and provided for.

The Schuman Plan has become institutionalized and—as far as one can now judge—permanent. It is not socialism, and it is not paternalism. It can perhaps best be described as a kind of democratic welfare state. The Schuman Plan pattern of labor participation was only partially carried over into the European Economic Community, and scarcely at all into Euratom.

II

The European Economic Community

A. The Treaty Provisions

The European Economic Community Treaty also contains, in article two, a reference to the standard of living, but it is very much weaker than that of the Schuman Plan. The Schuman Plan Treaty speaks of "the mission . . . to contribute to . . . the improvement of the standard of living . . ." and goes on to effectuate this in a practical way. The E.E.C. article says:

> It shall be the aim of the Community, by establishing a Common Market and progressively approximating the economic policies of Member States, to promote throughout the Community a harmonious development of economic activities, a continuous and balanced expansion, an increased stability, an accelerated raising of the standard of living and closer relations between its Member States.

And the implementation, except for the European Social Fund, is very meager. There is, for example, no concrete provision for housing construction. Labor has neither direct representation on the executive organ nor nearly the indirect impact it enjoys under the Schuman Plan. As a matter of fact, the labor unions have complained vociferously over their exclusion from policy-making functions. There is, of course, union participation, but most of this is limited to the European Social Fund. Labor is also represented on the Economic and Social Committee, but only as one of many categories of economic and social life. Furthermore, the Committee possesses only a restricted authority.

The European Social Fund is a device quite similar in purpose, but much more restricted in application, to the readaptation provisions of the Schuman Plan. Article 125 sets forth its purpose:

> 1. At the request of a Member State, the Fund shall, within the framework of the rules provided for in Article 127, cover 50 per cent of expenses incurred after the entry into force of this Treaty by that State or by a body under public law for the purpose of:
>   (a) ensuring productive reemployment of workers by means of:
>   —occupational retraining,
>   —resettlement allowances; and
>   (b) granting aids for the benefit of workers whose employment is temporarily reduced or wholly or partly suspended as a result of the conversion of their enterprise to other productions, in order that they may maintain the same wage-level pending their full reemployment.
> 2. The assistance granted by the Fund towards the cost of occupational retraining shall be conditional upon the impossibility of employing the unemployed workers otherwise than in a new occupation and upon their having been, in productive employment, for a period of at least six months in the occupation for which they have been retrained.
>   The assistance granted in respect of resettlement allowances shall be conditional upon the unemployed workers having been obliged to change their residence within the Community and upon their having been in productive employment for a period of at least six months in their new place of residence.

The assistance given for the benefit of workers in cases where an enterprise is converted shall be subject to the following conditions:

(a) that the workers concerned have again been fully employed in that enterprise for a period of at least six months;

(b) that the Government concerned has previously submitted a plan, drawn up by such enterprise, for its conversion and for the financing thereof; and

(c) that the Commission has given its prior approval to such conversion plan.

The Council of the European Economic Community has issued a regulation spelling out the operation of this fund. In part one, article one, of the Regulation,[16] it is emphasized that the Social Fund's part is primarily to reimburse "50% of the expenses incurred by the Member states or by bodies under public law . . ." for re-adaptation in its various forms. In other words, the initiative now is with the member countries rather than the Community. And benefits are less than under Schuman Plan programs. Furthermore, labor participation is limited to a committee consisting of representatives of governments and trade union and employer organizations.

B. Labor Liaison and Criticism

The International Confederation of Free Trade Unions has established a union secretariat for the three communities with headquarters in Brussels. The former head of the Luxembourg liaison bureau, Harm G. Buiter, is now general secretary of this office.

The unions, realizing the narrow treaty base upon which it must operate, place hope in the E.E.C. Commission for expanding the functions of the Economic and Social Committee and at the same time strengthening labor's role in it and in the executive. They also call for democratization of the European Parliament by direct election of its membership.[17] In this way, the unions hope to bring to bear on the E.E.C. some of the prestige they already possess in the Schuman Plan.

On the positive side the unions admit that, in consolidating the statistical services of the three communities under the former Schuman Plan personnel, the many benefits of a reliable and comprehensive survey are now made available on the basis of the whole economic picture, rather than being limited to the coal and steel industries. Another stride forward for labor was the election on September 29, 1960, of Ludwig Rosenberg, vice president of the German Federation of Trade Unions, to the presidency of the Economic and Social Committee for a term of two years.

C. Conclusion

The European Economic Community is too new to permit a definitive judgment on the role of labor. In fact, as far as labor is concerned, it is still in the developmental stage. Although lacking a treaty base—such as exists in the Schuman Plan—

---

[16] COUNCIL OF THE E.E.C., REGULATION No. 9, CONCERNING THE EUROPEAN SOCIAL FUND, PUB. No. 342/60-E (1960).

[17] Declaration on European Integration by the International Confederation of Free Trade Unions" European Union Secretariat, Brussels, Belgium, Nov. 28, 1960.

the European unions hope eventually to raise their status in the E.E.C. to the same level. They believe this can be done in two ways; first, by liberal interpretation of the E.E.C. Treaty; and, second, by consolidating organs and offices of the three Communities into one for the sake of efficiency. If, for example, the High Authority of the Schuman Plan and the Commission of the E.E.C. become identical, then it is fair to assume that at least one of the labor men on the former will be carried over into the new executive body. And the same principle applies to the administrative staff. Labor, therefore, can expect to receive more and more recognition in the European Economic Community, though perhaps never quite so much as it enjoys in the Schuman Plan.

III

EURATOM

The role of labor in this third of the communities is peripheral. The European Atomic Energy Community is the most parochial of the three, and has the least direct impact on labor. This circumstance is reflected in the Euratom Treaty, which is almost bare of references to working people or their organizations. Again the aim is to raise living standards, but here only "by the creation of conditions necessary for the speedy establishment and growth of nuclear industries."[18] There may be schools for training specialists, and provisions for safety and health.

The only real labor participation is on the Economic and Social Committee, which under the terms of the Convention signed on March 25, 1957, will have a common membership and operation with that of the European Economic Community. Thus, Ludwig Rosenberg, vice president of the German Federation of Trade Unions has not only been elected chairman of the Economic and Social Committee of the E.E.C., but for Euratom as well. Also, if labor succeeds in expanding the functions and effectiveness of this committee, it will in the same measure apply to Euratom. Otherwise labor has little recognition in this presently smallest, though potentially most promising, of the three communities. Thus, for labor, the model remains the Schuman Plan, which is still a rarity for union participation on such a scale in the free world today.

[18] Euratom Treaty art. 1.

Published for the
PARKER SCHOOL OF FOREIGN AND COMPARATIVE LAW
by
OCEANA PUBLICATIONS, INC.

A Bibliography on Foreign and Comparative Law Books and Articles in English,
Two Volumes: the first to 1953, the second 1953-59
by Charles Szladits   1st v. 1955; 2nd v. 1962 $15.00 each volume

Guide to Foreign Legal Materials—French, German, Swiss
by Charles Szladits 1959 $11.00

The French Legal System
by René David and Henry deVries 1958   5.00

Foreign Law—A Guide to Pleading and Proof
by Otto C. Sommerich and Benjamin Busch 1959   5.00

The International Status of the United Nations
by Guenter Weissberg 1961   7.50

International Contracts: Choice of Law and Language
Parker School of Foreign and Comparative Law Symposium 1962   5.00

The Soviet Legal System
by John N. Hazard and Isaac Shapiro 1962   12.50

Manual on Foreign Legal Periodicals and Their Index
by Albert P. Blaustein 1962   9.00

Bilateral Studies in Private International Law

These books deal exclusively with relations between citizens of two individual countries. A complete exploration of private law including the right to work, foreign judgments, proof of foreign law, marriage, etc.

1. **American-Swiss,** 1959
   Nussbaum, 2nd ed. $5.00
2. **American-French,** 1961
   Delaume, 2nd rev. ed. 7.50
3. **American-Dutch,** 1961
   Kollewijn, 2nd rev. ed. 5.00
4. **American-German,** 1956
   Domke 5.00
5. **American-Colombian,** 1956
   Eder 5.00
6. **American-Greek,** 1957
   Ehrenzweig, Fragistas,
   Yiannopous $5.00
7. **American-Danish,** 1957
   Philip 5.00
8. **American-Australian,** 1957
   Cowen 5.00
9. **American-Brazilian,** 1959
   Garland 5.00
10. **American-Chilean,** 1960
    Etcheberry O 5.00

PUBLICATIONS OF CURRENT INTEREST on

The Common Market
The European Regional Communities
International Trade, Finance and Law

Available direct from the Publishers

HAUSER, Rita E. and Gustave M.

A GUIDE TO DOING BUSINESS IN THE EUROPEAN COMMON MARKET Volume I: France and Belgium

This basic guide for lawyers, businessmen, investors and government officials analyzes the European Common Market and discusses the key aspects of the French and Belgian private and public law affecting business. 1960 $7.50

KRONSTEIN, Heinrich; MILLER, John T., Jr.; SCHWARTZ, Ivo E.

MODERN AMERICAN ANTITRUST LAW, A Guide to Its Domestic and Foreign Application

The Treaty on the new European Economic Community includes strong-worded and far-reaching general provisions against restraints of trade and monopoly, influenced in part by American law and philosophy. Published for Georgetown University Series, No. I. 1958 $7.50

METZGER, Stanley D.

INTERNATIONAL LAW, TRADE AND FINANCE: Realities and Prospects

The legal limitations and mechanisms employed in international political and economic problems, dealt with in the context of significant treaties and agreements. Published for Georgetown University Series, No. 3.   1962 $6.00

SHAW, Crawford

LEGAL PROBLEMS IN INTERNATIONAL TRADE AND INVESTMENT

Fourteen articles based on papers delivered by America's leading attorneys and government advisors at the 1961 Conference. Published for The World Community Association, Yale University School of Law, Legal Problems in International Commerce Series, No. I.   1962 $12.50

SHIMM, Melvin G., Editor; EVERETT, Robinson O., Special Editor

POPULATION CONTROL

The gathering "Population Explosion" will drastically affect the political, social, economic and ethical life of every person living today and for generations to come. Published for Duke University School of Law, Law and Contemporary Problems Series, No. I.
      1961 $6.00

SHIMM, Melvin G., Editor; BAADE, Hans W., Associate Editor; EVERETT, Robinson O., Special Editor

EUROPEAN REGIONAL COMMUNITIES

Presents a prognosis that Europe has made giant

strides toward political, economic and juridical union through exploration of the three European Regional Communities — the Coal and Steel, Atomic Energy and Economic Regional Communities. Published for Duke University School of Law, Law and Contemporary Problems Series, No. 2. 1962 $6.00

SMITH, T.B.

STUDIES CRITICAL AND COMPARATIVE

Deals with influences of French and Dutch legal thought on Scots law, a bridge between the European systems and English law. Co-published with W. Green & Son, Ltd., Edinburgh. 1962 $12.00

WALLACH, Frederick

INTRODUCTION TO EUROPEAN COMMERCIAL LAW

A very realistic picture of Continental Commercial Law as it affects United States' position in commercial transactions. 1953 $6.00